Grassroots Pacifism in Post-war Japan

Grassroots Pacifism in Post-war Japan presents new material on grassroots peace activism and pacifism in two major groups active in the post-World War II peace movement – workers and housewives.

Mari Yamamoto contends that the peace movement, which was organized in tandem with other activities to promote democratic, economic and humanitarian issues, served as a popular lever which helped to eliminate feudal remnants that lingered in Japanese society and people's individual attitudes after the war, thereby modernizing the political process and the outlook of the ordinary Japanese.

The book includes extensive primary material such as letters, essays, memoirs and interviews. Specialists in Japanese history, peace studies and women's studies especially will appreciate the richness of the text supporting Yamamoto's narrative of how workers' and women's political awareness developed under the influence of organizational and ideological interests and contemporary events.

Mari Yamamoto currently works at Nihon Keizai Shimbun Inc., and earned her D.Phil. in Modern History at St Antony's College, University of Oxford, England.

**Sheffield Centre for Japanese Studies/
RoutledgeCurzon Series**
Series Editor: Glenn D. Hook
Professor of Japanese Studies, University of Sheffield

This series, published by RoutledgeCurzon in association with the Centre for Japanese Studies at the University of Sheffield, both makes available original research on a wide range of subjects dealing with Japan, and provides introductory overviews of key topics in Japanese Studies.

The Internationalization of Japan
Edited by Glenn D. Hook and Michael Weiner

Race and Migration in Imperial Japan
Michael Weiner

Japan and the Pacific Free Trade Area
Pekka Korhonen

Greater China and Japan
Prospects for an Economic Partnership?
Robert Taylor

The Steel Industry in Japan
A Comparison with the UK
Hasegawa Harukiyo

Race, Resistance and the Ainu of Japan
Richard Siddle

Japan's Minorities
The Illusion of Homogeneity
Edited by Michael Weiner

Japanese Business Management
Restructuring for Low Growth and Globalization
Edited by Hasegawa Harukiyo and Glenn D. Hook

Japan and Asia Pacific Integration
Pacific Romances 1968–1996
Pekka Korhonen

Japan's Economic Power and Security
Japan and North Korea
Christopher W. Hughes

Japan's Contested Constitution
Documents and Analysis
Glenn D. Hook and Gavan McCormack

Japan's International Relations
Politics, Economics and Security
Glenn D. Hook, Julie Gilson, Christopher Hughes and Hugo Dobson

Japanese Education Reform
Nakasone's Legacy
Christopher P. Hood

The Political Economy of Japanese Globalisation
Glenn D. Hook and Hasegawa Harukiyo

Japan and Okinawa
Structure and Subjectivity
Edited by Glenn D. Hook and Richard Siddle

Japan and Britain in the Contemporary World
Responses to Common Issues
Edited by Hugo Dobson and Glenn D. Hook

Japan and United Nations Peacekeeping
New pressures, new responses
Hugo Dobson

Japanese Capitalism and Modernity in a Global Era
Re-Fabricating Lifetime Employment Relations
Peter C. D. Matanle

Nikkeiren and Japanese Capitalism
John Crump

Production Networks in Asia and Europe
Skill Formation and Technology Transfer in the Automobile Industry
Edited by Rogier Busser and Yuri Sadoi

Japan and the G7/8
1975–2002
Hugo Dobson

The Political Economy of Reproduction in Japan
Between Nation-state and Everyday Life
Takeda Hiroko

Grassroots Pacifism in Post-war Japan
The Rebirth of a Nation
Mari Yamamoto

Japanese Interfirm Networks
Adapting to Survive in the Global Electronics Industry
Ralph Paprzycki

Globalisation and Women in the Japanese Workforce
Beverley Bishop

Grassroots Pacifism in Post-war Japan
The rebirth of a nation

Mari Yamamoto

LONDON AND NEW YORK

First published 2004
by RoutledgeCurzon
2 Park Square, Milton Park, Abingdon, Oxon, OX14 4RN

Simultaneously published in the USA and Canada
by RoutledgeCurzon
270 Madison Avenue, New York, NY 10016

Routledge is an imprint of the Taylor & Francis Group

© 2004 Mari Yamamoto

Typeset in Times by Taylor & Francis Books Ltd
Printed and bound in Great Britain by Antony Rowe Ltd,
Chippenham, Wiltshire

All rights reserved. No part of this book may be reprinted or
reproduced or utilized in any form or by any electronic, mechanical, or
other means, now known or hereafter invented, including
photocopying and recording, or in any information storage or retrieval
system, without permission in writing from the publishers.

British Library Cataloguing in Publication Data
A catalogue record for this book is available from the British Library

Library of Congress Cataloging in Publication Data
A catalog record for this book has been requested

ISBN 0–415–33581–7

For my mother and the memory of my father

Contents

List of tables xi
Acknowledgements xii
*List of abbreviations, acronyms and names of
    Japanese organizations* xiv

Introduction 1

PART I
The peace movement and organized labour 27

1 Early years 29
2 The Korean War and the peace treaty 43
3 The Takano years 60
4 The labour movement under Mindō
   leadership and the *Anpo Tōsō* 77
5 Elements of the peace activities of organized labour 104

PART II
The women's peace movement 125

6 Prehistory and the early post-war years 127
7 The rise of a grassroots peace movement 152
8 Reflections on war and self 182

Conclusion 204

Appendix I: The Constitution of Japan 222
Appendix II: The Third Peace Declaration
by Women of an Unarmed Japan 224
Notes 226
Bibliography 276
Index 296

Tables

7.1	Membership of women's organizations	173
7.2	Size of Japanese women's groups	173
8.1	Women's responses to the end of the war	183

Acknowledgements

In the course of preparing this thesis, which has taken such a long time, I have been fortunate to get acquainted with a large number of people, to whose generosity my research owes an overriding debt.

I would like to express my heartfelt gratitude to all my interviewees, who so kindly helped this struggling novice researcher. It was so inspiring to get to know all these peace activists who were already involved in peace and other social movements right after the end of World War II, and have remained actively committed to their cause even to this day. Needless to say, my work has benefited a great deal from their assistance, but talking with and learning from them has enriched my personal life as well.

Special thanks go to Higuchi Tokuzō, who has demonstrated inexhaustible patience to see me through to the end of the chapters on labour unions. I am also greatly indebted to Negami Masayuki and Takeuchi Motohiro, who generously offered me use of their personal writings and assisted me with great enthusiasm.

I also owe a great deal to Professor Fujiwara Osamu of Tokyo Keizai University. My work would not have even got started if it were not for his advice regarding the basics about peace research.

I also thank David Hurwitz and David McNeill for reading through my draft. Their time-consuming effort to assist me and their active interest in my work have been so encouraging for me.

I was also privileged enough to receive insightful comments from Professor Glenn Hook and Dr Ann Waswo, who helped me greatly to improve upon my original work.

Thanks to the active efforts of Stephanie Rogers at RoutledgeCurzon to get this book published, my long-held dream has finally come true.

My supervisor Arthur Stockwin patiently saw me through my numerous trials and errors until I finally completed this work. I am privileged to have been able to rely on one of the most experienced and caring educators I have ever known.

Of all the people who have been generous with their help, I thank my parents most for their support and affection, which knows no limits.

My mother, Yamamoto Kazuko, has done everything in her power to help her wilful daughter to complete her undertaking. Her encouragement and exquisite sense of humour have given me the strength to continue my work whenever I needed it.

My father, Yamamoto Masao, passed away without seeing me complete this thesis. But I would never have even thought about undertaking this research if I had not inherited his sensibilities about war and peace issues. I am certain that its completion would mean as much to him as it does to his daughter.

Abbreviations, acronyms and names of Japanese organizations

Anpo Tōsō	The 1959–1960 protest movement against revision of the Japan-US security treaty
Fudankyō	The Association of Women's Organizations, a grouping of women's organizations of both the political right and left
Gensuikyō	Gensuibaku Kinshi Shomei Undō Zenkoku Kyōgikai
GHQ	The General Headquarters of SCAP
Gōka Rōren	The Japanese Federation of Synthetic Chemical Workers' Unions
Heiwa Mondai Danwakai	The Discussion Circle on Problems of Peace, a group of leftist and liberal academics debating peace issues
Heiwa Suishin Kokumin Kaigi	The National Congress for Promotion of Peace
ICFTU	The International Confederation of Free Trade Unions
JCP	The Japanese Communist Party
Kaiin	The All Japan Seamen's Union
Kokubō Fujinkai	The Women's Society for National Defence
Kokurō	The National Railway Workers' Union
LDP	The Liberal Democratic Party
Minpukyō	The Japanese Democratic Women's Association, an association of left-wing women's groups
National Congress	The National Congress to Block the Revision of the Japan-US Security Treaty
Nikkō	Nihon Kōzan Rōdō Kumiai, the Japan Miners' Labour Organization
Nikkyōso	The Japan Teachers' Union
SCAP	The Supreme Commander for the Allied Powers. Also means the occupation authorities.
Rōdōsha Dōshikai	The Workers' Association, a group of centre-left Sōhyō officials who pushed for the adoption of the four peace principles,
Sanbetsu	The Congress of Industrial Unions of Japan

Sanbetsu Mindō	The League for Democratization of Sanbetsu
Sangyō Hōkokukai	The Movement of Industrial Service to the Nation, collaborative wartime associations of employers and workers
SDF	Self-Defence Forces, the Japanese armed forces
JSP	The Japanese Socialist Party[1]
Shimbun	Newspaper
Shin Sanbetsu	The National Federation of Industrial Organizations
Shitetsu Sōren	The General Federation of Private Railway Workers' Unions of Japan
Sōdōmei	The Japanese Federation of Trade Unions
Sōhyō	The General Council of Trade Unions of Japan
Tanrō	The Japanese Coal Miners' Union
Tokyo Chihyō	The Tokyo Local Council of Trade Unions
Tokyo Congress	The Tokyo Congress for Joint Struggles to Preserve Peace and Democracy
WFTU	The World Federation of Trade Unions
Zendentsū	The All Japan Telecommunications Workers' Union
Zengakuren	The All Japan Federation of Student Unions
Zenkoku Kinzoku	The National Trade Union of Metal and Engineering Workers
Zenkōwan	The All Japan Harbour Workers' Union
Zenrō	The All Japan Trade Union Congress
Zenrōren	The Sanbetsu-dominated umbrella organization for labour unions
Zensen	The Japanese Federation of Textile Workers' Unions
Zentei	The Japanese Postal Workers' Union

Introduction

When the US-led coalition forces went to war against Iraq in January 1991, the attack was aimed at countering the Iraqi invasion of Kuwait, and it won the sanction of the United Nations and appeared to enjoy the near-unanimous support of the international community. As the US's key allies sent their troops to the Persian Gulf, the Japanese government looked sorely embarrassed as it took an apologetic stand, pleading the constitutional constraints which prohibited it from extending military support.

The Constitution was not the only reason that Japan was unable to fight in the war: an overwhelming majority of the public was against sending the Self-Defence Forces for an overseas war effort.[1] The Japanese responded to the Gulf crisis just as they had reacted to all of the major wars waged since World War II by the US. With their sensibilities shaped by decades of post-war pacifist school education, their main concern was the inevitable casualties which would be suffered among the Iraqi civilians. They voiced strong opposition against the proposed dispatch of the SDF to the Gulf in the belief that Japan would lose its innocence after managing not to send a single soldier abroad for nearly fifty post-war years. They feared Japan's record of not killing anyone outside its borders since the end of World War II could be sullied through their country's participation in the Gulf War. This despite the fact that their government had given vigorous logistical as well as moral support to the US during the Korean War and the Vietnam War. Japanese pacifists continued to regard anything related to the military with a great sense of foreboding, and feared ominous implications of taking an active role in any military effort.

I was living in Britain as the Gulf crisis developed into a full-blown war and ended with the coalition forces' victory. I observed the rest of the world's bafflement at Japan's inability to take a clear stand regarding the war. Opinions expressed from Tokyo sounded garbled, reflecting the dilemma of Japan, which was torn between diplomatic exigencies to fulfil its 'responsibility to the international community' as called for by the US on the one hand, and strong anti-war sentiment at the grassroots on the other.

This is how I decided to embark on a project to explain the Japanese attitude to war and have ordinary members of the public do the explaining.

2 *Introduction*

At the time of the Gulf crisis in October 1990, one irate politician of the ruling Liberal Democratic Party rebuked a senior foreign ministry official for preparing for the SDF's participation in the anticipated war without resolving the conflict between such an act and the no-war clause of Japan's Constitution. The politician declared

> Given the Constitution, Japan has no choice but to pursue an independent pacifist policy (*ikkoku heiwa shugi*). This is the experiment, whereby Japan has been trying to develop such a policy as an integral part of its people's way of life for the past fifty post-war years, no matter whether the international community understands such a policy or not.[2]

The LDP politician Koizumi Junichiro radically shifted his position after he became Prime Minister in 2001 by paving the way for the SDF's participation in the war on terrorism in Afghanistan from that year, and its assistance to the US forces in post-war Iraq in 2003. Apparently, he abandoned his grand experiment without making any specific effort to help it produce further results. Opposition parties and peace activists, who shared a similar vision, have also been unable to come up with a viable strategy to develop their belief into concrete policy measures.

As the memories of World War II receded and those who survived the war continued to pass away, Japan's peace movement increasingly lost its vitality. Lamenting widespread public apathy about war and peace issues in general, a growing number of pacifists have begun to mourn the loss of pacifist principles (*heiwa no kokoro*) among fellow Japanese.

Over most of the post-war era, the Japanese have made a singular claim to what they professed to be a unique kind of peaceful attitude or quality. Is this claim valid? If so, how did the Japanese come to cultivate such unique tendencies?

With such questions in mind, this book will discuss the popular attitude to peace in Japan during the fifteen-year period following the end of World War II, and the impact of the peace movement formed during the period on the nation's popular outlook. The book will analyze the meaning of people's peace activities in terms of previous Japanese experience with war and peace questions, as well as in the context of the radical changes that took place after 1945.

Popular attitudes to peace: an overview from the Meiji era to Japan's surrender

If the word pacifism is to be understood to mean a principled stand against war and violence in general, this kind of attitude did not spread among a wide sector of the populace before the end of World War II, because Japan's political and economic condition prior to the war had largely deprived the people of incentives to embrace such a belief.

Following over 200 years of their country's isolation from the outside world,[3] ordinary Japanese became conscious of matters regarding war and peace with foreign nations for the first time in their modern history when a US naval fleet came to Japan in 1853 to force open its doors.

Widespread poverty, lack of education and the absence of a democratic political system, however, made it extremely difficult for people to develop rational and informed ideas about war and peace issues.

People regarded Japan's new military, which was established in the Meiji era (1868–1912), in both positive and negative light. While some considered the military to be a modernizing force, providing people with an important vehicle for career advancement and job creation, others were critical of its brutal and repressive nature. Of those who were critical, their negative views of the military tended to consist of several strands other than that inspired by pacifism, the theme of this book.

When the Meiji oligarchy introduced military conscription in 1873, in the process of vesting Japan with the accoutrements of a modern state, the move met with significant popular resistance for the first dozen or so years, because the measure was perceived to be adding considerably to the economic and other burdens on the poor. The draft, which was dubbed the 'blood tax', also fuelled the fears of farmers and others, who were concerned that the government might literally make them pay the 'tax' with their own lives. There are no known incidents from those days of refusal to join the military on pacifist grounds. Even when people tried to avoid this new type of public duty, almost no one appears to have pondered the right or wrong of confronting a domestic or foreign adversary with military force or engaging in acts of killing.[4]

According to historian Ōe Shinobu's research on popular sentiment during the Sino-Japanese War of 1894–5 and the Russo-Japanese War of 1904–5 – the two first major wars following Japan's opening to the outside world – soldiers' writings and popular songs mostly reveal their querulous attitude or a sense of resignation about the hard life inside the military and the misery of being separated from their loved ones.[5] Yosano Akiko wrote her famous poem *Kimi Shini Tamō Koto Nakare* [Don't Die on the Battlefield], desperately pleading with her younger brother to come back alive from the Russo-Japanese War, and it can be assumed that her sentiment was shared by most Japanese who had relatives in the military. Still, aside from the riot sparked in 1905 by the outcome of the peace treaty ending the war, there were no major protests in which ordinary Japanese vented their grievances stemming from the conflict. What touched off the 1905 riot was neither anti-war nor pacifist sentiment. It was the fact that the treaty exempted Russia from paying reparations to Japan after all the suffering the Japanese had endured in terms of military casualties, the enormous tax burden and soaring prices.

The Taishō era (1912–26) saw an active movement calling for disarmament, which was triggered by popular resistance against the military's intervention in government over military build-up issues beginning in 1912.

4 *Introduction*

The movement was also stimulated by the general optimism about international peace among Western nations in the post-World War I era. The political scientist Ishida Takeshi, however, notes that a pacifist element was largely lacking in the attitude of most proponents of disarmament, because their arguments were premised on maintaining the ongoing state of armed peace, or a balance of power among the world's major nations.[6]

Riots and workers' strikes following the end of the Russo-Japanese War and World War I, some of them war-related and others connected with labour and tenant disputes or with the campaign for universal male suffrage during the Taishō democracy movement, often led to the massive callout of troops. Suppression of such disturbances by the army also engendered significant popular resentment against the military, but that sentiment again had little to do with any pacifist belief or opposition to war in general.[7]

The brief period of the Taishō democracy movement was followed by a reactionary backlash from the government, which gradually consolidated its hold on the nation's ideology amid the onset of the Sino-Japanese War in the 1930s. The repression of freedom of speech, severe restrictions on political activity, and a government policy that exacted total loyalty to its wartime ideology did much to stifle the social atmosphere. Amid a media blackout, most Japanese supported the war and many eagerly followed the activities of the Japanese military abroad, relying mostly on government-censored news reports.

Therefore, no major war Japan conducted from the start of the Meiji era met with any significant popular movement opposing it.

Grassroots sentiment manifested itself in vigorous support for the war being waged at any given time. The Liberty and Civil Rights Movement (*jiyū minken undō*), the nation's first pro-democracy movement, was transformed into one offering popular support of the Sino-Japanese War of 1894–5. Although there were some newspapers that opposed the Russo-Japanese war, repression by the government was not the key reason why they later each began supporting the war. Papers that initially expressed anti-war views, had to back down, fearing a steep decline in their circulation because the public was zealously calling on the government to start the war against Russia. There was also considerable pro-war sentiment among the public on the eve of the Pacific War, though most Japanese recall that the news of Japan going to war with the US came out of the blue. According to the journalist Tahara Sōichirō, Tōjō Hideki, in his first fifty days as Prime Minister, received more than 3,000 letters from all over the country urging him to 'smash the US and Britain', and succumbed to public pressure as well as to pressure from the military when he decided to go to war.[8]

A limited amount of material available on anti-war activities between Japan's dispatch of troops to Siberia in 1918–1925 and the Pacific War suggests that in most cases, activists were influenced by socialist thought and/or were motivated by rancour against the brutal treatment meted out by the Japanese military, or concern about the well-being of their families.[9]

The Japanese on the whole remained largely strangers to the idea of pacifism until the end of World War II. While views expressing joy were conspicuous in the immediate wake of the attack on Pearl Harbour, voices predicting dire consequences were hardly audible.[10] The public was largely under the sway of government and media propaganda which claimed that victory in the war would serve as an effective springboard to advance Japan's status to that of a leading world power (*ittōkoku*).[11]

A very small number of communists, socialists, other intellectuals and adherents of various religions opposed the wars, but aside from those motivated by religious faith, it appears there were very few Japanese who refused to join the military because of a belief that it was wrong to kill. Accounts abound of young men who feigned illness or fled in an attempt to dodge conscription. Some others who had serious doubts about whether it was right to kill another human being, even for the good of their country, were reduced to confiding their thoughts in their private writings, and mostly joined the fighting while keeping their views secret. A minority who voiced criticism against Japan's war in East Asia frightened their acquaintances by daring to harbour thoughts that diverged from the government view.[12]

Unlike pacifist dissidents in the United States, Britain and some other European countries, where conscientious objection was already institutionalized, the very few Japanese who took a stand against war on moral grounds were isolated and forced to put up a lonely, solitary fight.[13]

As the government strengthened police powers and cracked down on dissidents amid the war, most Japanese were cowed into silence and did not dare take issue with the government's war policy. The obedient attitude towards the authorities, which had been ingrained amid feudalistic social mores, can be assumed to have encouraged the overt and often sycophantic display of enthusiasm about the war among the public.

On the other hand, however, it is difficult to imagine that the moral code that exacted total dedication on the part of the public to their country's cause could have had an unbreakable hold over most people's minds. If casual observations of those who experienced the war are any guide, the public attitude in general was characterized by varying degrees of patriotism, moral rectitude, sycophancy to the authorities, opportunism, a you-can't-fight-city-hall mentality, cowardice, indifference to political events and a secret desire to put one's own interests first rather than the public good.[14] In the final days of World War II, the mix of such disparate feelings appears to have given way to widespread war-weariness, and even recrimination toward the authorities, who continued to wage the war.[15]

Towards the end of the war, survival was the issue that dominated the minds of most Japanese. In a landscape that had been reduced to rubble, ideologies such as Japan's imperial mythology and historical materialism were totally irrelevant. Despair had crushed every other emotion in many Japanese, who were just paying lip service to the official line.[16]

Following the end of the war, however, a radical ideological shift was engineered at the initiative of SCAP.[17]

Japan's surrender and subsequent military occupation by the Allied powers made it easy to debunk the myth about Japan's war aims, as the Japanese mass media had no choice but to convey SCAP's interpretation of the war to the Japanese people. Revelations of Japan's war crimes during trials held by the Far East Military Tribunal between 1946 and 1948 especially served as a sobering experience for ordinary Japanese, many of whom until then had no knowledge of atrocities committed by the Japanese military. Memories of the brutal nature of the military leadership that had exacted a terrible human toll within Japan, combined with SCAP's demilitarization efforts, were to give rise to a widespread revulsion against the military.

While the people were still shocked and distraught at the devastation of the war and struggled to survive, the occupation authorities tried to promote peace and democracy as the new norms towards which Japan was to strive. While previous governments had fought claiming they were fighting to achieve peace in the world, the new post-war government preached renunciation of war and arms as the nation's sacred contribution to world peace.

The shift to the new tenet of peace appears to have been easily accepted by the public. According to the results of a nationwide public opinion poll published in the 27 May 1946 issue of the *Mainichi Shimbun*, 69.8 per cent of all respondents, most of whom were intellectuals or those with a relatively high education, said 'yes' and 28.4 per cent said 'no' when asked if the war-renouncing Article 9 of the new US-authored Constitutional draft was necessary. It can be assumed that the shift to pacifism – the exact meaning of which is discussed below – was relatively easy for the rest of the nation as well because most people probably had wished for nothing but a cessation of the fighting and their own hardship towards the end of the war. Their earnest wish for an end to their suffering now was extolled by the authorities as an ideal to strive for. With Japan's military and industrial capacities devastated, renunciation of war also must have appeared to many Japanese as obvious, while some accepted the Constitution with a sense of resignation, thinking it was impossible to resist the US.

Against this backdrop, the occupation authorities encouraged popular initiatives to reform and rehabilitate the nation from its desperate condition. The new Constitution, besides renouncing war, guaranteed the sovereign power of the people, basic human rights, freedom of speech, thought, conscience and academic activities, and banned discrimination on the grounds of race, creed, gender, social status, property or income.

Readily abandoning the nationalistic moral code exhorting self-sacrifice for the state, ordinary Japanese blithely sang to the new tune of pacifist and democratic ideals upheld by the new Constitution. Taking their cue from the Potsdam Declaration, which pledged to remake Japan into a democratic, peace-loving nation, intellectuals and the mass media broke out in a chorus of 'peaceful nation' (*heiwa kokka*) and 'cultured nation' (*bunka kokka*), meaning Japan should redeem itself through its rebirth as a peaceful nation contributing to world peace. The historian Sodei Rinjirō argues that the entire Japanese nation, sensing that justice was on the occupying power's side, quickly changed sides in a wholesale act of apostasy (*tenkō*).[18] The way the Japanese so easily adapted themselves to the new principles raised some concern that another shift in the political winds might prompt them readily to shed faith in them, or that the Japanese might lack the moral fibre to fight for them when faced with an adverse political climate.

The challenges to the new ideals came as the Cold War deepened in the late 1940s. Amid the so-called reverse course, the occupation authorities prioritized policy measures to wage the Cold War over the continued democratization of Japan. The period saw the return to public life of politicians who had been implicated in Japan's war effort, and they augmented the conservative camp that advocated rearmament and constitutional amendment to excise the national charter's war-renouncing clause.

The conservative backlash, which went hand-in-hand with the crackdown on communist, labour, peace and other centre-left activists, forced leftist intellectuals seriously to rethink the earlier communist-dominated labour and other social movements, which were characterized by an elitist and inflexible top-down approach. The intellectuals, who had turned activist out of a sense of remorse for their failure to resist the wartime government, began to rethink their relationship with ordinary people to enhance the effectiveness of their social movements. It was then that the mass line of communist China, called *taishū rosen* in Japanese, captured the imagination of intellectuals and activists (for more on the Chinese mass line see Chapter 4).

According to the sociologist Hidaka Rokurō, the mass line, which called for learning from the masses instead of teaching them how to think and act, was embraced by activists throughout Japan by 1955. Hidaka noted that at conventions of the Japanese Teachers Union (Nikkyōso), rank-and-file teacher unionists and pupils' mothers, who were ordinary housewives, began taking over the podium from academics as ordinary people acquired an aura of authority in the eyes of intellectuals and political activists, due to the adoption of the new people-oriented approach.[19]

The historian Naramoto Tatsuya noted that activist historians and other academics spelled out a policy to organize informal cultural activities (*sākuru katsudō*) with ordinary people to 'establish a union between intellectuals and people in the spheres of social activism and academic thought'.[20] The historian Ishimota Tadashi is said to have given a strong impetus to the popular movement to write about one's personal history, by emphasizing the need to record the history of obscure people, especially women, who belonged to the lower strata of society, as against the history of great men.[21] Intellectual magazines such as *Shisō* began in the mid-1950s to give increased coverage to the grassroots activities of ordinary people.

8 *Introduction*

Amid this milieu, in which they 'discovered' ordinary people, intellectuals and other activists sought close cooperation with the general populace, and such activism proved crucial to the spread of a nationwide grassroots peace movement.

Intellectuals found a significant reservoir of receptiveness to their ideas amongst the public, which often acted of its own accord to organize peace and other social movements, as in the case of the nationwide ban-the-bomb movement triggered by the Bikini hydrogen bomb test by the US.[22] The newfound activism of ordinary Japanese was such that it began to make itself felt in the political process.[23]

The power and depth of popular sentiment regarding war and peace issues far eclipsed the influence of intellectual opinion. A group of progressive academics, called the Discussion Circle on Problems of Peace (Heiwa Mondai Danwakai), got together in 1949 and the early 1950s and tried to present their case for peace in as non-partisan a manner as possible, by discussing peace as an issue to be treated separately from Marxist ideology. But their call for a comprehensive peace with all of Japan's former enemies largely failed to win the support of the public, as the academics were generally perceived to be sympathetic to the socialist camp, and the mass media faulted their view as unrealistic. Any impact they had on public opinion was a far cry from the outpouring of anti-war sentiment unleashed by the Bikini nuclear test on a nationwide level. The past misery and fears of another war, which were stimulated by what was perceived to be the ominous turn of events, did far more to grip the mind of the populace than a case for peace expounded from the academic pulpit.

Considering the far greater influence of pacifist views formed at the grassroots level as compared with media or academic opinion in cultivating the nation's overall outlook, this author believes the attitude of ordinary Japanese towards peace deserves more scholarly attention than has been paid to it in the past.

Defining pacifism

Here it is important to distinguish the meaning of the word 'pacifism', generally used in the context of Western tradition, from the meaning of the phrase 'popular pacifism' that the author uses in this book in depicting the attitude of ordinary Japanese.

The international relations expert Martin Ceadel traces what he calls two strands of proto-pacifist thought, Christianity and Enlightenment rationalism, to eighteenth-century Europe, and argues that these fused in Britain as rational Christianity began to evolve into liberalism.[24] Since then, peace activities flourished in countries, mainly Britain and the United States, where Protestantism in religion and liberalism in politics as well as a free enterprise economy provided a favourable setting.[25] The type of pacifist attitude nurtured in the two countries, as Charles Chatfield argues, was historically oriented to liberal values – the primacy of the individual, distrust of economic and political concentrations, the value of voluntary association, and appeal to experience and reason.[26]

Whereas the oldest and most durable inspiration for peace activities in the West has been Christianity, political ideologies such as socialism and anarchism began to make new contributions to Western peace thought in the late nineteenth century. From the inter-war period, to cite Ceadel, 'attempts began to be made to justify pacifism not on the basis of any religious faith or secular equivalent, but on the basis of war's effects on net human happiness and suffering'.[27]

Ceadel identifies two strands in the attitude informing people's actions calling for peace, which was born of this Western tradition, namely pacifism and pacificism. Pacifism usually means absolute pacifism, which is an unconditional refusal to support war. Pacificism, on the other hand, sees the prevention of war as its main duty and accepts that, however upsetting to the purist's conscience, the controlled use of armed force may be necessary to achieve this. It believes that some defensive uses of force are acceptable in the short term, and that war can be abolished eventually by reforming international or domestic politics. There are as many varieties of pacificism as there are ideologies, and they encompass the anti-war arguments of socialism, feminism and ecology. Both pacifism and pacificism constitute principled objections to war transcending mere war-weariness or anti-military sentiment stemming largely from personal grievances.[28]

Also according to Ceadel's classification, pacifism, with its perfectionist implications of refusing to take part in any war, in essence is a personal, moral creed that would only have a chance if a national policy of total disarmament were in force, because such a policy alone would prevent a sharp conflict arising between the pacifist's conscience and his duty as a citizen. Therefore, it is not a political idea.[29] This view is echoed by David A. Martin, who defines pacifism as a religious faith of minority groups, or the historian Henry Kamen, who terms as complete pacifism the stand of Anabaptists who practise their anti-war belief through non-involvement in the affairs of the state.[30] The view is shared by the Japanese Christian pacifist Uchimura Kanzō, who denounced the organized church as prone to support war, and promoted 'non-church Christianity' as in the days of the ancient Christians.[31] In contrast, Ceadel says,

> Essentially, it [pacificism] is a political idea since it believes that implementing reforms at the political level – rather than waiting for profound changes to occur in men's consciences offers the only realistic chance of limiting the use of force and of curbing warfare as a human institution.[32]

The complex realties in Japan, however, defy the distinction between pacifism and pacificism as defined by Ceadel.

While minorities of religious adherents and socialists who had opposed the war continued to espouse their anti-war beliefs, for a vast majority of Japanese, embracing the new pacifist policy of the government meant an abrupt break with their previous position.

As Japanese society largely lacked the kind of religious and liberal tradition prevalent in Britain and the United States that caused many individuals to become committed pacifists, intellectuals in Japan derived much of their inspiration from Western ideas.

At the grassroots level, ordinary Japanese, in thinking about war and peace issues in general, tended to derive their chief inspiration from their own experience of the war, and to develop their ideas in terms of their own existential questions posed by such experience, rather than embrace ideas elaborated from an international perspective.

Another characteristic of the popular peace movement in Japan is its predominantly secular nature. Though a small number of Buddhist and Christian groups cut a prominent figure in the peace movement, their members made up a tiny fraction of overall peace activists. Religion was not the key inspiration for pacifism among the population, most of whom, although not atheists, maintained only tenuous links to organized religions, whether established or unorthodox. This is another reason why most Japanese people had little else but their own experience to fall back on in developing their ideas about peace.

Acute economic privation caused by the war and criticism of the wartime regime stimulated introspection, whereby people reflected on the issue of peace in the wider context of all the problems that brought misery to their lives. Their struggles for a better economic well-being and advancement of their human rights, which were ineluctably intertwined with their notion of peace, often far outweighed diplomatic issues in their importance. Their attitude to peace therefore cannot be understood simply by examining whether it should be categorized as pacifism or pacificism, since the two philosophical strands essentially stand for ideas contesting issues of war and peace as such.

It is also impossible to find a single term for the attitude of a vast number of ordinary Japanese who engaged in the peace movement or otherwise demonstrated anti-war tendencies, because their outlook on peace varied from one person to another. The attitudes of many were quite contradictory, and do not fall neatly into any ideological pigeonhole. Their attitude, moreover, is torn or oscillates between pacifism and pacificism as defined by Ceadel. The Japanese word most frequently used to depict a peace-loving attitude is *heiwa shugi*, which is a combination of the Japanese words for 'peace' and 'ism'. As the peace researcher Fujiwara Osamu points out, there is no English word that is a precise equivalent of *heiwa shugi*. The ambiguous nature of the term might have helped to make most Japanese oblivious of the need consciously to clarify whether their own attitude stood for absolute pacifism or pacificism, or conditional opposition to war.[33]

The creation of the Police Reserve, the forerunner of today's Self-Defence Forces (SDF) that was established in 1950 at the behest of SCAP, in effect nullified the war-renouncing clause of the Constitution. In the face of the deepening Cold War, very few Japanese took a policy of total disarmament seriously. Most peace activists or proponents of peace also tended to conduct rationalist arguments in opposing many government policies regarding peace and security issues, and tried to demonstrate why a given government policy aimed at building up the military or tightening the military alliance with the US, among others, was unwarranted by the prevailing international situation. Very few took a fundamentalist stand to insist on immediately practising the absolute pacifism called for by the Constitution, or were ready to do so without the implementation of further reform both at home and abroad that would ensure enduring peace. Their attitude, therefore, was pacifistic.

On the other hand, the widespread war-weariness in the early post-war period suggests that many Japanese viewed the devastation of the war they had suffered as the ultimate apocalypse, recurrence of which was simply too terrifying to visualize. Such views gave rise to a 'never-again' reflex of total rejection. By the time of the ban-the-bomb movement in the 1950s, the staunchly anti-war stand of activists acquired a moral aspect which made people determined to oppose all wars to prevent the recurrence of the kind of suffering A-bomb victims in Hiroshima and Nagasaki had experienced. As the moral element of their attitude to peace came to the fore, it began to eclipse rational considerations about how to resist all wars in this imperfect world that was still unable to live up to the pacifist beliefs of the activists.

It should be noted also that many ordinary Japanese, even when genuinely inspired and moved by the idealistic aspirations expressed by the Constitution, were too busy with the business of making a living and only had limited time deeply to ponder policy issues regarding war and peace. Many also lacked the intellectual skills to do so, and whenever they gave thought to the war they had experienced or peace issues in general, they often did little more than engage in a mental exercise of stirring up moral fervour and reflecting in a serious frame of mind. Due to the limited understanding of their own attitudes, but with the pacifist Constitution being a powerful source of inspiration, many peace activists in particular appear not to have doubted that they were pacifists, even when the actual policies they advocated fell short of abolishing the SDF, and they did not thoroughly consider whether they should refuse to fight even in self-defence.[34]

This potpourri of anti-war attitudes, which defies distinction between pacifism and pacificism, leaves this author little choice but to term the anti-war outlook of many ordinary Japanese as 'popular pacifism'. Although the ideas of most Japanese did not stand for absolute pacifism in the strict sense of the term, the main focus of this thesis is on a more or less principled stand that people took against war.

Research purposes and approaches

Ceadel's definitions of 'pacifism' and 'pacificism', when used as a conceptual tool, also needs to take into account external influences and other political dynamics that affect people's outlook on peace. Ceadel applied the method to analyze the British peace movement between 1914 and 1945, during which time peace activities thrived following World War I and then waned amid the onset of World War II. The historical context for the period this study addresses is radically different, and was defined by Japan's experience of the unprecedented devastation of the war and the introduction of institutional reforms and new ideas after the war. Whereas the British peace movement built on its Christian and liberal political tradition, the Japanese post-war peace movement began through repudiation of the wartime ideology. The abrupt discontinuity from the previous political tradition took place while peace activists made conscious efforts to acquire a new political ideology and values in order to make a cogent case for peace. In the process, a new political culture, which was conducive to the spread of peace campaigns involving a large number of grassroots activists, was created for the first time in Japan's history.

As the following chapters will demonstrate, the peace movement in the early post-war years had multiple objectives, some of which were only indirectly related to peace. In the process, activists also had to learn about the new political system introduced after the war, and reflected upon their past and present situations. As a result, the peace movement, besides sometimes helping to achieve political victories for the activists, produced a significant change in their outlook.

This author's contention is that the peace movement, which was organized in tandem with other activities to promote democratic, economic, humanitarian and various other issues, served as a popular lever, which helped to eliminate to a significant extent feudal remnants of the past that lingered in Japanese society and in people's attitudes after the war, thereby modernizing the political praxis and the outlook of ordinary Japanese. Their peace movement involved a struggle to establish anew a personal identity for the peace activists themselves and a national identity for their country.

The adjective 'feudal' or 'feudalistic' that Japanese peace activists used in the period addressed by this thesis generally meant unthinking subservience to authority as was evidenced by people's embrace of or quiescence towards the imperial ideology of the government during the war, or their frequent inability to assert civil or human rights sanctioned by post-war legislation. The adjective was used as an antonym for the word 'modern', which generally was synonymous with progress, rationality or the establishment of democracy in the nation's political praxis. In this thesis, however, another meaning of the word 'modern', which pertains to a personal attitude, is particularly important because it is vital in triggering people's spontaneous participation in the peace movement. I therefore use phrases such as a modern attitude or outlook to mean people's willingness to tackle wider social issues that transcend their own immediate personal interests even when there is no coercive outside influence, such as government propaganda, as was the case in wartime Japan. A willingness to speak up or take autonomous action by defying, if need be, unfavourable opinions or prejudice from other members of the public as well as the establishment will also be taken to mean a modern trait. Among the multiple meanings of the word 'democracy', egalitarian socio-political relationships between the people and the government, between labour and management and between genders figured prominently in the concerns of peace activists, as the following chapters demonstrate. These meanings of the words 'feudalistic', 'modern' and 'democracy' as understood by the activists of those days will serve as working definitions throughout this book.

Political activists in those days made diligent efforts to learn about the normative ideas introduced by the occupiers in the fields of the political system and education. The difficulty of assimilating them into their attitude in the immediate wake of Japan's previous historical, political and social legacy prompted activists to try and devise principles that would govern their political praxis, as well as the conduct of their everyday life, in a manner that would best suit their circumstances.

The international relations specialist Sakamoto Yoshikazu argued that the unique circumstances under which ordinary Japanese lived and staged their peace activities helped to 'indigenize' pacifist and democratic values inculcated by their Western occupiers. The purpose of this thesis is to clarify how the peace movement helped change people's attitudes, and to examine the process of the 'indigenization' whereby various strands of pacifist thought crystallized at the grassroots level to contribute to the nation's outlook, while giving an account of the dynamics of the peace movement in the period 1945–60, which ended with the *Anpo Tōsō*.[35]

There were three key factors that stimulated people's political activism. One was the institutional reform introduced by SCAP. Among all democratic legislation, universal suffrage no doubt had the most crucial impact, as electoral politics serves as a key weapon with which voters can assert themselves *vis-à-vis* the government. The second was a rise in the standard of living that allowed people to consider wider social issues beyond immediate concerns regarding their own livelihood. The third was a desire to live up to one's values.

Activism prompted by the first two factors can be explained with the resource mobilization thesis that became dominant in academic research on social movements in the 1970s and early 1980s. The paradigm that premises development of social movements on the acquisition of material resources and political opportunity holds true to a certain extent in the case of early post-war Japan. It is particularly relevant in considering the effects of the end of the Allied occupation and a rising standard of living from the mid-1950s onwards on the peace movement. It was after the departure of the occupation forces, for example, that *Asahi Graph* magazine did a special on the atomic bombings of Hiroshima and Nagasaki, and raised public consciousness on the issue of nuclear weapons prior to the Bikini incident. It should also be noted that in contrast to the peace movement of the early 1950s, which was dominated by the political left, peace-related activities from around 1955 saw a massive increase in the participation of people who did not subscribe to any particular ideology, against the backdrop of a steady improvement in the economy.

On the other hand, however, while dire poverty is not normally conducive to a climate in which peace activities can flourish, it is notable that peace campaigns began to be organized from the very first post-war years in Japan, when she had yet to achieve a level of economic development comparable to that of the major Western nations. The historian Wada Haruki contends that pacifism began to enjoy a powerful ideological sway ever since the emperor's call for the establishment of a 'peace nation' in a speech delivered on 4 September 1945 at the opening of the Diet immediately following Japan's surrender. According to Wada, both media and intellectuals subsequently began advocating pacifism as the nation's policy, apparently taking their cue from the emperor's speech.[36]

It should also be noted that people formed countless, grassroots mutual-help networks in the immediate aftermath of the war amid acute economic hardship, when they were unable to survive without joining forces with their neighbours (see the following chapters). This kind of grassroots infrastructure often served as a vehicle for spreading a peace movement. Admittedly, peace activities through the early 1950s were a far more limited affair as compared with the peace movement from the mid-1950s onward. Nevertheless, it is important to note that those peace campaigns, which were first stimulated by the ideological inspiration of government propaganda immediately after the war and assisted later by grassroots networks, preceded activists' acquisition of material resources – if such resources are to be understood in terms of economic means.

The social mobilization paradigm may also be inadequate to fully explain why there was no widespread peace movement during the Korean War, for example. The general apathy at the time of the Korean War has been often attributed by past researchers to the SCAP-led crackdown on the peace movement and Japan's low economic standard, under which most Japanese were preoccupied with how to make ends meet. But I believe that even if the occupation authorities had not suppressed peace activities, or if people had had at their disposal sufficient economic means that could have enabled them to spare some thought to issues other than their immediate personal concerns, any motivation on the part of the public to protest a humanitarian crisis abroad would still have been largely absent, in contrast to the days of the Vietnam War more than ten years later.

An engagement with public issues that were of no direct relevance to their own lives, such as international conflicts and human suffering abroad, became possible only after a greater number of Japanese, who lacked a tradition of political activism, gained sufficient awareness to motivate them to contest wider political issues through their own action. Only after some more years of learning did they come to recognize, for example, at the time of the ban-the-bomb movement from the mid-1950s, a fundamental injustice in the plight of A-bomb victims, whose basic human rights had been largely ignored amid the old mores of Japanese society. The protest against nuclear weapons also evolved from a movement driven by the health concerns of the Japanese into one aimed at benefiting the international community. The change that occurred in this process suggests a shift in people's value systems that subsequently helped promote a greater public readiness to organize collective action in the struggle for the wider public good.

The foregoing serves to buttress the arguments of critics of the resource mobilization approach who contended that it ignored the importance of values, grievances, ideology and collective identity in producing movements.[37] Given the underdeveloped state of Japan's economy and democratic institutions in those days, another important school of thought, the theory of new social movements, in which activists act in protest to mainstream social and political institutions and seek to create a counterculture that will repudiate a large bureaucratized state, is not relevant here. The theory is premised on the existence of an advanced industrial democracy, in which a large number of people chafe at the invasive influence of government control on their lives and act outside conventional channels of participation such as political parties and interest groups.[38] Japan's early post-war peace movement, which did not contest the issue of extensive government control, and relied heavily on traditional movement organizations, cannot be categorized as a new social movement.

Proving the ascendancy of the third of the above-cited three factors, namely a desire to live up to one's values, over the other two, or over institutional reform and a higher standard of living, is beyond the scope of this book. This study, however, will focus mainly on the transformative experience of peace activists that shaped the belief system at the grassroots regarding war and peace issues, and the self-definition of participants in the peace movement. The subject is important particularly because the depth of feeling that arose from the traumatic experience of the war, and the bewildering process of reorientation to the new post-war norms of peace and democracy, served as the driving force behind Japan's peace movement in the early years of the post-war era.

The peace movement in the period addressed by this book ended in defeats for activists in many of their crucial battles, for example, over the peace treaty, rearmament, and the signing and revision of the Japan-US security treaty. The fact that Article 9 of the Constitution nevertheless continued to enjoy majority popular support in later years, in glaring contradiction to the actual defence policy pursued by the government, suggests that whatever victories there may have been for peace activists were attained largely in the moral realm. The popular discourse that emphasizes

16   *Introduction*

the human tragedy aspect of war endured for decades following the end of World War II, and became part of the nation's spiritual legacy, which is another reason why this book will focus on the ideological aspect of the grassroots peace movement.

There were three major groundswells of popular activism aimed at the empowerment of the people between the beginning of the Meiji era and the start of the Sino-Japanese War in the 1930s: (1) The liberty and civil rights movement in the late 1870s up to the mid-1880s; (2) The Taishō democracy movement in the late 1910s up to the mid-1920s; and (3) the socialist movement in the 1920s and 1930s.

Unlike the above three incidents, where the initiative for social movements came from the Japanese themselves, the fourth popular movement in modern Japanese history emerged after receiving its initial impetus from SCAP following Japan's surrender. The fact that the new reform policy was imposed from above by SCAP and the government immediately after the war, helped to enhance the inspiring power of the new national tenet of peace and democracy in the minds of ordinary people, whose attitude was still characterized very much by obedience to higher authority. The pledge to renounce war enunciated in the nation's Constitution also provided a vital focus around which Japan's peace movement could rally.

The 1950s, which opened with the resurgence of the political right, saw fierce political strife between peace and other leftist activists and their opponents. The *Anpo Tōsō* marked arguably the final paroxysm of the major conflict between the political leadership seen to represent Japan's wartime authoritarian values and the pacifist camp promoting post-war values. The issue at stake in the anti-security treaty protest was those values as much as the Japan-US military alliance itself. Faced with a frenetic protest movement, the government subsequently opted to modify the way it dealt with highly sensitive war and peace issues. Against this backdrop, the percentage of Japanese opposed to amending the Constitution kept climbing and achieved a plurality already in 1955, despite stepped-up government efforts in favour of revision.[39] A rising number of ordinary Japanese apparently began to embrace the ideas embodied by the Constitution from the mid-1950s, in either explicit or implicit defiance of government pressure.

From the mid-1950s onward, the growing activism of a large number of both male and female peace campaigners not affiliated to established political parties or other mass organizations, gave rise, especially among intellectuals, to the vaunted myth of common men and women who would become key agents of historical change and act out the Japanese intellectuals' idealized view of Western democracy and civil society. This prompted leading thinkers such as Maruyama Masao, Kuno Osamu and Hidaka Rokurō to dream about the role that an engaged citizenry might play to promote an ever more civilized and liberal political system.

The political scientist Takabatake Michitoshi argues that intellectuals were the leaders of the *Anpo Tōsō* and that the protest movement escalated because the influence of intellectuals on society, which had grown as a result of a number of previous cultural and peace-related activities, reached its zenith at that time.[40] Intellectuals indeed had an undeniable influence on the grassroots peace movement. It is, however, debatable whether most ordinary Japanese were organizing vigorous anti-nuclear signature drives or demonstrating in the streets in hopes of realizing the idealized vision of a new world as conceived by progressive intellectuals. Since ordinary Japanese developed their ideas about peace through their association with labour unions, local community services and like-minded hobbyists, the sensibilities they cultivated often differed from the idealistic visions of intellectuals. It will be shown in the following chapters that the popular peace discourse forged in this milieu significantly diverged from the vision of Heiwa Mondai Danwakai intellectuals, which was premised on the role of enlightened citizenry modelled on an idealized view of Western civic tradition.

With a view to analysing the peace thought at the grass roots, the author has decided to focus on male unionists and housewives, both of whom were important pillars of the peace movement in the early post-war years.

Both groups, compared with academics and students, attached more importance to defending their own livelihoods in conducting their peace campaign, and as a result their peace movement appealed to a very wide sector of the populace. It is fair to say that their attitude to peace represented the bulk of the nation's sentiment or beliefs that made up what this author terms popular pacifism. Whereas many students easily changed their ideas or ended their participation in the peace movement once they graduated, both workers and women had to ponder their positions about peace over a longer term, as employees and in the case of women as individuals who would remain housewives/mothers for the rest of their lives. As for farmers, who also made up a sizable sector of the nation's population, they did not play any significant role in peace activities and so do not deserve much attention in this book.

In discussing the activities of the two groups, however, different approaches will be taken for the following reasons.

In addition to a gender difference, unionists and housewives differed in that they conducted their peace campaigns on distinctly dissimilar principles. The unionists' peace movement was to a large extent conditioned by their status as organization men, and was inseparable from the overall goals of the labour movement. Women's peace campaigns were supported largely by obscure grassroots activists. A majority of these were motivated by maternal concern for their children, as well as the past and present difficulties they had to suffer because of the war and their status as women. Many women also took part in the peace movement as individuals rather than as members of a large organization.

In conducting research on the outlook of individual activists, it is easier to collect relevant material on women because of the availability of women's newspapers and monthly magazines that continued to follow ordinary female readers' opinions throughout most of the first fifteen post-war years, while there were no comparable publications for male unionists. As members of large, hierarchical organizations, male workers often had little alternative but to obey their leadership or subordinate their personal interests to the objectives of their unions or the overall labour movement. The sway of socialist thought that dominated the unions' ideology also tended to stifle independent thinking among individual workers, and official statements made by unions sounded like little more than leftist cant.

While attempts will be made to analyse individual workers' thoughts by quoting their written opinions, much in the chapters on organized labour will deal also on the ideas of the leadership and the dynamics of the union peace movement. How to harness the energies of rank-and-file workers, who were radicalized as a result of the traumatic events during the war and their harsh economic conditions in the early post-war years, was a key concern for the union leaders. The policies they devised to utilize workers' energies speak volumes about the general tendencies of ordinary workers. Policies formulated at the top were often a reflection of the labour movement considered desirable by rank-and-file workers. The ideas and actions of the leadership were often a function of tendencies prevalent at the grassroots level. Also, although available material that sheds light on the development of workers' attitude to peace is limited compared with the literature on women, unionists' enthusiasm for peace issues can be gauged by the extent of their participation in peace activities and a leftward shift in their ideology. These therefore will also become key considerations in discussing the union peace movement.

War and peace had previously been a crucial part of the agenda of labour movements, both in pre-war Japan and the rest of the world, which were inspired by socialist ideology. A case in point is the Second International, which promoted a bond of socialist brotherhood to oppose the wars, militarism and imperialism of the ruling classes. The communists of wartime Japan also resisted the country's war of aggression from a similar standpoint. Socialist thought helped underpin much of the union anti-war movement, which saw the cause of advancing labour's struggle for social and economic power as synonymous with opposition to capitalist wars.

Such views also provided vital theoretical underpinnings to the ideas of peace activists in Japan's post-war labour movement. However, socialist thought alone does not sufficiently explain why both the leadership and rank-and-file of Japanese labour organizations so zealously devoted themselves to the peace movement, a political matter that often appeared far removed from their immediate economic concerns.

In the early post-war years, Japan's political scene was dominated by factors that propelled the expansion of labour union activities into the political sphere. Among such factors were the war itself; the economic and social chaos in its aftermath; the US occupation – which, although benevolent in many ways, was in effect a military dictatorship – Japan's political and economic leaders, who were still wedded to the ways of the pre-war authoritarian regime; and the Cold War.

To describe the way Sōhyō (the General Council of Trade Unions of Japan) expanded its activities beyond the economic sphere into the political sphere, the social policy specialist Ōkōchi Kazuo came up with the phrases 'internalization' (*naihōka*) and 'externalization' (*gaienka*) of the labour movement.[41] Internalization means to limit the activities of labour unions to traditional pursuits, such as pressing for wage increases and other economic benefits. Externalization means to expand union activities beyond the traditional bounds of trade unionism.

The labour movement during this period was marked by frequent and dramatic bouts of externalization, as a result of which, according to the former Sōhyō ideologue Shimizu Shinzō, the Japanese Socialist Party (JSP), Sōhyō's political ally, was driven to adopt the most left-wing stance of all the world's social democratic parties.[42]

Labour unions in those days had in both their leadership and ranks a significant proportion of workers who saw labour issues as part of a greater social movement aimed at transforming society. In the views of many activists inspired by socialist philosophy, union activities aimed at fighting poverty and unemployment, which they believed stemmed from capitalist control of markets, were supposed to eradicate the root cause of war. Thus, in the words of such activists, the labour movement itself was a peace movement.[43]

On the other hand, the number of apolitical union members was also significant. In contrast to the situation in Europe, where workers joined industrial unions of their own free will and as individuals, about 90 per cent of Japanese labour unions were in-house.[44] Japanese workers automatically became members of the unions at their workplace upon joining a company. This closed system tended to turn members' attention to the internal affairs of their own company, and labour unions faced considerable institutional drawbacks if they tried to play an active role in any kind of social movement beyond the company. The way organized labour staged its peace movement, therefore, was conditioned by the clash between the socialist goals of the overall labour movement and the economic exigencies at individual firms.

Labour unions suffered also from the bureaucratic inertia inherent in any organization of significant size, which tended to sap individual initiative among members, who depended on their leaders to tackle the tough issues. Unions, therefore, had a tendency to turn into organizational behemoths which, even when they managed to mobilize huge numbers of workers in a demonstration of their muscle, often failed to sustain the momentum of their campaign. How to organize an effective peace movement with unwieldy organizations that had not been purposefully set up to pursue peace activities, was an issue which greatly taxed the minds of union leaders and activists who were aware of the importance of the peace movement to advance organized labour's interests.

Despite these impediments, the labour unions' peace movement was driven to a considerable extent by the spontaneous participation of ordinary workers. Workers' commitment to the peace movement, as the following chapters will demonstrate, was more often than not proportionate to the level of their unions' militancy. Most militant unions placed the peace movement at the top of their agenda.

It was its heavy involvement in peace and other political activities that so bolstered the influence of Sōhyō on the national scene that the union federation's clout was compared, with a touch of hyperbole, to that of the former Japanese army.

The following chapters will attempt to analyse strands of thought at both leadership and rank-and-file level that compelled workers to engage in peace activities, and thereby clarify the relationship between the labour and peace movements. Light will be also shed on the change in workers' attitudes and conditions over the passage of some fifteen years, so as to ascertain how this affected their peace activities.

The author will also examine how interactions or tensions between leadership and rank-and-file affected the development of their peace activities. Special attention will be paid to the role of union activists, or *katsudōka*, who often acted independently of their leadership to address the peace movement as well as other union affairs.

The first fifteen years of the post-war period also witnessed a revolution in China, the Korean War, and other serious international conflicts that flared up amid the Cold War. How the ideological fallout resulting from these events that took place outside Japan affected the union peace movement will also be a subject of this study.

While these points will be examined in a survey of the fifteen-year post-war period in the first four chapters, Chapter 5 will look at specific examples of peace activities at individual unions to analyse the mechanism and characteristics unique to the peace campaigns conducted by organized labour.

This study will focus mainly on the Congress of Industrial Unions of Japan (Sanbetsu), Sōhyō, and the National Federation of Industrial Organizations (Shin Sanbetsu), and will mostly exclude unions that did not join or seceded from Sōhyō. The activities of the Japanese Teachers Union (Nikkyōso), a key Sōhyō member, are not discussed despite the pivotal role it played in the peace movement. The subjects of this research are predominantly other public-sector or industrial blue-collar workers, whose chief adversaries were company managers. Teachers in contrast were white-collar workers who conducted their peace campaign with the aim of resisting the policies of the school authorities and the education ministry, and winning over pupils and parents to their pacifist cause. The challenges teachers faced, therefore, were widely different from those confronting blue-collar workers, and are the subject of a separate discussion conducted in Part II, which deals with the women's peace movement.

The women's peace movement in the period discussed here was mostly an urban, middle-class affair, so this group is the main subject of discussion. Attention, however, will also be paid to those in rural or regional areas, many of whom were almost as important income-earners as their husbands, working as farm hands or co-managers of family businesses. As is already fairly well known, their participation in the peace movement was quite limited, and the condition of their lives, which was quite different from that of urban housewives, prompted them to react in a different way towards peace issues. Attempts will be made to study the contrast in attitudes towards peace between urban middle-class housewives and their counterparts in rural areas.

The discussion of the women's peace movement is divided into three chapters. Chapter 6 covers the first five or so years of the post-war period between Japan's defeat in World War II and the outbreak of the Korean War in 1950. This was the first time in the nation's history that a significant number of women voluntarily organized a peace movement. Any peace movement organized against the backdrop of the Cold War, however, was also gravely affected by a serious rift between the political right and left.

Previous studies of the women's peace movement during this period do no more than describe it as an affair that revolved around the controversy between conservatives, who fought against the radicalization of the peace movement, and those on the left, who tried to link the peace movement to other political and economic struggles.[45] In this study, attempts will be made to examine in more detail the contentious issues in the peace debates conducted during the period, and to clarify how the views of conservatives and leftists differed from each other.

Women's response to the Korean War will also be analyzed in this chapter. The war, which gave rise to public fears of Japan getting embroiled in the fighting, posed a severe test to the thinking of earlier peace activists, which derived its chief inspiration from the absolute pacifism propagated through the post-war Constitution. The chapter will seek to determine whether women in general reacted to the war from a pacifist point of view. With regard to the peace treaty debate, public appeals making a case for a comprehensive peace, which were issued by female intellectuals, will be analyzed to clarify the ideas behind their arguments.

The key question of Chapter 6 is whether conservatives or those at the centre of the ideological spectrum were less pacifist than those in the leftist camp. Was the case as clear-cut as many leftist historians and other writers have previously depicted it?

Chapter 7 spans the subsequent decade through to the *Anpo Tōsō*. This period saw the participation in the peace movement of a significant number of ordinary women, whose outlook had been shaped by the turbulent events of the war and its aftermath. Chapter 7 will consider the quantitative and qualitative change that women's peace activities went through in the mid-1950s, which helped to turn women, despite their lack of any great organizational structure comparable to that of labour unions, into an important force behind Japan's peace movement. The key questions in this chapter are: What factors increasingly facilitated the participation of ordinary women in peace activities, in contrast to the earlier days when women were inhibited from taking political stands? And: What arguments did women use to justify their actions?

The chapter will also explain why women in rural areas, who accounted for about half of the female population in the late 1950s, largely failed to take part in any peace movement.

Chapter 8 examines the elements that made up women's peace thought by looking at their writings and attempting to identify the hallmarks of their attitude that lent a unique spirit to their peace movement. Of interest here is what chiefly inspired their ideas; whether a sense of remorse concerning their own past conduct affected the way women thought and acted; and whether women were pacifists in the exact or usual sense of the word.

The feminist aspect of the women's peace movement will also be considered. Previous researchers broadly agree that feminist aspirations for elevating women's social status tended to be weak in women's grassroots social movements in this period, since maternal concern for their children dominated their agenda for peace. Indeed, few women appear to have engaged in peace activities with the aim of transforming gender relations in a fundamental manner. While the implications of a peace movement prioritizing maternal concern over the issue of gender relations will also be analyzed in Chapter 8, the point will be made that challenges women faced in conducting the peace movement amid the evolving post-war society compelled them to change their old ways, and that this helped to lay the foundation for a feminist movement in Japan's post-war period.

Most previous historical accounts of Japan's peace movement have dealt primarily with left-wing activism, thereby creating an impression that it was the political left which single-handedly led the campaign for peace. But it must be noted that in the case of the women's peace movement, a significant number of people with a conservative political outlook also played an important role, a point seldom acknowledged by left-leaning historians and writers, many of whom have taken an undisguised partisan stand in their writings, and depicted the attitude of conservative women as something to be deplored.

Conservatives often opposed the left's approach to the peace movement, and stiffly resisted its attempts to link the anti-nuclear movement to other political issues. As a result, they were often disparaged by the left for 'being apolitical' or lacking 'the right kind of political consciousness'. Whether or not that was indeed the case, however, it must be admitted that most women did not politicize the peace issue to the extent that those on the left did. Most women also did not translate their abhorrence of war into political action. Their yearning for peace, which was more or less apolitical in nature, also deserves serious study because it is a key ingredient of women's collective attitude toward peace.

The final chapters of each part of this book deal with reflective and other traits of the peace movement that cannot be addressed chronologically. They nonetheless constitute aspects that are integral to the discussion in this book, and are therefore considered in separate chapters.

The peace movements of organized labour and women are a study in contrast, and the widely differing ideologies of the two groups often became a source of mutual antipathy. Even when they cooperated and demonstrated together during the *Anpo Tōsō*, there was no significant meeting of minds on an ideological level. While battling the same enemy, the two groups continued to fight battles that were quite distinct from each other. Their ideologies differed mainly because organized labour sought to organize a movement of the working class, whereas the attitude of housewives, who were actively involved in peace activities, reflected traits of middle-class values largely devoid of socialist inspiration.

Frank Parkin, in his study of the Campaign for Nuclear Disarmament (CND), whose activism peaked in the late 1950s and early 1960s, distinguishes the tendencies of middle-class activists, who made up the bulk of Britain's ban-the-bomb movement, from those of working-class activists as follows:

> whereas working class radicalism could be said to be geared largely to reforms of an economic or material kind, the radicalism of the middle class is directed mainly to social reforms which are basically moral in content. Again, whereas the former holds out the promise of benefits to one particular section of society (the working class) from which its own supporters are drawn, the latter envisages no rewards which will accrue to the middle class specifically, but only to society at large, or to some underprivileged groups. It is argued in fact that the main pay-off for middle class radicals is that of a psychological or emotional kind – in satisfactions derived from expressing personal values in action.[46]

Parkin then cites terms used by Peter M. Blau to argue that the actions of middle-class CND supporters can be considered *Wertrational*, which means although they are not calculated to obtain specific advantages, their conduct, which is oriented to the pursuit of ultimate values, is not necessarily irrational. The concept stands in contrast to the counter-concept *Zweckrational*, which is used to indicate actions geared to attaining goals more concrete than the attainment of ideals or absolute values.[47]

This type of analysis based on the European type of class society in general, and that of Britain in particular, is not so relevant in the case of Japan in the period studied in this book. The neat dichotomy between middle-class and working-class behaviour is difficult to sustain in the face of Japanese realities of the time. Class distinction was not as clear cut in postwar Japan as was the case in Europe, and although unionists identified themselves as members of the proletariat or working class, their professed identity belied the socio-economic trend, in which sociologists increasingly began to identify the expansion of the middle class through a wide sector of the population in the mid-1950s.

While the union peace movement was always aimed ostensibly at serving workers' economic interests, many unionists believed their activities were inextricably linked to the reform of Japanese society and foreign policy, and transcended their narrow economic interests. A distinct moral element was also evident in the women's peace movement, but the middle-class housewives who took part in peace campaigns were mostly of far more modest means compared to their British counterparts of the 1950s. The Japanese women's movement therefore was also geared towards meeting their material self-interests in the immediate wake of the war, when there was an acute material shortage, or following the Bikini H-bomb test, whose fallout led to a widespread food scare. The issue of class was not necessarily a key factor in causing the two groups to act differently, unlike the case of Britain.

Traits of Europe's working- and middle-class movements crossed over between the two Japanese groups studied in this book precisely because the experience of the war, which had a cataclysmic impact on the nation's moral belief system, prompted both of them to live up to the values they acquired after the war.

As pointed out by Wesley Sasaki-Uemura, some Western researchers argue that social movements, whose formation is highly dependent on particular social and cultural contexts, cannot be accounted for with a fixed general theory.[48] The brief discussion of existing theories on social movements in the foregoing also suggests that application of any particular theoretical approach is unlikely to be effective in elucidating the subject matter of this book. I shall therefore use historical and empirical approaches in order to understand what the terms 'peace' and the 'peace movement' meant to the ordinary Japanese, and shall rely heavily on the discourse analysis of their statements and writings.

Another topic covered by the book is the issue of war responsibility, in both domestic and international contexts. The matter, which is inseparably bound up with the issue of how one interprets Japan's as well as individuals' roles in World War II, should constitute an integral part of any study of popular pacifism. This is because if pacifism is to be understood as a certain moral stand concerning war and peace issues, the moral high ground it claims would be in doubt if the nature of one's country's war and one's own conduct during that war failed to become a subject of serious examination by people who espouse pacifism. People's attitudes regarding these matters should therefore be an important gauge of the degree of their peacefulness.

Sources

Despite a vast amount of writings produced by both intellectuals and ordinary Japanese about their experiences in World War II and peace issues in general,

Japan's peace movement remains a largely untapped area as a subject of academic research, except for Fujiwara Osamu's seminal work establishing the process, in which the ban-the bomb movement, drawing on Japan's experience of the Hiroshima and Nagasaki atomic bombings, created for the first time a popular peace discourse in the mid-1950s, which was shared on a nationwide basis.[49] Among the books that do deal with Japan's peace movement, those with broad titles claiming comprehensively to cover most peace activities during the post-war period were written by peace organizations or activists, and their arguments are highly polemical and advanced apparently with the aim of promoting their peace activities.[50] Books written in English with similarly broad titles are sketchy overviews, and appear to have been written to inform readers abroad about basic facts concerning Japan's peace movement.[51]

Similar things can be said about existing historical accounts of the labour movement and women's social movements in the period. Most are little more than general overviews of such activities,[52] and were written by those representing organizations that were involved in the labour or other social movements. Almost none of them focus on the peace activities of labour unions or women.[53]

The post-war labour movement, however, attracted much wider scholarly attention as compared with the grassroots activism of women. Andrew Gordon, for example, conducted detailed studies of the way the socialist ideology of Japanese labour unions drove their economic struggles in the early post-war years, before organized labour later adopted a highly cooperative praxis *vis-à-vis* management.[54] His works, however, make little mention of the union peace movement. The political scientist Ōtake Hideo has written briefly about the radicalism of the JSP and Sōhyō, but his work relies on a highly limited number of primary sources and he appears to have interviewed neither current nor former members of the JSP or Sōhyō.[55] As a result, as will be pointed out in the following chapters, Ōtake underestimated the importance of Sōhyō's peace activities for the labour movement as a whole.

Among the vast amount of literature available on the *Anpo Tōsō*, George R. Packard's book, which seeks to survey the entire sweep of the protest campaign, serves as a standard reference on the anti-security treaty protest. But his comprehensive account of the movement, which presents a detailed analysis of actions by the government and the ruling Liberal Democratic Party in addition to the opposition camp, does not focus on grassroots protest. As the author himself says, his focus was on the political process and he did not conduct a deeper examination of the motivation of major actors in the campaign, such as labour unions, intellectuals and students.[56]

Most other work on the *Anpo* has also tended to focus on intellectuals, union leaders and political parties, and there has been no extensive research using primary material documenting the actions and ideas of grassroots activists.[57] So this book is an attempt to fill the void left by previous studies.

Because of its focus on grassroots anti-war sentiment, the book draws heavily on views expressed by ordinary Japanese in newspapers, magazines,

26 *Introduction*

and the organs of labour organizations and women's groups, as well as publications by the JSP and the Japanese Communist Party (JCP). Among daily newspapers distributed nationwide, I chose the *Asahi Shimbun* because this paper, due to its liberal bent, attracted a large number of readers with pacifist views and paid close attention to trends in public opinion, especially that of women.[58]

The archives I used in researching this book include those at the National Diet Library, the Tokyo Central Library, Sophia University, the Japanese Institute of Labour, the Ohara Institute for Social Research at Hosei University, Sōhyō Kaikan, the Japanese National Railway Union, the All Japan Harbour Workers' Union, the Takano Minoru collection of Shinshu University, the Japanese Teachers Union's library at the Japanese Education Centre, the National Women's Education Centre, the Institute for Gender Studies at Ochanomizu University, the Fusae Ichikawa Memorial Association, the Mothers' Congress, and the Tokyo Regional Women's Organization.

The subject of this book is the nameless Japanese, the vast majority of whom lack written accounts of their lives. Therefore this account deals with how they perceived many of the key events that took place during the period and why they reacted to those events in the way they did, an area which has remained largely undocumented to this day. In order to find answers to those questions, the author interviewed people who worked as peace activists in that period. The interviews and private writings of some of the interviewees were used to complement information gathered from libraries and other archives.

Among unionists who were interviewed, my informants include both former senior officials and lower-ranking activists, most of whom belonged to dissident camps rather than the mainstream Mindō faction. The choice was largely constrained by the availability of those who agreed to talk to the author, but I believe that the large number of dissidents who operated close to the grassroots was extremely helpful in understanding the labour movement from the point of view of rank-and-file workers.

My female interviewees are members of key women's organizations, and represent a wide ideological spectrum, from conservative to communist. They include roughly equal numbers of former senior officials and grassroots activists. But most high-ranking officials were themselves housewives, and there appear to have been few significant ideological differences between the leadership and the rank-and-file among female activists.

Part I
The peace movement and organized labour

1 Early years

The emergence of activist workers

Ordinary workers

Japan's pre-war labour organizations split and regrouped amid repeated crackdowns by the authorities. The labour movement had been virtually banned since 1937, before all labour organizations were disbanded in 1940. Independent unions were replaced in 1938 by Sangyō Hōkokukai (the Movement of Industrial Service to the Nation), which were collaborative associations of employers and workers. Sangyō Hōkokukai became the nation's only legal workplace organizations and were actively enlisted to support the war effort.

Some labour disputes did occur even during the war, and widespread sabotage and absenteeism were observed towards the end of the war as work and living conditions seriously deteriorated. But workers' resistance was severely limited, and organized labour took practically no concerted action against the government's war policy.

Due to the general ineffectiveness of the pre-war labour movement, the percentage of unionized workers was a mere 7.9 per cent at its peak in 1931. When the war ended after almost ten years of no union activity, the vast majority of workers had no experience of unionism and were not ready to take the initiative when SCAP encouraged the formation of labour unions as part of its demilitarization and democratization efforts.[1]

The initiative to organize unions came in many cases from company management. They were quicker than the workers in sensing the changing times, and managers hurried to set up labour unions to comply with SCAP's requirement. According to Yoshida Sukeharu, former head of Sanbetsu, many elected officials of the union federation and its affiliated unions were junior company managers.[2] Those who had some experience in the pre-war labour movement, and other social or left-wing political activists, also took a leadership role in union activities, while others, who were joining a union for the first time, relied on such leaders and other intellectuals to provide necessary organizational skills.

In contrast to the intellectuals who assumed the leadership role in the labour movement shortly after the war, the attitude of ordinary workers was hardly the stuff of militant left-wing politics pursued by numerous unions amid the radicalization of the labour movement.

In the pre-war days, a high proportion of unskilled industrial workers had migrated to urban areas because they were the younger sons or daughters of farming households unable to make a living in their home villages. Their abject poverty made them the butt of contempt, and these workers themselves were ashamed of their status. An essay by an industrial worker that won first prize in a contest held by a labour organization in 1918 was titled 'I want to live like a human being'.[3]

Pre-war employers had tried to prevent labour militancy by spreading the myth that a company was one big family in which workers were supposed to obey their employer unquestioningly. Paternalistic employment practices, through which employers sought to improve workers' welfare to a certain extent, were increasingly adopted to counter growing restiveness among workers following the Rice Riots of 1918.[4]

Amid the general poverty of pre-war Japan, having their children hired by the national railway or post office was a cause for celebration for families of modest means. Railway and postal employees were some of the most privileged workers in the country because they received salaries guaranteed to satisfy their basic economic needs. A range of benefits offered by the railway, such as free rail transport for workers and their families, the railway hospital, and pensions, were powerful incentives for people from poor families to cling to their jobs despite harsh conditions and a rigid workplace hierarchy. Authoritarian and paternalistic at the same time, the national railway's employment practices exemplified Japan's pre-war industrial relations, which were geared toward subordinating workers to the employer's will.[5]

'Feudalistic' was the most commonly used adjective to depict the attitude of railway men who worked uncomplainingly under such conditions. Surveys and other sociological studies conducted shortly after the war's end attest to the poor self-image of unskilled blue-collar workers who lived in destitute conditions and whose attitude was characterized by shame and resignation to their lot.[6] Sociologists and economists in those days attributed this attitude to their background in rural farming communities, and compared them to the labouring poor of Britain up to the late eighteenth century prior to the beginning of trade unionism.[7]

According to the social policy expert Ōkōchi Kazuo, during the rapid economic change brought on by the Industrial Revolution, British entrepreneurs came to believe the efficiency of their businesses would be enhanced if labour relations were handled through collective bargaining. Rational economic thinking on the part of employers combined with advances in the economy to help workers improve their job skills and status and modernize their outlook. In contrast, Ōkōchi argued, if Japan's pre-war experience was any guide, rather than remedy the ills of pre-modern society and ameliorate workers' living conditions, economic growth aggravated the plight of workers. This became all the more so as the economy expanded its reach beyond Japan. The seemingly intractable nature of the problem led many Marxist and other left-leaning academics to consider it a uniquely Japanese phenomenon that apparently doomed workers to their abject condition.[8]

Though SCAP pinned its hopes on Japanese workers to combat the authoritarian and warlike tendencies of Japan's political and economic establishment, most workers would have to start from a very low base if they were to act as the leading force to carry out the onerous task of democratizing Japan as the occupation authorities hoped. Pessimists feared that obedience to higher authority and passivity were second nature to workers, and were concerned that union activities began to flourish after the war simply because SCAP guaranteed the total safety of unions.[9]

But even low-ranking workers appear to have picked up the art of militant trade unionism quickly, as they demanded a living wage and struggled for their very survival. According to Yoshida Sukeharu of Sanbetsu, in October 1945 after SCAP announced five major post-war reform measures (one of which was the protection of workers' rights to unionize), ordinary workers also began taking an active part in organizing unions. Ōtsuka Masatatsu, then a young official with the Japanese Postal Workers' Union (Zentei), recalled how blue-collar workers started playing a vigorous role in deciding the union agenda and articulating their demands on their own from around 1947 or 1948. Such workers also became union officials around that time.[10]

Workers also flocked to labour unions because union activities provided them with the only means to ensure their survival. Some began taking an active role in the labour movement because trade unionism appeared to be the wave of the future and they simply feared missing the boat.[11] In contrast to quite a few intellectuals who joined the labour movement to act out their moral or ideological principles, there were many who took part in union activities hoping to advance their careers or make money. Whereas the army had been regarded as a premier vehicle for career advancement in the past, the swift escalation of industrial action across the country turned labour unions into a social climber's dream.[12] All this helped to push up the percentage of unionized workers to a post-war high of 55.7 per cent in 1949.[13]

Young intellectuals and experiences of the war

While many ordinary workers followed the instructions of more senior employees at their workplaces to join unions in an almost automatic process, other, mainly intellectual, types tried to overcome the moral crisis they had suffered after the war's end or practise their political beliefs through trade unionism.

Unions attracted a large number of young men in their late teens and twenties. This age group had been students or young soldiers during the war, and had suffered ideological dislocation as the war they had supported with great moral fervour came to a catastrophic end and was condemned overnight as a war of aggression.

The experience of Higuchi Tokuzō, a sixteen-year-old naval cadet at the end of the war, is typical. Higuchi lost three of his five brothers in the war, and saw his mother grieve silently without ever shedding a tear. Despite fighting for what he thought was a sacred cause, the war was condemned as criminal, leaving him ideologically and morally stranded.[14]

Higuchi read voraciously in quest of anchorage in the bewildering postwar world. The subjects of his reading ranged from philosophy, history and literature to the biographies of great men, and included the works of Kagawa Toyohiko, Kurata Hyakuzō, Kawai Eijirō, Marx and Kropotkin. But more than anything else, his personal experience of the war helped to shape his later thought. Higuchi concluded that what Japan called its war to liberate Asia was after all an imperialist war to invade China and other Asian nations, and that while his brothers had died seeking nothing for themselves, *zaibatsu* conglomerates made fortunes from the war.[15]

The example of communists, who had predicted that Japan's war of aggression would end in its defeat, and some of whom had persevered in prison for as long as eighteen years to oppose the war, came to Higuchi as a revelation. He joined the Japanese Communist Party (JCP) in the belief that poverty and unemployment had caused the war and that he could help to prevent another conflict by strengthening the labour movement.[16]

Ōtsuka Masatatsu, who joined the postal workers' union shortly after the war, said:

> The experience of no more than six months [the time Ōtsuka spent as a soldier] became a historic moment in my life that became etched deep in my memory. I gave up my plan for an academic career and found my life's aim in labour activities not just because the peace Constitution was enacted. I became involved in the labour movement because of my anger at Japan's dehumanizing pre-war society and because I believed it was my duty to dedicate myself to the labour movement for the sake of those who had died during the war. To work for perpetual peace and reform of the society that had resorted to war was the historic mission assigned to survivors of the war and especially to my generation.[17]

Takeuchi Motohiro, who was thirteen years old when the war ended, was distraught because his zealous support of Japan's 'moral cause' of liberating Asia from Western colonialism had come to naught. He felt betrayed by his father, schoolteachers and other grown-ups, who had abetted militarism and ultranationalism. Thereafter he decided to learn things on his own because others could not be trusted. The university he attended, like almost all other institutions of higher learning in those days, was home to the vigorous activities of societies for social studies, which were led by communists. The urge to try something radically different from the now-discredited wartime teachings also drove many young men to embrace socialist thought. Arcane debates on Marxist ideology and talks with friends about the future, as well as participation in JCP activities as young recruits, led young men like Takeuchi to seek their careers in organized labour.[18]

Inspired by such ideas, intellectuals sought to achieve much more than just redressing workers' grievances at individual workplaces, and aimed for fundamental changes in society, whether or not the term 'revolution' was used to describe their objectives. Young workers, who had expected to die before reaching the age of twenty-five because of the war, began channelling into the labour movement their unbounded energy, fuelled by the joy of being freed from the threat of death. Uchiyama Mitsuo, former head of the Hokuriku Railway Union, said young people were all the more enthusiastic about rebuilding the nation through union activities because they had previously given themselves up for dead.[19]

Traits moulded during the war help to explain how young activists so abruptly carried out the transition from the wartime ideology to left-wing thought. The wartime propaganda, in a process aptly termed by the sociologist Tsurumi Kazuko as 'socialization for death',[20] had inspired in the young the moral zeal with which they prepared to die for their country and the emperor. When the vaunted nationalist myth was debunked after the war, the subsequent disillusion and fury of the young made them channel their moral fervour into activities aimed at advancing a widely different cause. Their dedication to a moral crusade, carried over from the war years, thus fuelled the movement of the post-war left. Among those activists were young pilots who had been assigned to *kamikaze* suicide attacks but who had survived the war.[21] Young people, who had identified themselves with the destiny of the nation and keenly followed international events during the war, retained their attitude shaped during the war years and continued to brood over great public issues. The new cause they believed worthy enough to die for was a revolution to liberate the oppressed. Ardent youths fired by such a belief formed a core of young Turks in the labour movement, whose attitude was marked by the daring with which they tackled union issues without giving the slightest thought to how they could achieve personal success or even make a living.[22]

The young, who had married themselves to the glory and destiny of the nation, considered Japan's defeat to be a national tragedy. Takada Yoshitoshi, who broke down in tears at the emperor's announcement of the surrender, was distraught at what he regarded as 'the demise of the nation'. He revealed, however, that he savoured a kind of romanticism even in the darkest moment of despair, and that he shortly went about rebuilding the nation with the same sense of romanticism:

> After [Japan's] defeat, the transition from right-wing to left-wing ideology took place quite smoothly because the nationalistic romanticism I embraced as a military pilot transformed into another kind of

romanticism that drove me into the post-war, left-wing movement to rebuild the nation. Both types of romanticism subsumed a single self into a collective whole. A self had only a marginal value. The moral belief that continued to sustain me in the post-war years was that my life was not my own to live but was entrusted to me. The nagging sense of guilt I felt towards friends who had died in the war prodded my efforts to rebuild the nation. While leaders who had been involved in the pro-democracy or labour movement since the pre-war days relied on their intellect [in conducting the movement], emotions were the primary driving force for our actions.[23]

Nationalism continued to be a key element in the thought of young activists. The threat of a national crisis, a theme that had persisted since the war years, fuelled nationalism this time from a left-wing perspective.

Labour unions became the most readily accessible vehicle for young political activists. Many regarded unions as a bastion of the movement to rebuild a world free of war,[24] and considered the working class to be the vanguard of people's fight for peace. One railway worker said:

We don't renounce war and call for peace just because we have lost the war. ... It is because of our hatred of aggressive militarism itself and the belief that only workers can contribute to the progress of society and create a new culture that we oppose war which would bring us nothing but suffering. ... Come what may members of the working class will continue to fight in the firm belief that they are the leaders of the new society.[25]

A postal worker who had become disillusioned with the military also pinned his hopes for social reform on the labour movement:

There was no freedom or respect for human rights [in the military]. [While I was in the military] I felt hatred levelled against the [working] class and thought about the criminal nature of the war. Now black markets and prostitutes reign supreme in Japan, which was defeated in the war. I tried to recover [from the war] on my own but couldn't. I realized that solidarity of a large number of people alone can save our mother country. The government's current cultural policy is to dish out nothing but pornography and decadence. Although young men are yearning for beauty, everything is going to rot under colonial rule. We are being called upon to put up an earnest fight against these things.[26]

Young people such as these enthusiastically responded to the communist-dominated Sanbetsu's more radical left-wing agenda, as compared with that of rival labour organization the Japanese Federation of Trade Unions (Sōdōmei), and assisted the radicalization of Sanbetsu-affiliated unions.

It is often said that most workers with a modicum of political conscience joined the JCP in those days. Many of them had not even read the works of Marx or Lenin. Most joined the JCP because of their admiration for communist labour leaders and activists, who demonstrated fearless militancy in labour disputes and vigorously defended the interests of their fellow workers.[27] Yet popular support for the JCP should not be overestimated. The Japanese Teachers Union (Nikkyōso) was often compared to a redheaded crane because only a handful of its officials were JCP members, but the sobriquet applied to all labour unions.

The young Higuchi used to work at the Toshiba Corporation's plant in Horikawachō, Kawasaki, in Kanagawa Prefecture. The union at the electrical machinery maker's plant was said to have been one of the most militant in the late 1940s, with its strength matching the high proportion of communists in its ranks. However, Higuchi estimates the number of JCP members at the plant at 380 out of a total of 4,500, or about 8.4 per cent, shortly before the Red Purge in 1949. According to Higuchi, very few unions matched that percentage, and if the percentage of communists at a union totalled 5 per cent, that was generally considered to be quite high.[28] Based on another estimate that puts the total of JCP members at 150,000 as of mid-1950, the ratio of communists to the total of some 5.77 million unionized workers comes to about 2.6 per cent. The figure would be lower if JCP members who are not unionists were subtracted.[29]

The cold war and escalating labour strife

A split within Sanbetsu and Sōdōmei

The high hopes that many workers placed on the role of labour unions notwithstanding, intervention by the JCP in union affairs and internal rivalry within major labour organizations began to shake the unity of the labour movement in the late 1940s. The internal dissension that ensued made many unionists aware of the need to redress the top-down approach of the union leadership and bridge the gap between the leaders and the rank and file.

Within Sanbetsu-affiliated unions, naivety on the part of ordinary workers, who were unable to conduct rational criticism of party policies, as well as their readiness to defer to authority, helped to create the myth about JCP infallibility. The postal union official Ōtsuka, who was a JCP member between January and May 1949, noted that workers tended blindly to accept party instructions just as they had uncritically obeyed the wartime authorities. He recalled that when he tried to question what seemed to him to be wildly unrealistic policies, he was dissuaded by other party members, who told him that decisions made by those brilliant people, who had gone through so much during the war, were not to be disputed.[30] Sanbetsu's repeated policy zigzags of the late 1940s are generally attributed to the absence of criticism among a large number of workers and their inability to form independent opinions to counter their leaders' actions.[31]

The heyday of Sanbetsu was short-lived. In 1948 dissidents in the union federation established the League for Democratization of Sanbetsu (Sanbetsu Mindō) in protest against their leaders, who allowed the JCP to hijack the labour organization's policy agenda and give priority to the JCP's goal of establishing a 'people's government' through direct confrontation with the authorities. The rebellion was also aimed at redressing the yawning gap in opinion and hierarchical standing between Sanbetsu's leadership and its rank-and-file. The Mindō dissidents rapidly gained influence as they won the support of an increasing number of workers who were disgruntled with the JCP's heavy-handed approach.

Sōdōmei, a rival labour organization, was in similar turmoil. The more conservative of the two major labour organizations was an uneasy cohabitation of a centre-right faction led by Matsuoka Komakichi (1888–1958) and a left-leaning group headed by Takano Minoru (1901–74). Especially during the Cold War, Sōdōmei was wracked by fierce rivalry between the two factions, and preoccupied with its effort to rally as many unions as possible to strengthen the overall labour movement and fight the JCP. Hirasawa Eiichi, who was then a young Sōdōmei official, recalled that the labour organization was too busy to pay much attention to the needs of individual workers or labour disputes at small workplaces.[32]

While issues of Sōdōmei's organ *Rōdō* in the late 1940s give no clue as to the general attitude of members with regard to peace issues amid the onset of the Cold War, Hirasawa's account gives some indication of the mood among junior officials and other young members of the rank-and-file. According to Hirasawa, he and his young colleagues were critical of the fierce internal struggle that went on among right-leaning groups, and their collaborationist approach to dealing with management and the government. Young workers were increasingly attracted by Takano's more combative and flamboyant style of union activity. Moreover, Takano was an advocate of a peaceful revolution to be achieved through the active participation of workers and other ordinary people. That had powerful appeal for the young Hirasawa, who was opposed to the JCP which, after the loss of so many lives during the war, apparently still refused to renounce violence in its pursuit of revolution. The group led by Takano, who rode the crest of young workers' aspirations, captured the leadership of Sōdōmei in November 1949.[33]

Hirasawa actively tried to win over workers to the Takano group in 1949, saying:

> Capitalists are certain to go on the offensive soon and the JCP is likely to collapse. Dire things could happen if the labour movement then adopts right-wing tactics. That could even lead to another war. We have to do something to protect Japan's peace and democracy.

Hirasawa, however, admitted that was no more than *tatemae*, or a pro-forma statement of ideals. The overriding concern that underlay his argument for peace was how to banish old-fashioned labour leaders who collaborated with the authorities. He then aimed to rally workers around leaders like Takano, who had gone to prison before the war for calling for freedom and peace, and to organize a new united front in the labour movement.[34]

The episode reveals that in both Sanbetsu and Sōdōmei, disaffected lower-ranking unionists sought to change the power relationship between the leadership and themselves in their favour. Hirasawa's account also suggests that the rank-and-file activism that drove Sōdōmei's political stand leftwards made the labour organization more sympathetic to other left-wing political activities, including the peace movement. Grassroots radicalism exerting pressure on unions to become more involved in peace campaigns and other left-wing political activities, is a pattern that occurs again and again in the later post-war years, and will be discussed in subsequent chapters of this book.

The spectre of war and the radicalization of workers

The ideology of the left-wing labour movement, together with what was perceived to be an ominous turn of events both at home and abroad, became the prime elements that shaped workers' attitudes toward war and peace.

Mindō dissidents began to break ranks with the Sanbetsu leadership during the onset of the Cold War and a wave of massive job cuts. GHQ[35] shifted its labour policy and began clamping down on militant labour unions following the aborted 1 February 1947 general strike, which was called off at GHQ's behest.[36] This coincided with heightened international tensions and the looming shadow of war, which workers feared could break out somewhere in the world at any time. Meanwhile, the austerity budget introduced by SCAP in 1949 led to widespread misery and added greatly to popular anxiety. The resulting pessimism in the popular mood raised the spectre of a throwback to the war years, and made the use of a war metaphor seem quite apt in describing people's struggle to defend their livelihood. When the machinery producer Hitachi announced 5,500 job cuts out of a total of 32,000 employees, the headline of the Sanbetsu newspaper declared: 'Hitachi is hell-bent on its path towards war'.[37]

An old woman who was at the scene of the Hitachi labour dispute said:

> A layoff as awful as this is certain to be followed by war. When we demanded a raise back in the old days, that was followed by the sacking of workers and then came the war. And who profited from the war while we were forced to work hard without getting enough food? It was you capitalists.[38]

Another woman explained the link between the plight of workers and the possibility of another war as follows:

> Capitalists and reactionary bureaucrats in this country are working together mercilessly to sack admirable workers who are trying to rebuild a democratic and peaceful Japan. The number of violent incidents in which workers' resistance is suppressed in a bloody manner is increasing by the day. If things are left untended, there is going to be World War III as they desire and fascists will again turn us into their slaves.[39]

Ordinary workers saw a parallel between their current economic misery and their pre-war experience, and suspected 'intrigue' by the ruling classes to make workers suffer with starvation wages, punishing work loads and high taxes, in preparation for another war. A column in the *Zentei Shimbun*, the organ of the postal workers' union, explained the link between the privation workers were suffering and war as a matter of simple economics. According to its view, war is caused by the destitute condition of workers, which saps their will to work for peace, as well as the exploitation of the working class, which takes money from people and squanders it on preparations for war:

> If you become inured to the low standard of living and poverty, that means you are being groomed for the war they [capitalists and a fascist government] try to throw you into at any time. If we are made to suffer unbearable privation and our purchasing power plummets, that means we are being forced unwittingly to prepare for war in the name of rebuilding the nation. When we oppose war, we are not veering away from addressing the immediate problems of union members because a struggle to raise our living standard will help to prevent war. They get our money by lowering our living standard and charging taxes but what are they using that money for? ... Newspapers say the government is planning to set up a national defence force.

The column concluded by repeating its author's fear that the government might be trying to impoverish workers in order to spend money on the military.[40]

Reflecting this vein of thought, the mayor of the major industrial town of Amagasaki, Hyogo Prefecture, said the plight of workers, who had barely enough to eat whether they had a job or not, must be remedied by getting the government to sign a comprehensive peace treaty.[41] The May Day of 1950, called the 'Anti-war May Day', is said to have drawn a record 600,000 demonstrators, who gave vent to their economic grievances and called public attention to the plight of countless families committing suicide out of despair.

Meanwhile, Zenrōren, the Sanbetsu-dominated umbrella organization for labour unions, superimposed on the views of ordinary workers the Leninist theory of the relationship between the development of a capitalist economy and the outbreak of an imperialist war. According to Zenrōren, fascist rule was gaining strength amid the economic degradation and loss of rights of workers and an increase in production for military purposes. This was happening because international monopoly capital, in its efforts to overcome inherent flaws in its system, was pursuing an imperialist policy that stressed production for military purposes. Such a policy would turn Japan into a base from which a new war of aggression against the peoples of the Soviet Union, China and other Asian nations would be prosecuted, and the Japanese people would be forced to assist.[42] To counter this, Zenrōren argued, workers of the world, led by those of the Soviet Union and China, should rally around the World Federation of Trade Unions (WFTU) to frustrate the imperialist conspiracy.

The increased hostility of workers to those they characterized as war-mongering capitalists went hand-in-hand with the radicalization of their attitude.

While the JCP adopted a policy calling for a 'peaceful revolution' immediately after the war's end, the party continued to abide by the so-called 1932 thesis, which put top priority on 'toppling the absolute monarchy that rested on the power of the parasitic land-owning classes'. That made the communists' professed commitment to a 'revolution through peaceful means' doubtful. The so-called local popular struggles (*chiiki jinmin tōsō*) of Sanbetsu-affiliated unions turned into something far surpassing mere labour disputes in their radicalism, and became more like power struggles aimed at combating government authorities.[43] These combined with the fatal railway incidents of 1949,[44] which were blamed on communists, and put in doubt the JCP's peaceful intentions in the eyes of the general public.

The chief concerns of workers in those days – acute food shortages, unemployment and reconstruction of the nation's industry – issues which their employers at first neglected or refused to address, all required the attention of the government, and compelled labour unions to tackle political issues besides immediate problems within their own workplaces. The early post-war years saw for the first time in Japanese history the mass participation of rank-and-file workers in political struggles.

As they conducted political campaigns to defend their livelihood, workers increasingly turned militant. Negami Masayuki, a former official with the National Railway Workers' Union (Kokurō), tells of blue-collar workers who used their bloodied fingers to seal a written protest against the massive public-sector layoff of 1949. In a desperate struggle, the blue-collar workers thus tried to signal their determination to resist the layoff. The episode is indicative of how fast the railway workers had cast aside the vestiges of their 'feudal' attitude amid the heat of labour strife.[45]

The iconoclastic mood of workers gained added fuel because the government had lost credibility as a result of the war. The massive dismissal was meant to eliminate the redundancies caused by the repatriation of soldiers, so workers felt they were doubly victimized by the government and the railway authority that had tyrannized them during the war.[46] Iida Hichizō, a JCP member who was an official of Kokurō's Mitaka chapter in Tokyo, was fired because he had taken part in a strike staged in protest at a proposed cut of 95,000 railway workers' jobs. Iida said the workers' anger was compounded because the government had made them go through hell during the war, and had now decided to throw them out of work unceremoniously and with no promise of compensation.[47] The series of fatal railway incidents in 1949 and the Red Purge[48] that began in July 1950 put a virtual end to the 'great national railway family'.

Peace movements prior to the Korean War

Japan's first major peace gathering, the Japanese Convention in Defence of Peace (Heiwa Yōgo Nihon Taikai), which is said to have drawn 1,200 participants including members of Sanbetsu, was held in Tokyo in 1949. The convention issued broad statements that called on the public to oppose fascism, warmongers and a military alliance with the US, and promote pacifist culture, education and peacetime industry. It also called for the early signing of a peace treaty to achieve Japan's independence, and for cooperation with all peace-loving peoples. It is, however, unclear what impact the meeting had on the overall labour movement or the outlook of individual workers.

The peace movement, organized mainly by communist activists during the occupation years, was characterized more often than not by ideological intolerance. Kokubun Ichitarō, who was a JCP member in those days, noted that although peace rallies were held with the explicit aim of bringing together the widest possible cross-section of the populace regardless of their ideology, religious faith or economic or other interests, the JCP totally lacked the skill to unite people from different walks of life in a peace campaign. According to Kokubun, peace rallies held in those days were more like rabble-rousing sessions, in which workers, farmers or other delegates who took the podium took advantage of the occasion to air the demands of their own interest groups, in total disregard of whether their opinions clashed with the interests or beliefs of those representing other groups.[49]

As peace activities were linked to the unions' economic struggles, and the fiery rhetoric aimed at pressing union demands tended to dominate, antiwar sentiments nursed by ordinary workers appears to have received scant attention and failed to become a major issue in the peace debate.

In the late 1940s, *Rengō Sensen*, the Sanbetsu organ, printed only two letters in which ordinary workers voiced their views on peace issues. One was written by a print worker, who suggested a peace organization should be established to involve as many different kinds of people as possible and cooperate with people around the world.[50] His suggestion received enthusiastic support from other workers, one of whom contributed her letter, saying:

> I often despair, recalling the day when an ominously dark sky dropped a rain of fire and reduced our houses, clothes and even my favourite book of Ishikawa Takuboku's poems to ashes. I earnestly hope for a peace organization everyone can join.[51]

The historian Takahashi Hikohiro argues that Sanbetsu, as befitting its top-down style of running trade union activities, paid scant attention to the anti-war sentiment of ordinary workers, such as that expressed in the above letter, which was based primarily on their personal experience. Takahashi criticizes Sanbetsu for making no attempt to organize its peace activities in a manner that would reflect the wishes of those at the grassroots.[52]

Whether or not Sanbetsu was disregarding popular sentiment in its peace activities, it was in disarray at the time, as it was losing its members in droves to the Mindō dissidents. Besides crackdowns by SCAP on pro-Soviet peace activities, the antipathy of both non-Sanbetsu unionists and the general public to the communist-inspired peace movement compounded Sanbetsu's difficulty in organizing peace activities. As was the case with both the 1949 peace convention and the 1950 Stockholm Appeal anti-nuclear signature drives, peace activists prior to the outbreak of the Korean War, whether they came from Sanbetsu or other groups, tended to take their cue from the ideas and activities of the pro-Soviet World Peace Council, which limited their popular appeal.

It is also doubtful that the reservoir of anti-war sentiment at rank-and-file level, if tapped more actively, would have advanced the peace movement in any significant way. Anti-war feelings inspired by the Cold War and domestic economic privation tended to be vague and poorly defined, as long as the chief source of fears was the insidious menace to peace inherent in the capitalist system. It can be assumed that the lack of issues of a more specific nature probably made it difficult for the diffuse anti-war sentiment of the populace to coalesce into more focused pacifist thought. The absence of more real and present dangers appears to have been one factor that prevented individual workers' yearning for peace from achieving the critical mass needed to influence organized labour's policy actions.

The idea of peace that figured in the labour movement between 1945 and 1949 was to a large extent of notional and symbolic importance in the supposedly inevitable conflict between the capitalist and working classes. Though quite a few ordinary workers expressed their fears that events both at home and abroad might eventually lead to another war, the sheer scale of economic chaos and the workers' plight generally pushed peace issues off the agenda of the labour movement. Prior to the outbreak of hostilities in Korea, war was little more than an ominous shadow that hung darkly over workers' lives.

Newspapers published by major peace groups such as the Heiwa Yōgo Nihon Iinkai (the Japanese Committee for Protection of Peace), another JCP-affiliated body, tended to offer only dry accounts of numbers of anti-war signatures collected and rallies held by various peace groups. While giving extensive coverage to developments in the international peace movement, the papers hardly ever printed opinions expressed by grassroots Japanese peace activists, as if they regarded individuals taking part in the peace movement as anonymous toilers merely collecting signatures and swelling the ranks of those attending peace rallies.[53]

But around mid-1952, the papers began to give more coverage to the spontaneous activities and views of ordinary people, which suggests that those taking part in the peace movement at the grassroots became numerous and vocal enough to merit attention after the end of the Allied occupation.

By that time, Sanbetsu and its communist members had borne the brunt of the massive job cuts and the Red Purge, and as a result had surrendered their leadership of the labour movement to the newly formed Sōhyō. Though Sanbetsu officials were no match for the concerted efforts of SCAP and the Japanese government to expel them from labour unions, the labour federation's top-down power structure, which made its leaders neglect to cultivate close, durable ties with the rank-and-file, compounded their vulnerability and accelerated their loss of power.[54]

2 The Korean War and the peace treaty

The war's impact on the labour movement

The Korean War (June 1950–July 1953), the first major hostilities near Japan after the end of World War II, posed a major challenge to the Japanese peace movement. But rather than organize a protest against the war from a pacifist viewpoint, Japanese workers mostly had their hands full coping with the domestic, political and economic fallout.

The outbreak of the Korean War coincided with a period of decline in the labour movement, which hit its nadir during the Red Purge of 1950. Gone was the euphoria that marked the earlier post-war years, when organized labour went on the offensive, taking advantage of GHQ's backing and of disarray among corporate management in the immediate aftermath of the war. By the time of the Korean War, organized labour had already been put on the defensive. After the general strike planned for February 1947 was called off at the behest of SCAP, labour unions were increasingly constrained by tighter government regulations on their activities and crackdowns on activist union members, and many unions were compelled to surrender agreements they had won over wages and terms of employment.

Japanese unions included junior managers and others in supervisory positions who had taken the initiative in forming unions immediately after the war. But this upper layer in the union hierarchy became the first to succumb to the fresh onslaught from management, and it retreated from union activities. The massive public-sector layoff of 1949, the arrest of communists that followed the series of fatal railway incidents in 1949, and the Red Purge struck fear into ordinary workers. Hino Saburō, a former employee of Japanese National Railways, recalled the subdued atmosphere of most workplaces, where workers would not dare take part in union activities and would not even carry a union leaflet for fear of getting fired.[1]

Labour organizations were in no condition to take up peace activities when the Korean War broke out and turned Japan into the most important logistical base for the United Nations armed forces fighting in Korea.

Sōhyō, the new umbrella labour organization that took over leadership of the labour movement from Sanbetsu, was created with SCAP's active backing less than a month after the start of the war. Sōhyō's leadership supported the 'UN police action' in Korea while Sanbetsu, which opposed the war, was a mere shadow of its former self after the exodus of unions taken over by Mindō dissidents and the Red Purge.

With many of its militant activists thrown out of work, and with the general morale of labour unions suffering a severe blow, the labour movement lost considerable ground both on the economic and political fronts. The murky origins of the Korean War, which gave rise to controversy over whether the North or the South had started it, compounded the difficulty for labour unions seriously to deal with the implications of the war.

Amid the ideological muddle and the general disarray of the labour movement, working conditions at companies at the forefront of logistical support for the war seriously worsened. Workers in the metalworking industries, including shipbuilding, steel and automobiles, as well as those in sectors such as maritime transport and telecommunications, saw a dramatic increase in their workload, and some took on such hazardous work as the production and transportation of ammunition, including napalm bombs.[2]

The war had a particularly enormous impact on the national railway. The railways provided the vital infrastructure for transport of military matériel. The steep increase in transportation work threw railway operations into turmoil, and railway workers often had to work around the clock to handle the huge workload. Safety rules were ignored as meeting US orders became top priority.[3] Looking back at those days, Hino Saburō said railway workers were utterly exhausted and had no strength left to do anything but sleep after work.[4]

Tight supervision by armed police and the generally subdued atmosphere of workplaces made it impossible for railway workers to organize protests. Moreover, the government had refused to meet union wage demands for years, which widened the gap between the salaries of railway workers and those of private-sector employees.

While their rancour over their work conditions accumulated, railway workers routinely handled damaged tanks shipped from Korea that were stained with blood and stuck with bits of human flesh. The stories of soldiers' corpses unloaded at ports in northern Kyushu spread through the railway grapevine all over the country, and there was other evidence that pointed to the extremely bloody nature of the war. Although the circumstances at Japanese National Railways made it impossible to organize a vigorous anti-war movement, railway workers got wind of the horrors of the war in Korea, which made them wonder if any war causing that magnitude of human suffering could ever be justified.[5]

The JCP publication *Zenei* reports that at their October 1950 convention held in Matsue, Shimane Prefecture, delegates of the National Railway Workers' Union (Kokurō), especially those from Tokyo, Osaka and Hiroshima, expressed nationalistic-tinged anger at being treated by the US armed forces like dumb animals. Delegates also complained of a ban on paid holidays, not being paid for overtime work, and being forced at gunpoint to transport explosives. They voiced fears that further cooperation with the UN would disadvantage their wage negotiations. Workers were also fearful that much of Japan's national budget would be spent to support the American war effort and fund the Police Reserve, a forerunner of Japan's armed forces newly created at SCAP's behest. They feared such expenditures would leave little money available for their pay.[6]

Anti-American sentiment also grew among railway workers. Seto Sadao, who was a young Kokurō worker in those days, recalls that railway workers were often infuriated by the arrogance of American soldiers, who, for example, scattered a handful of cigarettes on the ground and enjoyed watching the Japanese eagerly scramble for them.[7] Petty episodes like that, combined with the punishing workload and occasional fatal accidents, made the epithet 'US imperialism' seem like an apt term to describe what railway workers regarded as their colonial existence.[8]

Since the massive layoff, the Red Purge and the Korean War were all conducted in the name of anti-communism, with the result that their labour union came to grief, some workers, though critical of the JCP, became resentful of the kind of anti-communism espoused by centre-right Mindō leaders, who supported the UN action and Japan's rearmament. In the novel Seto wrote under the pseudonym Ashigara Sadayuki, such leaders are depicted as collaborators with a management which did practically nothing to alleviate the harsh conditions of workers. Workers in Seto's novel regard them as puppets of US imperialism who should be banished from their union.[9]

While resentment and anti-war sentiment at a personal level increased in individual workplaces, concern grew among union leaders about what they perceived as a major challenge posed by the war to Japan's overall economy and industrial relations.

The Korean War, which generated massive military procurement orders, breathed new life into Japanese industry, which had been reeling from the effects of the government's austerity budget. Some workers as well as corporate managers welcomed war-related orders. But other unionists began to question the soundness of an economic revival that depended entirely on the war, and concern was expressed also about serious problems resulting from the war boom.

Chief among such problems were wage rises that lagged behind the pace of increases in production. Other sources of concern included companies filling job openings with day labourers or short-term contract workers, whose pay was far lower than that of permanent employees; excessive workloads that caused illness and accidents; and a handful of large corporations getting the lion's share of military procurement contracts.[10]

Workers in major public-sector unions such as Kokurō, Zentei and Nikkyōso, which made up the bulk of Sōhyō-affiliated unions, did not benefit economically from the Korean War. The economic benefits were quite unevenly spread, even among private-sector companies that won military contracts, so it can be assumed that the boom did not provide a sufficient economic incentive for a majority of Sōhyō unions to support the war.

It should also be noted that while the industrial production index (1932–6 = 100) in October 1950 exceeded the pre-war level, consumer spending in Tokyo recovered to the pre-war level of 1934–6 much later in 1954, and was still quite low by world standards. Though household spending on food in 1954 was on a par with the pre-war level, expenditures on clothing and housing were about 18–25 per cent lower.[11] The data suggest that whatever economic gains that were enjoyed by the average worker were quite modest.

On the other hand, there were appreciable signs of economic improvement as more food suddenly became available and construction activity increased. But for workers of the socialist persuasion, an increase in demand for their companies' goods and services was hardly a cause for celebration. They feared good economic times could fatten their capitalist foes and hamper the struggle against them (the possibility of robust demand resulting in fatter paycheques for workers was ignored in this left-wing thinking). The tendency of companies to cope with increased orders by sharply raising their employees' workload often made leftist accusations about capitalist oppression of workers sound reasonable.

Employers, knowing that the war would end sooner or later, tried to meet increased demand by hiring temporary factory hands. Company managers knew that if they hired workers as permanent staff, they would be bound to face bitter labour disputes later when they tried to get rid of redundant staff after the war's end. The sudden rise in the number of such short-term contract workers fuelled concern that the ruling classes were pursuing a policy to create a dual-structure economy in which a vast sector of the working population would be condemned to the status of expendable temporary labourers or unprivileged workers at small subcontracting firms. The Korean War, therefore, was perceived to be creating new distortions in the economy with the potential of seriously jeopardizing workers' interests.

Towards the end of the war, however, partly due to the peace overtures made by the Soviet Union and China after the death of Stalin in March 1953, Sōhyō, which had supported the US war effort in Korea, called for the earliest possible end to hostilities, by early April of that year, so as to prevent Japan from becoming embroiled.[12] Sōhyō's U-turn, however, had taken place much earlier and was attributable more than anything else to the debate on the peace treaty that began in the late 1940s.

The peace treaty debate

Shin Sanbetsu's initiative

Unions began conducting their first active debates on war prevention and Japan's peace treaty with its former enemies amid the onset of the Cold War in the late 1940s. With Eastern European nations falling into the Soviet orbit one by one, the European mass media conducted a series of interviews with European communist leaders, such as French Communist Party chief Maurice Thorez, and Palmiro Togliatti, who led Italy's communists, asking them what they would do if the Soviet Union were to invade their countries. In 1949, Thorez made waves by saying that his party would cooperate with the Red Army if it ever invaded Paris. While the JCP leader Tokuda Kyūichi neither approved nor opposed Thorez's comment, it gave rise to active debate in union circles as to whether the eventual revolution in Japan should be violent or peaceful.[13]

With regard to Sōhyō, most historic accounts are vague about how the newly created non-communist labour organization derived the ideas of the so-called four principles on peace – signing a 'comprehensive' peace treaty with all of Japan's former enemies including the Soviet Union and communist China, diplomatic neutrality, opposition to military bases and a ban on rearmament. Many historic accounts have Sōhyō adopting the principles after they were first conceived by the JSP. But an account by the National Federation of Industrial Organizations (Shin Sanbetsu) tells a different story. The labour federation held an independent debate on the peace issue, as it considered the matter critical to the very *raison d'être* of organized labour and would vitally affect the future conduct of the labour movement.

According to this version, Sanbetsu Mindō, which seceded from Sanbetsu in 1948, began to discuss the matter and raised the issue of Japan's neutrality in the summer of the same year. This was shortly after the formation of the Cominform in 1947, which had heightened international tension. Sanbetsu Mindō conducted a further debate after the US State Department announced, following the communist revolution in China in 1949, that the US was to begin preparations for the signing of a peace treaty with Japan. The American statement fuelled fears among Sanbetsu Mindō officials that Washington was trying to pre-empt the issue instead of going through a consensual process with the other Allied powers. Sanbetsu believed the possibility of an armed conflict between the world's two adversarial camps in the nuclear age made it all the more urgent for Japan to clarify its stand on the peace treaty. Sanbetsu Mindō convened to prepare for the formation of Shin Sanbetsu in July 1949, and drew up a policy statement, which noted that the conflict between the world's two camps was causing division in the labour movement. It announced that Japan must opt for diplomatic neutrality because that would be the only way the country could regain its sovereignty and promote peace and democracy.[14]

At its founding convention on 10–11 December 1949, Shin Sanbetsu voted for a comprehensive peace as well as diplomatic neutrality. The group worked closely with the youth section of the JSP. Its policy became a great inspiration for the young JSP members, who pushed the party leadership hard to embrace the three principles on peace – a comprehensive peace treaty, diplomatic neutrality and opposition to military bases. The party subsequently adopted the principles that December.[15]

The left-wing faction of the JSP youth section, which had embraced pacifism more zealously than older JSP members, seized on Shin Sanbetsu's ideas and mounted an all-out effort to get their party to adopt a new pacifist policy following the union federation's line. An overwhelming majority of young political activists in those days were members of the JCP, and only a small minority joined the JSP youth section. Many young JCP activists held a low opinion of the socialists and social democrats, who used to be members of parties that were the forerunners of the JSP, because they had supported Japan's war effort, unlike the communists. The substantial number of prominent academics who joined or supported the JCP also enhanced the party's appeal. Thus the JCP enjoyed greater moral and intellectual prestige among the young compared with the JSP.

Shin Sanbetsu's policy line, however, provided young JSP members with a precious opportunity to gain the upper hand over the JCP and the right-wing of their own party.[16] At its seventh party convention in January 1951, at the insistence of its youth and women's sections, the JSP decided to call for a ban on rearmament, which became the fourth principle on peace.

The JSP had been struggling to come to terms with the implications of the Korean War while being wracked by a division between its centre-right and centre-left factions which dated back to pre-war days. But collaboration between Shin Sanbetsu and the party's youth section tilted the JSP towards the four principles before the newly created Sōhyō could clarify its own stand on the matter.[17]

Around the same time, a group of progressive academics began debating peace issues in the autumn of 1948, and later formed the Discussion Circle on Problems of Peace (Heiwa Mondai Danwakai), the first post-war academic group that tried to discuss peace as a universal issue in a way that was distinct from the communists' political agenda. The group's ideas, which were disseminated through three public statements, helped shape the agenda for peace activists in the early post-war years.[18]

Mito Nobuto, however, a former senior official of Shin Sanbetsu, claims that Sanbetsu Mindō initiated the debate on the peace issues independently from the JSP and the academic group.[19]

At its inception, Shin Sanbetsu vowed to practise what it called militant and free trade unionism, on the grounds that a labour union should fight for freedom from capitalists, the government and political parties to ensure its independence. Hosoya Matsuta (1900–90), the leader of Shin Sanbetsu, noted that labour unions tended either to lurch leftward to come under the thumb of the JCP, or veer rightward to be controlled by employers. Hosoya said such tendencies were symptomatic of the flawed state of Japan's democracy, and that labour unions should strengthen themselves by combating them. Shin Sanbetsu also contended that it was critically important for unions to seize the peace treaty issue as a way to wean themselves from GHQ's patronage and stand on their own two feet.[20]

The JCP urged labour unions to protest against 'the US intervention in Korea's civil war', and in compliance with the party's instructions, Sanbetsu unions combined their struggle against layoffs with the anti-war movement. Shin Sanbetsu, however, distanced itself from the JCP by pointing out Japan's duty to accept the terms of occupation. Still, the labour group also argued that unions should not forget their duty to resist the government and capitalists who, it argued, were trying to take advantage of the emergency in the Far East to oppress workers. At a central committee meeting in July 1950, Shin Sanbetsu accused 'reactionary' forces within Japan of trying to embroil the Japanese people in the war, and voiced fears about the resurgence of the influence of the pre-war militarists and fascists.[21]

At its second annual convention in November 1950, Shin Sanbetsu repudiated the view that defined the rivalry between the world's two camps as that between capitalism and socialism in order to justify defending democracy against communist invasion. Noting also the Stalinist regime's expansionist moves to create a sphere of influence in Eastern Europe, Shin Sanbetsu argued that the US and the Soviet Union embodied two different varieties of imperialism.

At its third annual convention in November 1951, Shin Sanbetsu affirmed the 'revolutionary' role a third force could play to counter these two kinds of imperialism. By 'third force' was meant the developing nations struggling to win independence in the aftermath of World War II, militant labour unions in Western Europe, and countries such as Yugoslavia, which were taking an independent stand within the socialist camp.[22]

For Shin Sanbetsu, neutrality was of paramount importance. It feared that pledging allegiance either to the US or the Soviet Union would heighten the risk of getting Japan involved in war. If things ever came to that, it was afraid that labour unions would lose their independence and would be reduced, like the wartime Sangyō Hōkokukai, to a subordinate organ assisting the government's war effort. War had to be resisted by all means because it would undermine the very existence of the labour movement.[23] While Heiwa Mondai Danwakai and many other peace groups invoked the peace Constitution to construct their arguments, Shin Sanbetsu argued that labour unions had to work for peace regardless of what the Constitution said.

Shin Sanbetsu's emphasis on neutrality posed a subtle difference from the stand of the JSP. Kihara Minoru, a former member of the JSP youth section, recalled that the JSP in those days was feeling constrained by the JCP's assertion that it was impossible to maintain neutrality in the conflict between socialism and capitalism, while not wholeheartedly concurring with that view. The party did not take neutrality to heart as much as Shin Sanbetsu did because many JSP members found it difficult to appear aloof from the communist camp by insisting on diplomatic neutrality. According to Kihara, the JSP continued to have qualms even after it voted for neutrality.[24]

The leaders of Shin Sanbetsu were also aware that Japan's labour unions, which were predominantly in-house, tended all too easily to become oblivious of the need to advance the interests of the working class as a whole, because they were engrossed in matters affecting their own workplaces. Shin Sanbetsu officials believed that unions should remedy such tendencies by becoming actively involved in the peace movement. They argued that unions would be unable to make much progress unless they abandoned that narrow focus on their immediate economic interests and worked instead for greater humanitarian and political causes. They believed that the peace movement could serve as a bond that would unite the working class and play a vital role in the advancement of the labour movement.[25]

Sōhyō's policy shift

Initially Shin Sanbetsu did not join Sōhyō, on the grounds that Sōhyō might be compromising its principles by so readily accepting the backing of SCAP, which, it argued, called into question Sōhyō's independence as a labour organization. Shin Sanbetsu was also critical of what it perceived as the bureaucratic way Sōhyō was organized. Shin Sanbetsu feared such bureaucratism could stifle democracy, whereas democracy would be vitally important if the labour organization was to avoid repeating labour's wartime collaboration with the authorities.[26]

Shin Sanbetsu, however, later joined Sōhyō under the slogan 'Let's change Sōhyō' to take the initiative in the peace treaty debate at Sōhyō's second annual convention in March 1951. Three proposals on peace were presented at the convention as follows:

A In accordance with the spirit of the peace Constitution, we oppose rearmament and military bases, pledge diplomatic neutrality and call for a comprehensive peace treaty and thereby conduct our struggles to preserve peace and win Japan's independence.
B We consider it incumbent on Japan's working class to call for a comprehensive peace treaty, pledge diplomatic neutrality and oppose military bases, and will fight rearmament to achieve peace and Japan's independence.
C We will promote a comprehensive peace treaty and will struggle to achieve Japan's speedy independence, which will guarantee freedom and equality.

Proposal A was presented by the Sōhyō leadership, Proposal B by Shin Sanbetsu and Proposal C by the Japanese miners' union (Nihon Kōzan Rōdō Kumiai, or Nikkō).

Mito of Shin Sanbetsu, explaining his group's stand, argued that Japan's labour unions should not take any part in the Korean War, which was waged as part of the rivalry between the US and the Soviet Union. He also warned against going along with the argument of those who asserted Japan's right to self-defence in calling for rearmament.[27]

Proposal B won the highest number of votes. A delegate from Kokurō explained the reason for his support of Proposal B, saying that it spelled out struggles for peace and Japan's independence as the self-evident mission of the working class. A representative of Nikkyōso also backed Shin Sanbetsu's idea, saying teachers should not send their students to war ever again, whether there is a peace Constitution or not.

Nikkō, which submitted Proposal C, the most moderate of the three, was a Sōdōmei-affiliated federation of unions at small and medium-sized mines, and was known for its 'backward' hierarchical organization in which senior unionists dominated the rank-and-file.[28] Its proposal was backed by conservative unions, which made up a small minority within Sōhyō. An official of the All Japan Seamen's Union called the four principles on peace unrealistic and nonsensical, and voted for Proposal C, arguing that the task of labour unions was not to promote a certain ideology but to defend the actual interests of workers.[29]

In the first round of balloting, Proposal A won 86 votes, Proposal B, 108 and Proposal C, 28. Since none of the three proposals gained the required two-thirds majority vote, Zentei presented an alternative proposal which stated, 'We will achieve peace and Japan's independence by opposing rearmament and military bases, pledging diplomatic neutrality and getting the government to sign a comprehensive treaty'. Sōhyō subsequently adopted Zentei's compromise statement, which won 202 of a total of 241 votes.[30] Through its adoption of a neutral stand, the labour organization dropped its earlier support for the US war in Korea.

At the convention, Sōhyō also voted to drop its earlier plan to join the International Confederation of Free Trade Unions (ICFTU) en masse, and to leave it to individual unions to decide whether they would join or not. The pro-Western ICFTU supported the UN action in Korea and called on Japan to sign a security treaty with the US and rearm itself. That the ICFTU was unsympathetic to independence movements of developing nations also prompted Sōhyō-affiliated unions to drop their plans to join the international labour organization and opt to ally with labour groups in Asian nations instead.[31] Ōta Kaoru, leader of the Japanese Federation of Synthetic Chemical Workers' Unions, which overwhelmingly rejected the proposal to join the ICFTU, attributes the result to the strong opposition against the pro-Western organization, especially among rank-and-file workers.[32]

The implications of the decision by Sōhyō-affiliated unions to adopt the new principles on peace were manifold:

A partial peace had to be opposed on both security, economic and moral grounds: Japan should clearly indicate its sense of repentance for the war, pledge never to commit aggression against other nations and seek reconciliation with all of its former enemies. If Japan failed to sign a peace treaty with the Soviet Union and China, that would threaten Japan's security and also deny it opportunities to trade with these countries, which would be crucial for rehabilitating the Japanese economy.

A partial peace treaty and a Japan-US security treaty that would allow US armed forces to stay in Japan would be in violation of the war-renouncing Constitution. The two treaties also disguised the intention of the government and capitalists to rearm Japan and oppress workers in their pursuit of imperialist goals.

Labour unions also tried to deal with the contradiction of the situation in which unions, who started out with an avowed aim to work for peace to promote workers' well-being, were either supporting the war effort in Korea or not actively resisting it. They desperately needed to reaffirm their commitment to peace so as to map out a future course of action. In so doing, Sōhyō managed to distance itself from both the JCP and the political and economic establishments by calling for the promotion of what it called a third force, which was distinct from the Soviet camp and the capitalist West. Sōhyō envisioned the third force as a bastion of peace, comprised mainly of countries that had recently achieved independence such as India, Ceylon and Burma.

Sōhyō continued to condemn the peace movement organized by the JCP, including the Stockholm Appeal anti-nuclear signature drive, on the grounds that the JCP's peace activities were conducted at the behest of Moscow. It established a separate peace organization, the National Congress for Promotion of Peace (Heiwa Suishin Kokumin Kaigi), in cooperation with religious and other grassroots groups, instead of joining forces with the communist-affiliated Peace Committee.[33]

Sōhyō also managed to dispel the fears of many unionists who thought its close ties to SCAP and its support for the US war in Korea compromised the principles that any self-respecting labour organization was supposed to uphold. Sōhyō had looked on when JCP members and other left-wing activists were expelled from their workplaces during the Red Purge on the grounds that they deserved it considering the excesses they had committed in the past. Some Mindō union officials even went so far as to collaborate with employers to eliminate their adversaries through the Red Purge, which many workers regarded as despicable acts of betrayal.[34]

Mizuno Aki, who attended Sōhyō's founding convention, said the event was as lively as a funeral despite its claimed membership of 4 million workers. Those who participated were conscious of the fact that it was not they but SCAP that had won in the fight against the JCP, and that Sōhyō owed its leadership over the labour movement entirely to the occupation authorities.[35] The view is echoed by one labour ministry official who was in charge of union affairs. He said Sōhyō desperately needed to figure out a way to dispel the suspicion that it was a mere lackey of SCAP. He noted that the major policy shift was welcomed by early critics of Sōhyō, among whom the phrase, 'a metamorphosis from a chicken into a duck' rapidly caught on.[36]

From then on, Sōhyō vowed to take a principled stance as befitting a labour organization that would stage all-out struggles to fight the 'fascist' government and capitalists. Sōhyō thus revised its earlier anti-communist stance in the face of criticism that the union federation, preoccupied with its fight against the JCP, was neglecting the 'class war' aspect of the labour movement. The adoption of the peace principles was followed by Sōhyō's decision to take on other struggles, including the fight against the government's legislative move to restrict union activities in the name of clamping down on the JCP. Sōhyō pledged to work harder to win wage increases and additional benefits, especially for workers who had been compelled to handle excessive workloads and perform hazardous work to assist the war effort.[37]

Nationalistic rancour against the US occupation authorities was also an important element prompting Sōhyō's policy shift. Though the communists had welcomed the US occupation as an act of liberation immediately after the war, they began talking about the spectre of 'US imperialism' after the aborted general strike of February 1947. A nationalistic song, the 'Song of the Action Group for the Nation's Independence' ('Minzoku Dokuritsu Kōdōtai no Uta'), became popular from around 1950, reflecting a rise in anti-American sentiment among union and other activists.[38] Even among non-communist workers, there were numerous grievances against the US occupation forces. Supervision by armed policemen at factories and other workplaces supporting US forces during the Korean War was reminiscent of conditions under martial law. Adding to the frustration and fear of ordinary workers were summary arrests of those who were suspected of sabotaging the occupation administration, as was the case with the fatal railway incidents of 1949. A host of SCAP directives issued in contravention of existing laws made many workers question the gaping gulf between the realities in Japan and the post-war laws introduced to embody the vaunted democratic and pacifist ideals spouted by the occupiers. Andō Jinbei (1927–98), who was a young communist activist in those days, recalled that many people around him thought the idealistic Constitution was merely a sham or an empty gesture by the grandstanding and self-promoting MacArthur.[39] Hino of Kokurō said he felt the peace Constitution and laws guaranteeing workers' rights were nothing more than a piece of trash as long as American forces occupied Japan.[40] It was against this backdrop that independence from the US assumed particular importance in labour's peace movement.

The political scientist Ōtake Hideo argues that Sōhyō developed an 'inordinate' interest in diplomatic issues because it tried to alleviate the frustration over its ineffectiveness in economic struggles by battling the government over political matters. According to Ōtake:

Many unions lost confidence in their ability to conduct militant union activities in the face of management's resolute opposition. Sōhyō therefore took a strong interest in struggles against the US and the issue over rearmament because it sought to take out workers' frustration over union setbacks at workplaces on distant enemies such as the Japanese government and the US. Any struggle against such distant enemies would be safe because it was unlikely to hurt the unions or cause internal division within the labour movement. Sōhyō activists channelled all their energies into election campaigns, which were guaranteed as a civil right, also because they tried to make up for their setbacks in union activities.[41]

It should be noted, however, that defying SCAP directives in occupied Japan often resulted in summary arrest and sometimes the death sentence, as in the case of the workers who were arrested for allegedly causing the fatal railway incidents of 1949. Taking on the US as an adversary through peace activities, therefore, involved serious risk. It is true that some individual workers did take part in the peace movement out of frustration with union setbacks on the economic front. But when Sōhyō-affiliated unions adopted the four peace principles as the governing tenets for the labour movement, the move in effect signified a declaration of their resolve to put up a more earnest fight on the economic front as well. It was their battle cry rather than an attempt to take refuge in safer activities. Weak unions doing poorly in their economic battles would not dare take on political battles to press issues that were not of immediate concern to their own well-being, and risk a crackdown by SCAP.

The revival of union activism

Sōhyō's new-found militancy helped to lure back into the labour movement disgruntled workers who had yearned for the more confrontational style of Sanbetsu. According to Shimizu Shinzō, this period saw a marked increase in union activists who volunteered their services both inside and outside the workplace.[42] Sōhyō's adoption of a new stance on peace issues helped it to overcome the ideological muddle that had hampered the labour movement after the Red Purge and the outbreak of the Korean War. It helped to clarify union members' thinking, and the objectives they were supposed to work for.

This rise in the number of union activists was accompanied by a matching increase in the strength of labour unions, which helped them to conduct both their economic and political struggles to their advantage. Kokurō was one of the first to recover from labour's setbacks in the late 1940s. The newly resurgent labour movement resulted, for example, in a sixty-three-day industrial action by coal miners' unions in late 1952, and added to the acrimony of wage negotiations in 1953, which were marked by strikes and lockouts.[43]

Another celebrated case of a labour dispute aided by the resurgent morale of unionists inspired by the peace principles, was that of the union at the Nippon Steel plant in Akabane, Tokyo. The plant, which had been put in charge of repairing tanks and other armaments during the Korean War, had become East Asia's largest military plant and been placed under tight security by the US military, which severely restricted the union's activities. But union protests over low wages and harsh working conditions began gaining momentum from around 1952, as these were aided by labour's peace movement against US military bases. Union activists from neighbouring areas gathered in support of the Akabane plant workers in the belief that their industrial action would help Japan to achieve true independence from the US and counter the Japanese government's move to restrict strikes. It was the very first strike staged in defiance of the US military, and the Akabane workers brought it to a victorious conclusion.[44]

Sōhyō's renewed commitment to peace and other political activities was necessary also to enhance solidarity among different labour unions and thereby enable the labour movement as a whole to progress.

After the Red Purge expelled communist workers and other activists from their workplaces, labour unions were put on the defensive and turned their attention to more immediate matters, predominantly wage and other economic issues.[45] But as Shin Sanbetsu officials were quoted above as saying, as long as labour unions fought lone battles focusing on 'selfish' interests, they would be unable to get the government and management to address matters that concerned all workers.

The drawbacks of in-house unions, the perennial issue that taxed Japan's labour movement, were made up for, to a considerable extent, by Sōhyō's political campaigns which tackled issues that transcended the immediate concerns of individual unions because they appealed to workers' class consciousness or sense of brotherhood. Peace, being an overarching issue that concerned everyone who had been traumatized by the war, provided a badly needed nexus to bring together workers across the boundaries of individual unions.

Its newly adopted pacifist stance enabled Sōhyō to co-opt the diffuse antiwar sentiment of rank-and-file workers. The four principles of peace, which were formulated on the initiative of intellectuals and union officials, were welcomed on the whole by most union members.[46]

One man working for the Tokyo subway, for example, lamented the fact he had to take great care in choosing his words at his workplace because he could no longer trust his union, which had cooperated with management to draw up a list of workers who were to be sacked in the Red Purge. He then went on to say:

> Everyone is worried about the peace treaty and whenever I talk with colleagues I trust, we voice our concern that there might be another war. But in public, we can never debate peace issues. There is a union boss at every station and they keep in touch with one another to watch out for everything union members do or say. I often think it is unbearable, but can't do anything rash because that might cost me my job. All other conscientious union members feel like I do.[47]

In contrast to the militant rhetoric used by labour unions against the Japanese and US governments as well as corporate management, letters contributed by ordinary workers to Kokurō's in-house organ, the *Kokutetsu Shimbun*, are plaintive in their tone:

> We should never go to war again if we are to protect the happiness of our mothers and fathers, little brothers and sisters and ourselves, who have finally become able to take a respite after experiencing the worst conditions imaginable after the defeat in the war.[48]

> Japanese workers don't want to do anything that might cause another war because they hate war. I don't think it's cowardly because ... we just can't recover from the trauma caused by the war.[49]

Negami Masayuki, who was in charge of the campaign to disseminate the new policy, said although he was quite confident that it would appeal to war-weary workers, he was also aware that most of them needed to be educated about its implications. Kokurō enlisted some forty academics from the Union for Democratic Scientists, called Minka for short, to conduct a nation-wide educational campaign. The appeal of the new policy was made all the more powerful as it came from the mouths of top union officials and professors from prestigious universities, which left ordinary workers awestruck. In their naivety, workers simply lapped up the new policy, according to Negami.[50]

The adoption of the new principles on peace also entailed an important shift in the power structure of many labour unions. The Sōhyō leadership consisted of individuals who subscribed to left-wing ideology, though they were critical of the JCP, and those who were opposed to both the JCP and left-wing ideology. The centre-left group took a confrontational stance, organizing 'class struggles' against the ruling classes, which required externalization of union activities to tackle political campaigns. The centre-right group was generally against Sōhyō's political struggles, including the peace movement. It was pro-West in its outlook on the Cold War, and tended to be moderate or even collaborationist in its relations with management. This group tended to share the attitude of many pre-war union leaders who were opposed to capitalism, fascism and communism. Of these, hostility to communism was its most pronounced characteristic.

When labour unions opted for the four principles on peace, the centre-left group consolidated its hold on power and the centre-right group's influence began to wane. This shift in power is dramatically illustrated by the case of Kokurō.

At the Kokurō convention in June 1951, at which delegates gathered to decide the union's annual policy, Hoshika Kaname, deputy head of the union, dismissed a comprehensive peace as unrealistic and sounded a patriotic note in calling for Japan's independence and opposing the peace movement, which he said was incited by the 'fifth column' of the JCP. He reiterated the need to oppose the pro-Soviet peace movement and urged his colleagues to cast in the union's lot with the pro-West ICFTU. Hoshika also said the union should focus on concrete economic issues rather than divert its energies to the peace movement.[51]

A younger union official named Yokoyama Toshiaki began his counter-argument with an overview of the international situation, pointing to what he characterized as the nefarious intentions of the US. In reiterating the need for a comprehensive peace, Yokoyama drew the audience's attention to the formidable situation facing all labour unions. He pointed out how the conservative camp was revising laws to restrict union activities while resurrecting *zaibatsu* conglomerates, boosting the powers of the police and restoring war criminals to public life. He claimed that big businesses were regaining their strength thanks to the Korean War, and that capitalists were promoting economic cooperation with the US in hopes of benefiting from another war. Yokoyama argued that while such a policy premised on a partial peace was likely to be conducted at the expense of people's economic well-being, Japan's growing reliance on the US would further weaken its economy, which was all the more reason to call for Japan's independence. In countering Hoshika's accusation that the peace movement would divert the union's attention from urgent economic issues, Yokoyama, who was younger and knew at first-hand about the realities of individual workplaces, used his mastery of detail concerning union issues to the full to point out how important it was for the union to put up an earnest fight against the authorities.[52]

Younger unionists argued that labour unions would end up supporting the repressive policies of Prime Minister Yoshida Shigeru's government if they accepted a partial peace, and as a result unions would stray from being a labour movement inspired by class consciousness. They also opposed the 'patriotic' labour movement advocated by Hoshika, saying people's lives had been squandered in the name of patriotism during the war.[53]

The Constitution was frequently invoked to promote the idealistic aspect of the peace principles. A delegate from Hiroshima pointed to the ravages of the modern war being waged in Korea, and argued that Japanese workers should fight in the spirit of the peace Constitution, which embodied the idealism of the new post-war nation, and avert any recurrence of atomic bombings anywhere in the world.[54]

Hoshika's proposal was rejected, with an overwhelming majority voting for the three principles calling for a comprehensive peace, neutrality and opposition to Japan's rearmament. Hoshika and like-minded union leaders, who made up the centre-right faction of the railway union, subsequently suffered a precipitous fall in influence. Rank-and-file workers' anger against the old-guard leadership reached boiling point when it agreed with the railway authorities to settle for a semi-annual bonus whose sum was much lower than the original union demand, and tried to drop from the union's agenda the fight against the Anti-Subversive Activities Law.[55] Amid the resurgence of militancy among its workers, Kokurō defied the authorities' threats of dismissal in late 1952 to engage in direct action including sit-ins, overtime bans, work slowdowns and workers taking time off en masse, and finally won a wage increase.[56] The railway union became the first major union to recover from the setbacks experienced by organized labour.

Similar power struggles were observed elsewhere until around 1952. Right-leaning leaders of the Japanese Coal Miners' Union, accused of striking a deal with the Ministry of Labour to end the fight against the Anti-Subversive Activities Law, were brought down by votes of non-confidence. During the above-mentioned labour strife at the Akabane plant, too, a group of JCP and other left-wing workers ousted right-leaning officials from their posts.[57] Similar changes of leadership took place in other miners' and steel workers' unions. In the process, the involvement of ordinary workers in union affairs increased as they seized the initiative from their union superiors in workplace struggles.[58]

The decision by Kokurō, one of Japan's largest unions, to adopt a new policy on peace, greatly encouraged officials and activists, who were pushing for the adoption of the peace principles by other unions. The railway workers' move was followed by other key constituent unions of Sōhyō, most of whom saw overwhelming majorities of their officials vote for the pacifist principles.[59]

Within Sōhyō itself, the Rōdōsha Dōshikai (Workers' Association), a group of centre-left union officials pushing for the pacifist policy, gained the upper hand over centre-right officials.[60] With such leaders collaborating across the boundaries of industrial federations, lower-ranking activists stepped up cooperation on a widening front in industrial actions, which helped to strengthen the overall labour movement.[61] According to Shimizu Shinzō, while Takano and other older leaders, who had been involved in political activities since pre-war days, appeared to be concerned primarily with the possibility of another crackdown, the younger officials of Rōdōsha Dōshikai showed little fear, and single-mindedly worked to disseminate their ideas on peace.[62]

The economist Takashima Kikuo noted that as a result of the leadership change, union leaders who derived their strength mainly from the backing of ordinary workers gained ascendancy. This was the case, for example, with Kokurō, Zentei and the General Federation of Private Railway Workers' Unions of Japan (Shitetsu Sōren). According to Takashima, newly ascendant leaders took advantage of pressure from the rank and file to conduct successful negotiations with management.[63]

As a result of the leftward shift in Sōhyō's policy, four major unions seceded from the labour organization, opposing its increased involvement in political activities. Of the unions that denounced Sōhyō's peace movement, the rump Sōdōmei, after its split with its left-wing unions that joined Sōhyō, was known for its tendency to avoid confrontation with management and supported the Right JSP after the JSP broke up to form two separate parties in 1951, over differences with regard to the peace treaty and the Japan-US security pact.

Two of the four organizations that left Sōhyō, the Japanese Federation of Textile Workers' Unions (Zensen) and the All Japan Seamen's Union (Kaiin), were known for being rigidly controlled by their leadership.[64] About 80 per cent of Zensen members were poorly paid female factory hands, who generally played a passive and subordinate role in union activities. Kaiin was known for its militancy in the early post-war years, and became Japan's first union federation to get management to institute a minimum wage. Its leadership, however, was dominated by ageing officials in their fifties and sixties, and rank-and-file members of Kaiin were unable to take an active part in union activities because they were often at sea.[65] During the Korean War, Kaiin, confronted with the choice over whether to support the war led by the US, decided to cooperate by having its seamen assist transport in war zones, and not a few members lost their lives. The union argued that refusing to cooperate with the UN would be tantamount to condoning North Korea's invasion and contributing to the UN's possible defeat in the war.[66]

Leaders of these unions approved rearmament, a partial peace treaty and the Japan-US security treaty. The unions, which stayed out of the peace movement, were characterized by a lack of internal democracy, which tended to stifle rank-and-file activism. In contrast, Sōhyō made greater efforts, as the following chapters will demonstrate, to stimulate rank-and-file participation, and became increasingly radical as a result of its tactics.

SCAP, which had originally intended to create an anti-communist labour organization to its liking, was severely disappointed as Japanese workers, whose attitudes were moulded by their recent history, went their independent way to fulfil their own aspirations. The dynamics of the labour movement conditioned by the unique corporate, economic and political circumstances in Japan, was simply beyond SCAP's control.

3 The Takano years

Sōhyō's first five years, until mid-1955, were marked to a significant extent by the defining role played by its leader Takano Minoru (1901–74). Takano considered the grassroots initiative in the labour movement to be of particular importance and his ideas, which shared a significant commonality with those of low-ranking workplace activists, did much to stimulate and promote ordinary workers' participation in union, peace and other activities. In this chapter, Takano's views about the kind of labour movement he thought should be promoted will be discussed in order to better understand the context of the overall situation surrounding ordinary workers, who took up various workplace and non-union activities.

During those five years, Takano's stance shifted rapidly leftward from support for the US war in Korea to support of what he called the peace forces, suggesting that organized labour should forge a closer relationship with socialist nations as against the 'war forces' of capitalist nations. Takano's new stance ran counter to that of other Sōhyō leaders, who subscribed to the third-force thesis of the Left JSP and wished to keep a distance from the communist camp. The row eventually led to Takano's downfall.

Takano's approach to the labour movement

When he first led Sōhyō, Takano, like other top officials of the newly created labour federation, toed the SCAP and Japanese government line with regard to the Korean War. Shortly after the war broke out, Takano took the view that labour unions should follow the orders of SCAP, since the US was fighting for democracy as it tried to counter the North Korean incursion. He even went so far as to encourage labour unions to profit from war-related work.[1] While the stand he took with regard to the Korean War later haunted him, Takano apparently feared for the survival of the newly launched Sōhyō and wanted to avoid confrontation with SCAP.[2]

Considering the fact that he stuck to the centre-left position in the labour movement throughout his life, Takano's support of the Korean War appears quite out of character. The economist Takashima Kikuo, who was an advisor to the Sōhyō leader, said Takano later told him he had no choice but to support the Korean War because he might risk passing up the precious opportunity to establish a left-wing labour federation that would succeed Sanbetsu if he incurred SCAP's wrath. According to Takashima, Takano, who knew very well how powerful the US occupation forces were, struggled to find a way to make Sōhyō independent of US patronage, and the debate over the peace treaty provided him with an opportunity to do so. Therefore, Takashima said, Takano could have opted for nothing other than a comprehensive peace treaty.[3]

Prior to Sōhyō's adoption of the four peace principles, Takano kept his distance from Rōdōsha Dōshikai, a group of left-wing union officials who were vigorously trying to organize support for the peace principles, and adopted a centrist position within Sōhyō. But Takano also cultivated ties with leading academics of the day, including Shimizu Ikutarō, Nakano Yoshio, Yoshino Genzaburō, Uehara Senroku and Nanbara Shigeru, many of whom belonged to Heiwa Mondai Danwakai, the academic group that supported the peace principles. Collaboration with such intellectuals played a key role in Sōhyō's 'chicken to duck' metamorphosis, which suggests Takano was working behind the scenes to promote the adoption of the peace principles by organized labour.[4]

Takano started his career as a union activist long before World War II, and was a founding member of the first Japanese Communist Party in 1922. He was arrested several times and even tortured. Takano was imprisoned for about three years after being arrested in the Popular Front Incident of 1937 with other intellectuals belonging to the Rōnō school of Marxism, including Arahata Kanson, Yamakawa Hitoshi and Takano's mentor Inomata Tsunao. They were charged with obstructing the war effort and organizing Japanese leftists at the behest of the seventh Comintern.

Shimizu Shinzō argued that Takano was a confirmed communist and quotes Takano as saying he was 'a true communist' (unlike other phonies who called themselves communists).[5] Shimizu recalled that in the autumn of 1952 Takano privately expressed his support for the JCP's party platform of 1951, which was premised on the view that Japan was under the complete domination of the US.[6] The Rōnō theoreticians, who were members of the Socialism Association (Shakaishugi Kyōkai)[7] and worked closely with Sōhyō, considered Japan to be an independent capitalist state and believed that the immediate goal of the working class was to stage a socialist revolution.[8] According to Takashima, while Takano was close to the Rōnō group and sought its cooperation in co-opting young activists within Sōhyō, he differed with the Rōnō school of thought in that he believed that a nationalist people's front should be organized to achieve Japan's complete independence, and therefore was sympathetic to the JCP platform.[9]

The communist strain in Takano's thought is apparent also in industrial actions he led in the early 1950s, which enlisted workers' families and local communities in what were called *gurumi tōsō*, or struggles by everybody.

62 *The Takano years*

Takano's strategy called for paying close attention to the needs of individual workers and tapping their energies to build momentum for the labour movement from below. Even when he was still a senior member of Sōdōmei, Takano had actively organized young workers in efforts to consolidate the power base of left-wing unions. According to his son Tsumura Takashi, Takano was inspired by his mentor Inomata Tsunao, who had been a member of the American Communist Party and like Takano was a founding member of the JCP. Under Inomata's tutelage, he learned to attach great importance to the role played by union activists, and organized what he called 'initiative groups' of rank-and-file activists who would work to enhance the class consciousness and militancy of individual unions, industrial union federations and regional groupings of unions.[10]

To quote Takano's own words:

> It is important that people at the very bottom rung of workplaces and of society should be encouraged to make their demands public and that [the labour movement should be organized in a way that will] let such people take the initiative and vent their frustrated energies.[11]

In Takano's grandiose vision, workers acting on their own individual initiative should unite with others within local communities to enlist people from all walks of life, including farmers and small shop owners, eventually to form a vast united front on a national level. According to his ally Takashima Kikuo, Takano envisioned a grand people's front to achieve a revolution, which revealed an affinity with the style of JCP activists who worked their way upward from the smallest workplaces.[12]

Takano was wont to expound his romantic and somewhat sentimental vision of the popular movement, involving workers and the rest of the nation he so idealized, in very simple terms as follows: 'Workers can win their battles only when they join forces with their suffering brothers throughout the nation.'[13] The peace movement therefore lay close to his heart as a means to bring workers and the rest of the nation together in a grand popular movement. To quote his words again, 'If labour unions spearhead the peace and anti-nuclear bomb movements, then they will no longer be isolated and will be able to fight alongside farmers and citizens.'[14]

Meanwhile, the focus of Sōhyō's policy debates shifted from the peace treaty to the Japan-US mutual security act (MSA) designed to finance Japan's rearmament with US economic aid. Since the Japanese economy had gone into a slump when the boom created by the Korean War came to an end, many business leaders pinned their hopes on the MSA. It was hoped that US economic assistance for Japan's rearmament would revive Japan's arms industry, and that arms exports to strife-torn Southeast Asia would help to further the country's economic development. That raised concern among union circles that the MSA would assist in a militarization of the economy.

Sōhyō organized peace activities to oppose the MSA and convened meetings of its officials and academics to formulate alternative ways to develop a 'peace' (i.e. non-military) industry as against a 'war' industry reliant on arms production. Sōhyō became the nation's foremost opposition force, and began playing a role resembling that of an opposition political party, forming a shadow cabinet.

The early 1950s, during which Takano led Sōhyō, saw a chain of events that generated wide public concern. Acrimonious labour strife that erupted as a result of corporate restructuring in the steel industry in 1953 and 1954 spread to local farmers and commercial interest groups as well. Other key social issues that added to public anxiety included US military installations scattered across the nation that seriously disturbed the lives and livelihoods of local residents, a highly destructive typhoon that devastated western Japan in 1953, the exposure of Japanese fishermen to a hydrogen bomb test at Bikini Atoll in 1954, and widespread poverty.

Sōhyō's 'chicken to duck' transformation, which helped the labour movement to resume its militant posture and regain lost ground, boosted the union federation's prestige in the eyes of those involved in other social movements. Those outside organized labour, including small proprietors, agricultural organizations and a wide variety of grassroots groups, turned to Sōhyō for help in dealing with their problems. Subsequently many non-labour groups began to attend Sōhyō's annual conventions.[15] With Sōhyō greatly expanding the scope of its activities to tackle a wide range of political issues that were far removed from the traditional concerns of labour organizations, Takano, with a touch of grandiloquence and melodrama, claimed that the labour organization had been tasked to take on the whole nation's suffering.[16]

Despite his somewhat stiff and puritanical demeanour, Takano won a significant following among union leaders and a great number of activists working at the grassroots, because he was known among his admirers as a man who would never collude with the capitalist class and never let rank-and-file workers (*taishū*) down.[17] As Taguchi Fukuji noted, Takano's own words suggest that he regarded his leadership role in the labour movement as a kind of calling: 'My life as a guardian of labour unions.' 'I humbly take responsibility for the lives of union members' families.' 'We have the responsibility to meet the expectations of anonymous workers by fighting through to the end no matter what obstacles lie ahead.'[18] Considering labour unions to be the vanguard of a national movement to advance people's interests, Takano led the labour movement with messianic zeal.

A romanticized view of ordinary workers, together with radical national reform to be carried out through grassroots initiatives, constituted two key ingredients of Takano's philosophy, and he attracted support from the most activist sector of the labour movement, which was inspired by similarly romantic visions. The days of the Takano leadership coincided with the emergence of numerous union activists who were encouraged by their unions' policy shift over the peace treaty. Yoshioka Tokuji, a former head of the All Japan Harbour Workers' Union and a supporter of Takano, recalled that there were numerous activists who volunteered their services both within and outside their unions in the 1950s, regardless of the nature of union leadership. Such activists gained significant moral support from Takano's policy, according to Yoshioka.[19]

The peace forces debate

The so-called peace forces debate, which eventually forced Takano's resignation as Sōhyō's secretary-general, was kicked off when Sōhyō policymakers held discussions prior to the labour organization's annual convention in July 1953. During the policy debate, Takano proposed that Sōhyō should forge an international alliance with the world's peace forces to promote peace.[20] By the term 'peace forces', Takano said he meant any grouping of countries or peoples who wished for peace. He argued that countries such as the Soviet Union and India were part of the peace forces, and that British Prime Minister Winston Churchill, too, represented the peace forces when he criticized US Secretary of State John Foster Dulles.[21]

Takano's argument implicitly called for siding with the Soviet Union and China, thereby breaking with the third force thesis of the Left JSP. The idea drew a sharp response from other Sōhyō leaders of the Mindō group. They were shocked by Takano's 'about-face', because he had supported the US in the Korean War only two years before and now suggested that the US was a 'war force'.

Takano's 'leftward shift' is variously attributed to a trip he made to Burma in January 1953[22] or his bid to consolidate his hold on power within Sōhyō.[23] Ōta Kaoru, for example, presumes Takano was inspired by the united front of the Burmese socialists and communists when he attended a convention of Asian socialist parties there.[24] The new policy stand Takano took, however, had been prompted by shifting trends on the international scene and within organized labour in Japan, which the Sōhyō leader considered to be propitious in putting into practice his own vision of the labour movement.

Of all the international developments in those days, the communist revolution in China in 1949 had the greatest impact on Japanese unionists. While the Japanese in general felt a centuries-old ethnic and cultural affinity with China, reports about the new Chinese leadership fuelled Japanese workers' admiration for the country. Despite Japan's invasion of China, the Chinese People's Liberation Army was reported to have committed no atrocities against the Japanese in retaliation. The contrast with the Soviet Union on this point made China look all the more appealing. There was widespread hatred of the Soviet Union among the general public in Japan because it had violated the Japan-Soviet neutrality pact by invading Manchuria in the final days of World War II. The mass killings, looting and rapes by the Russians that ensued gave rise to enduring resentment among the Japanese. But towards the Chinese, many Japanese felt a sense of guilt about the suffering Japan's invasion of the country had caused.

Sympathetic chroniclers such as Edgar Snow and Agnes Smedley, and accounts of Japanese politicians and others who visited China and raved about the young state's remarkable progress in nation building, also did much to boost the admiration of Japanese workers for a country they had never seen.[25] Such reports helped to cultivate the impression among Japan's political left that the new Chinese government was the embodiment of morality and discipline.

Both the communists and left-wing members of the JSP, as well as some Mindō union leaders, enthusiastically hailed the establishment of a workers' state in the neighbouring country. China became a powerful source of inspiration, especially for the young, and the writings of Mao Zedong became essential reading for union activists. The Five Principles of Peace announced by Zhou Enlai and Jawaharlal Nehru in 1954 greatly promoted China's status in the eyes of Japanese workers as the nation working hardest for international peace.[26]

Another aspect of China that Japanese workers greatly admired was the Chinese Communist Party's egalitarian approach embodied in its 'mass line' (*taishū rosen*) policy. China's mass line differed from the approach taken by the Russian or other communist parties, which styled themselves as the vanguard that would lead the backward masses. The new Chinese approach, in a break from such left-wing elitism that exacted unquestioning obedience to party pronouncements, sought to serve people by aiding their awakening to a higher state of political consciousness through daily struggles and other experiences. The idea was embraced in particular by many Japanese unionists working at the grassroots, prompting them to introduce the Chinese method into their own unions.[27]

The leading ideologue of China's mass line, Liu Shaoqi, argued that in organizing people at the grassroots, the leadership should eliminate any gaps between the needs of the leadership and those of the people, and that the leaders, while educating and offering support to the people, must encourage their initiative. In doing so, leaders should neither be condescending nor peremptory. Leaders should tap the opinions of the people to draw up a programme for action and get the people to try that programme. The people's response should then be taken into account to perfect the programme. This process is to be repeated indefinitely (with a view eventually to reaching a state of perfection).[28]

Takano, too, appears to have been significantly influenced by Liu's ideas, and the hallmarks of such Chinese thought are apparent in his writings. He declared, for example, in his book published in 1952:

> You cannot enhance the power of the working class just by indoctrinating them with certain ideology. Although indoctrination is

important, it is the personal experiences of the workers that would make them truly embrace that ideology. Workers will cultivate their class consciousness through what they see and hear and their own struggles. They will learn things on their own instead of being taught.[29]

In the same book, he also said:

You have to believe in people and fight alongside them. At the same time, you should never lose your hold of them. Prepare for your struggle by holding up a mirror that reflects people's needs, holding fast onto the people and getting closely involved in their lives. ... You have to present people with the objective of our struggle and the scenario in which one struggle will lead to another struggle. Emphasize what we have achieved in our past struggles to boost their confidence. Help them to learn to make sacrifices and take a heroic stand. Lead people with the authority of your union but take responsibility for your actions.[30]

With a population of some 600 million people joining the socialist camp, the international situation appeared to have significantly altered in favour of socialist nations. This prompted Takano to remark:

Last year [in 1952] it was argued that the conflict between the US and the Soviet Union would not be resolved easily. But this year the prospects for achieving peace have been considerably enhanced thanks to the progress China has made on nation building. Any argument that underestimates this point is no longer of any use.[31]

The Chinese revolution also fuelled hopes for the independence movements in Asia and the Middle East. The Soviet Union, meanwhile, mounted a 'peace offensive' following the death of Stalin, prompting some Japanese leftists to consider it as a peace force.

Unions in Japan were also strongly influenced by the ideas of the labour movement in France and Italy, which stressed unity on an extensive front. On a visit to Japan in September 1953, WFTU Secretary Jack Woddis won a significant following in Japan when he urged Japanese unionists to cast aside sectarianism to enable cooperation among wide sectors of the working population. Around the same time, ten Japanese union officials attended the WFTU's convention in Vienna in October 1953, and their reports and the minutes of the convention later published in Japan made converts of many Japanese workers.[32]

The WFTU's idea was a revelation, especially for communists and left-wing JSP members.[33] Communist activists, who had followed their party's violent guerrilla tactics,[34] were already aware that their policy had been an utter failure and felt alienated amid the hostility of the general public. The idea of united action, which they learned about in their moment of desperation, sounded irresistibly appealing. The communists had believed that they should first fight the Mindō group and the JSP as they had faithfully tried to act out Stalinist doctrine, which argued that the communists must defeat social democrats before taking on monopoly capital, their most formidable enemy. The idea promoting unity was inspired also by the Chinese communists who, in contrast to the Japanese Communist Party, which had always sought to monopolize power as in the days of the Sanbetsu-led labour movement, had ceded considerable power to the rival Kuomintang during their war against Japan. The WFTU's idea also prompted some left-wing JSP members to consider burying the hatchet with the communists. Japanese unionists sought to borrow from the Chinese and European approaches, as well as from radical workplace struggles conducted during Sanbetsu's heyday (see the following section), to formulate a model that would best suit the situation in Japan.[35]

All these developments must have led Takano to conclude that the turn of events on both the international and domestic fronts was preparing an ideal environment for conducting the style of labour movement that was dear to his heart.

From early on Takano had been an advocate of unity based on an antifascist popular front promoted by the seventh Comintern convention of 1935. Shortly after Japan's defeat, he had envisioned a grand alliance in the labour movement that comprised both communists and conservative unionists led by Matsuoka Komakichi. It was his belief that the people's struggle to banish imperialism completely from Japan must tie up with similar movements in developing nations, including China and other Asian countries, and he was therefore supportive of united action by the international labour movement as promoted by European unions.[36]

As pointed out above, Takano appeared to be a convert to China's mass line, and tried to introduce the Chinese approach with a view to realizing his idealistic vision for a labour movement that would derive its strength from the initiative of individual workers. Takano was aware of the idealism of the young, who had been inspired by the promise of socialist nations and aspired to build a new society by emulating what they considered to be the peace-promoting and humane aspects of socialism. Takano believed that growing enthusiasm among the young would serve as a lever to help to realize his vision of the labour movement. It was natural that he should try to rally support of the young with his peace forces thesis, and it is difficult to imagine Takano acting any other way.

Takano's peace forces thesis primarily concerned an international relations issue, but Hirosawa Kenichi, a former JSP politician, argues that the peace forces thesis was also a message to union activists that they should continue their community-based struggles at the grassroots and break with the ways of corrupt union leaders, who paid lip service to the cause of class struggle but routinely compromised with management.[37] The leaders Hirasawa referred to here were those belonging to Sōhyō's mainstream faction, known as 'left-wing Mindō', who mostly subscribed to the third force thesis of the JSP.

Since his days as the leader of Sōdōmei, Takano had often been accused of making sudden policy reversals, and was branded as an opportunist by some critics.[38] Many also regarded him as a tactician with an uncanny ability to detect in which direction the political winds were blowing.[39] Indications are, however, that Takano was merely dissembling when he supported the US during the Korean War, and that he remained faithful to his Marxist agenda all along. Rather than have an abrupt 'change of heart', he appears to have been biding his time before showing his true colours. According to Shimizu Shinzō, Takano began acting like his true self during the strikes against the Anti-Subversive Activities Law in 1952 after the end of the US occupation.[40] Shimizu says:

> During the three and a half years [between 1948 and 1951], Takano put top priority on uniting the labour movement and used all his wiles to eliminate any obstacle to that objective. He demonstrated a degree of dynamism unmatched in other periods of his life and as he changed his tack so quickly, his actions and views expressed [during this period] were at variance with his actual thoughts.[41]

Although Mindō leaders opposed Takano's peace forces thesis, it carried the day in Sōhyō's peace debate due to the support it received from union activists, who responded enthusiastically to the dramatic rhetoric used by the man dubbed a 'quiet agitator'.[42]

The row over the peace forces thesis, which seriously strained Takano's relationship with the JSP as well as with Sōhyō's Mindō officials, continued during the debate over the Left JSP's new platform in the autumn of 1953, in which Takano put forward a proposal drawn up by Shimizu Shinzō.

Sōhyō and the JSP had joined forces before the party's split-up in 1951 to promote adoption of the four peace principles. Many of Sōhyō's ideas behind its support of the principles were borrowed from those of the JSP, which were expounded with Suzuki Mosaburō (1893–1970), a key politician representing the party's left wing, and Sone Eki (1903–80), a former diplomat belonging to the JSP's centre-right faction, playing the leading roles.[43] To ensure Japan's security, for example, Sōhyō and the JSP both called on the UN to take responsibility for protecting Japan from aggression by other countries.

The JSP's four principles, however, were informed largely by security concerns. The party's arguments focused on the need for Japan to enhance its security by signing a peace treaty with all of its former enemies, which was crucial if Japan was to win a security guarantee from the UN and achieve economic independence through trade with socialist and Asian nations.

Sōhyō, however, believing the very survival of the labour movement hinged on the outcome of the peace debate, adopted the peace principles for its own reasons. Its ideas focused primarily on how to protect workers' economic interests, and reiterated how rearmament would divert public funds away from peacetime industry and welfare programmes, and lead to the exploitation of workers.[44]

In 1953, when the Left JSP prepared to draw up its new platform, Shimizu Shinzō (1913–96), a right-hand man of Takano Minoru in those days, faulted the party platform on the grounds that the four peace principles as promoted by the party boiled down to purely diplomatic matters, and lacked a vision for achieving a socialist revolution. Shimizu argued that the four principles should go hand-in-hand with a viable strategy to free Japan's working population from the double scourge of US imperialism and Japanese monopoly capital. He said the policy on peace should be fleshed out with concrete measures aimed at uniting workers, farmers, small proprietors, intellectuals and sympathetic business people, and thereby lay the groundwork for establishing a truly independent government. Shimizu said that if JSP politicians lacked a concrete programme to tie its peace policy to the workers' fight against low pay and legislation to restrict their activities, and focused only on parliamentary activities and elections, the party would be unlikely to win the backing of workers, who faced harsh treatment on a daily basis. Though Shimizu's idea was rejected by the JSP, it won significant support from left-wing and young unionists.[45]

Shimizu also argued that the JSP had never made it clear whether the neutrality it supported stood for a diplomatic policy to keep an equal distance from both the capitalist and communist camps, or whether it signified an active opposition to the imperialism of both camps. In his view, the labour union's stand should definitely be the latter. Shimizu noted that because the JSP did not distinguish between the two meanings of its neutral stand, the party succeeded in appealing to the pacifism of less ideologically oriented citizens and securing the support of anti-imperialist unionists at the same time.[46]

After Shimizu's proposal, which had Takano's full backing, was rejected by the JSP, Takano contributed a paper to the organ of the Socialism Association, attacking the Left JSP's policy on the four peace principles. Takano argued that if the working class took a sectarian stand to insist on adherence to the four peace principles, it could never conduct joint struggles on the widest possible front. Any policies that would alienate certain sectors of the populace, because of their stance regarding the communist bloc, must be repudiated, according to Takano. His paper triggered a division within the association, subsequently driving Takano out of the group.[47]

The debate over the peace forces thesis and the JSP platform became so intense precisely because it reflected the dynamics within Sōhyō's labour movement, which was marked by growing grassroots activism.

The following section will look at what prompted an increasing number of rank-and-file workers to become union activists, and how they played an important part in radicalizing Sōhyō during Takano's leadership.

70 *The Takano years*

The rise of grassroots activism

Peace and independence

The major setback suffered by organized labour during the Red Purge and the Korean War was an extremely dispiriting experience for workers. But the impasse in the labour movement served as an occasion for introspection, and forced workers, especially young workers, to ponder a way somehow to break out of the deadlocked situation.

Amid the subdued atmosphere at workplaces shortly after the Red Purge, many rank-and-file workers dared not become involved in union activities for fear of losing their jobs, and the union leadership was unable to rely on them to implement their orders. Young workers, however, sought to divert themselves somehow and quench their thirst for art and culture to fight the depressing mood. From around 1952, they began forming societies (called circles or *sākuru* in Japanese) with their fellow workers, to take up such activities as choral singing, performing arts, essay-writing and flower arrangement, as well as studies of economics and history.[48]

At Kokurō, workers got together at first to gripe about the oppressive atmosphere at their workplaces shortly after the Red Purge.[49] In the summer of 1951, Kokurō's Hino and his young colleagues decided to have fun on a nearby beach because SCAP had banned meetings and other group activities at work. They set up a makeshift stage with sand and enjoyed singing with members of the Central Chorus (Chūō Gasshōdan), a JCP-affiliated choral singing group. The workers subsequently formed their own choral society.[50] Informal gatherings like this rapidly caught on in unions across the country, as workers sought to do something to cheer themselves up.

Group activities were also organized by activists concerned that the democratic reforms introduced by SCAP were being undermined. They were also aware of the gap between the ideals of the post-war democratization effort and the backward attitude of the general public, who had yet to measure up to those ideals. So they conducted their group activities with a view to eliminating that gap by modernizing and democratizing workers' attitudes.[51] Some activists also engaged in group activities as a way to criticize the policies of the union leadership.[52]

Political events also provided an important theme for workers' cultural activities. The departure of the US occupation forces in 1952 greatly enhanced their sense of liberation because workers no longer had to fear they could be sacked at the whim of General MacArthur.[53] But although the country's long-awaited independence had come, the Japan-US security pact ensured that US military bases remained in place, much to the fury of trade unionists.

The financial burden endured by the Japanese people in helping maintain the US installations, as well as the cost of Japan's rearmament, were perceived as continuing to oppress the people, thereby fuelling popular indignation at the condition of Japan, which workers believed was still subjugated to US interests. Even after the end of the occupation, 'peace and independence' became the slogan activists openly used to conduct their labour and peace movements, and anti-base campaigns erupted in many parts of Japan.[54]

Peace and independence also became the theme of countless poems written by workers. An excerpt from Kawamura Yasuo's poem, *A Foreign Country in the Midst of Our Motherland*, reads:

> Lost are our fields of wheat,
> Lost are our roads,
> Lost are our buildings,
> Lost are our parks,
> Lost are our maidens and work,
> A foreign country stands in the midst of our motherland,
> A foreign country extends over our land,
> Our eyes stare at those letters in the pouring rain,
> We see our country lost,
> We stare at those letters with anguish in our chest,
> Off-limits to Japanese.[55]

Other amateur poets wrote about their resentment of police brutality; of an American officer who manhandled a worker employed at a US base or a contractor working for the US military, and sacked him only because he stared back in defiance; and of employers who oppressed workers with unbearable working conditions. These enemies were depicted in their poems as oppressors who literally threatened their lives and against whom workers were called upon to risk their lives to resist. Poems calling for 'the liberation of the nation' became redolent of the sentiment informing the *Marseillaise* of revolutionary France.[56]

Liberation of self

As mentioned above, the first five or so tumultuous post-war years that ended in a humiliating setback for the left-wing political movement prompted young activists to rethink their strategies.

Takada Yoshitoshi was banished from the JCP following the party's split triggered by Cominform criticism in 1950 of the JCP policy that aimed for a peaceful revolution. Takada, who had been an ardent patriot during the war and wholeheartedly supported Japan's military effort, joined the communists after the defeat to dedicate himself as selflessly this time to the socialist cause. After being betrayed by the wartime government, he went through a second major disillusionment when he experienced the vicious infighting within the JCP. When all the activities in which he sacrificed his own personal interests for the sake of a greater cause, appeared to come to naught for the second time, Takada began to see the need to reflect and better understand the situation surrounding him. After considering suicide, he sought to regain his mental and moral bearings by learning to value his own self more, and discovered new values after becoming involved in workplace societies.[57]

Workplace societies were designed to provide a forum where young workers would learn together to cultivate an independent mind, and this gave rise to a personal sphere of workers' mental lives that was distinct from the public spheres stressed by the wartime moral code and post-war union ideology. The wartime ideology propagated during their school days, and the brave class struggle advocated by union ideology, both of which emphasized achievement of a public good, tended to diminish the importance of the personal sphere of individuals. Some young workers questioned both types of moralism and searched for a new set of principles that would harmonize the public good with the happiness of individuals. Young women workers at the Toa Wool Spinning and Weaving Company's factory in Mie Prefecture exchanged essays with young men in their home village and formed a choral society together. They were critical of older people, who insisted on self-sacrifice for the public good. Through their discussions, they pondered methods of social engineering whereby the happiness of individuals would lead to promotion of the public good.[58]

A choral singer with the All Japan Telecommunications Workers' Union (Zendentsū) said:

> We have decided to conduct our society activities mainly to improve unique qualities each of us has and enjoy ourselves instead of thinking too much about the peace movement and other [political] campaigns. A majority of us believe we can contribute to peace better that way.[59]

According to Kido Noboru, who organized informal society activities, the ceasefire in Korea, Japan's independence achieved through the peace treaty and a measure of stability in the domestic political and economic situation as compared with the late 1940s, allowed activist workers to pay more attention to their own personal lives. Workers subsequently began writing more about their own lives and work in addition to poems and other writings with political or social themes.[60]

Self-reflection was encouraged in these cultural activities, and the process of introspection often began with dark musings about the harsh realities of workers' lives. Many essays and poems were about the misery caused by the writer's poverty, painful memories of the war, and loved ones and opportunities lost to the war.[61]

Choral singing became the rage in the 1950s, but it was totally different from today's karaoke singing, which is aimed primarily at self-gratification. Singing by such workers' societies was called a singing movement (*utagoe undō*), in which workers tried to gain new insight by communicating their painful workplace experiences to the audience. The combination of raw emotions and music proved explosive, and the singing movement spread on a nationwide scale.

The chief objective of these group activities was to liberate workers' minds, and they were encouraged to think and act on their own rather than mimic the phraseology of union slogans or blindly accept their leaders' ideas. Another aim of such society activities was to create a workers' culture that was distinct from 'decadent pop or colonial culture dished out by the US and the Japanese mass media'.[62] It was hoped that workers would acquire a culture of their own so that the working class would become able to resist the culture of the enemy class.

Workers engaged in society activities with great enthusiasm, and as their spirits rose they began to develop highly pro-active attitudes. Negami, who was in charge of cultural affairs at Kokurō, explained the process of that change in attitudes as follows: Any worker trying to hone his or her artistic skills goes through a process of deep introspection. A worker trying to write a novel, for example, must first closely look at people and gain insight about them. The writer then turns his attention from individuals around him to society at large, and in the process develops a keen awareness of social issues. Workers involved in cultural activities all went through a similar process of deep reflection, whether they were learning to sing, dance, act or even practise flower arrangement.[63]

A young Kokurō worker, Seto Sadao, who wrote a novel about the hardship of railway workers during the Korean War, said he came to realize as he wrote the importance of organizing his colleagues from below, and became a member of the JCP.[64]

One worker in Fukushima Prefecture said he had found solace in writing poems ever since he graduated from high school. But as he wrote, he became interested in the 'substructure of society' because he thought he would be unable to write good poems unless he knew why the world was so full of suffering and hardship. He subsequently began studying economics.[65]

Choral societies were under the strong influence of the JCP-affiliated Central Chorus.[66] It was led by the musician Seki Akiko, who had been working since the pre-war days as a member of a left-wing artists' group that promoted proletarian culture. The choral group sent its members around Japan to organize workers' musical activities, and often went to scenes of labour unrest to sing in support of workers. The group's policy was to encourage workers to deepen their thoughts about the realities they faced, and express their will to fight through singing.[67] Its performances at workplaces in the midst of acrimonious disputes helped to raise workers' spirits. Sometimes impassioned workers, roused to vigorous action by the singing, overwhelmed management with the sheer intensity of their fervour and won their disputes. Seki Akiko, who was moved by such incidents, said, 'Singing is the force to promote peace' ('utagoe wa heiwa no chikara'), which became a catchword among choral singers and peace activists.[68]

A worker in Nara Prefecture explained why workers' singing would promote peace as follows: She was distressed that whenever she and her colleagues talked about peace or tried to start choral singing, people immediately attacked them as communists. She also deplored the fact that her country was soiled by US soldiers who brought back from Korea the stench of blood and gunpowder. She wanted to get rid of the oppressive atmosphere that tormented her both within and outside her workplace. She said that when she stopped whispering in fear and began singing out loud, she learned for the first time that singing was a force for promoting peace. She said, 'We can't really enjoy singing unless we live in peace. We will sing songs of peace ever more loudly just to defend our right to enjoy singing.'[69]

Through the intoxicating experience of choral singing and other group activities, workers bonded with their colleagues, which enhanced their sense of solidarity. Yoshioka Tokuji of the All Japan Harbour Workers' Union recalled that workers, who normally engaged in seemingly non-political hobbies, demonstrated remarkable enthusiasm and activism during labour disputes and attributed that to the 'We're all in this together' mentality they had cultivated through group activities.[70]

Workers' singing groups became an important feature of industrial action and the peace movement in Japan as they took on the task of raising the morale of other workers and peace activists.[71] Many choral singers are reported to have been quite eager to rush to scenes of labour strife to cheer on workers at other companies.[72]

Ōtsuka of Zentei said that since those involved in society activities formed independent opinions about the labour movement, they were quite different from members of the youth sections of Sanbetsu-affiliated unions in the late 1940s, who obediently followed the orders of their communist leaders.[73] The new breed of young activists often criticized the union leadership for its conservatism. Many activists began working as union officials themselves from the late 1950s or the early 1960s, thereby effecting a shift in their unions' power structure.[74]

Most cultural activists were under the sway of left-wing political thought and Hino, who led the choral singing society at Kokurō, said that because many workers admired socialist nations, choral singing groups gained considerable prestige when Moscow awarded Seki Akiko the Stalin International Peace Prize in 1955.[75] It is possible that the radicalism of the JCP-affiliated Central Chorus rubbed off on amateur choral singers. It is also true that many members of workplace societies were communists. Still, most societies appear to have managed to maintain the non-partisan nature of their activities. There are many stories about societies which resolutely resisted JCP operatives' attempts to bring their groups under party control. Most workers joined societies primarily to have fun, and would have none of the communist politicking that would ruin their enjoyment. The historian Naramoto Tatsuya, who surveyed society activities in those days, said that almost no societies appeared to be under the control of a political party, and that societies on the whole were functioning as voluntary grassroots groups.[76]

Company management, however, often tried to disband workers' societies because they feared the groups had been infiltrated by communists.

Sometimes union officials, who felt threatened by the growing independence of young workers, tried to ban group activities. But unions eventually discovered that the participation of society members in labour disputes was vital, and subsequently decided to promote their activities.[77]

Kokurō was one of the first major unions to promote such informal activities among its members. Fukuda Reizō, who was in charge of promoting society activities at Kokurō, said the idea was inspired by Liu Shaoqi's mass line. To implement Liu's idea, the railway union set itself a strict rule not to intervene in workers' societies but to extend vigorous support by offering generous funding and organizing events where they could perform.[78] Thanks to such encouragement, workers belonging to Kokurō were actively involved in cultural affairs, and the rank-and-file activism that was thus stimulated helped to mitigate to a certain extent the highly centralized, top-down organizational style of the national railway union.

Sōhyō, too, began promoting workers' cultural activities in the mid-1950s. At the request of Sōhyō, the Central Chorus divided the country into five regional blocs and sent its members to each bloc to organize singing groups. As choral singing gained in popularity, national events were held to bring together choral societies from across the country. A national event held in 1953 drew 3,000 participants. The figure jumped to 15,000 in 1954 and to 50,000 in 1955.[79] That year the educational and cultural activities section of Sōhyō spelled out a policy to respect the independence of workers' societies from their unions and offer assistance to encourage their activities.[80] Takano used his ties with academics to help establish the National Congress of Culture in Japan (Kokumin Bunka Kaigi) in 1955. The national body, made up of academics, professional artists and amateurs belonging to societies both inside and outside labour unions, was set up with the express purpose of promoting a 'culture of peace'.[81]

Workplace struggles

Another factor that helped to promote rank-and-file initiative in the 1950s was Sōhyō's policy to encourage workplace struggles (*shokuba tōsō*). The strategy is associated with the slogan 'Shift from leaders' struggles to rank-and-file workers' struggles', attributed to Uchiyama Mitsuo, who led the Hokuriku Railway Union's campaign against the US firing range in Uchinada, Ishikawa Prefecture, in 1953.[82]

A workplace struggle, as the phrase itself indicates, is bargaining with managers at the small workplace level by ordinary workers, who press their demands themselves. Sōhyō and its member unions promoted use of workplace struggles in the hope that workers, through direct negotiations with their bosses over workplace issues, would learn to commit themselves more actively to tackling union activities and acquire class consciousness. The method caught on, and spread among Sōhyō's constituent unions throughout the 1950s.[83]

A workplace struggle by and large started out with the modest aim of addressing minor complaints within a small workplace. Such struggles often served as a significant learning experience that helped workers to extend their horizons to think about issues outside the workplace. Sometimes, as a result of a tough struggle within their factory or office, workers who were normally averse to taking risks and would never dream of confronting management, became daring enough to imperil their jobs. As workers acquired pro-active habits and awoke to wider issues through workplace struggles, they found it impossible to remain complacent and just tackle in-house affairs, and began to take part in peace and other activities outside their companies. A celebrated example of a workplace struggle turning into a peace activity is that of the Hokuriku Railway Union's campaign protesting the installation of a firing range in Uchinada (see Chapter 5).

Such workplace struggles also helped to change labour relations in favour of workers. At times they strengthened workers' hands to the extent that managers became powerless and unable to control their employees. Such circumstances allowed Yokoi Kameo, a communist worker at a machinery maker's plant in Kawasaki, Kanagawa Prefecture, with a workforce of about 300, to take an unprecedented two months' leave to walk from Tokyo to Hiroshima on a peace march in 1959.[84] Higuchi recalled that in 1960 workers at his plant in Tokyo, where workplace struggles flourished, spontaneously left the plant to take part in a protest against the Japan-US security treaty, and their managers just looked on because they knew the workers could not be stopped.[85]

Union leaders initially took a dim view of workplace struggles. During Sanbetsu's heyday in the late 1940s, these often developed into wildcat activities, and Sōhyō feared losing control of small workplaces.[86] But union leaders were no longer able to ignore the importance of workplace struggles amid the popularity of the Chinese mass line, and in view of the vital role rank-and-file workers played in revitalizing the labour movement following the adoption of the four peace principles. Workplace struggles helped to produce a large number of union activists who would act on their own without waiting for instructions from their leadership. The role of such activists in the peace movement will be further discussed in the following chapters.

4 The labour movement under Mindō leadership and the *Anpo Tōsō*

The Takano style of labour movement came under strong criticism from economic 'realists' who wrested control of Sōhyō when Iwai Akira (1922–97) replaced Takano as secretary-general in July 1955. The row within Sōhyō that resulted in an end to Takano's leadership brought internal factional differences into stark relief.

The following will look at how the dynamics of Sōhyō's labour and peace movements were shaped by the rivalry among the three major actors in the run-up to and during the *Anpo Tōsō*. Discussed also is how the union peace movement was affected by fallout from overseas developments and the attitudinal change of workers from the mid-1950s to the early 1960s.

Major actors

Left-wing Mindō leaders

The largest group within Sōhyō, which captured the leadership from Takano and like-minded union officials, was the left wing of Mindō unionists. As stated earlier, the right wing either seceded from Sōhyō or saw its influence sharply decline during the debates over the peace treaty and the Anti-Subversive Activities Law. Left-wing Mindō officials vigorously pushed for the adoption of the peace principles, and played a key role in effecting a leftward shift in Sōhyō's policies. Although both Takano and left-wing Mindō leaders actively promoted Sōhyō's pacifist policy, the Mindō left broke ranks with Takano because it opposed his peace forces thesis and his 'excessive' involvement in political struggles. The economist Takashima Kikuo, who was an advisor to Takano, recalled that by 1955 almost all major private-sector union federations had come under the control of leftist Mindō officials, except for smaller members of the Japanese Federation of Iron and Steel Workers' Unions.[1]

After Sōhyō's leadership went to the Iwai Akira-Ōta Kaoru (1912–98) axis, it was assumed that the federation would tone down its involvement in political activities. The new leaders opposed Takano's policy on the grounds that he, in his effort to overcome the drawbacks of in-house unions, relied

78 *The labour movement under Mindō*

excessively on political activities and community-based struggles aimed at involving people and groups outside of labour unions. They argued that in so doing, Takano neglected workers' immediate concerns. Takano's peace forces thesis, with its anti-US, pro-Soviet and pro-China orientation, was opposed by Mindō leaders, who had retained a deep-seated resentment against communists ever since seceding from Sanbetsu.[2]

Takano's 'popular front' style of labour and other social movements had enjoyed significant support among leftist intellectuals, who lost some of their early enthusiasm about Sōhyō after Takano stepped down as its leader.[3] It was expected that after its ties with academics had weakened, Sōhyō would begin focusing on traditional union affairs.

But the new leadership became heavily involved in the anti-military base campaign in Sunagawa, Tokyo, right from the beginning, when the US military proceeded to expand its airfield in May 1955 by expropriating land from some 140 local farming households. Sōhyō had decided in May to oppose the expansion of the Sunagawa air base and all other military installations before Iwai became secretary-general in July. Sōhyō accordingly mobilized thousands of workers to campaign against the Sunagawa base.[4]

Explaining why Sōhyō devoted such energy to an issue that apparently had little to do with workers' economic interests, the federation's newspaper argued:

> It is evidently clear that a government that tries to expand a US military base, even if that entails bloodshed among its own people, would jeopardize the nation's independence and peace.[5]

In 1957, Sōhyō designated September as the month to step up a nationwide 'people's movement' (*kokumin undō*). The movement was supposed to tackle a wide range of issues that concerned the entire nation, such as price increases, government intervention in school education, nuclear weapons, military bases and minimum wages. To this end, Sōhyō decided to organize petition drives and propaganda activities in cooperation with the JSP and other organizations.

The Police Duties Law, aimed at boosting the powers of police, which the government of Prime Minister Kishi Nobusuke proposed in 1958, also turned into a war-and-peace issue as the government's alleged intention to restore the repressive regime of the pre-war days became the main bone of contention. The proposed law, as was the case with the Anti-Subversive Activities Law, united both centre-right and centre-left unions in their opposition because the matter concerned the freedom to engage in union activities.

After the government backed down and gave up plans to enact the new police law, Ōta, looking back at the way labour unions tackled the protest, said rank-and-file workers on the whole were not as committed to the protest as their leaders were. According to Ōta, Sōhyō leaders wanted to organize direct concerted actions against the law in quick succession, but there was insufficient worker participation to enable this.[6]

The protest against the revision of the Japan-US security treaty (*Anpo Tōsō*) escalated into the largest ever popular movement in Japanese history. But in its initial phase, there was a lack of interest in the issue among workers, and union leaders had to figure out a way to convince their members that revision of the treaty, which would incorporate Japan more tightly into the US military strategy, was inimical to their economic interests.

All this suggests that despite their reputation for focusing on economic issues, the new Sōhyō leaders on the whole were more committed to political struggles than the average union member.

One of the chief reasons why Sōhyō continued to remain actively involved in the peace movement after Takano's departure from its leadership was organizational. Vital economic issues – pay and working conditions – had to be handled by individual unions, and Sōhyō as a national umbrella organization could not negotiate such matters directly with management. Under the circumstances, Sōhyō could do little more than try to create an overall environment that would assist individual unions in bargaining with management. The peace movement provided Sōhyō with the vital means to carry out such a function. Thus the weight Sōhyō carried in peace activities, such as the movement calling for a comprehensive peace, protests against nuclear weapons, military bases and the *Anpo Tōsō*, far eclipsed the influence it could wield in wages and other economic issues within individual companies until the early 1960s, when *shuntō*, or industry-wide cooperation in wage negotiations, hit its stride.[7]

The newspapers put out by individual Sōhyō affiliates such as Kokurō, Zentei and the All Japan Harbour Workers' Union, were dominated by stories on wages and other economic matters and gave scant coverage to peace issues despite the leading role played by these unions in the peace movement. In contrast, Sōhyō's organ devoted extensive coverage to the peace movement and took up peace-related issues, including the Police Duties Law, in its editorials in almost every edition. So when the issue of the Sunagawa base came to a head in 1955, the new Sōhyō leadership tackled it with as much enthusiasm as Takano would have.

For both Iwai and Ōta, who were young men during the war, the issue of war and peace touched a raw nerve, and their anti-war stance sprang in large part from their personal experiences. Iwai had firsthand knowledge of the follies of Japan's war in China, and Ōta was wont to stress the catastrophic effects of the war on the economy.[8]

Just as important, both Iwai and Ōta were staunch socialists. Iwai had been a leader of the JSP youth section and played a key role as a young Kokurō official in getting his union to vote for the peace principles. Like Takano and Iwai, Ōta too was a member of the Socialism Association (Shakai Shugi Kyōkai). Both leaders regarded 'Japan's monopoly capital' and 'US imperialism' as the chief enemies of the working class. As such, the two leaders tried to press a socialist agenda that would transcend economic issues within individual companies.

The ideological penchants of individual leaders aside, the realities of industrial relations and widespread economic hardship facing Japan's working population were cause enough for Sōhyō to muster all of its theoretical as well as organizational prowess to counter corporate management and the government. Recalling the Mitsui Miike coal miners' 282-day industrial action in 1960, in which hundreds of thousands of workers took part, Ōta maintained that both management and government turned a deaf ear when he pleaded with them to do something about the coal miners' destitute condition, and that they began paying some attention only after the mass protests.[9] Sōhyō also decided to fight the productivity improvement movement initiated by the business community in the mid-1950s with the backing of the Japanese and US governments. It feared that an overwhelming majority of its constituent unions, which were in-house unions, already had a tendency to collaborate with management, and that they would irrevocably come under management's control once they started to cooperate with the productivity improvement initiatives.[10]

The new Sōhyō leadership's agenda also included annual industry-wide wage negotiations (*shuntō*), minimum wages, upgrading of temporary workers to permanent status, unionization of workers at small firms, and social security. Sōhyō continued to need broad unity within the labour movement to achieve these goals, and relied on socialist theories to counter the forces that might pull individual unions towards their own internal concerns. Whether coming from public- or private-sector unions, Mindō leaders, while critical of Takano's 'excessive' involvement in political activities, were in agreement about the vital importance of political activities to push the common agenda of organized labour as a whole.

When the peace forces issue came to a head, it can be assumed that Mindō leaders opposed Takano because they feared that growing radicalization at the grassroots level could split Sōhyō's labour movement. While Takano enthused about 'heightened political consciousness at the grassroots', Mindō officials were more sceptical. While aware of the increased militancy among activist workers, Mindō leaders were of the view that a vast majority of ordinary workers were far less activist, being preoccupied with the concerns of their in-house unions. Still, as was stated in Chapter 3, unionists of the Mindō school were also aware that they needed the active participation of rank-and-file workers in order to advance the labour movement, and Sōhyō continued to encourage workplace struggles in the late 1950s.[11]

The emergence of the government of Prime Minister Kishi Nobusuke (1896–1987) in 1957 helped to further divert Sōhyō's attention from economic to political issues. Kishi, a former alleged war criminal, who had been incarcerated in Sugamo prison, lent a sinister air to the new government in the eyes of the general public. On peace issues, Kishi supported the abolition of the Constitution's war-renouncing clause and deemed it constitutional for Japan to possess small-scale nuclear weapons for defence purposes. Legislative and other measures that the Kishi government pushed in quick succession, including teacher work assessments, the Police Duties bills and revision of the Japan-US security treaty, fuelled debates over peace and democracy to an unprecedented level in union circles. His staunch anti-communist stance further angered left-wing unionists because his policy to tie Japan to the US-led military alliance and alienate the socialist camp threatened to nullify everything the political left had worked for, including their pet project, trade with China. As time went on, any protest against government actions turned into personal attacks against Kishi, who arguably became one of the most widely reviled of Japan's post-war prime ministers. In opposing the Kishi government, the new Sōhyō leadership, which had sought to shift its emphasis to economic issues, ended up leading the most extensive political campaign in Japanese history.

Dissidents

Takano and his allies

Among leading figures who were critical of the Mindō leadership, Takano, without forming a formal group of his own, continued to wield influence over a small minority of like-minded union leaders and a large number of rank-and-file activists. He and his followers used a weekly publication named *Shūkan Rōdō Jōhō* (Labour Information Weekly) as their organ to criticize Mindō leaders for their 'neglect of political issues', 'bureaucratism' and 'disregard for rank-and-file workers'.[12]

Narrowly defined, the Takano group consisted of unionists who formerly had made up the left wing of Sōdōmei prior to the formation of Sōhyō. Their ties with Takano dated back to the pre-war years, and they had been arrested with him at the time of the popular front incident of 1937. Such unionists held key positions within regional groupings of labour unions in Japan's six largest cities, including Tokyo, Osaka and Nagoya. Union leaders who sided with Takano to oppose Mindō officials included those in the Tokyo Local Council of Trade Unions (Tokyo Chihyō), the All Japan Harbour Workers' Union (Zenkōwan), the National Federation of Printing and Publishing Industry Workers' Unions (Zen-in Sōren) and the National Trade Union of Metal and Engineering Workers (Zenkoku Kinzoku), which was Takano's home organization. In general, unions led by Takano's allies were mostly those at small or medium-size companies and were quite limited in number. His allies' control over major unions was severely weakened, with many unionists opting to side with the left-wing Mindō group that had taken power on one hand, and with the JCP making steady inroads into organized labour, on the other.

The main quarrel between the Mindō leaders and the Takano group lay in their approach to the labour movement. Takano had lost major battles during the massive community-based industrial action involving Nippon Steel's Muroran plant in Hokkaido and the Amagasaki steel mill in Hyogo Prefecture. In 1955, he was criticized by Ōkōchi Kazuo for expanding Sōhyō's activities far beyond the traditional bounds of the labour movement, or in Ōkōchi's words, 'externalizing union activities [*gaienka*]'. But unfazed, Takano stuck to his guns, saying, 'Why draw a line between "external" and "internal"?' Countering the criticism of the Muroran steel mill strike, in which workers' wives were mobilized to protest against the layoff, Takano argued:

> Housewives took part in the strike because they were desperately poor. This means people [outside labour unions] awoke to the fact that the causes of their suffering were capitalists, major banks and the reactionary government. What's wrong with co-opting these people into the labour movement?

He continued to contend that the egoism of unions that were concerned with their in-house matters would be remedied if they worked with forces outside the workplace, and that the working class would mature through such outside contacts.[13]

After he stepped down as secretary-general, Takano, ever a visionary, continued to call for a nationwide popular movement involving all kinds of grassroots activists. He urged Sōhyō to link wage issues to human rights issues, campaigns against nuclear weapons and the new government budget that would pave the way for an atomic war. He said that if Sōhyō demanded that the government use taxpayers' money on welfare programmes and peacetime industry instead of war, campaigners against military bases, A-bomb victims, welfare organizations, small business owners and many others would make common cause with Sōhyō to support its struggle for higher pay.[14]

Higuchi Tokuzō, who was a young worker and a member of the JCP in those days, though not a direct disciple of Takano, held similar views. Higuchi argued that the labour movement encompassed political, economic and cultural spheres, and that the province of union activities should be indefinite and unrestricted by boundaries.[15] In a similar vein, an activist with the Kyōdō Printing Company's union said he was against drawing a distinction between the labour movement and the peace movement, on the grounds that it was the destiny of workers to face the fiercest battle with the war force (*sensō seiryoku*), or those abetting war, at their workplaces. The problems that peace campaigners faced, the activist argued, were the same as the problems facing the labour movement.[16]

Whereas Takano and like-minded unionists believed in a labour movement whose purview could be extended without any limit, Mindō leaders, who also showed significant enthusiasm for political issues, were ambiguous about where to draw the line.

When it was formed in 1950, Sōhyō's platform set a goal of achieving a democratic revolution with a view to establishing a socialist society, which won the wide approval of both its centre-left and centre-right officials.[17] But according to Shimizu Shinzō, the dramatic connotation of the word 'revolution' became increasingly out of touch with Japanese reality by the mid-1950s, as the chaos of the early post-war years gradually subsided and international tensions began to abate amid rapprochement between the Cold War adversaries. As a result, the word 'revolution' was replaced by *kakushin*, or reform.[18]

Whether workers described what they were aiming for through union activities as a revolution or not, ever since they had been formed shortly after the war's end, unions had included a fair number of leaders and rank-and-file workers who were unable to content themselves with tackling strictly union affairs. One episode illustrates the reformist zeal of such union members. A massive typhoon hit the area around the Bay of Ise in western Japan in 1959. Organized labour predictably claimed that the damage caused by the typhoon was 'man-made' because the government had spent taxpayers' money for military purposes and neglected disaster prevention. The Tokyo Local Council of Trade Unions (Tokyo Chihyō) immediately sent relief supplies to typhoon victims the day after the storm and before any other relief organizations had taken action. Takeuchi Motohiro, former secretary in charge of political affairs at the Tokyo Chihyō, said it was not just sympathy for the victims that had prompted their action. The unionists were motivated by the belief that it was they who should take the lead in reforming society, according to Takeuchi.[19]

Takano continued to pin his hopes on union activists who, like himself, were attempting to expand the labour movement far beyond the boundaries of in-house unions. Takashima recalled that in the final days of Takano's leadership at Sōhyō, every idea Takano proposed met with opposition from three or four officials allied with Ōta, and that this paralysed the organization's decision-making process. Not knowing what to do, Takano and his allies decided to organize workers from below to regain lost ground, and relied on Tokyo Chihyō in doing so.[20] According to Takeuchi, it was more important for Takano to organize activists at the grassroots, and he was not that interested in how many of his allies took key positions within major industrial union federations.[21] In contrast, the style of Mindō officials, who eschewed heavy reliance on grassroots activism, was to control unions from above, and they dominated key labour federations, including those for steel, automobiles, chemicals and large public corporation unions. Except for Kokurō, the numbers of activists in Mindō-led unions tended to be small compared with those led by Takano's allies.

Mindō leaders who were at the centre of power showed an inevitable tendency to grow conservative in their actions, and despite their fiery left-wing rhetoric seldom resorted to strikes as they put priority on the need to protect their organizations. On crucial labour-related legislation such as minimum wages, Mindō leaders often accepted compromises that the JSP had negotiated with the government. Some Mindō leaders were also tainted with allegations of financial scandal. Takano in contrast was free of such scandal, and that helped to enhance his reputation as being incorruptible and a person who would never sell out to management or the authorities.

JCP members

Members of the JCP made up another key group within the labour movement. Following the Cominform's criticism of the JCP's policy to foment a peaceful revolution, the party switched to violent guerrilla tactics, and as a result suffered a steep decline in public support. After its clumsy 'military campaigns' failed miserably, the party formally rejected the policy in 1955, vowing to stop forcing its ideas on labour unions and to re-establish good relations with labour and grassroots groups. But turmoil continued within the party as members bickered over who was to blame for its weakened state. According to Takeuchi Motohiro's analysis of sales of the party organ *Akahata*, and police data, JCP membership continued to slide after 1955 until it hit bottom in 1958–9, before staging a modest recovery in 1960.[22]

But the party's self-criticism announced in 1955 helped significantly to improve its relations with peace and other grassroots groups. The party adopted a resolution stating that JCP members should make constant efforts to serve the interests of ordinary workers within labour unions, and that the public trust earned through such efforts should be the basis for campaigns to disseminate the party's ideology. The party criticized the way it had tried to appropriate to itself control over the labour and other mass movements, and pledged to cooperate with the JSP and the Rōnō Party in its crusade to liberate the nation from US imperialism. The party leadership thereby formally incorporated the Chinese mass line and the united action advocated by the WFTU into its policies. The JCP's new stance was widely hailed by both JCP and non-JCP activists working at the grassroots.[23]

It had become a tried-and-tested method of the communists, who had suffered repeated persecution since the pre-war years, to work themselves up from the very bottom of small firms or regional union federations. Many also worked their way into labour unions through grassroots organizations such as anti-nuclear weapons groups, associations to promote Japanese-Soviet and Sino-Japanese friendship, JCP-affiliated peace committees, and the movement to win acquittals for the people being tried for their alleged involvement in the fatal railway incident in Matsukawa, Fukushima Prefecture.[24] In view of the enduring hostility of Mindō unionists towards the JCP, communists within labour unions pretended to be followers of Takano or simply did not publicize their party affiliation. As long as they did not declare themselves to be JCP members, communists were sometimes allowed to hold key positions within union leadership.[25]

Grassroots activism at the JCP was particularly vigorous in the late 1950s because the top party leadership was still in disarray over the policy change, and was unable to exercise much control over rank-and-file members. In order to rehabilitate their battered party, many ordinary members in the mid-1950s made tireless and often selfless efforts to tackle union affairs, community work and other grassroots activities, and succeeded in winning a certain level of trust among non-communist unionists.[26] The JCP's monthly magazine *Zenei* noted in 1959 that many of the workers who had recently joined the JCP could not even tell the difference between socialism and capitalism.[27] The reasons workers cited for joining the party show that it was their fellow workers who were communists and stuck it out through hard workplace struggles who were their chief inspiration, rather than Marxist ideology.[28] Observers noted that in the southern part of Tokyo, which was home to numerous small companies, the number of those who joined the JCP through their union activities increased markedly after the party's self-criticism in 1955.[29] One official of the federation of private railway unions complained that whenever his union tried to encourage choral and other cultural activities, communists succeeded in winning new converts because JCP members played leadership roles in most informal workplace activities.[30]

With rank-and-file communists engaging in all forms of grassroots activities, they became accepted as regular members of almost all regional groups for collaboration in union and other local activities that proliferated in the run-up to the *Anpo Tōsō*, and totalled some 2,000 by the summer of 1960.[31] The sheer number of communists playing such a vital role at the grassroots level led Ōta and Iwai to announce Sōhyō's closer cooperation with the JCP in June 1959 in the campaign to block the revision of the Japan-US security treaty.

Generally speaking, workers called *katsudōka*, or activists who acted independently on union affairs and took up grassroots activities outside their unions, did not show particular interest in climbing up the union ranks, and regarded societal change effected through their activities as their chief reward. Many such activists were found among non-mainstream groups, such as Takano's followers and communists who were not at the party's or Sōhyō's centre of power. Collaboration between JCP members and Takano's followers also increased after the party's self-criticism in 1955.[32]

Overseas influence

Whether to adopt the third force or peace forces thesis became a highly contentious issue that divided the Takano group and the left-wing Mindō-JSP alliance in the early 1950s. The second half of the 1950s, however, saw Sōhyō steadily warm to the international socialist camp, making its professed adherence to the third force thesis virtually meaningless.

With regard to socialist nations, Takashima, who served as an advisor to Takano, recalled that while admiration for China rapidly grew at the grassroots level, China was almost a taboo subject among Sōhyō's upper echelons in the early 1950s. Takashima inserted praise for the Chinese people's efforts to build a socialist state in a draft of Sōhyō's 1952 policy statement, but his idea was immediately shot down by Takaragi Fumihiko, an influential Mindō leader who headed Zentei.[33]

By the mid-1950s, however, the peace forces debate appears to have died down. In 1954, nearly 100 Japanese union leaders are reported to have travelled abroad at the invitation of the WFTU, and presumably began to find it hard to resist the WFTU's policy for achieving unity on the widest possible front. The peace forces debate over whether to side with the Soviet Union and China had also lost much of its meaning now that the two countries began professing belief in the possibility of peaceful co-existence between the socialist and capitalist camps, and the 1955 Geneva summit talks between the US, the Soviet Union, Britain and France led to rapprochement on the international front. Many Japanese unionists were visiting the Soviet Union and China and returning to Japan favourably impressed, so it can be assumed that they began implicitly to become more sympathetic to the communist bloc. The 26 July 1955 issue of the *Asahi Shimbun* concludes that the peace forces debate had abated now that 'peaceful co-existence' had replaced both 'peace forces' and 'third force' as a trade unionist catchword.[34]

Communist China had become the darling of leftist workers, and its prestige tended at first to eclipse that of the Soviet Union in their eyes. Still, the dark image of the Soviet Union also began to improve after the death of Stalin. The pace of the country's industrial development, the success of its state-of-the-art space programme, Moscow's announcement of a unilateral end to its nuclear bomb tests in 1958, and both peaceful co-existence between the socialist and capitalist camps and the total disarmament advocated by Nikita Khrushchev, combined to win the hearts of many Japanese workers.

Khrushchev's denunciation of Stalin confirmed the doubts some leftist workers held about the former Soviet leader and they took heart from the new Soviet regime's break with Stalinist policy. The policy shift in the Soviet Union also appears to have prepared an environment that would help eventually to facilitate a working relationship between communists and non-communist peace activists. Sōhyō also welcomed the trend towards de-Stalinization as a sign of the Soviet Union's growing confidence in its peaceful development, democratization and pursuit of a flexible diplomatic policy.[35]

The Soviet invasion of Hungary in 1956, however, prompted some communists, including Zengakuren[36] students, to begin to have serious doubts about what they had believed to be the intrinsically peaceful nature of socialism in contrast to capitalism. But the event took place when Japanese workers were fighting the expropriation of farmland in Sunagawa for use by the US military, and the resulting anti-Americanism that heightened in workers' minds eclipsed any criticism they might have harboured against Soviet conduct in Hungary. While there was a large contingent of communist activists on the scene during the Sunagawa anti-base campaign, the JCP was not allowed to become an official member of the joint protest body comprising the JSP, Sōhyō and other groups. The ideological turmoil within the JCP caused by the Soviet invasion seems to have been largely confined to the party, and barely affected the overall protest movement in Sunagawa.

The impact of the invasion on Japanese leftists appears to have been far more modest compared with that of Western Europe's political left, presumably in part due to the information gap between East Asia and Europe.[37] The JCP did not conduct serious debate on either the Soviet Union's denunciation of Stalin or the Hungarian invasion, and the number of communists who left the party because of these incidents was quite limited.[38] Members of the JSP, though in varying degrees and to a lesser extent as compared with the JCP, were quite anti-US, which appears to have made them trivialize the significance of the Soviet actions in Eastern Europe, compared with that of the anti-base campaign in Sunagawa.

Sōhyō and the JSP, however, condemned the Soviet action in Hungary in November 1956.[39] But as its policy and rhetoric became increasingly radical in the late 1950s (see the section on the anti-security treaty movement below), Sōhyō began to sound like an apologist for the Soviet Union. Its fiscal 1957 policy statement attributed the invasion to the flaws of the Stalinist regime, which the Russian communists themselves had denounced at the Communist Party convention of 1956, and incitement by the capitalist camp.[40] Sōhyō became further critical of the dissidents in Hungary, denouncing them as anti-revolutionaries in the 29 January 1960 issue of its newspaper. Sakisaka Itsurō, the staunchly pro-Soviet doyen of the Socialism Association, which wielded considerable ideological influence on Sōhyō, opposed any study of dissidents fighting the Soviet regime, which appears to have helped to stifle debate over the Hungarian invasion within the labour organization, while ordinary workers were largely left in the dark about the actual situation in the socialist camp.

By the late 1950s, Sōhyō took the view that the Korean War had broken out because the imperialists had tried to block the nationalist revolution that was spreading from North to South Korea. The 1958 crisis over the islands of Quemoy and Matsu in the Taiwan Strait was blamed on the imperialist intervention by the US.[41] With regard to the unrest in Tibet that erupted in January 1959, Sōhyō contended that although China had been contributing greatly to the betterment of Tibetan people's welfare, a handful of reactionaries took the Dalai Lama out of Tibet at the instigation of the imperialists, and blamed the American intelligence agency for undermining the solidarity of Asian and African nations.[42]

The attention of workers continued to focus on the impressive pace of economic development in the socialist camp. Stories about a workers' paradise where there was no unemployment or exploitation retained a powerful hold on Japanese workers' imagination. Many continued to espouse utopian views of the socialist states until 1960, when the Sino-Soviet conflict first became known about.⁴³ Amid this revolutionary optimism, unionists frequently quoted Mao Zedong to argue that the east wind would prevail over the west wind and breezily predicted that the Soviet Union's economic and industrial prowess would exceed that of the US in seven years and that China would overtake Britain in fifteen years, with North Korea also soon surpassing Japan.⁴⁴

In contrast, the capitalist camp led by the US, it was argued, was suffering from contradictions inherent in its system and showing symptoms of depression. In a desperate struggle for their very survival, capitalist countries were forging military alliances in East Asia to capture Southeast Asian markets through imperialist war. While Japanese workers were confused by differing versions of news about repression within the communist bloc, the Suez crisis of 1956, the US and British armed intervention in Lebanon and Jordan at the time of the Iraqi revolution in 1958, and France's repression of Algerian workers, lent ammunition to Sōhyō's polemics against the West.⁴⁵

The rise of socialist nations' economic power, which was supposed to counter the power of the capitalist camp, was equated with the promotion of peace, and their arms build-up was either condoned or warmly supported despite workers' avowed pledge to defend the pacifist Japanese Constitution. A letter one worker contributed to a Zentei publication is indicative of the prestige socialist nations continued to enjoy among the young as promoters of peace:

> A speaker at the 20th convention of the Soviet Communist Party noted war was no longer inevitable because even if imperialists tried to start war, there was a powerful socialist force that could frustrate their adventurist move by dealing a lethal blow. It should be noted that the British and French invasion of Egypt in 1956 did not develop into all-out war because warnings from the Soviet Union, the nationalist movement of Arab nations and public opinion around the world averted it.
>
> It was evidently clear at that time that there was a powerful peace force that prevented the war and that the power of the socialist camp that made up the core of the peace force exceeded that of the imperialist camp. This was irrefutably borne out when the Soviets launched a satellite in 1957. The satellite launch tremendously boosted our morale because it proved to the whole world the superiority of socialism.⁴⁶

Hopes for peaceful co-existence, which continued to grow in the late 1950s, were dampened somewhat by the Soviet interception of the American U-2 spy aircraft in May 1960. The incident, which led to the collapse of the US-UK-French-Soviet summit talks and the cancellation of US President Dwight Eisenhower's visit to Moscow, appeared to contradict the view of left-wingers that although there were numerous signs that the international situation was growing ever more peaceful, Japan and the US were preparing for another war through the revision of the bilateral security treaty. Though the heightened international tension belied the leftist argument, however, the U-2 aircraft incident served to arouse popular anti-war sentiment and fuelled anger against the US, which was using military bases in Japan to violate the territorial integrity of the Soviet Union and China.[47] This gave added momentum to the protest movement against the security treaty.

In this international context, the Kishi government was believed to be working hand-in-glove with Washington, and aiming for imperialist war to avert a depression that would inevitably result from the capitalist system. So the primary duty of Japan's working class, Sōhyō argued, was to weaken the domestic ruling classes by winning higher wages, tax cuts and a better social welfare system. They believed they could thus act in solidarity with the socialist camp and nationalist movements in Asia and Africa, and contribute to peace.[48]

On the whole, the almost blind support professed by Sōhyō for the socialist camp, which went hand-in-hand with its increasingly vehement stand against the US and the Japanese establishment, appears to have been utilized to a considerable extent as a polemical instrument to fire up workers' morale and determination to conduct workplace struggles and peace campaigns in earnest. The Sōhyō leadership presumably believed the combative arguments premised on the contrast between the admirable communist bloc and the war-mongering West would facilitate strenuous resistance against what the labour organization considered to be the formidable power of the Kishi government. In the process, the views of left-wing Mindō leaders, Takano allies and communists regarding the fight at hand became hardly distinguishable from one another, although their tactics for organizing the labour/peace movement differed (see below).

Socialist biases aside, however, many workers tended to show keen interest in international trends because they still retained vivid memories of the war and feared the possibility of another conflict.

Networking at the grassroots

The run-up to the Anpo Tōsō

During the battle of Sunagawa, the bulk of the thousands of protesters admittedly were mobilized by Sōhyō-affiliated unions. But the protest against the military base saw a huge number of young workers who took part in the campaign voluntarily and sometimes came to Sunagawa from distant parts of the country.[49] Images of the desperate struggle of local farmers, who were resisting the requisition of their land because their economic survival depended on it, US military aircraft flying over the heads of protesters with a deafening noise as if impervious to the farmers' plight, police brutality which both Zengakuren students and workers faced unarmed, and the liberal bloodshed that ensued – all these served as perfect material to strike an emotional chord with young activists who had been conducting their struggle under the 'peace and independence' slogan.[50] Accounts of the confrontation at the base were communicated by word of mouth at the protestors' workplaces, galvanizing other workers into following their colleagues to the scene of the battle, according to workers in both the public and private sectors quoted by communist or communist-affiliated organs.[51] The experience of taking part in the most acrimonious movement against military installations ever, turned formerly apolitical workers into activists within and outside their workplaces.[52]

The Sunagawa campaign, which became for many workers a defining moment of their lives, did not end without affecting the labour movement, especially in Tokyo, which was the scene of the protest. Workers from different unions got to know one another and became close comrades in arms. Even after Sunagawa, they continued their cooperation in union affairs.[53] When some of their acquaintances from Sunagawa engaged in a dispute with their employers, others went to help them in their struggle. They formed regional groups to conduct joint action, which proliferated across Tokyo. Besides workplace disputes, joint bodies were organized to tackle political issues and ponder ways to foster cooperation on a nationwide level to advance their goals.[54]

It was around this time that labour disputes involving small firms took an increasingly vicious turn. Protests against plant closures and job cuts were quite common at small firms in those days, and it became the usual practice among employers to hire thugs to throw out workers occupying the plants. The violence and acrimony of such disputes was aggravated by active mobilization of the police. This became an established trend after the Police Duties bills were scrapped in late 1958. Labour unions, sensing the hand of national and regional employers' associations in the escalating workplace conflicts, came to believe that their struggle was part of an all-out battle between labour and monopoly capital.[55]

In the mid-1950s, Sōhyō began actively to organize workers at smaller companies. Sōhyō's backing and broad worker solidarity, strengthened by the Sunagawa anti-military base campaign, emboldened small-firm employees to fight management with increased tenacity. Although labour strife used to end in defeat for workers whenever the police were mobilized, now many workers held out for longer and sometimes won their battles.[56]

As workers stepped up their cooperation across the boundaries of individual workplaces, some employees at small firms turned activist and took up political activities, such as the campaign to free the Matsukawa railway incident suspects. They did so voluntarily, unlike those at large corporations, who normally received a modest remuneration from their unions when they were mobilized to take part in political activities.

Regional groups of labour unions continued to serve as a vehicle for grassroots political activities throughout the late 1950s in many parts of Japan.[57] In Tokyo in February 1959, local groups formed by labour unions with chapters of various grassroots organizations to protest such political issues as Sunagawa, the introduction of teachers' work performance assessments and the Police Duties Law, were integrated into the Tokyo Congress for Joint Struggles to Preserve Peace and Democracy.[58] Tokyo Chihyō played a leading role in the congress as it won high esteem for almost single-handedly organizing the Sunagawa campaign, which eventually compelled the government to end surveys aimed at expanding the air base. The union federation, which used to do little more than Sōhyō's bidding in organizing unions for May Day and other national events, subsequently began acting more independently of the national headquarters.[59]

Tokyo Chihyō leader Haga Tamishige was a Takano ally who had gone to jail with him in 1937. As stated in the foregoing, though major unions had come under the control of left-wing Mindō leaders by the mid-1950s, Takano's allies and JCP activists wielded a great deal of influence over unions at smaller firms. Tokyo was home to many such small unions, while large corporations' unions often had a more conspicuous presence in provincial regions because their plants were located outside urban areas. The concentration of small-firm unions in Tokyo, which included a fair number of activists in its ranks, goes to explain Tokyo Chihyō's militancy and active involvement in the peace movement.

A motley collection of local groups of unions and other organizations, whether in Tokyo or other parts of Japan, set aside their differences to work together, and wittingly or not, they conformed to the kind of approach aimed at achieving a loose unity that was advocated by Takano. Opinionated as he was, Takano was not a boss who would exact total fealty to his opinions from others, in contrast to the JCP leadership, which tolerated no opposition to party dogma.

Tsumura Takashi, Takano's second son, recalled that Takano attached paramount importance to taking action and believed that ideological differences were only of secondary consequence:

> Takano used to say, 'How rank-and-file activists act, that is the only thing that matters. So why engage in sectarian fighting or think only about one's own interest?' ... Takano was never versed in Marxist theories. He was impatient with both old Marxist academics and so-called New Marxists, who were obsessed with debates over forms of ownership and became bogged down in philological studies. Takano did not object to doing basic studies (of Marxism) but he believed Marxism would mean nothing if it did not translate into concrete strategies for conducting the urgent struggle against the enemy class.[60]

Takano derived the chief inspiration for his theory on how to organize popular movements from his mentor Inomata Tsunao, who called for broad unity among all left-wing groups and individuals, and Giuseppe Di Vittorio, a leader of the General Italian Confederation of Labour (CGIL) and the

WFTU, who held that labour unions should not become a transmission belt for the ideology of any political party. Vittorio also called for unity among communists, socialists and as many workers as possible to counter government economic policy.[61]

Though their actions were not dictated by Takano, local groups, having no choice but to opt for the kind of collaboration he advocated, worked together in a loosely knit federation. In this way, unity among wide sections of the population as advocated by the WFTU, which first inspired Japanese workers in the early 1950s, remained a guiding principle for joint social movements throughout the late 1950s.[62]

Takano himself did not head any exclusive faction of his followers. So-called Takano allies or followers included those of the left-wing Mindō persuasion, members of the Kakushin Dōshikai (the Association of Reformers) called Kakudō for short, and those with no affiliation to any political party or other group. Kakudō was affiliated with the Rōnō Party till the party merged with the JSP in 1957 and stood between the JSP and the JCP on the spectrum of left-wing ideology in Japan. But even when they did not subscribe to Takano's ideology, workers of differing ideological stripes were lumped together with Takano's followers and called Takano allies. They were his allies in so far as they followed Takano's approach to organizing labour and other popular movements and worked mainly through the grassroots rather than aim for centralized control from above.

The Takano approach emphasizing broad-based unity caught on among regional groups which, in part because of their physical distance from the national leadership of Sōhyō, the JSP, the JCP and major industrial union federations, independently worked out strategies for peace and other activities among themselves. Freedom from direct control by their national leadership helped weaken partisanship among local group members. Takeuchi recalled that whenever they convened to decide joint policies in the mountain resort of Hakone, Kanagawa Prefecture, member groups of the Tokyo Congress for Joint Struggles to Preserve Peace and Democracy easily agreed on a common programme for action.[63] The congress's programme, reflecting the enthusiasm at the grassroots level, tended to be more radical than the ideas of Mindō leaders at the centre of power, who were preoccupied with the need to preserve their organizations.

During the protest movement against the Police Duties Law, Tokyo Chihyō issued a statement which was dramatically called the 'declaration of a state of emergency', without the approval of Sōhyō. The extensive coverage the mass media gave to the statement provided a crucial impetus to the movement, as it prompted major unions to decide on direct action to protest against the proposed law. Tokyo Chihyō had already gained considerable prestige in union circles because of the role it had played in the Sunagawa campaign. It again led the pack by announcing its readiness to tackle the anti-Police Duties Law protest in earnest. Tokyo Chihyō was swamped by enquiries from other regional union federations as they looked to the Tokyo federation for leadership.[64]

The gap in radicalism between local groups and national union leadership widened further during the course of the *Anpo Tōsō*.[65]

The anti-security treaty protest

Although grassroots activism grew amid vigorous political and economic struggles from the mid-1950s, union leaders and activists, however, grumbled until mid-1959 that most workers showed little interest in the revision of the Japan-US security treaty. They had particular difficulty rallying employees at small firms to oppose the security treaty. In an effort to stoke up worker enthusiasm for the *Anpo Tōsō*, they coined the phrase *Anpo taisei*, or the Japan-US security system. In the somewhat contrived logic of the unionists, the *Anpo* system meant an entire complex of injustices on which the power of Japan's monopoly capital, the capitalist-supported government and US imperialism rested. That system, the argument went, was the cause of hardship for workers at small firms and lay at the heart of issues contested in their workplace struggles. The union at the medium-size printing firm Kyōdō expounded this point as follows:

> [Our company's] five-year business plan is aimed at ensuring the prosperity of the company at the expense of workers' happiness. The restructuring at our company is in line with the trend not only in the printing business but also in Japan's entire industry. The current wave of restructuring is called restructuring under the Japan-US security system and is bound to lead to war.[66]

The protest movement began gathering momentum from 25 June 1959 when major unions, including the Japanese Coal Miners' Union, the Tokyo chapter of Nikkyōso and private-sector unions, resorted to direct action to link the *Anpo Tōsō* with their struggles against corporate retrenchment, teacher work assessments and support for their brethren at smaller firms.[67]

Simultaneously, however, controversy over strategies for conducting the protest movement began to intensify. The Tokyo Congress had earlier unanimously voted to block the revision of the security treaty and bring down the Kishi government on the grounds that the two goals were inseparable. JSP and JCP activists, and members of other key peace groups who belonged to the Tokyo Congress, had all approved the two objectives. But a row took place on this issue in debate conducted within the National Congress to Block the Revision of the Japan-US Security Treaty, a body set up in March 1959 to lead the *Anpo Tōsō* on a national level.[68]

The JCP, which had joined the National Congress as an observer, objected to the slogan 'Bring down the Kishi government', arguing that it would alienate some protestors, who, while opposing the treaty, supported the Kishi cabinet. The JCP, which called for moderation on this point, insisted that the protest movement should target US imperialism as its chief enemy, on the grounds that the revision of the security treaty would further subjugate Japan under US control. The JCP demanded that the main thrust of demonstrations should be directed at the US embassy and President Eisenhower's envoy James C. Hagerty when he arrived in Japan. Others opposed this, saying the parliament building and the prime minister's official residence should be the primary targets. The protest movement was put on hold while the fierce wrangling consumed the protestors' energies for about two months.

In November, however, the JCP dropped its opposition to the call for toppling the Kishi government, apparently because rank-and-file communists' defiance of the earlier party policy forced its hand.[69] The JCP's change of tack proved an advantage for the overall protest movement, which began to pull itself together from that point. On 27 November, the date for the eighth joint direct action planned by the National Congress, workers, students and citizens turned out in numbers that exceeded the leadership's expectations. The Tokyo Congress organized the demonstrations so as to get as close as possible to the parliament building, but most congress members believed demonstrators would be unable to break through the police cordon.[70] Still, workers and students began massing around the parliament building, and taking advantage of a brief moment when police temporarily retreated, broke through the cordon and stormed inside the parliament building, to everybody's consternation.

Aghast at the escalation of the demonstrations, the leadership of Sōhyō, the JSP and the JCP blamed Zengakuren and some unionists for the rash action, and began toning down the protest movement. In the ninth joint action of 10 December, the National Congress, which was virtually led by Sōhyō, decided to focus on protests at workplaces and not to stage demonstrations around the parliament. The Sōhyō leadership began to fear that actions by union radicals could alienate the general public and that the *Anpo Tōsō* as a result would lose public support. In December, Ōta jumped at the suggestion by JCP leader Miyamoto Kenji (1908-present) that the National Congress should call off its planned demonstrations at Haneda international airport, which were aimed at preventing Kishi from flying to Washington in January 1960 to sign the revised security treaty.[71] In pursuit of its long-term goal of vanquishing US imperialism, the JCP called for achieving unity on the widest possible front, and insisted that no rash action should be taken, in order to win maximum popular support for the protest movement. The growing conservatism within the national leadership gave rise to resentment among rank-and-file unionists and unions making up regional federations.[72]

Sōhyō's policy zigzagged throughout the protest campaign. At first Sōhyō lurched leftward by allying with the JCP, which cost it the cooperation of Shin Sanbetsu and the All Japan Trade Union Congress (Zenrō), the most conservative of all major union federations. Sōhyō's leftward policy shift is also reflected, as has been seen, in the radical rhetoric it began using in the late 1950s to extol the Soviet Union and China and to denounce the warlike pursuits of the US and Japan's ruling classes, a rhetoric which hardly differed from that of the JCP.

While the growing influence of the Socialism Association on Sōhyō might have assisted the radicalization of its rhetoric,[73] Sōhyō's leftward shift appears to have been prompted largely by what its leadership perceived to be the realities facing the labour movement. Iwai Akira, explaining Sōhyō's 1958 policy to fight the Kishi government, said the policy was based on Sōhyō's reading of the current situation that suggested that tough times lay ahead for workers. Both Iwai and Ōta noted a sharp increase in arrests of unionists since the formation of the Kishi government, and argued that public prosecutors' offices, rather than the Ministry of Labour, were acting as if labour issues were their natural province. Sōhyō's increasingly combative arguments appear to be geared towards countering what unionists regarded as the growing confidence and might of the ruling classes.[74] In explaining why Sōhyō often diverged from the JSP policy line, Ōta Kaoru said that principles governing a political party and organized labour naturally differed from each other because unionists, unlike politicians, were constantly compelled to counter employers' efforts to exploit members on the production floor.[75]

Ōta's and Iwai's announcement of their intention to cooperate with the JCP, however, met with strong opposition from other Mindō leaders, and Sōhyō subsequently tried to backtrack from its earlier leftward shift and clarify its stand *vis-à-vis* the JCP. It therefore criticized the party's ambiguity about whether it really rejected its earlier 'military' tactics through the 1955 self-criticism, and aimed to attain a revolution through peaceful means.[76]

When the centre-right faction of the JSP left the party to form the Democratic Socialist Party in January 1960, causing division within Sōhyō's constituent unions, the Sōhyō leadership was compelled further to moderate its stance, and issued a statement entitled 'Japanese trade unionism' to clarify its policy with regard to political activities. In the statement, Sōhyō's Mindō leaders, while noting the importance of political activities, took the view that it was not the place of labour unions to contest political issues as if they were representatives of the whole nation. Such a role should be assumed, their argument went, by political parties, and if labour unions tried to assume that role, they would suffer internal division because many of their members would accuse them of neglecting their chief duty: to advance the economic interests of workers. But according to the Mindō leaders, the absence of political parties possessing the necessary organizational muscle to conduct political struggles on a nationwide level, and the unique circumstances under which Japanese workers found themselves – collusion with the US, Japanese monopoly capital and the Japanese government to trample on workers' rights to peace, democracy and a reasonable standard of living – left Sōhyō no choice but to assume the leadership role in the nation's political struggles.[77]

Sōhyō found itself in a dilemma as its ideological stand and activism among lower-ranking officials called for radical action, while realpolitik considerations compelled it to toe the moderate Mindō line.

Campaigners at the grassroots, meanwhile, went their independent way largely oblivious to the concerns of leaders at the national union federation. As stated earlier, the forerunner of the Tokyo Congress was a vehicle for enabling cooperation in labour disputes among unionists working for different small companies, and as such derived its inspiration for joint direct action from labour strife at individual workplaces. The sentiment at the local level, which was shaped by workers' personal experiences, inevitably differed from that of the Sōhyō leadership. The views of rank-and-file communists, who tried to link their struggles at their own workplaces to the *Anpo Tōsō* and make common cause with members of other groups in broad show of unity, also began to diverge from the policy of the JCP leadership. The same thing could be said about regional groupings of disparate organizations across the country, whose members tried to choose a course of action that best suited the specific characteristics of their regions, such as the composition of the local industry and population, while respecting the different conditions under which each of the constituent member groups worked. Such groups outside Tokyo often looked up to the Tokyo Congress rather than the National Congress for leadership, because the activism of the Tokyo Congress far exceeded that of any other regional group and because it was the virtual enforcer of actions planned by the National Congress.[78]

In compliance with the earlier decision of the National Congress to stage demonstrations at Haneda airport, regional groups around Japan collected donations to send their delegates to Tokyo. Over a thousand local delegates arrived in Tokyo, and voiced anger at the National Congress's decision to cancel the demonstrations. When the National Congress held a protest rally at a public auditorium in Tokyo in lieu of the demonstrations at the airport, one irate delegate climbed on to the stage in protest. He was a JCP assemblyman from Hiroshima who was enraged by the deal the party had struck with the National Congress to cancel the demonstrations.[79] The momentum of the protest movement was curbed again by leadership when Miyamoto Kenji and Iwai Akira met on 13 April and agreed to make the demonstrations scheduled for 26 April as 'orderly' as possible.[80]

The *Anpo Tōsō* reached its climax immediately after the government forced the security treaty bills through the lower house on 20 May 1960. On 4 June, Kokurō and other major union federations went on strike for a limited time. The nation's first joint strike contesting a political issue further fuelled excitement among protestors. Even though the revision of the security treaty was enacted on 19 June, the protest movement continued, shifting its focus from the treaty to the issue over democracy in Japan because of the

LDP's rough handling of the parliamentary process, and the *Anpo Tōsō* wore on till Kishi finally decided to step down as prime minister on 23 June.

The *Anpo Tōsō* mushroomed into the nation's largest-ever popular protest movement, as even normally conservative union leaders and ordinary workers were caught up in the excitement of the moment and took to the streets. But as the movement escalated, the rift became even wider between the Mindō, JSP and JCP leadership on one hand, and Takano allies, rank-and-file communists and other grassroots activists on the other.

The repeated instructions issued by the Mindō leadership and the JCP to moderate the protest movement often conflicted with the policies of regional groups.[81] The carefully nurtured local-level cooperative frameworks were seriously disrupted by the national leadership's policy shifts. Once the leadership decided to moderate the protest action, some JCP members, who displayed blind obedience to the decisions of a party that brooked no internal dissent, toed the party line. Workers, who came from unions at major public corporations such as Kokurō, Zentei and the All Japan Telecommunications Workers' Union, acted similarly as the centrally controlled nature of their organizations left rank-and-file workers no choice but to obey the leadership. Leaders of smaller private-sector unions making up the Tokyo Congress were dismayed by the policy changes of the National Congress, fearing the national body's call for moderation could dampen the morale of ordinary workers.[82]

During the *Anpo Tōsō*, workers jokingly fantasized about carrying out a revolution, although most did not believe such a thing would ever be possible.[83] In their lighter moments, they talked about a fictitious plan to have members of unions at military bases smuggle in weapons to immobilize US troops, or about planting time bombs on large gas tanks and then negotiating to extract concessions from the Kishi government. The ultimate goal of activists who worked at the grassroots, however, was not necessarily a revolution.

Takeuchi, a JCP member, and his like-minded colleagues in the Tokyo Congress, had grown increasingly disillusioned with the JCP, the JSP and Sōhyō and no longer regarded existing political or labour organizations as the 'vanguard' that would lead a revolution. They instead hoped the suprapartisan grassroots federation they were organizing would field their own candidates in both local and national elections in the future, and that these would defeat their conservative rivals to form a democratic government. No longer satisfied with parliamentary politics, in which political parties settled key issues among themselves, they envisioned a kind of direct democracy in which the democratic government would work in close cooperation with the grassroots federation. Their dissatisfaction with their leaders' moderate policies grew to such an extent that the centre-left media argued that the action of the rank-and-file transcended the leadership of the vanguard.[84]

The regional frameworks for cooperation that Takeuchi and others had painstakingly nurtured were to unravel during the *Anpo Tōsō*, as the national leadership's policy shift, aimed at curbing the radicalism of the protest movement, prompted many communists and members of major union federations to break ranks with other members of the regional groupings who stuck to their groups' original policies. The national leadership threw a spanner into the carefully laid plans to elect a democratic government, to the anguish of Takeuchi and his fellow activists. The initiative of rank-and-file communists, too, was gradually stifled as the JCP leadership recovered from its disarray in the mid-1960s and regained control over the party apparatus.[85]

The pragmatic Iwai laughed off some students' suggestions that they should storm radio and TV stations and the national police agency.[86] After the *Anpo Tōsō* ended, activists strongly criticized Sōhyō leaders for conducting the whole movement in step with the most moderate of campaigners, and denying others who were more committed the freedom to protest in a manner that most suited their varying degrees of activism.

Both Iwai and Ōta, however, were unrepentant. Iwai held that Sōhyō stuck to its policy to walk in step with the rest of the nation in the firm belief that the protest movement would never succeed otherwise.[87] Ōta argued that staking everything on the abolition of the security treaty would risk turning off most workers except for the most radical elements of the labour movement, and that such action would run counter to Sōhyō's basic policy. He insisted that the protest movement should be based on consensus among all participants. Ōta thus criticized Takano and other union radicals for ignoring the sentiment of ordinary workers, who had joined unions not to promote certain political ideology but merely to protect their livelihood.[88]

Changing of the times

The strength of the labour movement on the whole reached its zenith in 1960 when the *Anpo Tōsō* and the acrimonious labour strife at the Mitsui Miike coal mines greatly expanded the ranks of union activists.[89] By the time the *Anpo Tōsō* climaxed in late May, union funds to pay for demonstrators' transport had run out and workers were acting on their own without any instructions from union leaders.[90] As ordinary citizens began turning out in large numbers, unionists, noting that public opinion was on their side, forgot their fears that participation in the protest movement might cost them their jobs.[91] Workers from small private companies also cast aside their doubts that strikes would achieve nothing apart from hurting their boss and would not help them to attain the political goal of the *Anpo Tōsō*. Ōta noted that the National Congress, the JSP and the JCP lost all control over the protest movement towards the end.[92]

But a gradual process of decline in the left-wing labour movement set in immediately afterwards. Following the end of the *Anpo Tōsō* and the bitter defeat in the Mitsui Miike labour strife, Sōhyō leaders began to have second thoughts about the grassroots activism they had encouraged. Mindō leaders, who had a hard time reining in radical activists during the *Anpo Tōsō*, accused them of venting their frustrations through the protest movement to make up for their inability to win economic battles at their workplaces, and criticized their 'immaturity' and 'rashness'.[93] They also decided to tone down workplace struggles because the approach, which was highly effective in stoking up militancy, particularly that of the Mitsui Miike coal miners, served as a lightning rod that invited resolute attack by management.

While large private-sector unions were actively involved in the *Anpo Tōsō*, there were already signs foreshadowing their later withdrawal from the peace movement, as several key private-sector unions had lost major disputes during the 1950s and ceded workplace control to management. An umbrella organization for automotive unions, which spearheaded the peace movement during debates over the peace treaty, had already disbanded itself in 1954 after the union at Nissan lost a major battle against management in the previous year. Despite repeated strikes, unions at major steel makers lost their wage battles in the late 1950s to a determined management, while most major unions of the Japanese Federation of Iron and Steel Workers failed to stage strikes during the *Anpo Tōsō* due to internal division.[94] The union at Ōji Paper, the largest union in the paper and pulp federation, saw its strength steadily eroded by a resolute onslaught from management from the late 1950s. Rising salaries at large corporations also deprived their workers of incentives to cooperate with other unions, which helped to weaken the unity of organized labour. The economic boom of the 1960s further strengthened this tendency, as workers saw wages rise without their having to put up a fight against management. Productivity improvement programmes Sōhyō had resisted, also helped to prevent private-sector unions from tackling political activities outside their workplaces, as workers at many private companies had no choice but to participate in such programmes, and that helped to turn their attention increasingly to in-house matters.

Technological innovation from around 1955 brought on a rapid change in labour relations by eliminating the need for skilled factory hands, many of whom were union officials. As was the case in the period during the Red Purge, such union officials, who used to be in supervisory positions at workplaces, again dropped out of union activities. As factories became modernized, the number of workers on the production floor declined. Management also boosted its control over workers by exercising its right to transfer them to distant assignments and introducing promotion systems that had workers compete with one another. Cultural and recreational programmes organized by companies also won over employees from their own informal society activities. All this encouraged the atomization of workers and helped to break down their bonds of solidarity.

The emergence of younger generations and a significant attitudinal change among workers also made it increasingly difficult to continue practising the Sōhyō style of labour movement that had been effective in the 1950s.

From around 1955, sociologists began to claim that the values of the new Constitution were embraced by ever-larger sectors of the population and appeared to be taking root in Japan. The young who began working in the late 1950s took for granted the Constitution and labour-related laws that guaranteed workers' rights to form unions, and did not know how hard older generations had fought to have management accept the legitimacy of union activities. A growing number of young workers, who had only vague memories of the war, were generally more laid back in their attitude than older unionists. Older union officials, who had seen much tougher days, cast the labour movement in a grander light and viewed their struggle in terms of all-out confrontation between the working class, monopoly capital and fascism, which by extension concerned matters of war and peace. When they became union officials, they had to brace themselves for the prospects of job loss, imprisonment and sometimes even death. As they were ready to make great sacrifices in their monumental 'mission' to take on the establishment, they also exacted similar sacrifices from rank-and-file workers. But such union heroism was increasingly becoming a thing of the past.[95]

The sociologist Tsurumi Kazuko, who had surveyed women workers in 1947–8, also noted that although there was a significant number of union officials who professed they would sacrifice their own happiness for the sake of the labour movement, such heroic types became quite rare in the mid-1950s. Young workers found it difficult to suppress their laughter at the dramatic language used in union leaflets to exhort workers to class warfare. Tsurumi called such trends a 'return to the mundane'.[96]

Many young workers were the products of a transition from an early post-war age, and shared to some extent the traits of older unionists. But new tendencies among the young began to raise some eyebrows.

The union activist Takada Yoshitoshi cited a young worker who professed his belief in the possibility of a revolution. Unlike older unionists, the youth, who had not experienced any adversity in life, held quite an optimistic view that workers could drive capitalists into a corner by continuously winning concessions from them, which he said would prepare the conditions needed for a peaceful revolution. He argued that since rapprochement had been progressing on the international front since the mid-1950s, there must be a way to liberate the working class in a peaceful manner. His optimism appalled an older unionist, who believed in the overwhelming strength of capitalists.[97]

The writer Kamisaka Fuyuko noted the unlikely mix of altruism and self-love in her younger brother with much bemusement. Kamisaka's brother was actively involved in community services, showing slides on the Uchinada anti-military base campaign and holding lectures on social issues to educate residents of small villages. But his actions were partly motivated by fears that if things went unchecked, society might revert to the bad old days of war and that he could then lose his life, family, house and everything else. He said:

I will probably become a doctor as I have always hoped and join the middle class as an intellectual. I would never, ever give up this plan no matter what. I belong to the post-war generation and therefore can't make a total sacrifice for the sake of justice. But I will continue my modest efforts [for public good] in a relaxed manner to an extent that will not jeopardize my future.[98]

Here was the emergence of a post-war generation who were strangers to the morality of total self-sacrifice inculcated during the pre-war and war years. They were largely free from a sense of mission embraced by the young who had reached their adulthood immediately after the war's end and acted with considerable daring to fight acute economic privation and the system, dreaming of becoming the vanguard of a coming revolution. Older generations marvelled at the budding but unabashed individualism or even 'me-ism' in the new species of young Japanese.

The activist Takada, who had had to make a conscious effort to wean himself from his total devotion to the revolutionary cause, and learned to attach more importance to his own self through informal group activities in the early 1950s, realized there was a significant generation gap between himself and his younger brother. He noted that those in their late teens, like older generations who had enjoyed their lives as youths in the late 1920s, were very self-absorbed and did not need to learn the meaning of the words self-love or independence.[99] According to Takada, most people who began to work in and after 1955 took the capitalist system for granted and did not see the need radically to change the existing order because they did not feel oppressed by it.[100]

Materialism was another key trait of the attitude of young workers, who aimed for affluence rather than a decent standard of living.[101] As young workers thought increasingly in terms of personal well-being, they were unable to understand the mentality of slightly older workers, who agonized over the 'destiny of the nation'. Takada's younger brother said the JCP slogan calling for the independence of the nation did not appeal to him, although he understood a slogan relating to peace.[102]

In trying to enlist support for the *Anpo Tōsō* from young women workers at a women's magazine publisher, one Sōhyō official explained how their strike against their company, the aim of Nikkeiren (the Japanese Federation of Employers' Associations) to control the mass media, and the security treaty were all interconnected. But the young women were unimpressed and responded, 'Sounds too far-fetched.' The episode led the Sōhyō official to consider that the Constitution, with its peace and civil rights clauses, rather than left-wing ideology might enable old and young generations within unions to find common ground.[103]

In 1959, a Sōhyō official noted the emergence of a large number of activists at various unions, most of whom had taken part in workplace societies, and they were reported to have played an important role during the

102 *The labour movement under Mindō*

Anpo Tōsō.[104] But already from the late 1950s on, a decline in workplace society activities became apparent, which helped to erode grassroots radicalism in later years.

Many of the activists who organized workplace societies were JCP members, and most of them had followed the party policy to pursue an 'armed struggle'. But after the party renounced the policy in 1955 and conducted self-criticism on 'left-wing adventurism', many activists, anguished by a sense of failure and loss of purpose, ended their society activities, and the groups that lost their leaders were disbanded.[105] Some societies ran out of funding, and others were wound up because workers, particularly at large corporations, who became satisfied with their condition, did not feel any need to join workplace societies to divert themselves. An increasing number of workers in cities also sought pleasures beyond the workplace. Group activities remained popular among workers at smaller firms and among housewives, however, who continued to face a host of problems.[106]

The emergence of younger generations with an outlook significantly different from that of their older counterparts suggests that amid the onset of modernization, many workers began to acquire a new self-image and identity.

During the *Anpo Tōsō*, some workers began asking themselves whether they were demonstrating as members of the citizenry rather than of the working class.[107] Workers whose unions were unable to defy management to stage protests against the security treaty demonstrated in the streets on their own, but in doing so they had to conduct their protests outside the labour movement.[108] A growing number of intellectuals in those days were embracing the concept of citizenry or 'civil society' as a key actor to promote peace and democracy. According to Shimizu Shinzō, however, when Tokyo University academic Hidaka Rokurō propounded that idea, neither Ōta, Iwai nor Takano allies showed much understanding of such a concept.[109] Key union leaders and activists had retained their distinct mentality that set themselves apart from the sensibilities of ordinary Japanese outside the labour movement.

A survey of members of major unions suggests that the biggest concern of most workers during the *Anpo Tōsō* was war, and that their visceral hatred of war was a more compelling reason for opposing the security treaty than the left-wing argument that the 'Japan-US security treaty system' would jeopardize Japan's independence and add to their economic hardship. Asked why they opposed the revision of the Japan-US security treaty, 69–73 per cent of workers who belonged to Kokurō, Zentei and Zendentsū replied that they were opposed to war. About 40–45 per cent said they were mainly against the undemocratic nature of the Kishi government, and 25–30 per cent said they took part in the protest movement because they wanted Japan to achieve true independence. The percentage of those who linked their protest to the prospect of restructuring taking a toll on their wages was the smallest at 11–15 per cent.[110]

As the years passed, the growing influence of the mass media inexorably weakened organized labour's ideological hold on the minds of workers. Commentators conducted active debates on the emergence of the middle class, which was expected to erode class distinctions and the class consciousness of workers. The labour movement was again buffeted by forces that threatened to break up organized labour into isolated in-house unions. The subsequent decline in Japan's labour movement went hand-in-hand with the decline of its peace movement.

Unions at large, private corporations began to pull out of the peace movement in the 1960s, while major public-sector unions such as Kokurō and Nikkyōso, and unions at small firms including those belonging to Zenkoku Kinzoku, retained their militancy into the mid-1970s.

Meanwhile, union activists alienated by Sōhyō's leaders found little room for their independent activities amid a paradigm shift in labour relations during Japan's high-growth era which began in the 1960s. A minority of young workers, who inherited the radicalism of workers of earlier post-war years, formed an anti-war group around 1968 during the Vietnam War, mainly in urban areas, and joined the New Left activists who sought to organize an independent leftist movement that would be free from the dogma of the Soviet Union, China or the JCP. Many such activists joined the movement to protest against the renewal of the Japan-US security treaty in 1970. But their movement crumbled in the face of a determined attack by management and the government.[111]

With union leaders becoming preoccupied with economic affairs, and activists receding from the scene, Shimizu Shinzō began mourning the loss of a sense of mission in the labour movement as early as 1962.[112] Takano, true to his reputation as a class warrior, supported the New Left youths and continued to exhort workers to class warfare till the final hours before his death in 1974.[113]

As time progressed, the confrontationist Sōhyō-style labour movement became eclipsed by the new ethos of corporate culture that emerged during Japan's boom years. Workers shed their animosity to the capitalist enemy, and loyalty to their employers became one of the most salient characteristics of the archetypal Japanese 'salaryman'. All Ōta, Iwai and other left-wing Mindō leaders could do in later years was lament the irrelevance to Japan's new labour scene of their outlook, which was forged during the wartime and post-war economic hardship.

5 Elements of the peace activities of organized labour

While the activities of the union peace movement have been studied in chronological order in the preceding four chapters, this chapter will look at other traits of trade unionist peace activities, which were more or less apparent over the entire time sequence of the first fifteen post-war years.

The point of interest in all of the topics discussed below is the question of where lay the fine line between workers' commitment to the issue of peace as such, and peace as an extension of their economic well-being.

Sōhyō boasted a membership of about 3.7 million unionists in 1960, and at the height of the *Anpo Tōsō* many workers belonging to non-Sōhyō labour organizations swelled the ranks of the demonstrators. While a majority of those protesting in the streets during the anti-security treaty campaign were unionists, to what extent were individual workers committed to the peace movement?

As stated earlier, a good number of workers joined unions with the humanitarian goal of working for peace, and most leftist unions had manifestos avowing their mission to promote peace. But unions were not organized with the sole purpose of staging a peace movement, and as their in-house newspapers demonstrate, the issues that dominated union agendas were wages and other terms of employment. Most Sōhyō-affiliated unions normally devoted only a fraction of their efforts to peace issues. Union organs also suggest that while many young unionists spearheaded their unions' peace activities, the overriding concern for a majority of them was their meagre salaries, which made it impossible for them to marry and start a family.

Both Takano and left-wing Mindō leaders, however, were aware of the strategic importance of the peace movement, which could help unionists to make common cause with workers outside their unions, and even those outside organized labour. Sōhyō therefore exploited its organizational apparatus to the full in leading what it called *kokumin undō*, or the nationwide people's movement, and very often contested matters transcending the economic interests of organized labour in doing so.

The anti-nuclear bomb movement, in which unionists demonstrated for peace alongside a record number of women and other campaigners, opened some workers' eyes to the peace discourse outside union circles, and made them aware of the importance of joining forces with the rest of the populace.[1]

In Sunagawa, local farmers, who had nursed visceral hatred of red flags and communist-inspired workers, soon found activist workers to be invaluable allies who selflessly braved police brutality to help the farmers' struggle. Farmers quickly embraced the workers' views, expanding the ideological dimensions of their struggle to hold on to their land. Their struggle came to encompass broader ideals about peace and Japan's independence, as well as a fight against the airfield expansion, which was aimed at accommodating aircraft carrying nuclear weapons.[2]

Sōhyō's mass line approach to promote rank-and-file initiative helped to spawn a large number of activists, who screened anti-war films and slides in small communities as they took part in grassroots activities outside their unions. But the efforts Sōhyō and individual workers made to join forces with those outside organized labour had a limited ideological impact on popular peace consciousness.[3] Farmers and small proprietors mostly remained the natural constituencies of conservative politicians, and opinion polls reveal that they were far more supportive of the revision of the pacifist Constitution or of rearmament than were unionists.

Many workers, while engaging in left-wing politics in union circles, were said to revert to their conservative identities in their homes. In the words of one observer, workers were proletarians only during the day and *petits bourgeois* at night.[4] Workers who lived in provincial areas, in particular, often met with the scorn of more conservative neighbours and simply gave up efforts to disseminate their ideas in their communities.[5]

Community-based industrial actions promoted by Takano did not do much to bridge the gap in consciousness between workers and the rest of the population, because such labour strife tended to occur in a limited number of company towns where the economic existence of the whole community depended heavily on a single large corporation.

The organs of Sōhyō and its constituent unions, which were far more left-wing in ideology than the newspapers the average citizen read, suggest the ideological isolation of organized labour within the populace as a whole. Their polemics, bristling with diatribes against monopoly capital and US imperialism, would have simply turned off ordinary readers.

On the whole, workers and unions took part in the peace movement with widely varying degrees of commitment, and dedicated peace activists in union circles appear to have been a minority. Most labour leaders found it impossible to secure workers' continuous involvement in the peace movement, and union peace activities often turned into pro-forma gatherings to commemorate the atomic bombings of Hiroshima and Nagasaki and the end of the war. Peace activists outside organized labour often complained that many unionists refused to cooperate with their peace activities on the grounds that the primary duty of workers was to obtain higher wages and improved working conditions, which would ultimately help to promote peace to the benefit of all humankind.[6] In the anti-nuclear bomb campaigns, for example, many women, who engaged in the peace activities of their own accord, were often found to be far more enthusiastic than workers who were mobilized by their unions.[7]

The limited intercourse with activists outside unions inhibited the spread of the peace discourse of organized labour beyond narrow union circles. Under such circumstances, an uneasy balance or conflict, between the self-interest of unions and workers and an altruistic desire to work for the wider public good, continued to characterize the union peace movement throughout the post-war era. The point frequently recurs when the discussion is conducted from the following five perspectives.

Public- versus private-sector unions

Among the oft-cited factors deemed to have influenced unionists' commitment to the peace movement is the public/private divide. It was generally held at the time that workers in public-sector unions tended to espouse a stronger sense of class consciousness than their counterparts in the private sector, whose economic well-being was linked to their employers' business performance. Another contention holds that since workers in the public sector were hired by the government their union activities inevitably tended to be political. According to another generally held view, the wages of public-sector workers were limited by the government's budget, which left very little room for manoeuvre when it came to wage negotiations, so they devoted much of their energies to political campaigns and the peace movement.

The last view, however, is highly questionable, because for public-sector unions, too, wages were the most important of all union issues, and they conducted tough wage negotiations every year. Any union that did not fight for workers' wages would have soon lost its *raison d'être*. Former public-sector unionists this author has interviewed also hotly deny the notion that they were active in the peace movement only because their inability to negotiate economic matters left them with a lot of time on their hands.[8]

There are many examples of private-sector unions playing a leading role in the peace movement. When Sōhyō's Mindō officials attacked Takano for placing excessive importance on political activities, it was mainly leaders of private-sector unions who broke ranks with the Mindō leadership to support him. Among the unions that backed Takano were Zenkoku Kinzoku, the All Japan Harbour Workers' Union (Zenkōwan) and the National Federation of Printing and Publishing Industry Workers' Unions (Zen-in Sōren), all of whose constituent unions were highly active in the peace movement. Many celebrated peace activities were conducted by other private-sector unions such as the Hokuriku Railway Union which campaigned against the Uchinada firing range, and the union at Nippon Steel's Kawasaki plant, many of whose workers voluntarily participated in the Sunagawa anti-base campaign and the *Anpo Tōsō*.

The All Japan Federation of Electric Machine Workers' Unions (Denki Rōren), which was made up of private concerns and belonged to the Federation of Independent Unions (Chūritsu Rōren), a non-Sōhyō organization, also took part in the Sunagawa anti-base campaign and played an active role in the *Anpo Tōsō* by joining the National Congress to Block the Revision of the Japan-US Security Treaty. For example, according to the annals of Toshiba Corporation's union, a member of the federation, the union mobilized an unprecedented number of workers in protest against the security treaty. The reason Toshiba cited for joining the protest movement hardly differed from Sōhyō's argument. The union at this major electrical manufacturer contended that despite the international community's efforts to ease political tensions, the Kishi government was pursuing a warlike policy subserviently to support the US, and aimed to turn Japan into an American military base and send Japanese soldiers abroad to serve in America's wars.[9]

Although Zenrō, the most conservative labour organization, stayed out of the *Anpo Tōsō*, among members of the Japanese Federation of Textile Workers' Unions (Zensen), a Zenrō affiliate, some 2,000 in Aichi Prefecture, which were known for considerable activism at the rank-and-file level, are reported to have taken policies as militant as those of Sōhyō and to have taken part in the anti-security treaty movement. Activists at such unions are said to have encouraged militancy among their colleagues, in defiance of the policy of the Zensen leadership, ever since the major labour dispute of 1954 at Ōmi Kenshi, whose management had earned notoriety by their serious violation of workers' human rights.[10]

The degree of commitment to the peace movement by labour unions was usually matched by the degree that left-wing ideology held sway over unionists. The way both public- and private-sector unions attracted communists and other left-wing activists was a fairly random process, and private firms do not seem to have posed any greater difficulty than public companies to left-wingers trying to infiltrate their unions.

The example of Kyōdō Printing, which was said to be one of the three major bases for communist cells alongside Kōkan Kawasaki Steel and the Mitsubishi shipyard in Nagasaki Prefecture,[11] illustrates the process by which a private company union became actively involved in the peace movement under the leadership of left-wing officials.

The Red Purge that resulted in the dismissal of twenty workers was a dispiriting experience for employees at the medium-size Tokyo printing company, and union activities languished following the expulsion of leftist unionists. But in a process typical of many Sōhyō-affiliated unions which regained their militancy in the early 1950s, a group of leftist unionists at Kyōdō Printing took over from what appears to be centre-right Mindō leadership through a successful power struggle, and subsequently led a major strike in May 1953.[12]

108 *Elements of labour's peace activities*

After making significant headway in economic struggles, union leaders pondered ways to maintain the momentum of their activities. Again in a manner typical of a left-wing Sōhyō-affiliated union, the Kyōdō Printing union took a mass line approach and tried to link union matters to the current interests of rank-and-file workers. According to an official of the union's public relations section, most workers were interested in the anti-base campaign in Sunagawa, so the union decided to add Sunagawa to its agenda. The official described the situation within his union as follows:

> The union does not have any special section dedicated to peace activities and does not offer any guidance to workers regarding peace issues. But workers quite often talk about the peace movement reported by newspapers and the radio and the union won't get anywhere if it ignores workers' interest in it. Even when we are quite busy with issues over wages and work conditions, we have no choice but to take up peace issues when they present themselves. Union activities and peace activities are the same and we see no significant distinction between the two.[13]

Many union members are reported to have gone to the scene of the anti-base struggle of their own accord. The union also sent 10–12 workers every day during the peak of the battle in Sunagawa, about five of whom stayed there overnight. Kyōdō's workplaces were abuzz with the latest news reported by workers who had returned from Sunagawa, and the union drove a sound truck around Tokyo's Bunkyo Ward to campaign against the base. A union screening of an anti-nuclear film and another film on Sunagawa are said to have drawn an audience of 400. The company building was draped with four huge banners with anti-base slogans. After the work day finished, workers busied themselves preparing a photo exhibition for Hiroshima Day. The exhibition proved quite popular and travelled around Tokyo. Domestic news was not the only thing that interested the workers. They also showed a voracious appetite for learning about international developments such as the Suez crisis and the Soviet invasion of Hungary. Through vigorous peace activities, the union claims it succeeded in getting some 2,000 workers at the company engaged in union affairs.[14]

While it is doubtful that most workers in Japan were as interested in peace issues as those at Kyōdō Printing are said to have been, a mass line approach aimed at achieving successful synergy between economic struggles and peace activities was practised both by public- and private-sector unions. This is demonstrated by the participation of private-sector union officials from the coal, power, private railway, chemicals, steel, automotive and haulage industries in the group called Rōdōsha Dōshikai, which pushed for Sōhyō to adopt the four peace principles.

In contrast to private unions, large public-sector unions vested their leaders with extensive control over their financial affairs, bargaining with management and other matters, and were characterized by their highly centralized power structure, which often tended to stifle rank-and-file initiative. Smaller private-sector unions, however, could sometimes be easily swept up in the peace movement because of their size if a fair proportion of workers actively involved in peace activities managed to influence their colleagues.[15] All this suggests it was not whether workers belonged to public- or private-sector unions that was the decisive factor prompting their peace activities.

But public-sector unions, whose branches criss-crossed the nation, played a vital role in the peace movement because they were able to take advantage of their control over the nation's logistical arteries in staging strikes or mobilizing massive numbers of demonstrators or election campaigners. Thanks to their vigorous electioneering, organized labour was able to send a sufficient number of legislators to parliament to make their voices heard in the national political process when they pressed their peace agenda. The organizational prowess of public corporation unions generated a great sense of confidence among their members. They regarded themselves as leaders of organized labour, and often tried to act as such in the peace movement. The strike railway workers staged during the *Anpo Tōsō* was prompted in part by that sense of pride as leading champions of labour.[16] The audacity with which Kokurō struck for the first time to contest issues that had little to do with the immediate economic interests of workers, immensely boosted the morale of other campaigners against the security treaty.[17]

Public-sector unionists at railway stations, post offices, telephone exchanges and government offices across the country also took advantage of their close ties with local residents. Many of them played a leadership role in peace and other social movements in small local communities where they worked together with members of unions at small private firms and other grassroots groups.

The left-wing enthusiasm engendered through workplace struggles at major public unions also helped to stimulate unionists' participation in the peace movement. The 1948 law that deprived public-sector workers of the right to bargain collectively or strike kept their wages to a level comparable to those of small-firm employees, forcing public corporation unions such as Kokurō and Zentei to fiercely fight those impediments to their economic well-being. Kokurō strenuously resisted the railway company's restructuring policy, and frequently resorted to illegal direct action, with hundreds and sometimes thousands of staff later punished with a variety of disciplinary measures including dismissal.[18] Zentei fought for the right to collective bargaining by referring the case to the International Labour Organization. Zentei also tried to win permanent staff status for contract workers who, while doing the same job as other regular postal workers, received far lower salaries and enjoyed little job security. Amid their battle, contract workers also joined the *Anpo Tōsō* because of the supposed link between their own grievances and the so-called security treaty system.[19]

A link with economic struggles

Left-wing unions' militant workplace struggles derived their theoretical underpinnings from socialist ideology, which drew heavily on analogies between the injustices of the workers' situation and the injustices caused by the capitalist classes in the past and supposedly present imperialist wars. That made their active participation in the peace movement inevitable, with their peace activities often becoming an extension of their workplace struggles.

The union at Nissan Motor gained considerable ground in its economic battles through pioneering efforts to use workplace struggles to its advantage.[20] In 1951 during the movement calling for a comprehensive peace treaty, the auto workers' industrial federation, headed by the non-JCP Marxist Masuda Tetsuo (1913–64), who also led the Nissan Motor union, became the only labour organization to stage a strike. The federation became the leading force at a major peace rally held in Tokyo in 1951 by mobilizing some 10,000 of its 30,000 members, according to leftist sources.[21]

Striking over economic issues was daring enough. But if they were to stage a successful strike over a peace issue, which had little to do with workers' immediate economic interests, union leaders had to have secured considerable power *vis-à-vis* both management and rank-and-file in order to gain their approval for politically motivated direct action. It was impossible for union leaders to stage a strike aimed at achieving political ends unless ordinary workers united behind them. Leaders earned such trust only by demonstrating skilled leadership in handling union affairs or making vigorous efforts to fight for workers' interests.

The ability of the auto workers' union to strike for peace is testimony to the substantial achievements it had made through its workplace struggles, which made the union by far the most powerful in those days.[22] During the campaign for a comprehensive peace, other large unions such as Kokurō and Nikkyōso, which later assumed the leadership role in organized labour's peace movement, were still too weak to match the automotive union's initiative.

Another example of a union's workplace struggle leading to its participation in peace activities is that of the anti-military base campaign conducted by the Hokuriku Railway Union. Before it began spearheading the anti-base campaign, the union had engaged in active workplace struggles by alternately negotiating with management and staging strikes to win better terms of employment. Through such tactics, the union got the company to sign an agreement under which management would put on hold its decision to fire workers while the dismissal was being contested by the union. The union used the agreement as a weapon to resist the Red Purge and corporate retrenchment.[23]

Union officials linked their fight against 'corporate fascism' to protect workers' livelihoods to issues of peace and Japan's independence. According to them, the company's financial trouble was attributable to the Japanese government's economic policy of cooperation with the US, which they argued sacrificed Japan's peacetime industry to build up the country's military. They argued that the Hokuriku Railway Company was trying to alleviate its plight through cuts in wages and staff, and an increased workload for the remaining employees. The union explained to its rank-and-file members how the Japan-US security treaty aggravated the poverty of Japanese workers.[24]

The union became actively involved in May Day demonstrations and peace activities for one year after the peace and security treaties took effect in April 1952. In January 1953, the union concluded as follows:

> Japanese workers, farmers, small proprietors and Japan's peacetime industry are suffering under the laissez-faire economic system that forces the subjugation of Japanese people for the benefit of US monopoly capital. Japan will never become independent and we will never be liberated and achieve a reasonable standard of living unless workers fight by uniting with other oppressed Japanese people. We will pursue our wage struggle in a way that helps to form a united front [with other people] and promote peace and Japan's independence. Our wage negotiations are aimed not only at raising the wages of workers at Hokuriku Railway. They are aimed also at promoting cooperation with other Japanese workers, who are suffering from the policy [of the US and the Japanese governments] to enslave workers, and raising their wages as well.[25]

The union also vowed to collaborate with passengers and managers to block use of their railway for military purposes.

The political consciousness of the Hokuriku Railway workers was raised as they battled management over their economic conditions, and it was against this backdrop that the requisitioning of the nearby Uchinada sand dunes for use as a firing range site came to a head. The union's officials reached a quick decision to support fishermen's families who were opposing the requisitioning of the land. Carried away by the heady atmosphere that had welled up amid their workplace struggle, unionists decided to put their anti-war beliefs into practice by helping the locals to oppose the military base. They subsequently refused to transport supplies to the Uchinada range site and began leading the anti-military base campaign, teaching the villagers the basics about organizing demonstrations.[26]

Ōtake Hideo's repeated assertion that Sōhyō's radicalism regarding political issues stemmed from the need to make up for its setback on the economic front again requires examination. Ōtake argued that while workers could be punished by dismissal or loss of opportunities for promotion for their workplace struggles, their political struggles in the streets were legally guaranteed as long as such activities did not disturb their employers' business operations.[27] But as has been seen in the cases of the Nissan Motor and Hokuriku Railway unions, militant unions, which were making significant progress in their economic battles, often spearheaded the peace movement through strikes because they were confident of their strength *vis-à-vis* management. Some individual workers did take part in the peace movement to vent their frustrations over their union's ineffectiveness at the workplace. But union participation in the peace movement differs from that of individual workers because union peace activities were often accompanied by direct action at the workplace, and therefore constituted a highly daring move that put unionists' jobs on the line and risked arrests by police.[28]

Unions that were strong enough to defy management or government authorities to take an active part in the peace movement were the envy of weaker unions that were unable to win many workplace battles, let alone take direct action over political issues. Among weaker unions that took part in the *Anpo Tōsō*, a union of tax collectors overcame fears of dismissal facing civil servants who took direct action and joined the demonstration, saying, 'When can we fight if we can't fight this battle that seems to have aroused the whole nation?'[29]

Some unions are reported to have seen their effectiveness in workplace struggles enhanced after their members took part in the peace movement, as in the case of unions at firms located near Sunagawa, Kokurō's chapter in Tokyo's Shinagawa Ward, and the union at the Kawasaki plant of Nippon Steel, which also participated in the Sunagawa campaign.[30] The energy and enthusiasm workers displayed in the peace movement often carried over into their own workplaces. Many unions took the *Anpo Tōsō* all the more seriously in order to conduct wage battles, being tackled simultaneously, to their advantage.[31]

Small versus large company unions

During the *Anpo Tōsō*, some activists often complained that workers at large corporations had become complacent because of their rising salaries, and were not as committed to the protest movement as their more underprivileged brethren at smaller firms.[32] But such assertions appear to have been oversimplified and require re-examination.

Workers at small companies in the midst of fierce labour disputes admittedly were prone to radicalization. The ones who led the charge into the grounds of parliament during the *Anpo Tōsō* with Zengakuren students, for example, were members of the National Trade Union of Metal and Engineering Workers (Zenkoku Kinzoku) and other small-firm unions who had received their training through violent confrontations with police and strikebreakers.[33] Zenkoku Kinzoku was one of the very few union federations which were controlled by Takano allies from top to bottom, and consisted mainly of unions from small and medium-size firms.

A certain correlation was discernible between workers' active involvement in the peace movement and the acrimony of battles they faced at their workplaces. Shimizu Shinzō, for example, said small-firm workers, who were in the midst of fierce labour strife, were highly committed to political activities because they knew through their own experience how important it was somehow to shift the relationship between the capitalist and working classes in their favour.[34] Since it was impossible for them to improve their work conditions on their own, it was necessary to collaborate with unions at other companies. Peace campaigning and other political activities provided the vital link that brought together workers from different companies. So some small firm unions used the peace movement as a lever to lift themselves from their underprivileged status.[35]

Nevertheless, the ranks of small-firm workers that expanded the battlefront from their workplaces to political demonstrations appear to have been limited. At the height of the *Anpo Tōsō*, some 300,000 demonstrators massed around the parliament building, of whom about 80 per cent are estimated to have been members of labour unions, according to leftist sources. It was impossible to mobilize workers in such numbers unless large-corporation unions weighed in with the heft of their organizational muscle. Many small-firm unions more often than not had their hands full with their own labour disputes, which made it difficult to divert their energies to the peace movement.

Anpo Tōsō campaigners usually held a protest rally in Hibiya, Tokyo, after which they fanned out to demonstrate in all directions. On 25 June 1959, the National and Tokyo congresses tried a different tack, starting demonstrations in several locations in Tokyo to let some 30,000 marchers converge on a single rally site in Hibiya, according to the campaign organizers. The number of demonstrators was the highest ever, whereas in previous rallies, the maximum number unions could muster was believed to be no more than 10,000. Though they did not play a leading role, small-firm unionists who took part in the 'centripetal' demonstrations took heart from the sheer numbers of the protesters, because they thought they could put up a fight at their workplaces if they were part of such a massive movement.[36]

Unions that mobilized the bulk of demonstrators were those from large corporations. Kokurō, Zentei, Nikkyōso and the All Japan Prefectural and Municipal Workers' Union (Jichirō), which had chapters across the nation, were able to supply particularly high numbers of demonstrators. Among key private-sector industrial federations, the unions at steel, chemicals and electrical machinery manufacturers, even when they were unable to strike, kept a high profile in the protest movement. The weight that large-company unions carried in the *Anpo Tōsō* far surpassed that of small-firm unions.

Though workers at large companies enjoyed far better pay than those at small firms, unions on the whole around 1960 were engaged in frantic struggles to bring their wages up to the European level. Average hourly wages in Japan in those days were estimated to be equivalent to less than one fifth of those in the US and just under half the British and West German levels.[37] Complacency, therefore, was not an apt term to describe the attitude of employees at large companies.

114 *Elements of labour's peace activities*

Besides low wages, the 'pre-modern' industrial relations that still pervaded many workplaces around Japan appear to have continued to sustain rumblings even among workers at large corporations. According to Ōta Kaoru, widespread workers' discontent with undemocratic employment practices they experienced on a daily basis, as well as at the high unemployment rate, exploded when it combined with the *Anpo Tōsō*.[38] Ōkōchi Kazuo also noted that many employers, even in the early 1960s, continued to maintain an authoritarian attitude and tended to regard labour relations as those between master and servant, much to the fury of workers. Most managers regarded labour unions as nothing but a source of annoyance, and some considered them to be outright seditious, whereas most workers at large companies believed in equality between labour and management. According to Ōkōchi, worker indignation at what they believed to be the feudal attitude and intransigence on the part of management helped to keep alive the syndicalist tendencies of the pre-war days among post-war unionists, and prompted frequent strikes and other forms of direct action. Ōkōchi also attributed the rash tendency among workers to confront management to a sharp increase in the desire, especially among young workers, to enjoy the fruits of economic growth brought about through technological innovation.[39] The reservoir of radicalism among employees at large corporations therefore remained significant around 1960.

Involvement in the Korean War

Among other factors that triggered union peace activities was involuntary involvement in work related to the Korean War. As described earlier, the workers at the Akabane plant for weapons repair, together with national railway workers who had to suffer a punishing workload under tight security, made a dramatic response to their harsh conditions. Their anti-war sentiment grew hand-in-hand with their radicalization, which was fuelled by personal economic grievances.

Amid the crackdown on communists and other peace activists, and Sōhyō's policy of support for the UN action in Korea, the protest movement against the war was a severely limited affair. An eighteen-year-old worker, who found a job at a plant making military matériel after a long period of unemployment, quit after two weeks of sleepless nights, finding it unbearable to be producing bullets that would kill Koreans.[40] Meanwhile, some twenty out of the thirty workers at Tokyo's Shinjuku railway station, who had been assigned the task of transporting military matériel shortly after the outbreak of the war, did not turn up for work.[41] Some seamen refused to board vessels bound for Korea, and some factory hands deliberately made faulty military goods or tried to block their shipment.[42] One female phone operator, sobered by the fact that the phone calls she was handling could threaten peace in Japan and assist the slaughter in Korea, spent her month's salary on anti-war handbills that she distributed at her office. While the operator mounted her lone campaign, others, who listened in on phone calls conveying military orders and were made anxious by the presence of US soldiers who kept a close watch on them, vented their frustrations by singing *Peace Song*.[43]

But most workers, in fear of being tried by a SCAP military tribunal or for other reasons, went no further than make pious expressions of sympathy for the Koreans or mumble their inchoate anti-war sentiment, which was neither developed into a reasoned stand on the war nor channelled into direct action. Even among a limited few, who staged open and vocal protests against the war, a mere handful appears to have opposed the war from a purely pacifist point of view. A vocal peace movement appears to have gathered momentum only after the end of the US occupation and amid the communist camp's 'peace offensive' after the death of Stalin in March 1953.[44]

For the very few unions that opposed the Korean War, what was the chief motive behind their protest against the fighting?

One of the very few unions that protested against the Korean War with strikes was the All Japan Harbour Workers' Union (Zenkōwan). The stevedores' union opposed the war on the grounds that regardless of who had started it, the US had no business intervening in the affairs of Korea and wreaking havoc with the lives of Koreans. The union condemned the US for engaging in 'a war of aggression'. The argument is similar to that of the JCP and Sanbetsu, which instructed its constituent unions to stop producing and transporting arms and ammunition destined for South Korea. But Sanbetsu was already a mere shadow of its former self by the time the war broke out, and Zenkōwan, which had left Sanbetsu in February 1950, protested against the war on its own.[45]

The anti-war protest by the stevedores was driven by a mixture of humanitarian concern for the suffering caused by the war and their own economic grievances. They actively protested against the war in solidarity with Korean and other dock workers around the world, who were also resisting the war effort, and communicated with Japanese workers thorough handbills smuggled inside ships calling at Japanese ports.[46] Some stevedores did take up their anti-war protests primarily for humanitarian reasons. According to the writer Hayashi Eidai, workers at the port of Moji in northern Kyushu, who were handling consignments of military matériel for use in the war, dropped jeeps and trucks into the sea and damaged tanks and other equipment out of sympathy for Koreans and dead black soldiers, who were found in disproportionately high numbers among the corpses of American troops sent from Korea, as if they had been used as human shields for white soldiers. They told black servicemen in Moji about the high casualty rate and persuaded them to support their defiance against the US military police and hired thugs.[47]

But it is difficult to gauge the extent to which the union's anti-war strikes were motivated by humanitarian concerns, because the stevedores' grievances over their harsh work conditions might have far eclipsed their sympathy for the Koreans.[48] Following the outbreak of the war, their workload increased sharply and they often had to do night shifts for long periods while their wages were kept at subsistence levels. Though SCAP had banned strikes by the stevedores in June 1950, the workers defied the ban and won wage increases through a direct action that spread across the country from late 1950 to March 1951. The Osaka chapter of the union federation, which was one of the major epicentres of the direct action, was particularly enthusiastic about both its economic battle and its peace activities, and proposed a campaign for a comprehensive peace to other unions and grassroots groups.[49] The Osaka chapter explained its stand in a manner typical of left-wing unions: 'The struggle to raise our wages is aimed not only at protecting our livelihood but it is also a battle against the conspiracy of international imperialists, rearmament, war and colonial policy.'[50]

Being at the forefront of the logistical support for the war also prompted the stevedores to brood over the future of Japan's economy, as they saw how peacetime industry became only of secondary importance during the war. Stevedores saw war and transport vessels carrying military matériel keep civilian vessels from their ports. While workers at busy ports on the Pacific coast saw their workload soar, the amount of work at ports on Japan's other coast plummeted as maritime traffic dwindled in the Sea of Japan due to fears of mines. Stevedores who lost their jobs at ports along the Sea of Japan had to migrate to the Pacific coast in search of employment.[51]

Other day labourers who struck to oppose the war included in their ranks a significant number of communists who had lost their jobs because of the Red Purge. Many appear to have acted on the instructions of Sanbetsu and the JCP, which were in the midst of internal division and an ideological muddle about North Korea's 'war of liberation'.[52]

Workers at Nippon Steel's Akabane plant were employed for the sole purpose of supporting the war effort, and they were fully aware that the weapons they made or repaired would be used in Korea. Hirasawa Eiichi, a unionist who assisted in the strike at the plant, recalled that the combustible atmosphere during the labour dispute was compounded because workers were upset about having to handle bloodied tanks that reminded them of the carnage in Korea, as well as of the war they had experienced themselves.[53] But theirs was little more than an emotional outburst at their harsh work conditions, which were worsened by the association with the war, and as such the workers' attitude did not represent a committed pacifist stand against the war.

Many workers were involved in the production of weapons, including napalm bombs and ammunition, and other supplies for use in the Korean War, because they were unable to make a living in any other way.[54] An *Asahi Shimbun* correspondent reported that trucks he saw in Korea were all made by Japanese companies such as Nissan, Toyota and Isuzu, and that he saw Japanese-made weapons fired towards the North.[55] Though not openly supportive of the war, some unionists are reported at least tacitly to have welcomed the fighting in Korea because of the economic boom it brought.[56] The Federation of All Japan Metal Mine Labour Unions (Zenkō) is said to have tried as much as possible to obtain the fruits of the boom for its members when metal prices jumped during the war.[57]

One of the industrial union federations that showed the most active concern for peace issues during this period, as was stated above, was the federation of automobile manufacturers' unions. War-related demand revived Japan's motor industry, but the union at Ikegai Motor, for example, protested to management, arguing that 'It is unconscionable to work for the US military even if the company is unable to find other work.' But such anti-war stands appear to have been the exception rather than the rule in the motor industry.[58]

Thanks to the war boom, the Nissan Motor union regained the ground it had lost in 1949 when a large number of workers were fired. Still, unionists were far from content. They expressed fears that Japan's arms industry would prosper at the expense of peacetime industry and ordinary people's lives. As the automotive labour federation's stance became increasingly ideologically dominated, unionists actively discussed the state of Japan, which they feared was turning into a US colony. They also debated the question of US military bases, and called socialist nations a 'peace force' well before Takano Minoru proposed the idea in 1953.[59]

Following active debate on the war, the Nissan Motor union decided in February 1951 to focus on winning a wage increase and resisting excessive overtime work and the war economy. Meanwhile, loads of Nissan trucks were being shipped to Korea for use in the war. Saga Ichirō concluded that even the Nissan union, one of the most left-wing unions in those days, was unable to stage a peace protest unless its purpose was closely linked to workers' economic concerns.[60]

There are few clues as to how workers rationalized their position of opposing the war while remaining silent about the economic benefits they gained as a result of it. In the industrial city of Nagoya, many factories manufactured munitions during the Korean War, but about half of the workers interviewed by the *Asahi Shimbun* were reported to have expressed only nostalgia for the wartime past when their plants turned out advanced military aircraft. When asked about the contradiction of producing weapons while supporting a political party that opposed rearmament, a unionist at Mitsubishi Heavy Industry said 'We can't realize our ideals if we lose the means for our livelihood.' A union official at a Daidō Seikō steel plant producing artillery shells said about the weapons manufacture:

> It's a cross Japanese workers have to bear. If a worker at a company in a capitalist society refuses to make weapons, he is certain to lose his job. This is something not only up to Japanese politicians but also to the world's politicians to resolve.[61]

These unionists' views suggest that the social ills that left workers no choice but to make weapons in order to earn a living were to blame rather than the workers themselves, and that workers should not be called on to sort out the moral implications of assisting the war effort.

Even after Sōhyō dropped its support for the US war in Korea through its adoption of the peace principles, its 1952 policy statements focused on how big business profited at the expense of Japanese workers during the Korean War, and what it perceived to be the resulting 'militarization' of the Japanese economy. The labour federation's chief concern continued to be the current and future economic difficulties of Japanese workers, and it apparently could not afford to spare much thought to the suffering of Koreans.[62]

Remorse about World War II

The flowering of the workers' peace movement was made possible by a postwar law that guaranteed workers the right to work in their own self-interest, and the change that was brought on in popular consciousness about civil rights. The discourse that marked organized labour's peace movement revolved predominantly around the assertion of rights as a result. While many unionists regarded their peace campaigns as a righteous crusade for people's rights, however, it is difficult to tell to what extent workers confronted the moral implications of embracing pacifism immediately after taking part in one of history's bloodiest wars up until 1945. Any attempt to explore the moral aspect of the newly adopted faith would inevitably raise painful issues – remorse over the workers' own role in World War II and atonement towards and reconciliation with foreign nations.

Amid the chaos in the immediate aftermath of the war, many workers vented their pent-up anger by holding kangaroo courts to accuse company managers of causing all the suffering they had endured during the war.[63] According to Hosoya Matsuta, a former leader of Shin Sanbetsu, workers across the country were seething with anger at the government and bureaucrats who had made them suffer so much during the war, and they had demonstrated great enthusiasm for the 1 February 1947 general strike, which was eventually called off.[64] But any acts of retaliation to bring the managers to account for their 'war responsibility' were conducted in spasms and did not serve to engage seriously the issue of war crimes. After many such revolts had led to the ousting of corporate managers, workers summarily heaped all the blame for the war on the ruling classes, such as greedy capitalists and 'militarists'. Their rash actions shortly after the war's end contributed practically nothing to the nation's view on war responsibility, except for enduring grudges against the ruling classes.

A minority of Japanese, who held themselves at least partly responsible for the tragedy of the war, tended to keep silent. Gotō Jun-ichirō, a former Sanbetsu official who organized unions in Tokyo shortly after the war, said there were many junior managers at small and medium-size firms who had police records because of their past involvement in leftist activities, and who therefore had been rejected by large companies. Gotō said it was easy to form unions at such smaller firms because the junior managers, who had failed in their pre-war labour activities and had ended up supporting the war effort, showed great understanding for union activities led by post-war communists. According to Gotō, these managers, out of a sense of guilt about their earlier ineffectualness, refrained from taking the leadership role in the post-war labour movement while encouraging union activities at their firms.[65]

Labour disputes charging managers with war crimes took the most dramatic form at newspaper publishers. Some managers and reporters voluntarily quit their jobs because they found it impossible to continue working after serving as zealous cheerleaders for the catastrophic war. Immediately after the war's end, employees organized active campaigns to punish senior executives for their conduct during the war, and the top management of many newspaper publishers, including such major papers as the *Asahi Shimbun* and the *Mainichi Shimbun*, were forced to resign.

The most celebrated case of newspaper staff battling to banish war criminals from their top management was fought at the *Yomiuri Shimbun*, where workers succeeded in forcing the resignation of President Shōriki Matsutarō and took over the publishing operations. After the dispute ended, the paper's editorial on 12 December 1945 vowed that the *Yomiuri* would work for the realization of a 'democratic revolution'.[66]

According to Masuyama Tasuke, a former senior official of the *Yomiuri* union, however, the staff took the action in part because they feared that SCAP would either close down or suspend publication of the paper. This was because the *Yomiuri* had been the most vocal supporter of the war and did the most to indoctrinate the populace with the official militarist ideology. Masuyama said the Yomiuri staff's rebellion against top management, which they called an in-house democratization movement, was aimed at banishing the war criminals themselves so as to pre-empt GHQ's move to punish the company.[67] Masuyama recalls that both communist and non-communist reporters mostly shunned discussions about war responsibility because they did not want to talk about their wartime reporting.[68] Ariyama Teruo, who did detailed research on Japan's journalistic community of the early post-war years, also points out that the indictment of their managers by newspaper staff tended to lose sight of the responsibility of individual reporters.[69]

Any soul-searching that newspaper staff did about their war guilt was short-lived and appears to have had little impact on the nation's conscience. *Yomiuri* workers put out a paper that was as radical as the JCP organ during their brief moment of victory. But the situation was swiftly reversed when management regained control, with the help of GHQ and the Japanese government, in October 1946.

Meanwhile, the *Asahi* had issued a declaration entitled 'We will rise with the people', on 7 November 1945. In the statement, the *Asahi* apologized for not reporting the truth or resisting the government during the war, as a result of which it had kept the people in the dark till the very end. The newspaper vowed to work through the consensus of its entire staff and always be on the side of the people in reflecting their views. Ariyama's study, however, shows that despite its professed resolve, the *Asahi* and all other newspapers gradually lost their enthusiasm to investigate issues over war responsibility after their strike of 5 October 1946 failed. During the so-called reverse course, the *Yomiuri* turned into one of the most vocal critics of communist activity. Most newspapers were unsympathetic to Kokurō and other workers who were rounded up following the fatal railway incidents of 1949. Newspaper publishers in general put up little significant resistance in the face of SCAP censorship, or when communists and those regarded as fellow travellers were banished from their offices during the Red Purge.[70] Even after the end of the occupation, major newspapers never regained their radicalism of the early post-war years, and were widely disparaged as 'commercial' or 'bourgeois' papers by left-wing unionists.

As soon as the war ended, the political left categorically repudiated the conflict as a war of aggression. The entire blame for the war was laid at the door of capitalists, militarists or the capitalist system, making it easy to lose sight of war guilt at the grassroots level. Moreover, a sense of war guilt revealed by a minority of workers in the early post-war years, as well as the war responsibility issue that emerged at newspapers, were mostly domestically oriented. War responsibility in this context focused mainly on the roles of individuals in contributing to or failing to prevent the catastrophe that befell Japan.

Debate on the peace settlement around 1950 provided an important occasion for the Japanese to ponder the issue of war responsibility in an international context. But in union circles, as has been seen in Chapter 2 of this book, debate revolved around workers' economic interests, the survival of unions and the labour movement as a whole, and security considerations to ensure peace for Japan.

Proponents of the four peace principles, however, did express their remorse for Japan's aggression in Asia, and their desire for reconciliation with all of Japan's former enemies through a comprehensive peace treaty. At its founding convention in August 1951, the Japanese People's Congress for Promotion of Peace (Nihon Heiwa Suishin Kokumin Kaigi), which was formed by Sōhyō, the JSP and religious and other grassroots groups, issued a declaration which stated:

> We engaged in imperialistic aggression for half a century and invaded neighbouring Asian nations. We now have to prevent war for the sake of all humankind with a sense of contrition toward our Asian neighbours. In doing so, we should unwaveringly commit ourselves to non-violence and remain unarmed. Arms will never help to achieve peace. Peace will be achieved only through peaceful means.[71]

In a statement clarifying its stand on the draft peace treaty authored by the US, Sōhyō expressed the following view:

> We made enemies of Asian nations, which should have been our friends, through our acts of aggression and plunder. But Japan and other Asian nations have a common mission to fight poverty in underdeveloped Asia and improve its political status. Japan must pursue a policy to improve diplomatic relations with the rest of Asia because one of the greatest challenges facing the world now is how to bridge the economic gap between the US and Europe, and Asia. We wish to reconcile and achieve mutual trust with the US but we desire to cultivate such a relationship more than anyone else with Asian nations. Therefore, we could never accept the [US-authored draft of] a peace treaty that would antagonize Asia. We hope that the opinions of India and Southeast Asian nations will be respected and that the issue of two Chinese governments will be resolved as soon as possible based on facts.[72]

Such a frank admission of guilt to Asian countries was made in part because Japanese labour unions were aware of the need to make common cause with China, Vietnam, the Philippines, Burma, the Middle Eastern nations and other developing countries across the world so as to conduct Japan's own struggle for independence to its advantage. While acknowledging 'grave' responsibility for the unprecedented suffering of Asian countries that Japan had turned into battlegrounds during World War II, Sōhyō demanded that all claims to war reparations should be waived, pleading lack of economic means.[73] The union federation argued:

> The poverty of Japan's working population was one of the reasons for Japan's war. One of the chief causes of war can be eliminated by fighting the Japanese people's poverty. [Demands for reparations] could also fuel xenophobia in Japan. Establishment of a system within Japan that would preclude any future aggression against Asia should serve as the best reparations.[74]

Highly incensed at the reparations demands of some nations, Takano declared, in an editorial in the Sōhyō organ, that 'Countries that demand more reparations should be smacked on the ear with a wad of cash.'[75] Though the garbled reasoning of the editorial makes it difficult to tell what Takano really meant by that, it can be assumed that unionists who had firsthand knowledge of Japan's devastated industrial capacity considered the reparations demands unreasonably harsh. Trying to extract as many economic concessions as possible for themselves was also second nature to labour unions, so unionists might have found it natural to bargain for leniency on the matter. This attitude contrasts with that of female intellectuals, who issued a statement around the same time declaring that a lack of economic means should not exonerate Japan from its obligation to pay war reparations to its victims. (See Part II on the women's peace movement.)

When the issue over reparations for South Vietnam came to a head in 1959, Sōhyō opposed compensation on the grounds that Japan did not need to pay 20 billion yen for the negligible damage it caused in South Vietnam, which was equivalent to only 'three chickens'. Such reparations, Sōhyō argued, would be used only to build up military installations in South Vietnam and serve US military interests in the region.[76] Unions opposed reparations for Vietnam and other Southeast Asian nations in the late 1950s also because they were loath to see Japanese monopolists fatten themselves with lucrative government projects funded with the reparations.[77]

When labour unions and other grassroots groups sought to strengthen their ties with China, it was inevitable that they would face issues over Japan's war crimes. Under the initiative of the Japan-China Friendship Association (Nicchū Yūkō Kyōkai), labour unions of stevedores, coal miners and construction workers organized regional committees across the nation to collect the remains of their late Chinese colleagues, who had been forcibly brought to Japan and perished under inhumane work conditions at labour camps. The Japanese Coal Miners' Union, for example, instructed all constituent unions to cooperate with the initiative, saying that the working class should play a leading role in the project to promote peace between Japan and China.[78] The collected remains were honoured at Buddhist ceremonies in Japan before being shipped to relatives in China.

The project to honour the Chinese victims was conducted almost entirely on private initiative, with the central government refusing to cooperate.[79] It marked Japan's first significant act of contrition towards foreign victims of the war. At the height of the *Anpo Tōsō*, the communist-dominated Japan-China Friendship Association stressed its opposition to the security treaty on the grounds that Japan should not err twice against China[80] and organized a major memorial service for Chinese victims; the group claimed that this drew some 2,000 mourners, of which one third were said to be unionists.[81] But the Japan-China Friendship Association had originally taken up the matter in 1950 only at the insistence of Chinese residents in Japan.[82] It is also notable that workers, while courting the communist China they so idealized, did not appear to have staged any major initiative to collect the remains of the large number of Korean labourers who died under similar circumstances. Any sense of contrition expressed by unionists towards Chinese victims, therefore, appears to have been tinged with a socialist bias, which tended to emphasize the need for Japan's reconciliation with its former enemies from the standpoint of advancing the domestic and international labour movement.

All former union officials and activists whom this author has interviewed said they could not recall any instance in which Japan's unions formulated policies to deal with Japan's past war crimes, and noted how workers regarded themselves primarily as victims of the war. Public expressions of remorse about the war made by Sōhyō and other labour organizations tell us nothing about whether individual workers made any conscious effort to come to terms with their own conduct during the war. Takeuchi, who had been too young to take part in combat, recalled how older workers used to talk about the horrendous atrocities committed during the war without ever making it clear whether they, too, had taken part in them. According to Takeuchi, former soldiers talked about the battles they had fought merely as events that had happened in days long gone by. Hino of Kokurō remembered that older colleagues talked about their deeds in China only when they got drunk, and confided tearfully they could never forget the faces of the Chinese they had killed. Such workers, according to Hino, never talked openly about their conduct in China because they were afraid that they might be branded as war criminals.[83]

In explaining Japanese workers' inaction regarding matters concerning the foreign victims of Japan's war, Yokoi Kameo, the tireless peace marcher who worked for a small machinery manufacturer, said it was impossible for unionists to tackle anything more than they actually did.[84]

Workers' battleground for their economic and political struggles was generally restricted to the domestic scene, and their horizon as a result extended little further than the challenges facing them within Japan. As a result, Japan's war responsibility towards its foreign victims by and large failed to figure prominently in the unionist peace agenda.

Yamaguchi Kenji, a former leader of the JSP's youth section, expressed his view as follows, forty years after the 1960 *Anpo Tōsō*:

> Of the men I got to know through the labour movement after the war, almost no one seriously took the issue of rape during the fighting abroad as a personal matter. Those who admitted to raping women were better [than most who did not] and most appeared to think matters such as rapes were quite inconsequential. I questioned [left-wingers'] tendency to blame everything on the emperor. I probably might have been thinking about 'people's own responsibility for Japan's aggression', an issue for which I could not find any clear answer.[85]

Yamaguchi's appears to be a hindsight that most trade unionists failed to cultivate during the tumultuous early post-war years.

Part II
The women's peace movement

6 Prehistory and the early post-war years

Pre-war and war years

In expressing their sorrow over World War II, women, both in the early post-war years and even today, have often argued that women were the chief victims of the war. Japanese women who lived through the war generally consider the unequal laws and the traditional mores that pervaded Japanese society to have aggravated the injustices of the war, and this strengthened their sense of having been wronged by the government and the military.

Before moving on to discuss the beginning of their post-war peace movement, the following will briefly look at the condition of women in pre-war and wartime Japan with a view to shedding light on how the change in their legal and social status after the war affected their consciousness over war and peace issues.

Ever since Japan's authoritarian government, anchored in the emperor system, was firmly established at the beginning of the twentieth century, the government prescribed for women the role of virtuous, obedient and self-effacing members of their families and the state, serving their male superiors to help them to advance the good of their families and by extension the public good. In wartime, the government tried to exploit to the full this patriarchal system, under which women were supposed to make the utmost sacrifice to help the state achieve its war aims.[1]

The government's idea of the ideal Japanese mother, disseminated through school education, was a paragon of moral rectitude, who would stoically accept the entire burden of housework and totally dedicate herself to the service of her husband, in-laws and children. That was supposed to be the way a mother would raise her children, who in turn would become loyal subjects of Imperial Japan. When the nation was at war, so the official propaganda went, a mother should readily surrender her children for the good of the state without a word of complaint.

This type of patriarchal order, which sought to mould women into the obedient handmaidens of government policy, was often challenged by political and economic shifts following the end of the Russo-Japanese war. Those challenges included the rapid development of the economy and a resultant exodus of the rural population into urban areas, which disturbed the traditional *ie*,² or family system, and communal order in provincial areas. The pro-democracy movement following World War I also posed a serious test to the authoritarian regime, for as the number of working women rapidly increased after World War I, more women became actively involved in the labour movement and campaigns for women's suffrage.³

The government responded to such newfound political tendencies among women with repression and an ideological counter-offensive. Whenever it considered that women were straying from the officially approved ideological line, the government stepped up propaganda campaigns extolling its version of maternal virtues such as self-effacement and self-sacrifice.⁴

As the war escalated in the 1930s in China, the unprecedented national crisis facing Japan and the all-out mobilization for the war effort gave the government an excuse to bring all grassroots organizations under the single state umbrella of the Imperial Rule Assistance Association (Taisei Yokusankai), so that the budding political assertiveness of women was virtually stamped out. Many women's rights activists, including Ichikawa Fusae, who had earlier resisted the war, were eventually enlisted for the war effort.

Amid the onset of the war, the only public activities women were allowed to take up were those aimed at supporting the war effort. In the collective Japanese memory of the wartime years, the conspicuous role played by members of the government-controlled Kokubō Fujinkai (the Women's Society for National Defence) stands out. These were the women, most of them ordinary housewives, who zealously waved national flags at railway stations to send soldiers off to war, sent letters and bundles of goods to military personnel fighting outside Japan, and looked after the wounded or bereaved families of those who had been killed. Japan had never seen as big a women's organization as Kokubō Fujinkai, whose activities were made possible to a considerable extent through the voluntary action of women at grassroots level. The vigour with which the women of Kokubō Fujinkai engaged in their patriotic activities reflected a significant reservoir of pro-war sentiment among women.

While the law and prevailing social mores discouraged women from taking an active part in political or other activities outside the home, members of Kokubō Fujinkai were free to engage in public activities. After the war, some women who recalled those days said they had felt liberated and exhilarated when they were allowed to leave their homes and openly engage in something that would be good for their country. The vigour of their activities appears to have been fuelled by the sense of pride that women, too, were important members of society able to offer indispensable services for the wider public good.⁵

The women of Kokubō Fujinkai were often seen with right-wing politicians and members of right-wing organizations at the Osaka railway station. But the historian Fujii Tadatoshi sees no close link between Kokubō Fujinkai and rightists, arguing that members of Kokubō Fujinkai showed little interest in the nationalist ideology promoted by the army and that their frenetic cheer-leading was not prompted by any deep political outlook.[6]

Whether voluntary or not, the women of Kokubō Fujinkai took up activities prescribed or approved by the authorities, and as such there was little room for independent thought or action in their patriotic work. In hindsight, people have often expressed dismay at the sheer mindlessness that appeared to mark the zealous activities of the well-meaning but naive housewives.[7]

In the absence of reliable opinion polls, it is difficult to know exactly what ordinary women thought about the war while it was being waged. Economic hardship, and the generally repressive political climate that discouraged women from discussing politics both inside and outside the home, served as serious disincentives for women to form dispassionate and objective opinions on wider issues facing them and their country. Though some members of Kokubō Fujinkai quite willingly and happily busied themselves in good works, their actions can be attributed in part to the extremely circumscribed horizon of their political outlook. The historian Kanō Mikiyo has also noted that many women were often found to be more enthusiastic about the war than men, who had to fight, and attributes that to the news blackout that kept them ignorant about the war's realities.[8]

Looking back at those days, the historian Tatewaki Sadayo (1904–90) has noted that a majority of Japanese set aside their ideals and became quite realistic in the face of growing economic difficulty.[9] The socialist politician Yamakawa Kikue (1890–1980) has also noted the general superficiality of public discussion and the decline in independent thinking on the part of the public in those days. According to Yamakawa, after it had become impossible to campaign for their political rights, women stopped insisting on matters of principle and focused on pragmatic matters as trivial as cleaning the streets.[10]

Although under the law women were treated as second-rate citizens incapable of responsible action in matters of politics and business, and received little training to tackle the major challenges of life, their abilities were tested to the limit amid extreme deprivation and the onset of the war, under circumstances men would have found difficult to endure. Most women, who had been quite ignorant of the political situation, came face-to-face with the realities of the war for the first time in the form of air raids.[11] As women often said years after the end of the war, they were taken by surprise by the war and felt powerless to exercise any control over the unfolding turn of events.[12]

A view expressed by a thirty-six-year-old housewife in an essay written in 1963 was often echoed by other ordinary women:

[Shortly after the Pacific War broke out,] nobody really cared about the lives being lost in the war amid the generally festive mood. But as the war took a turn for the worse and when we saw numerous bodies burnt and disfigured beyond all recognition by air raids, we were shocked to learn people's lives were being treated as if they were of little value. But that realization didn't lead us to criticize the war because we thought it was part of some great destiny which we had no choice but to accept.[13]

The death toll sharply increased after the Sino-Japanese war began in earnest. But no matter how shattered they were, the families of dead soldiers were obliged to talk in public about the honour of serving their country, and express pride in their men fulfilling their duty by dying an honourable death. At no time during the war did the sorrows of bereaved families serve as an effective check on government policy, according to historian Fujii Tadatoshi. It was not until shortly after the war, when university students published the writings of their dead fellow soldiers, that sorrow over the deaths of loved ones became a driving force behind the anti-war movement.[14]

The example of the labour union activist Higuchi Tokuzō's mother was probably typical of the naivety of many women who had followed the official government line without giving much thought to its implications. It was only after the death of her sons that she came to realize the consequences of offering them up for the nation's cause.

Higuchi's mother Ryū was publicly honoured because three of her sons volunteered to join the navy. She dutifully and by all appearances mindlessly parroted the government line when speaking on the radio, saying, 'The boys are not mine [but my country's].' The words that came to Ryū's lips so effortlessly were just one variation on the frequently quoted response that a virtuous wartime mother was expected to give. In the June 1939 issue of *Shufu no Tomo* magazine, one woman was quoted as saying, 'I have given my son to the emperor. It makes me so happy that my son has won his Majesty's praise for dying for his country and that is enough for me to forget everything else.'[15] After losing all three of the boys, Ryū, overwhelmed, did not even know how to vent her grief.[16]

It was only in the catastrophic aftermath of the war that most women learned about its devastating consequences. Former members of Kokubō Fujinkai realized their tender feelings for poor soldiers they sought to comfort had been exploited and tragically betrayed. They later learned they had helped to send so many men to their deaths in an unjust war, and that their well-meaning action had put moral pressure on men to carry out their duties valiantly despite being in mortal fear.

After Japan's defeat, women remembered the war primarily in light of the loss of their loved ones and other harsh sufferings they had been forced to endure. As they felt that the wartime government had taken advantage of their frailties and ignorance, they later viewed the war principally as something that most oppressed the weak and unprivileged members of society. Recrimination against the injustices of the war, and a sense of being its chief victims, became the prime motif in women's views of the war.

A revival of grassroots activities and the post-war education of women

Immediately after Japan's surrender, most women desperately struggled to survive and had no time to think how and why things had gone so horribly wrong because of the war. SCAP, meanwhile, imposed its new pacifist policy from above to make the populace renounce their wartime ideology, and together with the Japanese government began trying to turn women into converts to a democratic political system, in view of the general absence of political initiative on their part.

Soon after arriving in Japan, SCAP, as part of its efforts to eradicate militarism, implemented a series of measures to emancipate women. The new US-authored Constitution guaranteed equality between the sexes, and the civil code was revised. Women accordingly were freed from pre-war laws that relegated them to the status of incompetents, and were granted inheritance rights, the freedom to marry and divorce, and equal rights as parents. The traditional *ie* system was abolished in principle.

SCAP also abolished the security police law that had banned women and minors from attending political rallies or joining political parties, and the Japanese Diet approved women's suffrage in December 1945, allowing women to cast their ballots in Japan's first post-war lower house election on 10 April 1946.

SCAP measures to liberate women won general public approval. According to a *Mainichi Shimbun* opinion poll in April 1947, 57.9 per cent supported the abolition of the *ie* system, while 37.4 per cent were opposed and 4.7 per cent said they did not know.

SCAP disbanded women's support groups for the war effort and encouraged the formation of grassroots women's groups. Liberal and left-wing women, who had been critical of Japan's pre-war and wartime regime, seized this opportunity to form independent organizations. One of the leading such new organizations was the League of Women Voters of Japan (Shin Nihon Fujin Dōmei), which was established in November 1945 with the professed aims of educating women about political affairs, combating feudalistic institutions and plutocracy, and promoting peace. Another new group, the Women's Democratic Club, was founded in March 1946 by the socialist politician Katō Shizue and liberal or leftist intellectuals such as Hani Setsuko, Miyamoto Yuriko and Sata Ineko, with the full support of SCAP. The group's stated goals were to emancipate women from feudal institutions and make full use of their abilities in order to democratize Japan. In August, the club published the first issue of its weekly newspaper *Fujin Minshu Shimbun*, and subsequently began setting up local chapters, organizing women at the grassroots to tackle immediate concerns such as inflation, food and health.

Women's political activities in the early post-war years were led mainly by groups such as the League of Women Voters of Japan, the Women's Democratic Club and the women's sections of labour unions and

132 *Prehistory and the early post-war years*

consumers' associations. Such groups and many ordinary housewives became actively involved in JCP-led struggles to demand rice from local authorities and protest against hoarding or misappropriation of rationed goods in their local communities. Gotō Junichirō, a former Sanbetsu official, recalled a large number of women taking part in collective bargaining with fishermen's unions at Tsukiji, Tokyo, to secure supplies of fish. According to Gotō, the zeal of their demands for food was such that it gave an important impetus to the local labour movement, with women urging their husbands to form unions to defend their rights at the workplace.[17]

Their militant struggle for survival demonstrates that women had quite readily repudiated the wartime propaganda that called for blind obedience to the authorities. As was the case with one district of Suginami Ward, Tokyo, where women won most of the executive posts in a neighbourhood association and took an active leadership role in forming a consumers' group, grassroots networks expanded apace in many urban areas, challenging the policies of local authorities and replacing local groupings that had served as cogs in the government's war machine.

On the whole, however, a majority of women had yet to awaken to the meaning of their newly gained political rights, and were strangers to the idea of asserting their human or democratic rights. Educating them about Western democratic principles became the urgent task of both SCAP and the Japanese government.

In addition to the government, the mass media also took it upon themselves to 'enlighten' ordinary women about the newly prescribed national tenets of peace and democracy. Newspapers such as the *Asahi Shimbun* printed editorials especially written for female readers to advise them on how to conduct themselves in the new post-war order. Early post-war issues of women's magazines such as *Fujin Kōron* and *Josei Kaizō* consisted mainly of articles written by male intellectuals that were aimed at teaching women about newly introduced democratic institutions and laws providing for the emancipation of women.

Immediately after the war's end, the women's movement was inspired by the Constitution, which guaranteed women's rights for the first time in Japan's history. Issues over equal rights stimulated active debate in the mass media for the first ten or so years of the post-war period.[18] Of the two overarching tenets of peace and democracy, democracy was of more immediate concern to most women. Some women have said that for them, the most memorable thing about the post-war reforms was the Constitution's war-renouncing clause.[19] In general, however, since Japan's total defeat had precluded any possibility of its resuming hostilities for the foreseeable future, the issue of peace did not assume as much urgency as democracy. For most women, newly introduced democratic principles such as equality of the sexes and voting rights were more directly relevant to their daily lives. Women in rural areas, who lived under feudalistic mores that forbade them from disobeying the male heads of their families, particularly welcomed

Article 24 of the Constitution, which stipulated that marriage should be based on the mutual consent of both parties, and that it should be maintained through mutual cooperation with the husband and wife enjoying equal rights. Although the Women's Democratic Club later became actively involved in the peace movement, its organ the *Fujin Minshu Shimbun* stressed the importance of the national charter's democratic clauses when it editorialized about the new Constitution, and made no mention of Article 9.[20] Immediately after it was promulgated, the nation's charter became generally known as the democratic Constitution (*minshu kenpō*) rather than the peace Constitution (*heiwa kenpō*), a name that became more commonly used in later years.

But SCAP's active initiative to encourage the formation of independent grassroots groups gradually ran out of steam amid the onset of the Cold War. The occupation authorities had initially opposed the Japanese government's effort to resurrect wartime associations that would automatically include all women of a given local district as members to be presided over by a local boss. That policy began to change as US officials travelled ever deeper into rural areas, because they began to feel that active re-education campaigns were necessary, particularly in backward parts of Japan, if the lowly status of women was to be improved.[21] In the end, SCAP had little choice but to rely on the network of old associations that dated back to pre-war days, if they were to help women to deal with the harsh economic realities and counter the influence of the increasingly militant women's sections of labour unions. Thus SCAP fell back on the former officials of wartime associations and promoted the formation of regional women's organizations, to be administered by local officials in charge of adult education.[22]

Other grassroots groups, such as the Women's Democratic Club, reacted to such developments with deep concern, fearing war criminals were taking over regional women's groups again. Clashes between the political right and left over control of local communities became pronounced in many parts of Japan,[23] and it was against this backdrop that women began creating Japan's first post-war peace movement, the conduct of which was complicated by the Cold War being waged on both the international and domestic fronts.

The Cold War

Newborn idealism

For a few years prior to the deepening of the Cold War, SCAP and the Japanese government presented the concept of pacifism, as stipulated by the Constitution, as a new ideal towards which the nation should strive. War-weary women responded favourably, and some of them embraced the new idea with a great sense of elation. They confidently believed the Constitution would forever prevent any recurrence of war and put a definite end to all the misery they had endured. One Christian minister's wife describes her joy at the enforcement of the Constitution as follows:

> In 1947, we were trying hard every day just to survive. Food rations either came late or never at all, and prices skyrocketed while we received only meagre remuneration from our church. ... It was dizzying because I was so busy trying to buy food for my family, attending services at the church and sewing clothes to eke out a living. But despite the heavy workload, how happy and serene I felt! It was because of the Constitution, called the peace Constitution, which came into force on 3 May 1947. The Constitution declared that Japan had renounced war and maintaining armed forces forever.
>
> Oh, we no longer have to go through those dark days of the war again. How liberating! This sensation reassured me during those hard days. While I worked, I often thought about this and couldn't help smiling.[24]

For this woman, the Constitution was a source of moral revelation, and Japan's renunciation of war was a spiritual legacy bequeathed by the tragedies of war:

> The war robbed my children of their smile and took away my brother, our house and all our possessions. But the only thing that remained [in the aftermath of the war] was the belief that there should be no recurrence of war. I was so happy that we have gained an irreplaceable treasure when our country, after losing everything, renounced war. ... [The Constitution] also accorded with the truth preached by Christ.[25]

Women also demonstrated great enthusiasm for Japan's official post-war propaganda, which exhorted the Japanese people to rebuild the country as a bastion of peace and thereby help to regain its honour. One widow in her forties, in the belief that the world expected Japanese women to work for peace, vowed to contribute to the task with a soaring ambition. But the method with which she aimed to attain peace is reminiscent of the civic duty promoted by the wartime government:

> Japanese women [who had no power outside their homes] now have their dignity publicly recognized and stand in the blinding limelight of the international arena. ... I will try to avoid buying in black markets as much as possible and save money so that I can make ends meet with a month's salary. Then my life, though still difficult, will become more comfortable so I can gain confidence in myself ... Even a person like me can do this much. Admittedly this is just a small thing but it will make our lives a little better and eventually lead to world peace. So, our sisters, rise up with a sense of responsibility and confidence![26]

But these women appear to have been some of the brave few, whose moral fervour made them forget their harsh existence, if even for a brief moment, to look at things in a broader perspective. Other letters that ordinary women contributed to newspapers and magazines in those days suggest their destitute condition had reduced them to despair, robbing them of any capacity for thinking about things beyond their immediate personal needs. One woman in Gunma Prefecture said

> There must be millions of homes in Japan this evening where women are preparing dinner. I wonder how many of them really feel happy while doing so. Most working women must be cooking, lamenting the small amount and the poor quality of food they can offer their families.[27]

Another woman in Saitama Prefecture said

> I am not asking for any luxuries. But wearing rags and spending all day looking for food, we are exactly like some lowly animals. I only wish for peace of mind that would allow me to enjoy watching my children grow.[28]

It can be assumed that many Japanese, whether men or women, could not help but express dismay over the stark contrast between the idealism of the brave new world envisioned by the Constitution and the realities of their lives.

A discourse of good versus evil

Any happiness inspired by the new pacifist thought, however, was short-lived and gave way to fears, in 1948, of the possibility of war. Reflecting the heightened international tension at the onset of the Cold War, people began wondering aloud whether there was going to be another war, and some housewives began talking about preparing to evacuate their families to a safer place.[29]

Newspapers and magazines for women were particularly quick to respond to the unfolding crisis. *Fujin* magazine and the *Fujin Minshu Shimbun*, for example, did specials on World War II in their August 1948 issues and tried to alert the public to the horrendous consequences of another war by emphasizing the suffering inflicted on civilians in Hiroshima, Nagasaki and other parts of the world during the war.[30]

Faced with crises in places such as Germany, Greece, Turkey and East Asia, which were entirely beyond their control, both female pundits and ordinary women expressed anxiety over the inexplicable nature of the threat to peace. While communists such as the writer Miyamoto Yuriko attributed the imminent crisis to 'fascists who are out to destroy peace',[31] other women, who were not of the socialist persuasion, shared a similar view premised on the dichotomy between the minority of warmongers who intended to profit from another war and the vast majority of others wishing to preserve peace. The writer Maruoka Hideko made the case in a series of rhetorical questions:

> There certainly should be a reason for the emergence of this shadow of death that has given rise to vague anxiety. Is there still a minority of people in the world, who try to disguise a gambling act of war with beautiful words such as the destiny of the mother country, and engage in narrow-minded intrigues to promote themselves? Is there still a minority of people, who try to use those in power who act like this and believe they can make money out of war?[32]

If the dynamics of international relations are to be understood in the light of evil versus good personal intentions, the machinations of those inciting war, so the reasoning goes, had to be combated by moral and spiritual force, and in the case of women by maternal love. Miyamoto Yuriko urged each woman to initiate a moral crusade and act on her maternal instincts:

> We have to recognize that if we are to preserve peace, each one of us has to put up an earnest fight against every influence of deep-rooted fascism, which is destroying the peace.
>
> Mothers of Japan, be strong. Aspire to become a member of world motherhood. If each woman possesses the qualities of a mother, she will follow her instincts to nurture her child and protest from the bottom of her heart the forces that destroy peace.[33]

The feminist thinker Hiratsuka Raichō (1886–1971) also sounded a moralistic note in rallying women to action:

> A peace movement cannot be complete if it is a movement whose sole purpose is to prevent war between countries. In tandem with such a movement, there has to be a forceful, spiritual peace movement aimed at establishing peace within the hearts of individuals.[34]

When the new Constitution was promulgated, the government and the political commentators mainly stressed the moral aspect of the new national policy, which was to redeem the nation as a bulwark of peace and thereby attain an honoured place in the world. Their arguments, which were long on the spiritual and short on the concrete measures Japan should take to prevent war, apparently left female intellectuals little choice but to make their case against a possible war in rather vague moralistic terms. Thinking of war and other world affairs in terms of the nation's moral duty was a popular method of discourse that dated back to the pre-war days.

At the grassroots level, meanwhile, women's groups organized peace rallies and issued statements expressing their resolve to resist all wars. Faced with a crisis of a rather indeterminate nature, however, women groped for a core of issues around which to develop their ideas, but largely appear to have failed to do so. They seem to have done little more than voice their opposition to war with the overused phrase, 'We want no more war' (*sensō wa iya desu*).

The League of Women Voters of Japan also issued a declaration in which it emphasized Japanese women's 'mission to debunk the demagoguery of those who incited war, and to prevent war in accordance with the Potsdam Declaration and the Japanese Constitution'. While the statement announced the group's resolve to cooperate with women in other countries to achieve eternal peace, it presented no programme for specific action aimed at realizing that goal.[35]

Critics among women activists were dismayed over the paucity of ideas expressed at peace rallies, and deplored the inadequate verbal skills of speakers, who were unable to offer any meaningful insights that would further enrich the philosophy behind the nation's nascent peace movement. Noting the lack of skill among Japanese women to express their ideas in an effective manner, a foreign observer who attended a YWCA meeting said they needed to acquire the intellectual abilities that would enable them to play a meaningful role in society. One contributor to the *Josei Shimbun*, a YWCA organ, quoted Joseph Dodge, the US envoy who drew up the government's austerity budget for fiscal 1949, as saying the Japanese should know that not only Japan but the whole world was suffering. The contributor noted the parochialism of many Japanese peace activists, who were unable to develop a broader vision that transcended their own personal needs.[36]

The immature state of political consciousness among women and their inexperience in political activism combined with the rift between the conservative and leftist camps seriously to disrupt women's collaboration in organizing the peace movement.

The clash between conservatives and the political left

Past accounts of the women's peace movement in the late 1940s, given mainly by leftist writers, mostly blame conservatives for the failure of women activists to form a united front in the peace movement, on the grounds that conservative women were averse to politicizing issues and were bent on making their arguments as innocuous and uncontroversial as possible for fear of directly confronting the government.[37] The following will examine whether things were indeed as clear-cut as that, and whether the depiction of leftist activists as righteous in comparison to their conservative counterparts, will stand scrutiny.

While the peace activities of many groups in the late 1940s suffered from a lack of specific programmes for action, those of the political left, notably labour union members, were more successful in devising theoretical underpinnings for their acts because they were in the midst of fierce workplace or other struggles, to which they linked their peace activities. Leftists saw immediate threats to peace primarily in domestic factors, namely the feudalistic remnants in Japanese society that condemned women to lowly status, and the dominance of monopoly capital, both of which had persisted from the pre-war days. The thrust of their activities, they said, should be directed at emancipating women by enabling them to exercise their democratic rights and win better wages, thereby countering the efforts of those who pursued their warlike aims by subjugating them.

But when activists tried to organize collective action by bringing together women from across the entire ideological spectrum, the effort resulted in serious discord. The attitudes of female participants ran the gamut from a starry-eyed idealism that considered peace primarily as a moral or spiritual issue, to the strident militancy of those eager for direct action.

The battle lines were broadly drawn between the conservatives, including the League of Women Voters, the YWCA and the women's section of the Democratic Liberal Party (Minjitō) on one hand, and the centre-left Japanese Democratic Women's Association (Minpukyō), which included women's sections of labour unions, the Women's Democratic Club and members of the JCP.[38]

The conservatives tried to premise their peace activities on the slogan borrowed from the UNESCO charter that stated, 'Since wars begin in the minds of men, it is in the minds of men that the defences of peace must be constructed.' This gave rise to a catchphrase in Japanese, *kokoro no heiwa*, or 'peace in people's hearts'. The phrase 'peace emanating from people's hearts', while striking a sentimental chord in women with an idealistic bent, was regarded by leftists as a ploy to discourage peace activists from taking political action, and to restrict their activities to expressing pious prayers for peace. The conservatives, on the other hand, were furious at the leftists, thinking they were trying to force their idea of class struggle upon the women's peace movement, and refused to budge from their 'peace of the heart' line.[39]

Both camps, however, somehow managed to agree on six slogans to be adopted at a joint peace rally. The compromise slogans included both 'world peace emanating from peace in people's hearts' and 'opposition to low wages that could pave the way for war'.

After the slogans were decided, a battle for leadership ensued. The leftists backed writer Matsuoka Yōko as the head of the movement on the grounds that she was qualified to represent working women. The conservatives supported the YWCA leader Uemura Tamaki because of her experience in the international arena. The row over the selection of the leader prompted the withdrawal of the left-wing activists from joint peace activities, and the two camps decided to hold separate peace rallies.[40]

In August 1948, the conservatives' rally, which is said to have been attended by 1,500 people, adopted slogans calling for a fight against hunger, full implementation of the terms of the Potsdam Declaration, a respectable standard of living for workers, and the repatriation of Japanese still stranded abroad. The left-wing rally, at which labour unions and consumer cooperatives played a dominant role, is said to have drawn an audience of 2,000. They vowed to fight against low wages, cutbacks in food rations and the oppression of workers, and demanded the resignation of the cabinet led by Prime Minister Ashida Hitoshi.[41]

In May 1949, women's organizations of both the political right and left, in an attempt to patch things up, formed Fudankyō (the Association of Women's Organizations) with the participation of forty-four groups, and managed to hold a joint peace rally in August. The two camps decided to bury the hatchet, according to the conservative newspaper *The Nihon Fujin Shimbun*, in the belief that if a war ever broke out, the vast majority of people would suffer while only a handful would benefit.[42]

The joint declaration adopted at the rally stressed the plight of housewives, who feared another war and whose worries were compounded by increased unemployment, pay cuts and heavy taxes. The statement equated women's struggle against poverty with their fight for peace, and pointed out the need to identify the cause of their anxiety and initiate a movement to preserve peace. It concluded on a militant note, saying 'We must act in solidarity to oppose those who try to destroy peace.'[43]

In 1950, the joint group cooperated again to organize a demonstration celebrating the Women's Day on 10 April, which commemorated the first exercise of women's voting rights in Japanese history. The group, which included female members of the ruling Liberal Party as well as the JCP, once again bickered over their slogans. Conservatives opposed left-wing proposals to protest against US military bases, worker layoffs and price rises as part of the campaign for peace. Liberal Party members naturally were against any statement opposing the party's economic policy.[44]

In the end, the two camps split up again as leftists, in violation of a prior agreement, hoisted red flags and placards proclaiming radical slogans during the demonstration. As a result, they incurred the ire of other participants. With women's efforts to put up a united front again breaking down, Fudankyō did no more than issue a vague blanket statement – 'We want no more war' – when the Korean War broke out. Women of the political right and left subsequently ceased all collaboration.

After their initial anger subsided, some conservatives began to admit that the political right also shared some blame. The conservative *Nihon Fujin Shimbun* criticized the right for demonstrating far less interest in the group's joint discussions. The paper also faulted the prudishness of the *petits bourgeois*, who failed to take as much action as their counterparts on the left.[45]

The view was echoed by other leaders at the centre. Saitō Kiku, a delegate of the League of Women Voters, held the centre-right participants responsible for the joint group's division because of their intransigence towards the left. Yamataka Shigeri, who headed the national umbrella for regional women's organizations, also faulted the centre-right women's apparent lack of enthusiasm for the joint activities, and criticized them for mobilizing only a small number of women.[46]

According to Yamataka, about two-thirds of the women who took part in the demonstration of 10 April 1950 were members of labour unions. The *Nihon Fujin Shimbun* estimates the number of left-wing participants, including members of the JCP, the leftist Women's Democratic Club and labour unions, at some 1,000. At Fudankyō's gatherings, the massive numbers of left-wing activists eclipsed the presence of centre-right participants, and they often tried to impress or intimidate others with thunderous applause whenever their colleagues took the podium.[47]

The overall political climate of the late 1940s, which was marked by massive layoffs and escalating labour strife, appears to have made suprapartisan cooperation among women virtually impossible. Female officials of the JCP said there were too many party members in the demonstration and that they were unable to persuade all of them to put down their flags and placards. They also admitted that they failed to win the understanding of rank-and-file party members, which suggests the implacable attitude of those involved in fierce struggles on a daily basis, and their determination to conduct the peace movement in a militant manner whether conservative activists liked it or not.[48]

The foregoing suggests that a majority of ordinary women with a conservative outlook were apathetic towards the peace movement. It should be noted, however, that a relatively small number of women belonging to conservative groups did react quickly to the political uncertainties caused by the Cold War. This is quite remarkable considering that amid the increasingly intolerant political climate of the late 1940s, the peace movement was stigmatized in the minds of the general public as being a creation of the Reds (*aka*). Conservative women defied such public censure presumably because of a sense of urgency fuelled by the perceived threat to peace.

Despite its differences with left-wing groups over how to conduct the peace movement, the League of Women Voters decided as early as May 1948 to organize a joint gathering with other women's groups in the cause of preserving peace.[49] The group had been led by Ichikawa Fusae, a leading figure in the pre-war suffragist movement. According to a report by *Josei Kaizō* magazine, while Ichikawa had been banned from public office because of her cooperation with the wartime government, a divisive debate was held between the group's right- and left-wing camps, in which the left insisted that the League should support left-wing political parties. The conservatives defeated the left and took control of the group, but it nonetheless continued to cut a prominent figure in the nation's peace movement.[50]

The YWCA also played a conspicuous role in the peace movement despite its small membership. Its leaders had close ties with overseas Christian groups, and had been aware from early on of the need to face up to Japan's war crimes, as they had contact with other Asians who had suffered from Japan's invasion. Watanabe Michiko, who later became chairman of the YWCA, recalled that although Christians had suffered persecution during the war, they were also aware that their conduct during the conflict was not entirely free of blame. And so the YWCA began its post-war activities by tackling the issue of Japan's war crimes.[51]

Christianity's emphasis on moral rectitude and spiritual matters generated a kind of conservative outlook that prevented women from undertaking bold political initiatives that would be out of line with the generally accepted sense of decorum. Indeed, the YWCA was not known for taking radical political action. Still, the group was active in the peace movement, whose hallmarks were a sense of contrition for Japanese aggression and an international approach aimed at promoting solidarity with women in other countries.

Among conservative political parties, the women's section of the Democratic Liberal Party was reported to be involved in the peace movement in an effort to win over untapped constituencies of ordinary housewives. The party argued that a sound conservative party was best positioned to promote peace in Japan, and put peace on its agenda because it was a topical issue that would draw the attention of a significant number of ordinary women.[52]

In previous historical accounts, it was often said that the main bone of contention in the peace movement of the late 1940s was whether to restrict the movement to seeking only the peace of the heart as demanded by conservatives, or to take a more left-wing line and make economic issues an integral part of the peace agenda. But a closer look at the activities of individual groups reveals the actual picture was not so clear-cut. One JCP official, for example, claimed to have cooperated closely through Fudankyō with the YWCA and regional women's organizations to call for a comprehensive peace, and work on economic issues that concerned ordinary households.[53]

Admittedly, any joint statements issued by Fudankyō, which comprised groups from across a wide ideological spectrum, were products of great compromise. Still, members making up the joint group shared a vague fear that peace was being jeopardized by an anonymous few who might be conspiring to profit from war, and Fudankyō managed to issue a resolute protest against 'those who were trying to destroy peace'. And as was noted, conservative groups could not afford to be indifferent to the serious economic issues that faced ordinary housewives.

Women's groups managed to find broad common ground regarding both the political and economic aspects of the peace movement, and found considerable scope for cooperation. Available accounts of the run-up to the collapse of their collaboration in 1950 suggest that the final split was caused by the political rivalry and intransigent attitudes of the extreme right and left, which became pronounced due to the intense acrimony of the general political scene, rather than by ideological differences.

The Korean War

The response of non-activists

The vague fears of the public concerning the possibility of hostilities starting in one or other of the world's numerous trouble spots amid the Cold War were vindicated by the outbreak of the Korean War. Major women's groups, however, had abandoned efforts to form a united front with regard to the war. With none of the groups wielding any significant influence on public opinion, the initial response to the crisis in Korea varied widely from one woman to another.

The primary concern of many women was peace solely for Japan. One Tokyo housewife said: 'I was genuinely shocked. I can hardly concentrate on my work as I keep thinking about how peace can be preserved for Japan.'[54] Some women voiced strong support for the United Nations forces, saying the UN was not waging a war in Korea but trying to achieve peace there. They said they wanted to see the UN punish the North Korean invaders, and expressed horror at the thought of what would become of Japan if it were not for the UN.[55]

Others unabashedly pressed their economic agenda because the economic fallout from the war mattered the most to them. An editorial in the Japanese Housewives Association's organ *Shufuren Dayori* lamented the oppressive mood and anxiety that had spread in Japan as a result of the war, and urged women to fight the coming economic hardship by mustering the same kind of courage they had demonstrated immediately after World War II. The newspaper, which said the primary goal of the group's peace movement was to fight inflation, mentioned nothing but the economic concerns of Japanese women. A vice-chairman of the association expressed her hope that the war would not have a serious impact on food supplies. In accordance with its primary concerns, the group called on the government to increase imports of daily necessities, prevent speculative buying and reduce taxes.[56]

Others, who were resolutely pacifist, summarily condemned all kinds of war whatever the cause of the fighting. Among such women, the head of the Zentei postal union's women's section said that though it was not clear who started the Korean War, she was totally against the use of military force to resolve disputes.[57]

But none of these ideas appear to have been compelling enough to prompt a large number of ordinary women into some kind of action to make their voices heard.

A dearth of newspaper stories about ordinary people's views on the Korean War is indicative of the degree to which censorship had been tightened by the occupation authorities.[58] The *Asahi Shimbun* printed few letters to the editor about the war. A letter from a housewife in Tokyo which appeared in the 1 July 1950 issue of the newspaper speaks of her sadness to see Korea engulfed in the war, and anxiety for her Korean friends who had so selflessly helped her after Japan's defeat. The letter expressed sorrow at

Prehistory and the early post-war years 143

events which were totally beyond her control, and ended innocuously enough with a pious prayer for Korea instead of a protest against the war.[59]

General reticence about the Korean War, however, does not seem attributable only to SCAP censorship and crackdowns. The women activists this author has interviewed say that although they continued to be involved in some kind of social movement during the Korean War, they recall few memorable things about the conflict except for the widespread public fear of Japan becoming embroiled in the hostilities.

A column in the *Asahi Shimbun*, for example, tells of people fearing they might have to evacuate to a safer place, and laments that in its preoccupation with personal concerns, the public appears to have forgotten to think seriously about world peace, although they had so earnestly wished for it briefly after Japan's defeat.[60] Reflecting the public's heightened materialistic concerns, the government, and the 7 August 1950 and 4 March 1951 issues of the newspaper, found it necessary expressly to urge housewives not to buy too much in advance just to beat inflation.[61]

One housewife who took part in a discussion organized by *Fujin Asahi* magazine said, 'It is inconceivable that we have any business directly fighting on a battlefield since we have [already] renounced the use of arms.' The remark suggests that she believed the Constitution had already totally obviated the need for Japan to consider how to respond to a war, because it went without saying that it would not fight. That said, people no longer had to busy themselves thinking about which course of diplomatic action Japan should take. The housewife continued:

> We housewives should stick to our obligation not to disturb the social order. For example, there are people who buy too much just to beat inflation now that prices have begun rising because of the Korean conflict and thereby disturb the public order. If we are influenced by the actions of such people, we will disturb our peace ourselves. We will make a step toward peace if we reflect upon our situation and fight the influence of those people.[62]

According to her, peace begins with the efforts of individuals to maintain decent moral conduct and preserve the stability of the small society in which they live.

Another woman admitted that when the housewives' association she belonged to agreed they should not buy too many goods to beat inflation, they made the decision out of nothing more than financial concern. She said:

> We are having such a hard time just to buy food for dinner each day so we don't want to think about deeper issues. The only thing we can do is refrain from speculative buying. We simply proposed that we should try to learn more from one another [about things in general].[63]

144 *Prehistory and the early post-war years*

These housewives were later criticized by other readers for worrying about the war only because of their own personal concerns and failing to express any resolute intention to oppose the conflict. Their critics also noted the general tendency among women to be concerned mainly about matters such as inflation, their own future and their children's education. Other readers from poorer rural areas expressed outrage that middle-class housewives had the luxury of worrying about speculative buying and their children's education while those in farming areas, who led a hand-to-mouth existence, were too poor to even think about such things.[64]

On the whole, the serious material difficulties they faced on a daily basis appears to have turned the attitudes of many women inward and made them avert their eyes from the war in Korea. One woman teacher noted that whenever she asked people she knew what Japan should do about the conflict in Korea, most cited the occupation and said, 'It can't be helped' (*shikata ga nai*).[65] Powerlessness in the face of the occupation appears to have sapped the will to give any deep thought to the war. Another woman recalled, 'I could see nothing but the absence of feeling that resembled a sense of resignation on the faces of other returnees [from the Asian mainland] who must feel [as intensely as] I do about Korea.'[66]

A lack of political awareness is also evident in the example of the above-cited housewife, who considered the role women could play to promote peace in terms of civic duties they were supposed to discharge in their capacity as housewives. Her idea hardly differs from the pre-war and wartime official propaganda, which called on women to know their place (strictly within their households), and exhorted them to contribute to the public good by fulfilling their duties at home, for example, by saving money and being frugal. Inane as the profession of her duties may sound, it is difficult to have expected her to think otherwise. Official post-war propaganda had done little more than expound in abstract terms Japan's new mission of redemption by transforming itself into a peaceful and cultured nation, and was quite short on specifics as to how individuals could play a role in helping to achieve such a grandiose goal. Most ordinary women were probably baffled by the wide gap between the new official propaganda's idealistic aspirations and their own mundane personal existence, which had not undergone as sweeping a change as the nation's official precepts. So she mouthed what decorum required her to say in a public forum. The parochialism of her view bespeaks the absence of change in women's political outlook four years after they were granted the right to vote.

The failure of ordinary women to protest against the Korean War appears attributable to widespread apathy and a lack of political awareness that made it difficult for women to think about matters beyond their personal concerns, rather than to any fears about a SCAP crackdown. As a result, most women appear to have lacked any deep understanding about the war.

Prehistory and the early post-war years 145

The response of activists and women's organizations

Following the outbreak of the Korean War, women workers belonging to the Sanbetsu-dominated Zenrōren labour federation began a peace movement at their workplace. The women's section of the JSP also voiced anti-war views and demonstrated a more pacifist stand on the matter than the party leadership, which condemned North Korea's invasion and gave moral support to the United Nations' 'police action' in Korea. Women members of the JSP called the war 'extremely deplorable', appealed for Japan's neutrality in the conflict, and criticized the party's stand on the war.

But on the whole, any open protest against the war was quite limited. Peace campaigners were hampered by the ideological muddle over who was responsible for the war, as well as organizational disarray because the Red Purge barred left-wing activists, who would have spearheaded anti-war activities, from openly leading the peace movement. Besides the harsh crackdown by SCAP that anti-war campaigners would inevitably face, the Allied occupation of Japan, which excluded Japan from the diplomatic process, made it difficult for Japanese pacifists to conceive any course of action Japan could take with regard to the Korean War.

The League of Women Voters' organ, *Fujin Yūkensha*, for example, admitted that Japan had something to do with Korea's current plight, given its past colonial rule of the peninsula. But it went on to say that Japan had no right to intervene in other countries' affairs because it had yet to conclude a peace treaty with the Allied nations or regain its sovereignty. The publication, however, concluded that

> It should be the duty of Japan actively to sue for peace if another world war looms, since it has voluntarily renounced war after its defeat and has become a genuinely pacifist nation. There is no doubt all Japanese are hoping the war that rages in Korea will end as soon as possible.[67]

Despite the earnest tone in which it professed Japan's duty, the statement also sounds like an admission that Japan could do nothing but pray for an end to the hostilities.

Even among leftists, only a few appear to have expressed vocal opposition to the war itself. At a peace rally held by Minpukyō, the association of left-wing women's groups, and PTAs on 25 July 1950, women agreed that the education of children was of particular importance if peace was to be promoted in Japan, and that children would not learn to love peace unless men learned to respect women. The participants also discussed household issues as part of the peace campaign. A resolution passed at another rally held by women's groups in Setagaya, Tokyo, on the same day, read:

> We never want any more war.

146 *Prehistory and the early post-war years*

> We will never let our beloved husbands, children, brothers or boyfriends take part in another war.
>
> We call on all countries of the world not to build any atomic or hydrogen bombs. Japanese women, who have experienced the atomic bombings of Hiroshima and Nagasaki, should spearhead the world peace movement.[68]

Women like these apparently braved the difficulty of conducting peace activities under SCAP's watchful eyes. But their frequently uttered anti-war statement, 'We want no more war' (*sensō wa iya desu*), gave no clear indication as to what kind of stand they took on the war in Korea and what should be done to stop the fighting. The anti-war sentiment voiced in the above-cited slogans draws exclusively on motivation stemming from their own personal needs or experiences; and whether intentionally or not, women activists seemed to be skirting the debate over the war in Korea.

Activists in those days recalled that 'peace' became a taboo word after the outbreak of the Korean War, and that to phrase their anti-war sentiment in the form of an appeal for a comprehensive peace was the most they could do during the Allied occupation.[69] Vigorous signature drives staged by some activists in response to the Stockholm Appeal called for a ban on the use of nuclear weapons, but fell short of constituting direct criticism of the Korean War. Kondō Yūko, former editor in chief of the *Fujin Minshu Shimbun*, recalled that many members of the Women's Democratic Club shared the view that US envoy John Foster Dulles's anti-communist diplomacy in South Korea and many other parts of the world had paved the way for the war, because they believed that impoverished North Korea could never have launched a military attack. But according to Kondō, the club was unable to organize an anti-war protest because its JCP members, who made up a significant proportion of the group, could no longer lead such activities.[70]

Following the split between the political right and left, major women's groups failed to hold their annual joint peace rally in August 1950. Those at the centre or centre-right of the ideological spectrum were either hesitant about expressing their opinions on the war or actively supported the US military action.

Regional women's organizations voiced caution about organizing a peace rally on the grounds that their peace activities had been hijacked in the past by those who had tried to turn them into a pro-Soviet peace movement.[71]

While keeping their distance from the left-wing peace movement, conservatives, including the YWCA, the women's section of the Liberal Party and regional women's groups, organized studies on how to achieve peace with the stated aim of cultivating critical thinking on issues relating to peace.[72] Since the women's sections of the Liberal and Democratic parties as well as the YWCA supported Japan's cooperation with the UN action in Korea, some of these women, including members of regional women's organizations and PTAs, and students at women's schools, did more than express moral support for the UN forces: they sent presents to UN soldiers, visited hospitals to comfort wounded servicemen and donated blood for the wounded.[73]

Amid the general political trend of the so-called reverse course, conservative activists appeared to be gaining the upper hand over their left-wing counterparts in the propaganda war. According to the 20 August 1950 issue of the *Fujin Shimbun*, women members of the Liberal Party actively promoted party policies shortly after the outbreak of the war, while other women's organizations generally refrained from staging any peace activities. Conservatives advocated anti-communism and continued to reiterate their usual 'peace of the heart' line to counter the influence of the political left.[74] They stepped up calls for women to stay home and concentrate on child rearing, and sounded a patriotic note, urging women to 'rearm their minds' in the face of heightened international tension.[75]

The war in Korea was the first major issue to prompt women peace activists to have serious doubts about their earlier peace activities, when they were unable to put forward any substantive ideas to support their anti-war sentiment and did little more than chant 'no more wars'. On 19 October 1950, the chairman of an entity called the Japanese UN Association spoke before some forty representatives from thirty women's groups, saying

> It has become evident the UN alone can preserve world peace. If the UN police force calls on Japan [to send its men to the war], we must resolutely comply with the request and we want ladies' understanding on this matter.

The audience, which included members of conservative political parties, the YWCA, regional women's organizations and the League of Women Voters, as well as those from the JSP and Nikkyōso schoolteachers, were rendered speechless as apparently even the political right was not ready for the consequences of their support for the UN forces, which might necessitate Japan to send men to the fighting.[76]

The 30 October 1950 editorial of the conservative *Nihon Fujin Shimbun* stated that if Japan were to conclude a peace treaty with the Allied nations and recover its sovereignty as soon as possible, it should discharge its responsibilities towards the free world so that it could get back on its own two feet. It declared that

> Our earlier vow to preserve peace even at the cost of our own lives would prove empty if we just look the other way, leaving an arsonist to his own devices, and do not catch him or put out the fire together with the peoples who love justice.

The editorial marked the newspaper's explicit break with absolute pacifism as called for by the Constitution.

Both the political right and left failed to clarify their stands with regard to the Korean War in a way that would justify either their belief in absolute pacifism in the case of liberals and leftists, or their calls for Japan's non-involvement in active combat in the case of conservatives. Left-wing women, while opposing all kinds of war, neither proposed concrete measures aimed at ending the war nor explained how it was possible to resolve the conflict without resorting to military force. Conservatives supported the UN action in the belief that Japan would not be called upon to take part in actual combat. But these women did not fully consider how their support for the UN action in Korea could square with their pacifist stance that took for granted Japan's non-involvement in any war, or whether Japan's support for the UN would eventually necessitate Japan's participation in a 'war aimed at restoring world peace'. Their stand implicitly revealed that they believed that the renunciation of war as called for by the Constitution was a principle that applied only to Japan.

The peace treaty debate

While the occupation of Japan and the lack of sufficient information about the actual state of the Korean War made it extremely difficult for the Japanese to tackle the issue beyond their own country, policy matters of direct concern to Japan, such as concluding a peace treaty with Japan's former enemies and rearmament, helped some women to explore ways in which Japan could pursue a pacifist policy, in somewhat more concrete terms. A well known initiative on this matter was taken by a group of female intellectuals.

Impatient with others who did not take any action, Hiratsuka Raichō drafted a request addressed to John Foster Dulles, calling on the US to work out a system under which Japan would continue to renounce war and remain unarmed in accordance with the Constitution after its independence. The document also stated that Japan should carry out its mission to work for world peace by maintaining absolute neutrality while helping the world's two adversarial camps to come to terms with each other through peaceful means and signing a comprehensive peace treaty that would guarantee non-aggression by other nations. It also expressed hopes that an international treaty pledging all nations to non-aggression against an unarmed Japan would deprive any country of any reason to maintain military facilities in Japan. The request, which was dated 26 June 1950, a day after the outbreak of the Korean War, was co-signed by Gauntlett Tsuneko (1873–1953), Uemura Tamaki (1890–1982), Jōdai Tano (1886–1982) and the writer Nogami Yaeko (1885–1985).[77] With the exception of Hiratsuka and Nogami, the remaining three women were all leaders of Christian groups.

These women sent another request to Dulles in February 1951, and another similar joint statement was issued in August of the same year by a larger number of women leaders.

In these statements, the signatories professed their belief in an absolute pacifism inspired by the Constitution, which they vowed to practise no matter how the international situation changed, and expressed hopes that Japan's pacifist policy would lead other nations to follow suit and pave the way for world peace. The women's third statement argued that the pacifism called for by the Constitution had become the moral underpinning of the new Japan that was reborn after the war. According to them, the new pacifist principle was to be defended even at the cost of suffering foreign aggression, because if Japan could not live up to that new ideal, it would lose its national identity and become prey to moral decay. They also called for a comprehensive peace on the grounds that Japan needed to achieve reconciliation with all of its former enemies (see Appendix II).

Rearmament, which would be in violation of the Constitution, was opposed also on the grounds that it could resurrect militarism, undermine democracy in Japan and force a heavy tax burden on the impoverished Japanese people.[78]

Like the JSP, the women also looked up to the UN to protect Japan's national security, but argued that Japan's security should be ensured through every conceivable effort except the use of military force. Hopes were expressed that Japan and the rest of Asia should make up the 'third force' that belonged neither to the US nor the Soviet camp.[79]

In opposing US military installations and rearmament, which they argued would heighten tensions in the Far East and could pave the way for war, the women said that they would not worry about any security vacuum that could result from the absence of a national defence, because they believed that the human spirit, supported by [universal] truth, was mightier than 10 million troops or any state-of-the-art weaponry. In concluding the third statement, the women conceded that politicians, diplomats and business leaders would most likely consider their ideas to be unrealistic. The women, however, pointed out that such experts tended to lose sight of humanism. The female signatories to the document pledged to think and act from the standpoint of humanism, as women and mothers who sought to protect invaluable human lives.

Hiratsuka Raichō, who took the initiative in the joint action, said she was seeking to break with the approaches of earlier peace activists, who just chanted 'no more wars' or based their peace activities on religious grounds. Hiratsuka said she was trying to present ideas that transcended political sectarianism and reflected the conscience of Japanese women.[80]

As Kanō Mikiyo and other researchers have made clear, it should also be noted that their communiqués confronted Japan's war crimes more squarely than any other major organization had done.[81] This presents a sharp contrast to Sōhyō's stand on the issue as unionists were absorbed in a desperate economic struggle. Sōhyō called for exempting Japan from paying war reparations due to the country's destitute condition. The women's second joint statement began by saying that Japanese women, while always wishing for peace, had not staked their lives on achieving peace and as a result had failed to prevent the tragic war. It was out of their sense of remorse, the statement declared, that they had resolved not to go to war against any country regardless of the circumstances. They said that Japan should pay compensation for the damage it had inflicted on its Asian neighbours through its aggression, and that its lack of economic means could not serve as an excuse for failing to do so.[82]

The passage appears to reflect the outlook of Christian women on Japan's war crimes as well as Hiratsuka's idealistic bent. As was stated earlier in this chapter, Christians had conducted rigorous self-criticism about their conduct during the war. The Tokyo military trials of war criminals had in particular served as an occasion of deep reflection for Christians. The sense of remorse expressed in columns of the YWCA organ *Josei Shimbun* is in line with the Christian confessional tradition, which attaches importance to coming to terms with one's sins. With regard to the trials, one writer said

> We shall all accept these sentences (handed down to the war criminals) with a deep sense of contrition. The 25 defendants at the trials are all reflections of ourselves. ... Japan's conduct over the last 40 years has been exposed [by the tribunal]. The Japanese have oppressed the weak and exploited and committed atrocities against others in the name of fighting communism and building a co-prosperity sphere. In the face of these revelations, we can't help but turn away our eyes. This is what our fellow Japanese, no, we ourselves planned and carried out.[83]

Leftists often criticized Christians for narrowing the debate over peace to the spiritual realm, and disparaged their oft-used phrase 'peace of the heart' as lacking in substance or offering no basis for concrete action. But the Christian activists considered 'peace of the heart' to be a vital matter of conscience that encompassed issues of Japan's responsibility for the war, and they believed it to be an integral part of their peace philosophy. Consideration of Japan's war responsibility was largely missing in leftist women's arguments regarding peace issues in the early post-war period, although they became more willing to consider the matter than their conservative counterparts in later years.[84]

Many of the signatories to the three documents were so-called conservatives, who had frequently been at odds with left-wing groups whenever they tried to organize joint peace activities. They were wary of any political party's attempt to exploit the peace movement for its own political gain because the bad blood between the political right and left became even more pronounced as time went by. Despite efforts to keep their distance from the political left, the women's stand on the peace treaty and rearmament was more or less the same as that of the Marxist-dominated left wing of the JSP, except that the women were even more explicit in their commitment to absolute pacifism, and on this point they were more radical than the JSP.

Their joint statements won broad approval from a wide sector of women activists, including those representing conservative regional women's organizations as well as those on the left such as the Women's Democratic Club, which incorporated the ideas into their peace activities.[85] The broad support enjoyed by the three statements demonstrates that despite their frequent spats, there continued to be considerable common ground between the right- and left-wing camps, as in the earlier years of the Cold War.

It should also be noted that not only Hiratsuka but also Uemura and Gauntlett drew their inspiration from the conscientious objectors of Western nations in advocating absolute pacifism.[86] As such, the intellectuals' three documents were a declaration of their moral faith as well as diplomatic policy recommendations, and that moral element was far more pronounced in their ideas than in the four peace principles advocated by the JSP and organized labour.

The moralistic and idealistic ideas set out in the three statements, however, owed much to the privileged status of the authors, which enabled them to acquire a wide knowledge about peace thought both in Japan and abroad. Thus their appeal might have been limited mainly to well-read members of the public and committed activists. While favourably received by peace activists, the statements apparently failed to attract a significant number of converts from among ordinary women.

Meanwhile, a new rift developed in the women's peace movement as those further to the right, such as conservative women MPs, broke ranks with other peace activists and failed to oppose rearmament, pleading party policy. Such women began to express doubts about the feasibility of practising absolute pacifism, and embraced 'realpolitik' to approve the US military presence in Japan and the establishment of Japan's own armed forces. They became increasingly critical of 'irrational' pacifists who opposed rearmament.[87]

7 The rise of a grassroots peace movement

It is well known that following the Bikini hydrogen bomb test of 1954, the number of ordinary women involved in the anti-bomb and other peace movements, became massive enough at times to force the government to deal with them. But what were the factors that inspired so many women to resort to direct action? Did any significant attitudinal change take place among women in the run-up to and after Bikini? And did their thoughts about peace issues evolve in a notable way from the late 1940s? The following will attempt to answer these questions.

Stirrings prior to the Bikini H-bomb test

The generally oppressive mood of society amid the political repression of left-wing activists during the Korean War, together with economic hardship, acted to blight the growth of political consciousness among ordinary women, as was seen in the previous chapter.

Against this backdrop, however, conscious efforts were made, mainly by schoolteachers, to encourage women to awaken to political matters. The following sections will divide women into schoolteachers, leftwing activists, and ordinary women with no political affiliation, and examine the nature of their activities and thoughts which prepared the conditions under which the ban-the-bomb movement was organized.

Networking by teachers

In the general absence of political activism at the grassroots, left-wing peace activists could not help but concede defeat when they were unable to organize an effective movement in the face of the Red Purge and the Korean War. But stirrings that later contributed to the rapid spread of the antinuclear movement were never stamped out, even when the overall peace movement hit its nadir. The single largest organization behind women's grassroots peace activities was Nikkyōso.

Though the teachers' union became one of the prime targets of massive public-sector job cuts and the Red Purge, its women's section persevered and it defied SCAP's threat to sentence its members to hard labour in Okinawa if it did not disband.[1]

The union, which had tackled mainly economic issues until then, rethought its earlier policy as a sense of crisis spread with the outbreak of the Korean War and the establishment of the police reserve, the forerunner of Japan's Self-Defence Forces. That prompted Chiba Chiyose, a female Nikkyōso official, to propose the slogan, 'Never send our students to the battlefield'. The May 1951 convention, where the union adopted the slogan, turned into a scene of tearful teachers owning up to their wartime responsibility for indoctrinating children with militarism and exhorting them to go to war. The union henceforth began to take up peace education in earnest.[2]

At Nikkyōso's annual conferences for pedagogical research, teachers engaged in heated discussions on the urgent task of giving children a decent level of education amid the general economic hardship. Pedagogical issues greatly absorbed teachers also because they had great difficulty teaching democracy to their pupils. For several years immediately after the war, the Ministry of Education and teachers cooperated closely in disseminating democratic ideals at schools as prescribed by the occupation authorities. Teachers, however, began to doubt their ability to teach democracy when the ministry started to back-pedal on its new post-war policy to promote democracy and pacifism in school education. By September 1950, the ministry began promoting the use of the national flag and the singing of the national anthem at schools. Teachers were at a loss about how to teach democracy also because many of them still had difficulty coping with the radical shift from the militaristic education of the wartime years. Debates at the union's annual pedagogical conferences in the 1950s became all the more earnest as teachers tried to devise a systematic approach to teaching democracy at school.[3]

Against this backdrop, women teachers decided to hold all-women research conferences.[4] One of the key topics at the first conference, which the union claims was attended by some 3,000 participants, was the rowdy behaviour of American servicemen and prostitutes around US military bases, which became a matter of particularly serious concern to women following the outbreak of the Korean War. The incidence of rape is said to have increased sharply as many soldiers went out of control before they were due to leave for Korea or during leave. Teachers discussed the influence of red-light districts on children and ways to banish the 'warlike' culture that had spread during the Korean War in the form of war toys. According to the former Nikkyōso official Hashiguchi Kazuko,[5] teachers and housewives conducted oblique protests against the presence of the US military in Japan through their campaigns aimed at banishing war toys such as toy guns and soldiers, which had become widely popular among children, because they were unable directly to oppose the American bases.[6]

At the second women teachers' research conference held in February 1953, Egashira Chiyoko, a participant from Nagasaki who had lost her husband, mother and four children to the atomic bombing, spoke about her experience, and she became the first A-bomb victim to tell her story on national radio.[7]

The third conference was held in January 1954, shortly before legislation was submitted to the Diet to ban teachers from engaging in political activities, and a sense of crisis prompted women teachers to decide to organize joint activities with the mothers of their students.

According to Nikkyōso's own claims, participants in the subsequent movement to form societies of mothers and women teachers (*haha jo no kai*) organized a total of 6,400 meetings in almost all municipalities across the country, which were attended by some 1.6 million people.[8] Some teachers also joined forces with housewives who had been organized by the labour unions their husbands belonged to. Such housewives demonstrated considerable militancy in support of their husbands' workplace struggles.[9] The focus of the small teachers' and mothers' groups was in most cases on immediate issues in the local community and personal matters facing mothers and children, rather than on national or other broader political issues. That helped to develop the infrastructure for regional activism in many parts of Japan, and later made it possible to organize anti-nuclear campaigns, as well as the movement for the Mothers' Congress, on a nationwide scale from the mid-1950s onward.

As of early 1954, or shortly before the Bikini test, activist teachers had not been conducting a peace movement as understood in the usual sense. Nikkyōso faced widespread criticism from the public, which had a visceral dislike of red-flag-waving unionists, and considered the actions of Nikkyōso members to be politically motivated. Many school authorities also discouraged teachers' attempts to offer peace education. Teachers themselves were also often stumped for ideas when they explored ways to conduct peace education.[10] The harsh economic and social realities facing their students' families also prevented them from developing political awareness on peace issues.

Nikkyōso adopted a slogan exhorting its members to participate in activities aimed at promoting peace (*heiwa o kakuho surutameno jissen*), and many teachers did this in the form of offering community services in poverty-stricken areas.[11] They argued that the condition of women and children in rural areas, who were resigned to their miserable existence and made no effort to improve their lot, was exactly the same as the social ills that had afflicted pre-war Japan and helped to prompt the country's slide into war. The teachers, therefore, worked to improve the economic condition of such women, and also tried to ameliorate their lowly family status on the grounds that their emancipation from material privation as well as efforts to have their basic human rights respected would help them to cultivate a more positive outlook on their own lives and society at large. The actions of the activist teachers were premised on the hope that peace would eventually emanate from the happiness of people resulting from the democratization of their personal relationships and the fight against poverty.[12]

Teachers conducted research into the lives of residents in their local communities, many of whom were struggling both economically and mentally as a result of the loss of family members to the war, as well as on the lifestyles of women and children, who continued to suffer from the feudalistic attitude of male heads of household and in-laws who paid scant attention to their need for self-fulfilment. Teachers argued that since the feudalistic social mores, which women and children took for granted and against which they had failed to put up any resistance, had done much to facilitate the escalation of Japan's war of aggression, both women and children should fight their tendencies uncritically to obey their superiors and assert their rights to happiness and freedom. Women and children were also urged to develop an independent way of thinking, and to learn to look at things from a more critical standpoint.[13]

Some teachers spearheaded campaigns against US military bases by educating local residents about the injustice of their lands being expropriated for use by the military.[14] Fostering a peace-loving attitude became one of their main methods of promoting peace, and some teachers urged their pupils to be kind to others and refrain from using bad language or denigrating others, in the name of peace.[15]

In a reversal of pre-war school education that sought to groom the young for death in the name of the emperor, Nikkyōso reiterated the importance of each individual life. For women, who had known little else but the daily struggle to provide for themselves and their families, it required some mental prodding to understand the relevance of this new idea to their own lives. One thirty-two-year-old female farmer from Akita Prefecture left her town for the first time since her wedding to attend a major convention organized by women teachers and mothers. On the first night of her trip, she worried about her cattle and apple orchard before giving any thought to her husband and children. But after attending the convention, she said it dawned on her that her children were more important than her cattle and apples and that she should not live for her livestock and orchards but for her children.[16]

A teacher from Shizuoka Prefecture said she had invited her pupils' mothers, who had been preoccupied with farm work, to write about their lives, and that such reflection helped many to develop an active interest in their children.[17]

The method of the teachers' peace activities was dictated largely by the dire condition in which their pupils' families lived, so they tackled peace issues as if they were indistinguishable from people's economic concerns and personal problems. Through this down-to-earth approach to the peace movement, as well as the genuine dedication they demonstrated in trying to alleviate the plight of the needy, women teachers achieved varying degrees of success in getting housewives to attend meetings and winning their support. This was by no means a small achievement because the prevalent conservative public attitude made it extremely difficult for many housewives to engage in activities outside the home. Women feared the disapproval of their families and neighbours for doing something other than housework. They were able to attend PTA and other gatherings organized by teachers because they were supposed to discuss their children's education, and were secure in the knowledge that people would not think they were indulging their personal interests. Activities by women teachers served in many cases as the initial catalyst for housewives' activism.[18]

Left-wing activists

The teachers' approach of linking peace issues to immediate problems facing ordinary people was commonly used by other activists in the left-wing camp to recruit housewives. In an apparent effort to facilitate women's understanding of the peace treaty issue, the Women's Democratic Club carried in its organ the *Fujin Minshu Shimbun* an article with the eye-catching title, 'How will the peace treaty affect your kitchen?' In the article, the academic and peace activist Hirano Yoshitarō explained to the two housewives who interviewed him the likely economic implications of Japan's decision on whether to conclude a comprehensive or partial peace treaty. The housewives asked Hirano whether the signing of a peace treaty would alleviate their economic difficulty, to which Hirano responded by saying that a partial treaty that would exclude China from the peace process would perpetuate Japan's reliance on the US, and make it impossible for Japan to attain economic independence because its international trade would be restricted.[19]

Leftists took a thoroughly materialistic view in explaining the cause of the perceived threat to peace. Six members of the Women's Democratic Club chapter in Suginami, Tokyo, who were eking out a meagre living by taking on manual piecework, asked one another why power rates, rice prices and public bath fees had suddenly begun to soar, while utility rates charged to industrial plants were much lower. The women concluded that the plants were allowed to use cheap electricity at the expense of ordinary consumers to make supplies needed for another war. The women subsequently began an anti-war signature drive, saying, 'People at the very bottom rung like us have no choice but to oppose war.'[20] By a similar logic, other housewives in many parts of Tokyo and elsewhere attributed rising prices to the government's intention to conclude a partial peace treaty and sought neighbours' signatures in support of their belief that people's economic condition would not improve unless Japan signed a comprehensive peace treaty. They argued that the government was severely hurting people's lives through its policy of squandering resources on the production of military supplies, and cutting Japan off from trade with China and other countries by concluding a partial peace.[21]

While Hiratsuka Raichō and the female Christian leaders wrote to John Foster Dulles, stressing the need for Japan to carry out its moral mission to practise absolute pacifism, many other women also wrote to the US envoy. Some such women sharing leftist views, however, appeared to have done so

The rise of a grassroots peace movement 157

out of personal economic concerns and to plead with him to work out a peace treaty that would alleviate their desperate condition. In a plaintive letter, one invalid housewife said

> I wonder if you know what a hard life many women, who have lost their husbands and children, are leading in Japan. I wonder if you know how many women are being forced to take up a shovel as day labourers to work with rough men or dying with their children in their arms because they no longer have the means to earn a living ... Mr Dulles, if you are a good man, I beseech you to work to bring peace to the whole world.[22]

Anti-war sentiment influenced by left-wing thought was demonstrated at its most dramatic among housewives organized by labour unions. Unions had been enlisting member's wives since around 1949 amid the escalation of labour strife. One group of housewives, for example, whose husbands worked for a printing company in Yokohama, turned into political activists after a labour dispute in March 1950 in which the company decided to hand over its plant site for use by the US military. Alongside the unionists, housewives squared off with hundreds of American MPs and armed police, and were detained overnight as a result of their involvement. The political lesson they learned through that experience turned the housewives into vigorous campaigners against rearmament.[23]

The attitude of female leftists towards the Korean War further makes it clear that their calls for peace were motivated primarily by domestic concerns. Their reticence about the Korean War was mentioned in Chapter 6 above, and was illustrated with a quotation from the 12 August 1950 issue of the *Fujin Minshu Shimbun*. Nine months later that attitude did not appear to have changed much, while the war raged on. Although a small number of leftists conducted vigorous street protests against a partial peace and rearmament, they concentrated almost entirely on domestic issues, as indicated by the slogans adopted at one peace rally held in 1951, apparently by left-wing women's organizations. The slogans read as follows:

> We will stake our lives to oppose a war to which we could lose our children, husbands and brothers.

> Let us conclude a peace treaty and be reconciled with all nations.

> We oppose a military build-up that would raise prices and taxes.

> We call on the government to protect the livelihoods of working mothers.

> Let us promote the education and culture that would be most suitable for our children, who will work for the betterment of the future world.

Let us improve our economic condition by calling for enlightened government policies.[24]

In the newspaper published by the left-wing women's federation Minpukyō, a columnist argued that the Chinese, who had fought the Japanese the longest and suffered the most, should not be excluded from the peace process, and that Japan should heed the opinions of Asian nations who had been victimized by Japan and were opposed to the proposed signing of a partial peace and a security treaty with the US. With regard to the Korean War, however, the paper criticized the war purely out of concern for the interests of the Japanese people. According to the paper, only big capitalists benefited from the war while workers' economic conditions worsened, and if people were to improve their standard of living, they had no choice but to cease the production of weapons and make goods they really needed instead.[25]

The JCP-affiliated *Heiwa Fujin Shimbun* carried an article opposing the shipment of Japanese-grown rice to Korea because a shortage of domestic rice might force the Japanese to eat imported rice, which was known to be of poor quality. The paper also reported on railway workers who refused to support the war effort and were consequently fired. The paper pointed out how the Japanese workers suffered from the government's policy of offering land for military use and thereby supporting 'foreign countries' terrible war'. It concluded, 'The railway workers' suffering will not end unless Japan concludes a comprehensive peace and all occupation forces leave.'[26]

Even for leftists, who generally demonstrated a higher degree of consideration for the victims of Japanese aggression throughout the post-war era compared with those in other camps, their own suffering served as the primary basis for their opposition to the Korean War, and the suffering of the Koreans largely remained a non-issue. The former Nikkyōso official Hashiguchi recalled teachers were not thinking about the fate of any other country but Japan when they adopted the slogan, 'Don't send our students to the battlefield.'[27] Then Nikkyōso Chairman Oka Saburō argued that the most essential thing was to discuss ways to prevent the bloody conflict in Korea spreading to Japan, and that the union's policy for 1951 must focus on defending workers' livelihoods, since 90 per cent of them were barely managing to eke out a living and could not afford to spare any thought to war or rearmament.[28] When the JSP tried to organize a peace campaign shortly after the outbreak of the Korean War to reflect the prevailing public opinion, the chief rallying cry was, 'Don't let Japan get embroiled in the war.'[29]

Housewives with no political affiliation

Amid the general apathy among ordinary women in the early 1950s, efforts by peace activists made little headway. Many women's groups began distancing themselves from political parties as the conflict between the right and the left became increasingly acrimonious. Some groups decided not to appoint as senior officials anyone who represented a political party, and not to support any party's peace activities. The JSP's peace movement is reported to have been unpopular because many women did not hide their mistrust of political groups that appeared to call for peace in abstract terms, rather than help to improve people's standard of living. That prompted the JSP to play down its party policy and shift its focus to domestic issues concerning female voters. Grassroots peace activists, meanwhile, complained that their petition drive calling for a ban on the use of atomic bombs was confused with the JCP's peace movement, and met with strong public criticism. Activists were also reported to have made little headway in winning over women to their cause when they worked through the PTA. One observer in December 1950 noted that those who had earlier made vocal appeals for peace appeared to have grown silent, even though the Korean War was taking an increasingly serious turn as time went by.[30]

Besides leftists, there had been other activists who sought to tie UNESCO (United Nations Educational, Scientific and Cultural Organization) in with Japan's peace movement. UNESCO provided occupied Japan with the only international forum to discuss peace issues with countries on the other side of the Iron Curtain, and many peace activists pinned their hopes on the UN organization as the Cold War deepened. Japanese peace groups tried to get UNESCO to call on Japan's political parties and labour unions to work for world peace, and engaged in educational activities aimed at enhancing the mutual understanding of nations around the world. Hopes were expressed in the mass media that the non-communist peace movement would attract a wider sector of the populace and help them to awake to the importance of peace issues.

The UNESCO movement in Japan originally started out as a grassroots movement in many parts of the country, with the first regional group formed in Sendai in July 1947.[31] As of September 1948, however, the *Nihon Fujin Shimbun* reports low turnouts of women at UNESCO gatherings,[32] and the movement began losing momentum a year later as the peace groups' educational activities failed to attract much public interest. The grassroots initiative was later stifled as both central and local authorities took control of UNESCO groups. Though a woman official of the movement noted in 1953 the need for women to make their voices heard, and expressed hopes that they would improve their social status by getting involved in UNESCO activities, the movement never became part of the mainstream post-war peace movement.[33]

Around 1950, newspapers and magazines as well as political commentators often expressed concern about the lack of political awareness among most women. A survey conducted by the *Fujin Minshu Shimbun* in 1948 asked women about the hardships they had suffered during the war and what they intended to do if there were another conflict. While a vast majority of women poured their hearts out in response to the first question, hardly any one responded to the second, leading the editor to conclude that most women were able to do little more than moan about their own personal experiences.[34]

One former newspaper editor noted in 1949 that women accounted for only about 3–7 per cent of those who sent letters to his paper, and that most women's letters were about food rations and other personal matters. According to him, they hardly ever mentioned broader social or political issues.[35] The 11 April 1949 editorial of the *Asahi Shimbun*, for example, noted that Japanese women would be unable to improve their intellectual capacities unless they were freed from their daily chores to read and reflect upon themselves. Noting a general passivity among women, the editorial declared

> [Japanese women] have been granted the vote and legal rights, unlike their foreign counterparts, who made their own efforts to win them. That probably makes it difficult for Japanese women to get accustomed to their new status, or maybe as a result of their long ingrained habit, they are resigned to their lot.
>
> Women should have the desire to improve their situation by tackling matters directly related to their lives, and assert themselves consistently in doing so.

Letters to the *Nihon Fujin Shimbun* in early 1950 also lamented the lot of ordinary housewives, most of whom did not have time to read newspapers carefully, and observed that a vast number of women trailed far behind the handful who were emancipated enough to lead a successful career.[36]

A survey conducted by the *Asahi Shimbun* in February 1952 showed that almost half of the women respondents said 'don't know' when asked whether Japan should have a military by amending the war-renouncing clause of the Constitution. The percentage of women who said 'no' was about the same as that of men.[37] While the poll suggests that women on the whole had yet to take any clear stand on issues such as peace and Japan's security, the *Asahi* also reports around the same time a sharp increase in letters to the editor sent by women, who expressed their views on issues such as rearmament and the 'reverse course' as well as on personal matters.[38] Women's opinions expressed in newspapers subsequently drew wide public attention because they were indicative of the changing times, in contrast to the pre-war days, when women who dared ever to read the newspaper were often criticized for their 'impudence'.[39]

As has been noted above, women had been wary of leftist political parties' arguments about peace. The UNESCO movement, which sought to educate people about the cultures and societies of foreign nations, also failed to win a significant following among women. Women's budding interest in political affairs appears to have been stimulated by matters of direct relevance to their lives.

Most letters which women wrote about peace issues expressed fears of another war, and as far as the letters sent to the *Asahi* are concerned, the frequency with which women readers expressed their concerns about rearmament suggests that of the so-called four peace principles, establishment of a military was the issue that most gripped their attention because it would have the most direct impact on their daily lives.[40] Some women who opposed rearmament argued that since it was inconceivable that war would break out in an unarmed country, the most effective way to prevent war was not to possess any arms.[41] Others voiced concern that Japan could rearm itself only at the cost of an effective social security system, and said that the government should spend taxpayers' money to get rid of prostitutes and slums, repair the roads and otherwise improve people's standard of living.[42] Worries were also expressed that rearmament might return Japan to the miserable war years.[43]

According to a January/February 1953 poll conducted by the *Asahi Shimbun*, about 30 per cent of women opposed rearmament while 20 per cent were in favour, regardless of occupation, level of education and location of residence; compared with about 40 per cent of men who were in favour and 20 per cent who were against, showing a clear contrast between the views of men and women on the issue.[44]

In January 1952, former prime minister Ashida Hitoshi said that although he favoured a constitutional amendment to allow Japan to rearm, this should be postponed for some time because women would oppose any amendment in a national referendum.[45] This shows that the position of women on rearmament was already influencing the political process.

With regard to the Korean War, *Asahi Shimbun* polls of both men and women showed their views of the war's effects on Japan remained largely unchanged throughout three years of fighting. The way the questions were put in the polls suggests that the predominant concern of the public continued to be how their own lives were affected by the war. The proportion of those who believed that the war had a negative impact on Japan stood at 34 per cent in a September 1950 survey, and at 36 per cent in a survey taken in January/February 1953, shortly before the ceasefire in June. The figure for those who said the war had a positive influence on Japan was 18 per cent in the earlier poll and 10 per cent in 1953. While respondents who said the war had both a positive and negative impact totalled 8–10 per cent, those who said, 'don't know' accounted for 31–43 per cent of the total. Although the results indicate the relative ambivalence of respondents, an impressive 85 per cent of all respondents in the later poll hoped for as quick an end to the war as possible, a response, according to the paper, which was universal among both male and female respondents.[46] The response, however, should not be interpreted as a reflection of the public's strong pacifist sentiment, because it is inconceivable that most people would say they wanted any given war to continue.

Concerning the US military, while 42 per cent of women expressed hopes for a continuation of the US presence and 18 per cent wished for the

162 *The rise of a grassroots peace movement*

departure of US troops in a May 1952 poll, the percentages were reversed in the January/February 1953 survey, in which 39 per cent wanted the US military to leave and 23 per cent wanted it to stay, indicating that women, who had earlier sought US protection, had begun with the passage of time to consider US military bases nothing but a nuisance.[47] Women's opposition to military bases, one of the four peace principles, appears to have stemmed largely from their annoyance at having such facilities in their vicinity rather than their desire for peace.

Whether on rearmament, the Korean War or US military bases, views expressed by ordinary women on the whole reflected their fears about another major calamity that might befall their lives, and their somewhat parochial concern with defending their interests.

Nonetheless, as mentioned above, signs appeared around 1952 that women were beginning to extend their horizons to matters outside of the home. The following will seek to shed light on how that came to pass by looking at the activities of ordinary women.

The formation of essay-writing and other grassroots groups

Peace activists suffered a succession of setbacks over the Korean War, the peace treaty, the Japan-US security treaty and rearmament, as they lost out to the government on all of these divisive issues. The same thing can be said about those who had been involved in labour and other grassroots political activities. On the eve of the restoration of Japanese sovereignty, the nation's future looked extremely bleak and uncertain to many activists, who despaired of their powerlessness in the face of the 'reverse course', in which the influence of the conservative establishment appeared to become resurgent.

The early 1950s, which saw the advent of the so-called San Francisco Treaty system premised on a partial peace and the Japan-US security treaty, was a time of deep gloom and reflection for those involved in the labour, peace and pro-democracy movements, and they brooded over what had gone wrong with their struggles. Many intellectuals and activists wondered whether peace and the democratic rights they thought had been won after the war's end were an illusion.[48] This sense of defeat prompted activists to try different approaches from the early 1950s.

One of the new approaches was to form informal essay-writing societies. A collection of essays written by schoolchildren from a small village and edited by Muchaku Seikyō, and another book on education through essay-writing authored by Kokubun Ichitarō, were published in 1951.[49] The schoolchildren's accounts of their lives, which showed small children making brave efforts every day to overcome the poverty and sorrow caused by economic hardship, moved a great many Japanese and prompted many adults to try their hand at essay-writing, which became a widely popular pastime in the mid-1950s.

According to Kokubun Ichitarō, although new ideas imported from the West after the war – such as democracy, peace and respect for human dignity, as well as American educational methods – all embodied worthy values in themselves, the Japanese tended to accept them too uncritically. Kokubun and other schoolteachers sought to remedy such drawbacks in Japan's post-war education by having schoolchildren write about their everyday lives, and thereby incorporate into their education unique traits long embedded in Japanese society and its culture, language and writing system.[50] The aim was to express ideas that were not borrowed from anybody else. An essay-writer was supposed to base his or her ideas on personal experience, and learn to articulate them in a unique way. The educational method promoted by Muchaku and Kokubun was also intended to initiate a kind of movement, because writers were called on to think as they wrote, after which they were to hold discussions in small groups, in order to distinguish between problems they had in common and problems unique to individuals, and try to find solutions to these problems together. It was hoped they would gradually learn how to resolve their problems and begin to ponder what kind of scientific or historical knowledge they should seek if their personal experience alone did not suffice.[51]

The sociologist Tsurumi Kazuko (1918–), who led a small essay-writing group of housewives, thought the publication of the children's writings was timely because many Japanese were searching for a way to practise their thoughts or ideals through action, or integrate their intellect, reason and emotions into a harmonious whole in a way that befitted their actual existence. Tsurumi argued that this kind of learning method was useful for adults, too, because they thought they had to start things all over again now that the new San Francisco Treaty system seemed to negate the ideals they had embraced as the principles of the new post-war Japan. With Japan appearing to achieve just token independence from the US, adults thought they needed to learn to emancipate themselves mentally and ideologically and think independently. In Tsurumi's view, essay-writing taken up by such adults turned into a kind of grassroots movement for a searching examination of oneself as well as society.[52]

According to the historian Nagahara Kazuko, people involved in group activities also studied political and economic issues in the context of their personal concerns – such as the household budget, bickering between a housewife and her mother-in-law, and love and marriage – so their activities attracted a good number of housewives who had never taken part in a social movement, and spread to many parts of the country.[53]

Against this backdrop, countless essay-writing groups sprang up throughout Japan. Some of these groups were led by university teachers or other intellectuals, who put together programmes to guide group activities. Others were formed spontaneously, even when there were no particular leaders, as many women gathered in a desperate search for solutions to their serious economic or other problems. Makise Kikue, who was a leading member of one such group in Tokyo, said

Our group included widows and we were all deeply traumatized by the war. Even when writing and thinking about something else in our everyday lives, we inevitably came to the conclusion that the source of all our problems was the war.

We decided to write for our children about the painful experience we suffered when we were unable to give them enough food to eat and gave them an unhappy childhood.

We began writing because it was the least that powerless housewives like us could do amidst the oppressive atmosphere surrounding us after the outbreak of the Korean War, and we didn't expect to do anything big. We just hoped to get the trauma gradually out of our system by talking and writing about it.[54]

One essay-writing group in the Tama area on the outskirts of Tokyo included many people who had to toil away from morning to night to eke out a meagre living, war widows with children, invalids or those who did not know what to do about their broken families. As they confided their problems to and bonded with one another, the group attracted many new members who sought the comfort and pleasure of other women's companionship. Collections of members' writings, which were distributed four times a year by about 170 members, totalled some 500 copies and were said to have earned the empathy of a great many neighbours.[55]

One housewife, who came from a poor farming village in Chiba Prefecture and was thirty years old when the war ended, looked back at the hard life she had led ever since she was a small child. She said she had long questioned the general tendencies of tradition-bound rural communities that showed almost no regard for women's human rights or their personal dignity and left them little freedom to form opinions of their own. She had been critical of the mores of rural society that regarded a woman as a subordinate being to her husband, and forced her to make great sacrifices for the family while giving her almost no benefits in return. She herself had been inured to a considerable extent to the generally oppressive social climate, and had been unable to resist it.[56]

But this woman detected a change in the times after the war, and began to hope that there might be a way to overcome the social forces that so oppressed women when they tried to foster the sound development of their personality. She took heart from reading the writings of other ordinary women because she learned that others were in a similar situation and that she was not alone. As circumstances did not allow the woman to confide in people around her, she began contributing her writings to the organ of a local PTA. Her writings, which were simple accounts of her daily life, encouraged many other women to write because they thought even they could write about such simple matters. These women, who had long kept their problems to themselves, also wanted to share their inner feelings.[57]

Women began first by looking at matters that were of direct concern to their lives, and wrote mainly about their children. But some later began discussing wider educational or labour issues as they started to think about society.[58] Since only a limited number of housewives in those days was sufficiently emancipated to be able to leave their homes and openly busy themselves with activities other than their domestic chores, the rare sensation of being free – even if only for a brief moment – to meet with other housewives, helped them to open their eyes to and reflect upon matters other than homemaking. Such a reflective process prompted some women later to get involved with the peace and other social movements.

Meanwhile, an increasing number of housewives were no longer content to stay at home, and began to exhibit a voracious appetite for learning. From the early 1950s they took up social studies, in many cases attending lectures given by academics.[59] The reasons for their desire to learn varied from woman to woman. But many said they wanted to learn more about the world they lived in because they were not sure whether they would be able to make the right decisions when exercising their newly accorded voting and other rights. Others expressed fears that they would be unable to keep abreast of the times because of their ignorance. One widow said:

> It was eight years ago that I lost my husband to the war and began working, because I had no choice but to do so. After hopping from one job to another, things have finally become easier for me and I have regained some peace of mind. Still, I am now saddened by lack of my education, and because of that I feel inferior to others at my workplace and am unable to improve myself. At home I have begun to lose confidence in my ability to educate my children. I want to attend a night-time course at high school so that I will be able to answer my children's questions correctly. At least some widows must be feeling truly sad just like me about the education gap between themselves and their children.[60]

A fifty-five-year-old woman from a rural area in Fukushima Prefecture expressed a similar view:

> Although they tend to fall behind the times, not a few housewives are trying to catch up when they can take time off from their farm work. We want to nurture this kind of new attitude that is now budding in housewives living in farming villages.[61]

Upon noticing such trends among women, national newspapers began devoting a section to letters to the editor sent by ordinary women.[62] Such newspaper features won a nationwide following of housewives, and their zealous devotees, who were dubbed 'Mrs Letters to the Editor' for habitually writing to newspapers, began forming small essay-writing societies of like-minded housewives.[63] As essay-writing groups sprang up across the country, they began networking with each other and exchanging ideas with their counterparts in distant areas, thereby creating informal networks of essay-writers crisscrossing the whole country.[64]

The writer Shimizu Keiko, who followed women's grassroots activities, noted that from around 1953, many women, impatient with the formal and stifling atmosphere of PTAs, which were under the thumb of a handful of leading officials, began forming informal groups outside PTAs, where everyone was encouraged to express their opinions. Some women became independent enough to give up the tutelage of local authorities, which prepared educational programmes consisting mainly of lectures that people listened to passively. After leaving existing women's societies, at least some women faced popular condemnation that branded them as 'Reds' (*aka*) but persevered to continue their group activities, as they wished to deal with problems in their own way.[65]

In its August 1959 report, the Ministry of Labour's Women and Minors Bureau noted a sharp increase in the number of such small, independent grassroots groups, and forecast their further growth across the country.[66] According to Maruoka Hideko, such informal groups no longer required any particular leaders because their members' enthusiasm was so great that they were capable of making independent decisions and acting upon them.[67]

Although most of these activities, which thrived both in urban and provincial areas, focused primarily on pragmatic matters such as home-making and hobbies, many later began tackling wider issues, with peace inevitably being one of them. After realizing the flawed nature of the education they had received before the war, members of Awata Yasuko's essay-writing society, the 'Hinata Group', mounted an active signature drive against bills presented to the Diet in 1954 to restrict school teachers' political activities. Fearing that such legislation, aimed at countering Nikkyōso's peace education, might spell a return to the pre-war education system, they even delivered political speeches in the street, a quite audacious act by the standards of most Japanese housewives in those days.[68] A group of housewives who studied in Suginami, Tokyo, under Yasui Kaoru (1907–80), a former Tokyo University professor of international law, played a crucial role in the anti-nuclear weapons movement right from the beginning. Another group of housewives in Umegaoka, a small town in Tokyo's Setagaya Ward, was also galvanized into action in 1954 upon learning about the Bikini H-bomb test. They collected 1,500 anti-bomb signatures in a couple of days without figuring out in advance what they would do with so many.[69] The activism of the Umegaoka women had been nurtured through years of study sessions they had organized on their own. Housewives in Nagasaki, who had also awoken to the need to act out the thinking they had cultivated through essay-writing activities, helped one young woman, whose legs had been paralysed by the atomic bombing, to acquire job skills to earn a living. That A-bomb victim in turn helped fifty other such victims to acquire job skills.[70]

Prior to the Bikini test of March 1954, there were sufficient levels of political consciousness and grassroots networks in place to organize a nationwide peace movement, in which a great number of housewives belonging to no major organization took a proactive role without waiting for instructions from the leadership.

After Bikini

The emergence of a nationwide peace network

The H-bomb test on Bikini Atoll in 1954, which injured Japanese fishermen and claimed the life of one of them shortly afterwards, galvanized a great number of ordinary citizens, especially housewives, into spontaneous protest campaigns because of the major health hazard posed by contaminated fish and rain.

Almost 20 million anti-nuclear signatures were collected by the end of 1954, according to the National Council of Anti-Nuclear Signature-collecting Movements (Gensuibaku Kinshi Shomei Undō Zenkoku Kyōgikai, or Gensuikyō). Prompted by the furore at the grassroots level, both chambers of parliament passed unanimous resolutions calling for a ban on nuclear arms, and almost all prefectural governments and some 250 municipalities passed similar resolutions within about six months. The government, which earlier had defended the US nuclear test, retreated from that stand to mollify public opinion.[71]

With local authorities and a large number of citizens with no political affiliation vigorously supporting the anti-nuclear campaign, the peace movement, which had earlier met with widespread popular criticism or even hostility because of its association with the JCP, gained respectability in the eyes of the general public. This was the first time in Japan's history that peace issues had engaged the attention of so many individuals, and that a grassroots peace movement had made a direct impact on politics both at local and national level.

The anti-nuclear campaigns that swept the country boosted the confidence of women, who collected the bulk of the anti-bomb signatures, and gave further impetus to women's groups to join forces with other organizations.[72] This brought together housewives and working women, as well as women from urban and provincial areas.[73]

The Mothers' Congress movement that began in 1955 also did much to bolster the nationwide networks of women activists. The first annual Mothers' Congress was held at local and national level in Japan prior to delegates being sent to the world Mothers' Congress in Lausanne, Switzerland. The mothers' movement was organized by a varied bunch of mainly centre-left organizations, including the Society for the Protection of Children,[74] the Women's Democratic Club, cooperatives and PTAs, as well as women's regional organizations.

168   *The rise of a grassroots peace movement*

The movement, which relied heavily on Nikkyōso's organizational muscle, brought together women from across the country, ranging from illiterate female farmers to full-time housewives married to middle-class, white-collar workers in suburban Tokyo. The mothers' movement helped to provide a vital network, by which women who had been isolated and had no means of ameliorating their lot could work with others to resolve their problems through the political process. Most societies of women teachers and mothers, whose activities were based within a given locality and focused mainly on children's education, affiliated themselves with the Mothers' Congress and thereby became part of the national movement to tackle a much wider range of political and economic as well as educational issues.[75]

The evolving political outlook

The slogan of the mothers' movement, 'It is the earnest desire of all mothers that the life they have created be nurtured and protected', struck a particularly resonant chord with countless women, many of whom still had difficulty providing a decent standard of living for their children ten years after the war's end.

The movement, which was funded by donations collected by volunteers who were total novices in organizing grassroots activities, brought together impoverished widows, coal-miners' wives living on starvation wages, day labourers putting up a desperate fight against job cuts, and others of society's downtrodden, who tried to use the forum to draw public attention to their plight.[76] Women traumatized by the harsh realities of both their past and present poured their hearts out at local and national meetings of the Mothers' Congress.

It was the first time in Japan's history that such large numbers of women had the opportunity to engage in a collective, tearful catharsis. The sensation of openly weeping over their own troubles in a public forum was totally new for many ordinary women because it stood in stark contrast to what had been called for by the official wartime propaganda, namely stoically to accept and endure any hardship.[77]

Leaders of the mothers' movement had to devise an effective approach in order somehow to enlist the participation of ordinary women, who were total novices in politics. They argued that banning the bomb and other esoteric debates involving international politics were not what peace was all about. They said peace must be achieved also by addressing small issues that directly affected ordinary people's lives. This made it easier for women to discuss peace issues, as they began discussions by talking about their personal concerns such as poverty and unemployment. Consequently, many women became involved in peace activities as part of a movement that sought to address all problems women faced.

The proselytising method was quite similar to that which Nikkyōso schoolteachers had used in the early 1950s to win over ordinary housewives.

Organizers of the mothers' movement continued to win a growing number of converts through the simple but proven formula.

While such arguments helped to enhance the legitimacy of their activities in the eyes of those newly initiated into the peace and other social movements, the developments, as described below, helped further to boost their belief in what women considered to be their righteous cause, and emboldened an increasing number of women to resort to direct action.

When the news of the Bikini test first broke, many women panicked over the potential health hazard, and reacted with nationalistic anger over the death of a fisherman who had been exposed to the radiation. While many women were furious about this third nuclear calamity that the Japanese had been forced to suffer, many activists began sending their anti-nuclear message around the world with a sense of mission. They believed that since the Japanese were the only people who had been victims of nuclear bombings, they had the credibility and duty to call for nuclear disarmament. Until then, many women had been encouraged to think about peace issues in terms of their personal lives. But after the Bikini test, the international and humanitarian dimensions of peace consciousness began to become evident for an increasing number of ordinary women, as they worked with unionists and other male participants to organize the first anti-nuclear international conference in Hiroshima in 1955. As if she knew she would soon die an untimely death, Yamashita Asayo, a Hiroshima housewife who had experienced the atomic bombing of her city, for example, indefatigably continued her peace campaign until she died of cancer in 1964, saying, 'I'm doing this to banish war from the world.'[78]

The Mothers' Congress in particular played a significant role in politicizing the women's peace movement. In encouraging political activism, organizers of the mothers' movement argued that issues such as poverty and the unfair treatment suffered by women both inside and outside their homes were attributable to the deeply entrenched structure of Japanese society. As such, they argued, redressing the ills of society required collective action by as many women as possible. A university professor who spoke at an annual gathering in Nagano told the audience they would get nowhere unless they understood the political situation well. He said, 'Politics is not about waiting for some authorities to give instructions to do something. Politics is about taking action.'[79] The arguments used by the organizers of the mothers' movement helped to make it less of a taboo for women to press their personal interests through the political process. The dire condition of many impoverished women, which cried out for immediate action, also helped to enhance the political activism of the mothers' movement, which prompted an inevitable leftward ideological shift overall.

Meanwhile, the intensified conflict between the Kishi government and the leftist camp, as has been seen above in the chapters on organized labour, also spread to ordinary women with no political affiliation. Of particular concern for housewives, besides the possibility of war that could be increased through the revision of the Japan-US security treaty and restriction of civil liberties by the Police Duties Law, was their children's school education, which they

170   *The rise of a grassroots peace movement*

feared was coming increasingly under government control.[80] Many housewives were reported to have differed with their husbands over the issue of the introduction of teacher work assessments, which both Nikkyōso and students' mothers feared would cow teachers into following the government's educational policy and perhaps lead to a revival of the authoritarian style of wartime education. As women continued their studies on school education at the grassroots level, their views also clashed with men running prefectural and national PTA federations.[81]

Amid the heightened political tensions, even the YWCA, which had usually eschewed active involvement in political matters, joined the campaign against the Police Duties Law, and a major essay-writing group named Kusanomikai (Seeds of Grass), also joined street demonstrations against the law. Kusanomikai, which was formed by women whose letters to the editor had appeared in the *Asahi Shimbun*, had been known for its members' reflective tendencies and had seldom taken political action.[82] Many of these women had to hide their faces when demonstrating against the Police Duties Law because they feared damaging their husbands' career prospects if they were recognized. But they discarded such caution during the *Anpo Tōsō*, and demonstrated openly after they unanimously decided to protest the revision of the Japan-US security treaty.[83]

As they became increasingly radical, more female activists began making common cause with labour unions. The historian Tatewaki Sadayo recalled many participants in the mothers' movement, who had earlier regarded labour union members as communists and shunned any cooperation with Sōhyō, considered unionists as comrades in arms during the *Anpo Tōsō*.[84]

Although debates on peace had attracted relatively small audiences in previous years compared with two other sessions dedicated to discussing children and women's rights issues, crowds overflowed at the 1959 Mothers' Congress's session on peace issues because of concern about the Japan-US security treaty. The increasingly outspoken and assertive attitude of women involved in the mothers' movement prompted the government and the LDP to step up efforts to undermine the mothers' movement,[85] but such tactics backfired and steeled women's will to fight the authorities, and participation in the mothers' movement continued to increase.[86]

Women's political consciousness grew with each protest movement, and observers marvelled at the way housewives animatedly discussed parliamentary politics and national security issues during the *Anpo Tōsō*, sensing a dramatic change in their outlook.[87] Women had made considerable progress since the early 1950s, when a vast majority of them were unable to form coherent views on similar security matters involving the peace treaty.

A split amid the climax

The political ferment, which was enhanced by the Kishi government's hardline approach, gave rise to growing intolerance on the part of both conservative and left-wing activists in the peace movement. The pattern of division was quite similar to that observed in the earlier days of political strife in the late 1940s.

In the early years of the ban-the-bomb movement around 1955, the political right and left set aside their differences to work together, and both communists and groups such as conservative regional women's organizations played a prominent role in calling for a ban on nuclear weapons.

While the left was suspicious of regional women's organizations' ties to the government and the LDP and criticized them for citing 'political neutrality' and 'peace of the heart' as their reasons for non-involvement in political activities, many such groups, however, were quite active in opposing the government's attempt to restore the *ie* system or revise the Police Duties Law and the Constitution. Yamataka Shigeri, who headed the national umbrella for regional women's organizations, for example, played a pivotal role in getting conservative rank-and-file members to join the anti-nuclear movement, by stressing the non-partisan nature of the act of opposing nuclear weapons, which was of concern for the whole nation.[88]

Despite left-wing claims of their reluctance to engage in peace activities, many regional women's groups defied those who smeared them as Reds to join the anti-nuclear movement and played an active part in organizing relief efforts to help A-bomb victims.[89] In 1958, when some regional group members opposed the policy of other anti-nuclear campaigners, who tried to stage a protest against teacher work assessments as part of the anti-nuclear movement, and insisted that they should no longer attend Gensuikyō's annual rally, they had to bow to other members of regional organizations, who pointed to grassroots opposition to such a move.[90]

The radicalization of some activists, however, caused a sharp division among women, which made it increasingly difficult to maintain a broad united front. As was stated above, the Mothers' Congress continued to attract ever larger numbers of housewives, who had taken up grassroots activities outside their homes for the first time. A large number of women hardly took any partisan stands on political issues, and expected of the Mothers' Congress little more than a place to find sympathetic listeners to their problems. These women began complaining about other women trying to politicize their activities. Meanwhile, other female activists with more experience became more knowledgeable about issues and more committed to their activities.

The anti-nuclear movement, too, began to suffer a serious rift between conservative women, who showed little interest in most political or ideological matters other than the bomb, and others, who were more actively involved in various political campaigns and impatient with what they regarded as the lukewarm or apolitical attitude of other participants.[91] Leftists and liberals deplored the attitude of those who belonged to regional women's organizations because they appeared to be interested in nothing but acquiring culinary and other practical skills, and enjoying themselves through recreational activities. Those on the left also criticized the passive attitude of rank-and-file members of such groups, who simply followed the instructions of their leadership.[92]

The way regional women's organizations were set up tended to constrain their mode of action, and became the source of conflict with left-wing groups. Regional groups automatically included as members women residing in a given locality, in contrast to left-wing groups, such as the Mothers' Congress, which consisted largely of volunteers. The ideological spectrum of regional groups' members encompassed the whole gamut, from far right to far left. Since the groups included communists as well as members of the LDP, they had no choice but to moderate their political stand if they were to preserve organizational unity.[93]

By 1959, some prefectural organizations of locally based women's associations dropped out of the anti-nuclear movement led by Gensuikyō, because Zengakuren students and other leftists were trying to use the movement as part of their campaign to bring down the Kishi government and oppose the revision of the security treaty, and because the wrangling among anti-nuclear campaigners had become increasingly strident.[94] Tanaka Satoko, a senior official of the regional organizations' federation, also argued that the rivalry between the JSP and the JCP, which later paved the way for the final schism in the anti-nuclear campaign in 1963, had taken such a nasty turn by the late 1950s that it became impossible for her group to remain in the ban-the-bomb movement.[95] The number of participants from regional women's bodies in Gensuikyō's annual international anti-nuclear rally dropped significantly in 1960, totalling just fifty-four delegates, compared with some 1,000 in 1955.[96] The group thereafter organized their own peace campaign, aiming for non-partisan activities that everyone could join. The group sent letters to the US and the Soviet Union in 1961 to protest against their nuclear bomb tests, and continued its assistance to A-bomb victims.[97]

Centre-left groups, which were bearing the brunt of the Kishi government's strong-arm tactics to undermine their protests, resolutely continued to go their own way, and the growing polarization among women's groups later helped to pave the way for the final split of the anti-nuclear movement in 1963.

The location of activism

Nameless housewives affiliated with no major organization continued to swell the ranks of activists taking part in popular protest movements, such as those against the Police Duties Law, and the *Anpo Tōsō*, so it is impossible to make an accurate estimate of the total number who took part in the peace movement.[98] But a look at statistics on women's membership of major groups gives some indication of the extent of their participation in the peace movement. Tables 7.1 and 7.2 below consist of excerpts from data compiled by the Ministry of Labour's Women and Minors Bureau as of April 1958.

Table 7.1 Membership of women's organizations[99]

	Organizations	Membership
Regional women's organizations	18,229	6,401,654
Women's sections of farm cooperatives	8,953	3,437,897
Women's sections of consumer cooperatives	36	89,958
Widows' associations	5,468	1,037,442
Housewives' groups organized by labour unions	1,480	303,935

Table 7.2 Size of Japanese women's groups

Group names	Chapters	Membership
Japanese Women's Christian Temperance Union	126	7,000
YWCA	99	12,000
Japanese Women's Peace Association (Nihon Fujin Heiwa Kyokai)	14	700
Zenkoku Tomo no Kai*	156	13,700
League of Women Voters of Japan	41	5,000
Women's Democratic Club	70	3,500
Japanese Association of University Women	29	1,500
Kusanomikai	n/a	1,200
Japanese Housewives' Association	187	n/a

* Zenkoku Tomo no Kai is a nationwide group of women organized by the women's general interest magazine *Shufu no Tomo*.

Source: Women and Minors Bureau of the Ministry of Labour, *Fujin no Genjō*, 11 August 1959, p. 91.

The Women and Minors Bureau classified women's groups into three categories:

1 groups based in local districts such as regional women's organizations, PTAs and the women's sections of agricultural cooperatives
2 groups formed regardless of geographical boundaries to achieve certain objectives, such as the associations of housewives and women voters, religious groups and the women's sections of political parties
3 labour unions, groups within labour unions, and craft unions.

174   *The rise of a grassroots peace movement*

Members of the second and third groups tended to demonstrate independent initiative in their activities, in contrast to the first group, which more often than not counted women residents in local districts automatically as its members. The percentage of women who belonged to the second and third groups was estimated at 6 per cent each of total eligible women voters, while about 63 per cent of adult females belonged to some kind of organization in 1958.[100]

As was discussed earlier, participation in the peace movement by regional women's organizations, which accounted for the bulk of women belonging to any group, was mixed. Women's sections of farm cooperatives, about 70 per cent of which were said to be headed by leaders who doubled as the heads of regional women's organizations,[101] do not appear to have played a significant role in the peace movement. Throughout the first fifteen post-war years, about half of the female population resided in farming communities, where a vast majority of residents were not involved in any peace activities.[102] It should also be noted that not all of an estimated 12 per cent of eligible women voters, who belonged to the second and third groups, were actively involved in the peace movement. Thus it appears quite clear that the percentage of adult women who took an active part in the peace movement was far lower than 50 per cent.

Groups such as the League of Women Voters, Kusanomikai and the Society for the Protection of Children had a great deal of difficulty winning new recruits. Those consisting mainly of housewives were chronically short of funds, and housewives were unable to take much time away from their housework, meaning that no women's grassroots group possessed the organizational muscle comparable to that boasted by major labour federations.[103]

Meanwhile, of the housewives actively involved in the peace movement, a significant increase was reported in the number of middle-class women from late 1958, when the movement against the Police Duties Law began. Many such activists were residents of Tokyo or its surrounding areas, who reportedly had years of experience in local community-based activities or as members of PTAs.[104]

Certain age groups, the middle-aged or the young in particular, appear to have produced a large number of activist housewives. Fujiwara Tei, who became a key official of Gensuikyō, said she was terrified that she might lose her child when the Korean War broke out, and that joining the anti-nuclear movement was quite a natural response for her. Fujiwara was surprised to find among anti-nuclear campaigners many other housewives who had raised small children during World War II just like she had. Fujiwara said they shared the feeling that it was incumbent upon them to work for peace, for the sake of those who had died in the war. She felt her generation was the main protagonist in the war because two thirds of the men who had been in her primary school class had died in the war, and one third of her former female classmates were widows.[105] Another housewife,

Numabe Tamiko, who joined Kusanomikai in the late 1950s, also says a majority of women in the group were mothers, who had experienced World War II.[106]

Older women were less actively involved in the peace movement presumably because they were less flexible than younger women in adapting to new ways.[107]

After the *Anpo Tōsō*, however, women's grassroots group activities began losing steam like any fad that runs its course over time. From the 1960s, the Mothers' Congress saw a generational shift in its participants in line with the demographic trend towards an increase in the working women's population. It was increasingly taken over by younger working women concerned with their own issues, whereas the chief concern of middle-aged housewives, who had been active participants in the congresses in the 1950s, had been their children rather than themselves.[108] The frenetic peace activities of housewives in the early post-war years, after peaking during the 1960 *Anpo Tōsō*, began gradually to taper off as their keen concern for politics was numbed into inactivity during years of growing economic affluence, and as the government took a low-key approach to skirt sensitive political issues such as the Constitution, national security and peace.

Peace movements in rural areas

This section will discuss the activities of women in backward rural areas, where local residents earned their living through primary industries, namely agriculture and fishing. It is quite well known that very few women in such areas took part in the peace movement. What, then, were the factors that limited their participation?

In rural areas, post-war land reform, which eliminated the heavy economic burden of farm rents and broke the control of large landlords over tenant farmers, gave women some breathing space. As their families' economic condition improved, they were to a certain extent liberated. Unlike densely populated urban areas, much of the countryside had been spared from air raids, and some residents benefited for some time from the severe food shortage immediately after the war, which raised the price of farm produce. Still, residents in rural areas also bore scars from the war, as they lost many of their men in battle and farmlands had turned desolate due to shortages of manpower and fertilizer. Government food requisitioning also added to their troubles.

In the early post-war years, there was a significant divide between Japan's major cities and its rural areas, in terms of standards of living and social mores. In economically backward areas many women, who were often dubbed human cattle, shouldered the crushing burden of both farm and housework. Many were still destitute in the mid-1950s, when the writer Ishigaki Ayako urged urban housewives to devote their idle time to 'more worthwhile activities' besides homemaking and thereby kicked off the so-called housewife debate.[109] The mentality moulded by the *ie* system was very much alive in the countryside, and many husbands and in-laws still showed precious little regard for housewives' human rights. Mothers-in-law often demanded from their daughters-in-law the same degree of uncomplaining obedience they themselves had been forced to give when they were younger, and treated them as harshly as their own mothers-in-law had done. Both their families and neighbours generally tended to disapprove of housewives who engaged in activities outside the home that were not related to their domestic work.

In order to improve the living conditions and lowly status of farm wives, local authorities organized various educational programmes for women. The number of such study sessions, called 'housewives' classes' (*fujin gakkyū*), held in rural areas appear to have been far higher than in urban areas because of the urgent need to educate and improve the conditions of women in provincial regions.[110] In the so-called living standards improvement movement (*seikatsu kaizen undō*) initiated by the agriculture and labour ministries from the late 1940s, instructors visited rural villages around Japan to help farmers to introduce new farming methods and adopt innovative approaches to housework so as to lighten the workload of farm wives. Such activities helped to improve rural living conditions and women's status within their families to a certain extent, as did the return of men from the war and an increased use of machinery and agrochemicals. It is also notable that thanks to the movement, the pursuit of a better material life, which used to be disparaged by rural residents as comparable to indulging in luxuries, was now increasingly viewed in a more positive light after the war.

From around 1953, however, when unseasonable weather devastated farm crops, rural residents began to question whether activities such as those aimed at remodelling their kitchens and changing their diet would improve their lives in any fundamental way. Thereafter, instead of just passively following the instructions of the authorities, the women's sections of agricultural cooperatives[111] and female farmers began organizing activities on their own to take a more active role in the running of family farms and their households. Such efforts contributed to the empowerment of women inside the home. As a result, they became increasingly committed to their farm work and began showing a keen interest in rice prices and political issues related to agricultural matters.[112]

By the early 1950s, when the hard times caused by inflation and the Dodge line austerity budget drew to an end, life had become somewhat easier for farm wives. From the late 1950s, a noticeable improvement was witnessed in their standing, which increasingly allowed them to engage in activities outside the home.[113]

The Ministry of Education, as well as local authorities, also encouraged women to conduct participative kinds of studies, in which women engaged in active discussion in small groups to talk about their poverty and the backward attitude of residents in their communities. In *fujin gakkyū* classes, women are reported to have begun showing active interest in wider issues besides the living standard improvement movement and hobbies.[114] In some areas, organizers of study sessions who were used to conducting such activities in towns, began to hold them in smaller localities, making it easier for women to engage in more open discussions.[115]

Kokubun Ichitarō noted that unlike in cities, where the occupation of a household head varied from one to another, residents in rural areas tended to form a more close-knit community because cooperation with neighbours was indispensable for farm work. This was also the case in their efforts to improve relationships with their in-laws, local bosses and others, who were still wedded to the traditional outlook based on the *ie* system. According to Kokubun, such close relations among neighbours easily generated a sense of solidarity, and there were many PTAs and *fujin gakkyū* joint study groups in rural areas that were far more active than their urban counterparts.[116] There are also reports of housewives and women teachers who were actively involved in the mothers' movement, and who conducted peace and other activities on their own.[117]

Some peace activists made considerable inroads into the remotest corners of the country. Anti-nuclear campaigners in particular served as trailblazers in Japan's peace movement, as local activists toured even the smallest villages in their prefectures, villages which had never been visited by such campaigners before, to educate local residents on the Hiroshima and Nagasaki atomic bombings and the new threat posed by the far more destructive H-bombs. In such activities, too, small local women's associations played a crucial part in fostering grassroots opposition to nuclear arms.[118] The mothers' movement, which sought to deal with all kinds of issues facing women, also won a large following in provincial areas, as many women tried to share their troubles with others or vent their frustration at a Mothers' Congress. Such women are said to have flocked to Mothers' Congresses held at the local level like Muslim pilgrims heading for Mecca.[119] Nikkyōso also provided a nationwide conduit through which peace thought elaborated in Tokyo was conveyed. PTAs and groups of women teachers and pupils' mothers played an important role in enlisting ordinary women into the peace movement, as campaigners sought to link the concept of peace to women's immediate concerns, many of which were unique to their localities.

Many such groups also took an active part in campaigns against the some 700 military bases around the country that remained even after the end of the occupation. The protest movement against the bases attracted even women in very modest farming and fishing communities because of the serious danger posed by such installations to their livelihoods and children; and it turned local women into radical activists as they fought over these life-and-death issues.

Essay-writing became a favourite pastime for women of modest means across the country because it allowed them to have some respite from their harsh existence, and to benefit from the catharsis produced by pouring their

178   *The rise of a grassroots peace movement*

hearts into writing. Tales of amateur writers turning into activists in their local rural communities are quite similar to those from urban areas cited above. Women in farming communities clarified their thoughts and put things into perspective through writing. When essay-writing was taken up by a group, collective self-reflection often led members to devise a strategy to cope with their problems, and spurred them on to vigorous community or other activities. One such women's society began selling seaweed and dried fish, and used the sales proceeds to organize a travelling library for use by local residents.[120] Others took up essay-writing to think more deeply about themselves and the world around them after they had engaged for some time in community work or other activities.

In the rural prefecture of Fukui, for example, a housewives' essay-writing group was formed in 1954. Fukui was home to a sizeable population of Buddhists belonging to the Sōtō and Nichiren sects, as well as large communities of farmers and numerous small businesses. The attitude of many Fukui women, who were impoverished and overworked, is said to have been characterized by a sense of resignation to their lot, which was attributed to the influence of their Buddhist faith.[121]

In an attempt to enlighten such women, the local newspaper, the *Fukui Shimbun*, started a letters-to-the-editor section for women in 1954. Unhappy and frustrated with their situation, women responded with enthusiasm and formed an essay-writing group among themselves. A total of forty members aged between eighteen and sixty-one, including a typist, a bus conductor, factory workers, widows and housewives, discussed such matters as child discipline, relationships between housewives and their in-laws and government spending cuts for schools. They also became aware of peace issues in the course of their activities.[122]

In another small rural community, farmers' wives saw a movie on the life of a woman raising silkworms in Nagano Prefecture, and the movie's heroine reminded them of their own harsh lives. The women began to think that something must be wrong with their lives, and started to participate actively in lectures and other study sessions held in the community to improve their economic conditions.[123]

After such consciousness-raising, the reaction of women was swift when in 1954 the government debated amending the Constitution and rearmament. Fearing another war, some 500 women formed a society to defend the Constitution, and organized study sessions to learn about the national charter and the post-war education law. At the time of the *Anpo Tōsō*, they mounted signature drives and went all the way to Tokyo to demonstrate.[124]

A collection of accounts of the war given by farmers' wives in Iwate Prefecture, where the number of casualties was especially high, tells of the great sorrow they felt when they lost their husbands or sons.[125] But despite their great suffering, they did not protest against their lot because they were hampered by social inhibitions that discouraged women from speaking up, and their own attitude, which resigned them to the harsh challenges of their lives.

The rise of a grassroots peace movement 179

But even in a small community in Iwate, female farmers began in the late 1950s to organize activities designed to lighten their heavy workload. Women initiated innovative projects to improve their health and reduce the infant mortality rate in Iwate, which was the highest in Japan at that time. They succeeded in getting the government to provide 100 per cent medical insurance coverage for new-born babies up to age one, and a subsidy of 10 yen a day to make milk affordable for pregnant women. Through such activities, women learned to appreciate the importance of their own and their children's lives. Their awakening to the value of people's lives led them to think about the war, and in 1961 to organize a society to discuss their wartime experiences.[126]

These examples of grassroots activities in rural areas point to the gradual awakening of women to their human rights, which ultimately led them to detect some linkage between people's human rights and peace issues. It was not just poverty that deprived rural residents of the time to think about peace issues. Their social conditions, which had contravened their basic human rights, had made it difficult for women to realize that a person's life was so important that its value deserved due consideration in discussions of war and peace issues.

Numerous accounts of such an awakening process given in newspapers, popular magazines and the histories of prefectures around Japan, suggest that there was a vast reservoir of popular sentiment that was receptive to this singular discourse of peace: that since war oppresses the underprivileged and vulnerable members of society the most, namely the poor, women and children, the establishment of a new social order that will empower them and respect their human rights is a crucial step towards achieving peace. Here, it should be noted that they perceived the unjust domestic system, which had inexorably embroiled the weakest members of society in the war without giving them any say in the matter, as the greatest threat to peace, rather than possible foreign aggression against Japan.

The above accounts of activism among women in rural areas, however, appear largely to be exceptions to the rule. While grassroots activities proliferated, most women in farming communities did not experience the kind of political awakening that their counterparts in urban areas went through. Housewives in rural areas, who had to struggle from a position of far greater disadvantage, appear to have had little time to develop any significant political awareness about peace issues. They were too busy fighting the poverty, and the reactionary mind-set of their relatives and neighbours, that so hindered their liberation.

Gekkan Shakai Kyōiku magazine, which surveyed grassroots activities across Japan, reported on many women in farming communities who earlier had never dared talk back to their husbands or in-laws, no matter how unfairly they were treated by them. Many such women later learned to speak up in public, and gained confidence in themselves as they acquired various farm and other skills by taking part in informal group activities. Women also cooperated to win permission to take a day off from farm work on a regular basis, and took part in group activities aimed at improving mutual understanding between younger women and their mothers-in-law. Most of them appear to have contented themselves with that kind of modest achievement, whereas many of their urban counterparts started out with similar group activities and went on to tackle wider social and political issues. Women in rural areas appear to have desired no more than to be able to express their independent opinions without worrying too much about being criticized, to have their dignity as human beings acknowledged just like their male relatives, and to relish the joy of learning with other women. Even when such women tackled activities outside their homes, they seem to have done little more than call for the introduction of a national health insurance plan, or engage in community work to open a nursery, for example.[127]

Newspapers and magazines frequently reported on a conspicuous lack of interest in the peace movement among rural residents. Even when women in rural communities did take part in peace activities, they appear in most cases to have been able to do so because JSP, JCP and other left-wing activists had made significant inroads into their communities, and the women relied on existing networks they had set up.[128]

Maruoka Hideko recalled that whenever she went to visit rural areas to do research, women invariably told her they never wanted to go through again what they had experienced during the war.[129] No matter how intense the depth of their feelings about the war, women in rural areas by and large appear to have been unable to organize a spontaneous peace movement on their own because their heavy workload[130] and the opposition of their relatives and neighbours to any political initiative, which was attributed to communist instigation, were too powerful a deterrent.[131] Activists who tried to organize peace activities in rural communities often reported on women who differed over war and peace issues with their husbands, who supported conservative politicians. Such women are said to have signed petitions opposing the revision of the Japan-US security treaty while pleading with the activists not to tell their husbands.[132]

Adult education in rural areas relied mostly on public initiative, and that also explains the lack of women's interest in the peace movement. The living standards improvement movement led by government authorities, though aimed at ameliorating women's status in rural communities and freeing them from back-breaking labour, tended to restrict rural women's horizon to practical matters concerning their farms and homes. Some local officials in charge of organizing adult education for women, admitted that their educational programmes largely skirted the issue of people's experiences during the war or other political matters. According to them, legislation on adult education, which was promulgated in 1949 amid the 'reverse course', was aimed at rectifying the 'excesses' of post-war democracy. The authorities tried to discourage any attempt to deal with the deep trauma that continued to afflict people after the war, or the continued US dominance over Japan even after the occupation ended, even though such issues were unavoidable if they were to discuss war and peace issues. Local officials also said that they failed to devise an educational technique that would help those enrolled in their educational programmes to establish a connection between the concepts of peace and democracy and their own personal experiences.[133]

Poverty; women's low level of education; the absence of readily available educational programmes on war and peace issues; grassroots networks insufficiently developed for generating a peace movement; and the local populace's deep-rooted mistrust and hostility towards grassroots political activity – all these factors combined to prevent most women actively taking part in the peace movement. Apart from displaying an emotional 'never again' reflex, a vast number of women in rural areas appear to have had no other means for articulating their opposition to war.

After Japan's economy began to take off in the late 1950s, most small grassroots groups disappeared from the scene amid an exodus of male workers from rural to urban areas, the modernization of agriculture, and major regional development projects that brought dramatic changes to farming communities. In the process, peace issues, which had never figured prominently on the agenda of farming communities, receded even further from the rural scene.

8 Reflections on war and self

This chapter will seek to analyze the nature of women's pacifist outlook by looking at where they chiefly derived their ideas from, whether a sense of their own responsibility for the war and feminism figured in their ideas in any important way, and whether they were pacifists in the exact sense of the word.

Sources of inspiration

Most women, who had been shut out of the political process, had to learn from scratch in order to acquire ideas that would serve as a basis for their peace activities. What were the major influences that helped to shape their ideas? Were there any female leaders who wielded a major ideological influence upon ordinary women? To what extent was left-wing ideology important in the peace thought of communist or other centre-left women?

Like their male counterparts, many former schoolgirls and young, unmarried women, who had believed in Japan's moral crusade in East Asia and actively supported the war effort, tell of how they wept profusely on hearing the news of Japan's defeat on 15 August 1945 and felt a deep sense of remorse over their inability to measure up to the emperor's expectations.

Though there appear to be few reliable opinion surveys on how women felt immediately after the war, many housewives and young unmarried women commonly expressed a sense of relief (*hotto shita*) at hearing the news about the war's end, rather than grief at the failure of Japan's 'moral mission in the war'. A poll of women conducted by the women's peace committee of Sōka Gakkai, a major lay Buddhist organization, yielded the results shown in Table 8.1. Women were asked the question: 'How did you feel when you learned that the war was over?'. Respondents were allowed to give multiple answers.[1]

In a far more limited survey in the late 1950s that polled twenty-eight respondents, most of whom were housewives between the age of thirty and sixty, twelve said they were shocked when the emperor announced the end of the war on the radio, while another twelve said they felt relieved.[2] Numabe Tamiko, who was a schoolgirl when the Sino-Japanese war began in earnest in 1937, said she was glad to hear that the war was over because she had been fed

Table 8.1 Women's responses to the end of the war

	Number of responses
Had an indescribable feeling	440
Felt relieved	431
Felt bitter (about Japan's defeat)	400
Couldn't believe it	253
Felt happy	197
Things were as expected	59
Japan should have continued fighting to the end	38
Didn't feel anything	2
Other responses	85
No response	6

Source: Sōka Gakkai Fujin Heiwa Iinkai (ed.) *Kappōgi no Jūgo* [Aprons and the Home Front], Tokyo: Daisan Bunmeisha, 1987, p. 206.

up with the petty bickering, caused by food and other shortages, that seriously soured her family's relationship with neighbours and other acquaintances.[3]

The significant number of women who voiced joy at the end to the fighting, and little else, is indicative of the passive attitude of women, who had been powerless to exercise any control over the on-going situation, no matter how much they resented their condition.

While the war had broken out without any women having their say in the matter, peace and democracy descended on women after the war quite out of the blue. Their reactions to the abrupt change ranged from rapturous enthusiasm and bewilderment to complete indifference. While those who had worked for the women's rights movement since the pre-war days joyfully accepted their newly granted rights, polls revealed a dearth of interest in political matters among ordinary housewives, especially in rural areas.[4]

As they began to study the new post-war principles and institutions introduced by the foreign victors, not a few women, while expressing joy at the equality of the sexes guaranteed by the Constitution, voiced bewilderment as well, fearing that they were not fully equipped to exercise their newly accorded rights.[5] They said their condition would not improve unless they studied hard so as to make informed decisions in exercising their rights, and acted effectively. Other women wondered aloud, 'How are we to understand new concepts such as democracy? Our old moral code consisted only of teachings like, "be kind to others".'[6] Some, who felt deceived by the wartime propaganda, were wary: Kondō Yūko, who later became editor-in-chief of the *Fujin Minshu Shimbun*, recalled that she was anxious that she might be duped again this time by 'democracy'.[7]

Maruoka Akiko, a young housewife at the time of Japan's defeat, recalled that a torrent of new ideas flooded into her life and immensely stimulated her curiosity. She pestered her husband, asking him the meanings of words such as capitalism and exploitation of the working class and wondered why workers were suddenly turning out in such massive numbers to demonstrate in the streets. Exasperated at her incessant questions, Maruoka's husband told her to read the three-volume book, *An Introduction to Socialism*, published by Iwanami Shoten.[8]

For many women, the window on the new post-war world outside their homes was opened by PTAs and the new education their children were receiving at school. Parents were often nonplussed by the newly acquired, assertive and straight-talking attitude of their children, who had imbibed new ideas at school. Their attitude stood in sharp contrast to earlier generations of schoolchildren who had endured the far stricter discipline of autocratic parents and teachers, elders who had sought to inculcate them with a sense of loyalty and obedience. Post-war children often bridled when parents tried to have their way, and chided them for being 'undemocratic'. Children were the first to insist that democracy and gender equality should also be practised at home.[9] This led many women to realize that the things taught at their children's schools were widely different from what they themselves had learned before the war, and that they would not be able to understand what was going on in their children's minds unless they learned more about the new post-war education system. It was this desire to understand their children and become a respected mentor that they could turn to, that was one of the chief motives that prompted many women to create informal study groups.

Besides democracy, women were also initiated into the idea of basic human rights through contact with their children's schools. Maruoka Hideko said that on returning home from China after the war's end, she became involved with the activities of the PTA at her children's primary school from around 1947. She began studying the Constitution with other women at the PTA. What struck Maruoka most about the new charter was that it gave back people's lives to the people themselves, whereas Japan's wartime policy, which regarded people's lives as a resource of the state, gave precious little thought to people's well-being.[10] Another woman also expressed surprise that the new school education made no mention of loyalty to the emperor.[11]

Numabe Tamiko, a housewife who had no affiliation with any political party, was greatly impressed by the way her children and their friends took an active part in primary school classes, in sharp contrast to her own schooldays, when she and other pupils obediently listened to their teachers' lectures. The liveliness of the children and the great enthusiasm of their teachers made her feel reassured that the war years would never return. She joined Kusanomikai in the late 1950s, in hopes of sharing the joy of the new post-war world with other housewives of her age. Her encounter there with women from various backgrounds later led her to take part in the peace movement.[12]

For ordinary housewives organizing a vigorous signature drive against nuclear weapons or engaged in other peace activities, the chief inspiration behind their actions seldom appears to have come from ideas propounded by intellectuals. In their writings about war and peace issues, ordinary women developed their ideas by drawing on their own personal experience, and hardly ever cited intellectuals. Peace activists this author interviewed mostly said they knew very little about what intellectuals thought simply because they had little time to study, and derived whatever insight they gained about peace issues while tackling a wide range of grassroots activities that addressed both peace and non-peace issues.

Intellectuals such as Tsurumi Kazuko, Maruoka Hideko (1903–90) and Shimizu Keiko (1906–91), who worked closely with ordinary housewives, were aware of the need to educate and awaken ordinary women to broader social issues. But they never tried to pontificate to them, and took great care to maintain as egalitarian a relationship as possible between themselves and the housewives. They encouraged women to think in their own manner and reach their own conclusions about issues.[13] The communist novelist Miyamoto Yuriko (1899–1951), who was one of the leaders of the Women's Democratic Club, also avoided taking a didactic approach. She tried to devise guiding principles from the thoughts of ordinary housewives, and to consider war and peace issues from the standpoint of the chief victims of war, such as returnees and widows.[14]

Far from preaching their ideas to 'enlighten' them, many intellectuals more or less accepted ordinary women as they were, and recognized the intrinsic value of their actions, prompted by their simple motives. Ichikawa Fusae (1893–1981), a leading figure in the women's rights movement, said that women did not need to engage in any arcane political debates to justify their stand against war, but that it would suffice for them to say they just did not want to have the children they had raised drafted by the military and killed in war. Ichikawa said that women should not mind being called foolish or stupid [for resisting war], but they should have the courage to demand what they wanted or make their feelings known through their actions, so that they would never be tricked again into giving up their husbands or children.[15]

In citing their reason for opposing war, most housewives placed their maternal concern for the lives of their children above all else, and argued that their motherhood entitled them more than anyone else to the right to call for peace.

Among intellectuals, Hiratsuka Raichō was well known for reiterating the importance of motherhood in her peace thought. Since the pre-war days, Hiratsuka had stressed the importance to society of the act of giving birth and raising a child, and argued that in view of the momentousness of the task they carried out, mothers should be granted the vote, so as to participate in the political process and play a major role in changing the society they lived in.[16]

Motherhood again became a central theme for Hiratsuka after the war. She elaborated her peace thought to argue that any society that did not value the act of giving birth would neither recognize the value of life nor have respect for children. Such a society, she argued, would not repudiate the mass killing that is war. According to Hiratsuka, peace would have a chance only in a society that valued motherhood, and the women's movement would become complete when staged in tandem with a peace movement.[17]

Ordinary women, too, invoked the sanctity of motherhood, which they considered vested them with more rights than men to take the moral high ground on peace issues, and most did so without ever having heard of Hiratsuka's ideas. The venerable feminist's point was vindicated by the actions of ordinary women, who spontaneously set about their peace activities without ever making a conscious effort to act out Hiratsuka's beliefs.

As has been discussed in the previous chapters, the factors that motivated the peace activities of leftist women did not necessarily differ much from those that inspired women with a more conservative outlook. Even for female communists and other leftists who worked at the grassroots, the chief inspiration for their actions came from actual problems they faced in their daily lives rather than Marxist ideology.

Kojima Senoko, who joined the JCP shortly after the end of the war with her husband, told her husband that she wanted to learn the basics of socialism by reading some works of Marx and Engels before joining the party. But he dissuaded her, saying that she should learn through the experience she would gain by taking part in activities aimed at addressing people's immediate concerns, rather than from books. For Kojima, one of the main sources of inspiration was her husband, who had been a left-wing activist since his university days, extended a ready helping hand to the needy around him, and treated her as an equal human being in the days when most other men took it for granted that women should play a subordinate role. Kojima exlained that trying to foment a revolution was the last thing on her mind.[18]

Ozawa Kiyoko, another communist, was initiated into left-wing politics when her two brothers were jailed before the war for leftist political activities. She said she had no time to read and learn about intellectuals' ideas as she tirelessly engaged in many forms of grassroots activities after the war while raising four children. Ozawa said whatever insights she acquired were gained while she busied herself with anti-nuclear signature drives and other activities, and did not recall any ideas which derived from intellectuals having a significant impact on her outlook.[19]

Articles in the communist-affiliated *Heiwa Fujin Shimbun* and the organs of the Mothers' Congress and the Women's Democratic Club, both of which included large contingents of JCP members, in the main are accounts of the plight of women in farming communities, female factory hands in the midst of acrimonious labour strife, or other women fighting poverty. Instead of expounding Marxist ideology, the papers, by reporting on such women, encouraged female readers to ponder the root causes of their own and other women's suffering, and realize the injustices of their condition. The papers sought to inspire in women insights that would result from an empirical thought process, rather than indoctrinate their readers with socialism.

While arguments attributing existing social ills to the Japanese government's 'militaristic' policy and the US are not entirely absent from these newspapers, the difficulties facing women across the country are described in mostly non-partisan language, and the papers reported on how such women were devising practical strategies somehow to improve their conditions. Their main contention was that if peace was to be achieved, the plight of millions of women who were suffering silently must be alleviated. Militant left-wing arguments premised on the fight against monopoly capital and US imperialism appear to be seldom used in the papers, indicating that socialist ideology was of far less importance for rank-and-file female communist activists than for their male counterparts. It can also be assumed that communists played down their Marxist rhetoric and tried to promote their ideas in the simplest possible terms in order to recruit poor women, who had little understanding of ideological matters and were fearful of communists.

China and the Soviet Union, admired by trade unionists as ideal socialist models, also inspired women. Women in both left- and centre-right groups, including the Japan Housewives' Association, expressed admiration for the zeal with which China and the Soviet Union were pressing ahead with the building of a socialist state, for their well developed social welfare systems, and for the ready availability of day-care centres for working women. Kojima Senoko and Ozawa Kiyoko both said they envied the Soviets and the Chinese, who enjoyed free medical care and school education, as well as a respectable standard of living guaranteed by the state. Kojima said she longed for a future when Japan would embrace the socialist model and she would be able to buy everything her children wanted.[20]

But apart from voicing such starry-eyed admiration, most ordinary women appear not to have borrowed any methods or ideas from China or the Soviet Union in organizing their peace activities, and to have focused primarily on immediate issues facing themselves and their families rather than work for the creation of a socialist state.

The women's peace movement appears to have been largely action-oriented rather than ideology-oriented.

A sense of remorse

Ordinary women had no political rights and the vast majority had no higher education and were poorly informed. For these women it was virtually impossible to understand the falsehood of Japan's wartime propaganda or to oppose the war. Many peace activists who were adults during the war, however, commonly expressed a sense of guilt for their own ignorance and inaction, and the sheer number of the dead among their compatriots weighed upon their conscience. That set housewives apart from the angry young men, whose peace activities were inspired by mistrust of and protest against the older generation responsible for the war.[21]

The sense of guilt towards the foreign victims of Japan's war was expressed mainly by intellectuals from early on. The independent upper house member Kōra Tomi recalled a question posed by an Indian philosopher, who asked whether the Japanese had forgotten their ideals, namely, the emancipation of Asia from Western colonial rule, which had made them dare to start a war against the West. Kōra in reply had to admit that those ideals had been false.[22]

The writer Yamashiro Tomoe recalled that she was deeply impressed by one lecturer, who urged his audience never to forget the shame of having sent a regiment from their home town which had committed incredible atrocities in China. Yamashiro said she began her peace campaign so that she would be able to atone for the war with other Japanese women, for the sake of whom so many Japanese soldiers felt pressured to fight, which resulted in the Nanking massacre.[23]

The poet Morisaki Kazue (1927–), who had grown up in Korea, said it was precisely her sense of guilt for Japan's aggression in Asia that made her feel that she had to start her life all over again after the war.[24]

The sense of guilt toward victims outside Japan was shared by liberal or left-wing intellectuals, many of whom were able to go abroad to visit Asia or think about the war in an international perspective. Still, not a few ordinary women expressed remorse for Japan's foreign victims. One housewife said, for example,

> [After the war was over,] we realized we had lost everything including our loved ones and fortunes. But most painful of all was the fact that it was we who had started the war and that we were responsible for the devastation in China and southern parts of Asia that was similar to what we ourselves were suffering.[25]

After the first national Mothers' Congress began with women venting their sorrow over their own miseries, the issue of women's own war guilt came to a head at the second congress in 1956, causing a sharp division among participants. One speaker claimed that the Japanese were oblivious to their own guilt and said since it was Japan which had begun the war, it should have no right to criticize the US for dropping the atomic bombs. She proposed that Japan should first apologize to the US and the rest of the world. Many women responded in anger, saying it was the government which was to blame and that they did not owe the US or anybody else an apology. But there were also many others who warmly applauded when a Buddhist nun said she and her fellow Buddhists engaged in peace activities to atone for their inability to speak in opposition to the war, and that nobody could completely deny their own responsibility.[26]

Kondō Yūko, former editor-in-chief of the Women's Democratic Club's newspaper, said she and her fellow activists involved in the *Anpo Tōsō*, both male and female, widely shared the view that the revision of the security treaty had to be opposed partly because they should not strengthen a military alliance with the US against China or any other country that had suffered at the hands of Japan's military.[27]

Most ordinary women, who never had firsthand knowledge of battles outside Japan, however, thought about their relatives and acquaintances when they expressed their sense of remorse, and many voiced their grief in the form of 'survivors' guilt'.

The publication in October 1949 of *Kike Wadatsumi no Koe* (Hear the Voices from the Sea), a collection of writings of university students written shortly before they were killed in the war, served as a particularly painful revelation for mothers, who realized that they had been totally unaware of the agony their sons suffered before being sent to the war. One woman said:

> I used to believe in Japan's cause in the war but now I have realized that it was totally wrong. The idea saps me of all strength and I often wish I could die, but I can't die because we have now earned peace and the great new Constitution that has abandoned arms, which my beloved (son) Yōichi sacrificed his life for. I believe I can honour his memory only if I work for peace for this world, in which my son so desperately wanted to stay alive.[28]

Another woman who had lost her son in the war was shocked when she read his diary, in which he wondered how anyone could approve of any war from a moral standpoint, since killing people was what war was all about:

> I was so foolish to believe that joining the military would build my son's character. ... But after I read my son's diary, I realized he had agonized over things I could have never imagined. Still, I was so foolish to think about nothing but to give him good food and keep him entertained when he was home on leave, and I now regret that when it is too late. ... My friends and I have decided never to support any war again, but how can this be done?[29]

The writer Okabe Itsuko (1923–), who was nineteen years old when she saw off her fiancé to the front, was shocked to hear him say before his departure that he did not want to die for the emperor in a war that he considered to be wrong, although he would be happy to die for Okabe or his country. Okabe was shaken because she had been thoroughly indoctrinated with the wartime propaganda and believed it was expected of everyone to die gladly for the emperor. Confused, Okabe was only able to say, 'If I were you, I would die happily [for the emperor].' Okabe later regretted not having asked her fiancé why he thought the war was wrong and not having chosen to die with him if he was so opposed to it. She thought she did not deserve the love of her fiancé, who had mustered the courage to criticize the war and speak negatively of the emperor at the risk of great danger to himself, because critics of the war were severely punished by the authorities. After his death, Okabe considered herself to be the chief culprit, who had sent her fiancé to the war, where he was forced to kill and then be killed himself. She said that although most women considered themselves to be the victims of the war, they should take responsibility for the great harm they had done by letting their loved ones be killed.[30]

The point was raised also by the poet Tanigawa Gan (1923–95) in a more provocative manner at the national Mothers' Congress in 1959. Tanigawa taunted the women who were present at the congress for shedding tears when such tears were no longer useful. He criticized them for their inaction during the war, when women could have done something to resist it by crying openly [over their children being lost to the fighting]. Tanigawa asked why they had not tried to listen to their sons, who were tormented at the thought of having to go to the war, or had not tried to understand their fears. He said he could not trust them when they campaigned for peace because he still remembered that the very same women now engaged in the peace movement had cheerfully waved flags to send him and other youths to the battlefield. The poet said many boys had died because of that, and women's peace activities would not be genuine unless they were ready to sacrifice their sons' lives this time for the sake of peace.[31]

Tanigawa's accusation shocked the audience and drew an irate reaction from most women, many of whom had attended the congress to indulge their sense of self-pity in the belief that they were the chief victims of the war. Tanigawa's provocation was meant as a brutal reminder for women, who had not stopped to think about the part they had played in the war or question its moral implications. While women who were present at the congress reacted strongly to his criticism, others, including intellectuals, were more or less bemused at the harshness of the poet's words, and his outburst does not appear to have prompted most women to ponder the issue of women's war responsibility.

Women in essay-writing societies, meanwhile, made patient efforts to improve their writings and deepen their insight into the war by listening to the criticism of others. Young men criticized them for wallowing in a sense of self-pity, and advised them instead to write about how they had viewed the war in the past and take a more critical as well as objective look at themselves. Such criticism by others prompted the housewives to debate how they should improve the way they conducted group activities, and led them to take up social studies using a book called *Today's Capitalism* as a text.[32]

Makise Kikue and her group took up such studies in the belief that unless their essay-writing activities were accompanied by social research they would end up just producing weepy accounts of the war, and would never derive any deeper insights. But the more they learned, the more ignorant they felt themselves to be. And a simple question raised by their children added further to their dismay over the extent of their own ignorance.[33]

Women read to their children harrowing accounts of the way they had suffered, expecting sympathy and hoping that the children would understand what a cruel toll the war had taken on people's lives. The children, however, asked their mothers why they had not done anything to stop the war if they were so strongly against it. They asked why they did not question it if they felt something was going wrong in the run-up to or during the war. The children asked, 'Were you such a silly person as to do everything others told you to do until that brought all sorts of disaster on you?' The mothers were shocked to realize their school education had never taught them to question in a critical manner what grown-ups told them, nor to think on their own. The question made them aware that their unthinking obedience during the war had made their situation look absurd in the eyes of their children. The women learned that in their children's eyes their own attitude represented nothing but ignorance and gullibility unworthy of a self-respecting human being. The children's blunt reaction gave the women the impetus to question their earlier outlook and attitude, as well as the value system that pre-war society had imposed on them.[34]

Makise recalled how mothers, while being ready to starve themselves to secure food for their children, had waved flags and sent them off to war as the official propaganda extolling patriotic motherhood had told them to do. She now saw how wrong the mothers were for suppressing their real feelings: that they did not want to lose their husbands or children to the war. Makise also noted that although most women believed themselves to be victims, they actually were accomplices of the government since they cooperated with the authorities because of their 'can't fight city hall' mentality, and put their personal interests first to avoid any consequences of insubordination. As a result, Makise concluded, they also harmed others, and those who were already adults during the war could never claim innocence by pleading ignorance. She said she and other women were unable to let bygones be bygones like the young, who could claim innocence, and that they were trying to delve further into the meaning of their experience of the war out of a sense of guilt.[35]

Tsurumi Kazuko noted that the process of awakening through writing about oneself probably met the unique needs of Japanese women because most Western women, for example, who had achieved a higher degree of independence and were far more individualistic than the Japanese, were able to articulate their thoughts more clearly and freely without putting them first into writing.[36] By contrast in Japan, although the law guaranteed freedom of expression, women had long been discouraged from thinking on their own or expressing their own opinions, so they required a patient learning process to master the art of self-expression. And Makise concluded that independence, the very antithesis of what had been considered female virtue in the pre-war days, was exactly the trait Japanese women should acquire so as never to err again.

She said they had unwittingly let Japan slide into the war because they had done nothing but devote themselves to serving their husbands and children, in the belief that being a totally obedient and self-effacing wife was the epitome of virtue. After the war was over, they felt as if they were new-born babies who knew nothing. Makise said:

> We want to cast off women's virtues such as obedience, self-effacement, readiness to dedicate and sacrifice oneself, patience and stoicism, so that we can become true human beings. We want to establish relationships with other members of our families that will not make us give up becoming a true human being for the sake of being an [exemplary] woman or mother.[37]

Through such a mental process, women came to repudiate the stoicism inculcated by pre-war morals, with which they sent their children to the battlefield without showing any emotion amid what Tsurumi Kazuko called 'socialization for death',[38] or the intense indoctrination by the authorities for an extreme act of self-denial for the good of the country. They consequently condemned the inhumanity of the wartime regime that denied its people their natural feelings, and discovered the sanity of acting in accordance with human nature and the desire to live.[39] During the *Anpo Tōsō*, a forty-one-year-old housewife recalled:

> As I saw orderly columns of students file out of their universities, I wished I could change places with them to demonstrate on their behalf. But unlike the days when we saw off soldiers who marched to battle, we were able to find solace in the fact that each one of the students this time was marching of their own accord to make the world peaceful and that they would live.[40]

The constitutional scholar Hoshino Yasusaburō, who attended the national Mothers' Congress in 1957, reported on how participants expressed their appreciation for the war-renouncing clause of the Constitution because it allowed them openly to show their affection for their children, while mothers had been forced to say, 'come back dead', when they saw off their children leaving for the battlefield.[41]

It was when women in Makise's essay-writing group concluded that they should try to atone for their ignorance that the *Anpo Tōsō* reached its zenith. It became impossible for the women to keep their silence in the face of the unprecedented popular protest against the Japan-US military alliance, which in their view threatened war.[42]

Most of the housewives were in their forties and fifties, and some of their children were involved in the *Anpo Tōsō* as student activists. When students increasingly put themselves in harm's way as the demonstrations escalated, the older women were again troubled by a sense of guilt, because they thought students were being forced to act to make up for the inaction of older generations. For fear of repeating the sins of omission they had committed during the war, all members of the essay-writing group took to the streets. For most of them it was the first time that they had engaged in such an open and public protest. Driven by maternal concern for the safety of young students, the women wept when the student activist Kanba Michiko died in a violent clash between demonstrators and police, and faulted themselves for their inability to protect young people like her.[43]

Reflections on their own war responsibility prompted Makise and other amateur writers in her group to resort to direct action, as well as deepening their insights about human rights and how women should conduct themselves. But women who owned up to their own responsibility were mostly limited to a relatively small number of intellectuals and others, who had spent a certain amount of time in self-reflection by writing essays or through other activities. The majority of women, who did not put their thoughts into writing, have left very few clues as to what they felt about their own responsibility. It can only be assumed that activist housewives, who took on the bulk of the endless clerical and other practical tasks besides their housework in the peace movement, such as the collection of anti-nuclear signatures, might have had little time to repent their past conduct. Considering the prevailing view that women were the war's chief victims, self-pity and a sense of recrimination appear to have loomed larger for most women than self-criticism.

Feminism and empowerment

Like female peace activists in many other countries, Japanese women in the early post-war years stressed what they claimed to be the innately peaceful traits of women. They argued that their motherhood and experience as victims of the war enabled them to take the moral high ground on the issue of peace, and accorded themselves singular claims to being natural proponents of peace, in contrast to men.

When women considered war and peace issues in gender terms, their empowerment also became an important topic. But when women talked about the need for empowerment, they were not aiming for the achievement of specific goals, as normally called for in today's feminist movement.

If textbook feminism, which became prevalent in the post-World War II era, calls for a gender revolution aimed at repudiating and vanquishing the male-centred worldview, value system and preconception about gender roles that has been predominant from time immemorial, the arguments of Japan's female peace activists were neither as audacious nor accusatory. The mind-set of ordinary women was not ready for that kind of militancy, and the word 'feminism' was seldom used in the arguments of Japanese female grassroots activists prior to the rise of the feminist movements in Western nations in the 1960s.

The feminist case that ordinary women made for peace largely falls into the category of 'gynocentric' feminism, in contrast to the 'humanist' feminism of later feminists, to use the terms employed by the American philosopher Iris Morgan Young.[44]

Many Japanese housewives engaged in group and other public activities on the pretext that they were doing so for their children's sake. Makise and her fellow amateur writers, who vowed to stop being just obedient wives and doting mothers, began writing in the hope of becoming better mothers. Makise said she conducted a searching self-examination because she believed she would not be able to get at the root cause of problems troubling her children unless she fought her own backwardness, dependence on her husband and other weaknesses deeply ingrained in her.[45]

Housewives invariably cited their children as the primary reason when they were asked why they were doing what they did. Such tendencies among ordinary women often prompted teachers and intellectuals to voice concern that they were unable to assert themselves unless they acted in their capacities as mothers, and were still far from shedding the backward attitudes with which they condemned themselves under the old social order.[46]

The diffidence and lack of independence that so eroded women's will to improve their own condition were far more prevalent in rural areas than in cities. When many women began contributing letters to newspapers in the mid-1950s to express their opinions on various issues, editors expressed dismay that so many of them were anonymous, even when the writers discussed issues that seemed the least controversial and delicate, which is indicative of the considerable inhibition felt by ordinary women about expressing their own views in public.[47]

Whether they lived in urban or rural areas, housewives were social novices groping for ways to get firmly on their feet in the world beyond their homes. Timid and diffident, women found it difficult to speak up even at existing regional women's organizations or PTAs, and formed their own smaller groups with like-minded housewives. They began their social activities by shedding their façades and establishing easy relationships with others, in which they could discuss everything about themselves frankly and enjoyably.[48] Women who had to learn the very basics about how to relate to the outside world never dreamed of transforming their society by battling male dominance.

Activists, therefore, had to explore ways to get such women to feel like fully fledged human beings. One method they devised to coax housewives into accepting their view was to use the argument that women would not be able to defend the rights of their children unless they respected their own rights.[49] They argued that children would not be able to attain sound development of mind and body, unless the relationship between men and women at their homes and workplaces was changed in a way that emancipated mothers from their heavy workload and ensured more respect for women's human rights. The feudalistic family relationship would have negative effects on children's education, while the world would move closer to peace if women were freed from the feudalistic mores that condemned them to lowly social status, and were allowed to work for the happiness of their children. Women, unlike men, attached paramount importance to life, so peace would have a better chance if the logic of women, who were committed to protecting life, were to counter the more warlike logic of men. Peace and the emancipation of women had to be tackled as two inseparable issues.

The rudiments of gynocentric feminism are apparent in such arguments. Women activists presupposed inherent female qualities that could be enlisted to counter the tendencies of male-dominated society, which they believed was responsible for numerous injustices, including war.

The essay-writing group Kusanomikai, for example, devised its own method of organizing itself in repudiation of the hierarchical relationship that bound the conduct of 'organization men', which its members argued had paved the way for the war. Kusanomikai women tried to have 'female principles' embodied in the way they organized themselves so as to prevent certain members from controlling the group, or they respected the freedom of individual members so the conduct of group activities would be in line with the principles of the egalitarian society they desired.[50]

The leader of the mothers' movement, Kawasaki Natsu (1889–1966), repeated her pet phrase, 'If mothers change, the whole society will change', which became the slogan of the Mothers' Congress. Most women leaders, however, urged women to acquire more political awareness, and called for their increased participation in politics in general terms. Apart from that, they presented few specific strategies for changing Japan's male-dominated society. While they reiterated the need to improve the status of women, they did not consider men or male chauvinism as their chief obstacle.

This contrasts with the position of feminists in later years. Nakajima Michiko has noted that women peace activists in the early post-war years never questioned the fundamental inequality in their society that differentiated the role of women from that of men. Nakajima faults early women peace campaigners for neglecting the fact that the inexorable force that accelerated Japan's militarization stemmed from an industrial structure that placed almost the entire burden of housework on women and paid them far lower wages than those given to their male colleagues. In a vein characteristic of humanist feminism, she argued that if war was to be prevented, women had to be liberated from a male-dominated system that was premised on the strict division of labour between the two sexes.[51] Amano Masako also points out that the women did not renounce their role as housewives or mothers, which had been prescribed by men.[52]

Indeed, seeking a role equal to that of a man was remote from the minds of most housewives of the early post-war years, who never dreamed of becoming anything other than housewives. Even among labour unions, except for Nikkyōso, whose women members began demanding equal pay for equal work shortly after the war's end, women workers appear largely to have focused on their needs as mothers and devoted most of their efforts to winning special conditions of work aimed at protecting their health prior to and during pregnancy.[53] They considered being a mother as their chief vocation in the social setting of the day, which still considerably limited their activities and left them little choice as to which roles they could assume as members of society. Although women strenuously resisted politicians' attempts to restore the *ie* system, a hotly contested feminist issue, they did so to prevent a relapse into the bad old days, and their resistance was not aimed at breaking the existing mould of their status as housewives and mothers.

Some women believed that the peace movement could serve as the means to improve women's status. Seeing there were as many women as men at the international anti-nuclear convention held in Hiroshima in 1955, Yamataka Shigeri (1899–1977), the head of the National Federation of Regional Women's Organizations, said: 'Has there been any gathering like this before in Japan's history? The anti-nuclear convention has proved that equality of men and women can be achieved only through the peace movement.'[54]

In 1952, members of the Kansai Housewives' Association (Kansai Shufuren) organized an anti-war march in which they dressed up as white apron-clad housewives cheering young soldiers during the war, military nurses, war widows in black, civilians doing air raid drills and fallen women who eked out a living by serving American soldiers as prostitutes. The procession served as a graphic reminder that women had come a long way since the miserable wartime and early post-war days. One demonstrator said she and other peace activists were making history in their struggle to emancipate women by plucking up the courage to stage a protest in broad daylight.[55]

Women in Uchinada and Sunagawa fought at the forefront of the campaigns against local military bases because they were the only ones available to launch the protest while their husbands were busy working. As a result of their brave struggle, the women came to enjoy greater respect within their families. But whether fighting against military bases or protesting against the use of nuclear weapons, women did so not with the chief aim of improving gender relations, and any modest progress in elevating women's status was more or less a largely unintended by-product of their peace activities.[56]

Admittedly, there were telling signs that the rapid pace of modernization was affecting housewives' attitudes. Many women sought bonds with others amid the atomization of relationships, and there were also women who took up social studies because they wanted to enrich their own intellectual lives. In 1960, Isono Fujiko questioned why a housewife should remain uncompensated for her housework even though her work created value, and argued that the issue had something to do with the status of a wife, who was not recognized as an independent human being. Isono's argument mirrored the social climate in those days, when a growing number of housewives began to reveal their discontent or self-doubt, and wondered whether it was right for them to stay the way they were and continue to look up to their husbands.[57]

Already in the mid-1950s, an article by the writer Ishigaki Ayako (1903–96) in a women's general-interest magazine, in which she urged housewives to work for their self-improvement, kicked off the so-called housewife debate (*shufu ronsō*) that lasted for several years. Ishigaki said that many housewives, freed from much of their housework thanks to the advent of modern appliances, were now wasting a lot of time on foolish chitchat with neighbours, and deplored the vacuity of the minds of such women, who she considered to be leading an idle, comfortable existence. Ishigaki argued that what housewives needed was critical self-appraisal so as to take their lives more seriously, and that in addition to homemaking they should engage in other worthwhile activities by finding a job or offering, for example, their homes as day-care centres for working mothers.[58]

But most housewives who could afford not to work lacked the skills to start the new careers they desired. Around 1960, married middle-aged women, if they were not going to teach in primary or secondary schools, would have had to settle for extremely poor work conditions.[59] One woman from the rural prefecture of Yamanashi, who wrote to *Fujin Kōron* magazine after reading Ishigaki's article, pointed out that the housewives Ishigaki criticized for leading idle lives must be the privileged few, because the wives of farmers and working-class women who made up the majority of the female population had no choice but to work to supplement their husbands' incomes, and many of them were overworked at homes that still had no electricity.[60]

Middle-aged housewives in urban or suburban areas also appeared to have been very much the product of the educational system of pre-war Japan. That tended to inhibit them from overstepping their bounds as prescribed by the old social mores, and made them cling to the age-old ideal of a good wife and wise mother (*ryōsai kenbo*). Awata Yasuko, a member of one essay-writing group, recalled that some of her colleagues had considerable reservations about spending too much time on themselves outside their homes, and hesitated to become actively involved in the peace movement. Such women clashed with more activist housewives, and disturbed the unity of Awata's small grassroots group.[61] Another essay-writing group, Kusanomikai, had difficulty appointing a leader, as housewives pleaded housework to avoid taking on the responsibility of becoming a group officer.[62]

Whether living in urban or rural areas, many women's views on their own status within and beyond their families were characterized by conservatism and complacency about their modest existence. A twenty-six-year-old housewife from Tokyo expressed approval for the writer Yamamoto Kenkichi's view that a person's life was a conglomeration of all foolish and trivial happenings that occurred on a daily basis, and that the wise way to go about one's life was to have respect for all those trivialities. The housewife said: 'Many people say they lead quite ordinary lives day in and day out. I believe people who lead ordinary lives are truly happy people.' A thirty-year-old housewife from Kumamoto said:

> Since my husband works diligently every day, we and our two children manage to lead a modest and peaceful life. Admittedly there is no limit to one's desires. But I think we will be as happy as we can be as long as we just lead an honest life as our circumstances allow.

They and many other women saw positive value in seeking happiness as a modest housewife without ever overstepping the bounds prescribed by a generally accepted notion of propriety.[63]

That attitude was also shared by Kusanomikai women, who mainly sought to deepen insights about their lives, and showed little interest in becoming something other than ordinary housewives. The modest statement of the group's goals professes that they would rather aspire to the modesty and steadfastness of 'durable grass that produces seeds in obscure places' than vie with one another to outperform their peers through showy actions.[64] In response to critics who urged activist housewives to stay at home where they belonged, one Kusanomikai member said she and other women took up outside activities precisely because their homes were so important to them.[65] Another twenty-six-year-old housewife complained that working women and social commentators, who reiterated the need for women to seek a career outside the home, sounded as if they were belittling the housewife's role. She said that being a housewife was her vocation, and that she would never be able to comprehend any social issue in a context divorced from her home.[66]

The poet Morisaki Kazue was involved in the group activities of housewives who were organized by the coal miners' union that their husbands belonged to (Tanpukyō). The wives of coal miners, whose union was one of the most militant in Japan, had more opportunities than most women to learn progressive ideas, but Morisaki lamented that even such women were still unable to emancipate themselves from the old mould of the saintly, self-sacrificing mother, and were more than happy to act as if they were their families' menial servants. In their study sessions, these women argued that they, the victims, would not be liberated unless they fought their husbands' male chauvinism. But they immediately forgot what they had said once they returned home and tried to act like exemplary mothers as called for by the old morality. According to Morisaki, they shunned the responsibility that would arise if they were to take action to change the existing order, and continued to enjoy the peacefulness that could be preserved through their inaction, although it was precisely the inaction of women that had made the world go horribly wrong. Though women learned new things through their activities that changed their sense of values, they made no effort to change their husbands' views or their relationships with them. Morisaki argued that if their husbands did not accept their new values, women should shock them out of their complacency by divorcing them, and aim for the ideal state of love.[67] But that was a tall order for women who saw new visions of the post-war world but were too timid and conservative to act them out.

While some intellectuals criticized housewives' inability to relinquish their old attitudes, there were many others who sympathetically viewed the progress ordinary women had made since the war's end.

The writer Shimizu Keiko, for example, countered Ishigaki's criticism of idle housewives by drawing attention to the remarkable traits many housewives demonstrated in those days. Shimizu noted that unlike in the old days when social activities were dominated by women from distinguished families, women members of labour unions, or students, who were unmarried and were free to engage in whatever they wished, it was now ordinary housewives who were spearheading the peace movement and other activities opposing price rises, political corruption and the establishment of red-light districts near military bases.[68]

Shimizu argued that ever since the Korean War, housewives had been trying to join forces with one another in the belief that their collective action opposing war, rearmament and attempts to deprive women of their civil rights, would somehow change the world. The age of housewives had just begun as women were now confidently making public statements through newspapers, PTAs and at other gatherings in their capacity as housewives. Whenever they sensed that something might be afoot that could pave the way for war, women rose up and began mounting vociferous peace campaigns, becoming the most politically conscious sector of the nation. According to Shimizu, housewives had finally come into their own and were valuable assets of the nation, who could brighten Japan's future.[69]

Many other commentators, too, took favourable views of housewives, who had just awoken to wider political and social issues and were struggling to find their feet in a new post-war world. Active involvement in peace and other social movements, however, made it extremely difficult for women to live up to the traditional role model of being a housewife. Engaging in various activities outside their homes and absorbing the new ideas that informed such activities, they were challenged to shed a mentality that was shaped in the past, and to seek a new role for themselves that befitted the new society their movements sought to create. Consequently, as the historian Itō Yasuko argued, the 1950s was the last post-war period when the key trait that characterized an activist housewife was her identity as nothing more than a mother.[70]

Strategies for peace: were women pacifist?

Pacifism in the usual sense of the term means an attitude invoking the categorical refusal to take part in any war as a means of settling disputes because of moral or religious principles. Then to what extent did Japanese women embrace the absolute pacifism normally connoted by the word, or as called for by the new Constitution? Or if they were not absolute pacifists, how did they try to secure peace for Japan?

Some women, as in the case of Hiratsuka Raichō, who had been more or less critical of the war, instantaneously converted to the new faith. They unambiguously maintained that renunciation of arms should be part and parcel of Japan's security policy. As was mentioned in Chapter 6, the pacifist arguments of female intellectuals were notable for their moralistic tone. In a breathtaking ideological shift, the poet Fukao Sumako, who had authored uplifting odes glorifying Japan's 'mission' in Asia during the war, became a vocal proponent of absolute pacifism. She now declared:

> Needless to say, we should take a stand against war, and rearmament is absolutely out of the question. How foolish it is to own guns and build tanks in an age of uranium.
>
> As the nation which began the Pacific War, we must by all means carry out that great undertaking – create an ideal world free from all conflicts for all humankind – to atone for our grave mistake.
>
> Is there any such demon who would harass or hurl an atomic bomb at a nation with such admirable intentions? We should do everything to create a peaceful, ideal world and even if the nation is annihilated because of that, so be it.[71]

For the upper house member Kōra Tomi, too, morality took precedence over devising any pragmatic security policy:

> It is defeatist to despair in the face of the difficulty of preserving peace. It would be unbearably humiliating [to take such an attitude] for a nation with a modicum of gumption. What we Japanese can't achieve due to lack of physical force, we can achieve with our moral force.[72]

Absolute pacifism was also professed by many grassroots activists involved in the peace movement. These activists commonly said that they wanted a completely disarmed Japan, on the grounds that international disputes should be resolved through the utmost efforts to negotiate the matter, and that no country would ever harm an unarmed nation, while an effort to rearm Japan could provoke aggression by another country. They put their faith in a moral deterrent that they believed would inhibit any country from committing aggression against a completely unarmed nation for fear of becoming the target of international censure. Some insisted on non-violent resistance, and said they would rather die than resort to war. Rearmament was also opposed on the grounds that the military might again attack other countries as well as oppress its own people. Pacifists contended that any effort at a military build-up would be useless in the face of state-of-the-art weaponry developed by the US and the Soviet Union, and opposition to spending taxpayers' money on arms rather than on welfare remained significant throughout the 1950s.[73]

Some were ambivalent with regard to rearmament while opposing the government's policy, because they believed that the government was planning a larger military build-up than was necessary for the purpose of self-defence. But they also argued that taking minimum measures for defence did not constitute the establishment of a military force.[74] While many women expressed strong anxiety about rearmament, especially in the early 1950s, opinion polls show women were more or less divided on the issue.[75] A view expressed by an official of the Tokyo federation of regional women's organizations on behalf of other members appears to reflect the widespread concern of ordinary women about rearmament, which did not necessarily spring from strictly pacifist sentiment. She said:

> We want female members of parliament to give much thought to the issue of rearmament from a woman's point of view so that our children will not be drafted in the future. While we don't know for sure whether Japan should rearm itself or not, we want women politicians to express their clear opinions about the issue instead of prevaricating or waffling. If it is absolutely necessary for Japan to rearm itself, we strongly demand that no draft system should be introduced but that only volunteers should be recruited into the military, because that is what many women earnestly desire.[76]

Ideas that spurred ordinary women to peace activities were not always particularly deep or insightful. Most housewives' writings on their experiences of the war talk of the unspeakable suffering they experienced, after which they conclude their writings with stock phrases such as, 'That is why we should never let this happen again and have to work for peace.' Most such accounts are long on the horrors of the war they had endured, yet precious little is said about what specific action they believed was needed to prevent another conflict.

Some women had seen children or invalids thrown into the sea to be preyed on by sharks because their boats, fleeing from Korea towards the end of the war, would otherwise never have been able to reach Japan.[77] Others had seen people's limbs and insides fly around amid a hail of bombs. Horrific as their experiences were, the moral that many women had drawn from the war often sounded mundane and sentimental, to the dismay of many intellectuals.

Most housewives were in no position to analyse the international situation on their own and reach their own conclusion concerning security issues, or matters that belonged to the realm of foreign policy. They were able to do little more than simply embrace arguments and theories put forward by political parties or intellectuals.

If they were unable to take part in policy-making, however, ordinary women could organize anti-nuclear petitions, demonstrate in the streets or make their views known through voting. But their writings suggest there was one more dimension to the women's peace movement besides taking political action. In letters to newspaper editors and other writings, women asked themselves what they could do to promote peace, even though they were humble individuals who could wield little influence either inside or outside their homes. The question often led to introspection, whereby women tried to determine new principles for governing their conduct in their daily lives.

Women's writings about peace issues were often statements of their new resolution to do their small bit to work for peace, and their ideas were often indistinguishable from the common-sense morality that exhorts one to become a better human being. In order to work for peace, modest housewives, fully aware of their inadequacies and unsure of themselves, vowed to muster their courage to think independently, mend their ways, improve relationships inside and outside their homes, speak up in public and fight their weaknesses to confront all kinds of problems in their lives. For many housewives, thinking about peace, no matter how naive their views might sound at times, often involved a dialogue with their inner selves, and sometimes led them to rethink their outlook on life.

One housewife began keeping a diary for her four children when the eldest entered primary school. In the diary, she urged her children not to repeat the mistakes of the adults, who had allowed their country to slide into war and had let so many people die, and told them to fight against anything that could threaten peace. Although she had begun writing to communicate her thoughts to her children, she realized that the writings had become exhortations to herself to overcome her weaknesses, to stop being dependent on her husband and to learn more about the world.[78] The housewives were fully aware of their limitations. Their struggle for peace involved fighting on two fronts: self-improvement, or efforts to live up to their moral beliefs at a personal level, and participation in the peace movement. For Makise Kikue, peace, like charity, began at home through her efforts as a housewife. She hoped that her insights, acquired from studies and other group activities, would inspire her family and transform their outlook, leading ultimately to peace.[79]

A comparison of female peace activists with trade unionists makes clear a fundamental difference between the workings of the two peace movements. Members of labour unions delegated much of the decision-making to their leaders, who decided whether or not to take part in peace activities. As a result, policy on peace issues sometimes fell victim to the vagaries of union politics, which supported or broke with the peace movement over the heads of ordinary union members. The sense of participation of rank-and-file workers in the peace movement was often watered down because their leaders made the key decisions.

But housewives, who were members of far smaller grassroots groups such as Kusanomikai, had no such leaders, and at the same time were eternal members of the rank-and-file. They had to make their own decision on whether to join a peace campaign in those early post-war years, when engaging in any political activity in an individual capacity risked provoking considerable public censure. Consequently, the women's peace movement was less vulnerable to the kind of organizational politics that governed the conduct of labour unions.

As modest members of the rank-and-file who were only just beginning to learn about the wider world, women put faith in things that could be understood empirically through experiences in their personal lives. As eternal grassroots activists who coveted little honour for themselves, they gave priority to the basic essentials, or things that mattered most in their own lives and the lives of their families. As the least privileged members of society, who desired little more than the fulfilment of their most basic needs, many women often took a more left-wing stand on peace and other political issues than their husbands, and were also free from the political considerations their husbands had to weigh. Women laughed behind the backs of their husbands, saying men styled themselves as communists at their workplaces because their union required it; on leaving their workplaces and getting on the train, men then acted like social democrats as befitted good citizens; on reaching home, they turned into conservatives who acted like autocrats towards their wives and children because the male chauvinism of pre-war Japan was still ingrained in them.[80]

Tsurumi Kazuko criticized the men's 'samurai spirit' that made them apply a double standard to their activities at work and at home, and attacked the duplicity of men as political animals. According to Tsurumi, it was precisely that samurai spirit that had to be combated if universal principles that would apply both to people's workplaces and homes were to be worked out, and that was what women activists were attempting to do.[81]

The pacifism of housewives was a way of life that encompassed the moral as well as political, social and economic dimensions of their existence. Peace was to be achieved eventually through the aggregation of efforts made at a personal level to become a better person, establish better relationships inside and outside one's home and resolve specific issues facing individuals. For women of the early post-war years, peace was not a matter that could be reduced to debate over rearmament or relations between countries.

Conclusion

In concluding this book, I will look at what overall effect the peace movement in the early post-war years produced on the nation's political landscape, based on the findings from the previous chapters.

The preceding analysis has demonstrated significant differences in the ideologies and organizational principles between the peace movements of labour unions and ordinary women.

As has been seen, the idea of peace as conceived by organized labour was quite different from the outlook shared by progressive intellectuals or the general public. Amid the onset of the Cold War in the late 1940s, Mindō union leaders seized the occasion to define the identity of organized labour as a countervailing force against the government and corporate management on the domestic scene, and against the two imperialist camps headed by the US and Soviet Union on the world stage. When they did so, their stand with regard to peace issues was geared towards maintaining the independence of organized labour, and was posited as an antithesis to their old ways, whereby they had collaborated with the wartime government. In the microcosm of the individual workplace, however, the workers' stand for peace was equated with their determination to battle management and the government.

The peace movement, often accompanied by massive demonstrations in which workers from across industries marched shoulder-to-shoulder, served as an occasion to confirm their sense of solidarity. It was also the first time in Japanese history that unionists had been allowed to stage such an extensive protest in broad daylight, which stood in stark contrast to the repressive atmosphere of the pre-war and war years. The peace movement therefore served as something of a festival, which boosted the confidence of trade unionists in the newfound power of the working class.

The level of union power cannot be gauged solely by labour's victories in wage negotiations, nor can it be determined by factors such as government regulations, corporate earnings and economic conditions. Public-sector unions such as Kokurō and Zentei, although quite powerful, had a rather mixed record with regard to the success of their economic struggles, due to the legal impediments banning their collective bargaining and strikes. Still, even when they were unable to extract significant concessions over wages and other economic matters, many unions wielded considerable power because they were able to exercise control over their workplaces, and were highly successful in defying company policy regarding personnel cuts and other corporate retrenchment measures. Highly intangible factors such as worker psychology and ideology, which are so elusive as to baffle any researcher's attempt to analyze them in quantitative terms, did much to enhance the effectiveness of the labour movement in the early post-war years. These intangible factors were strengthened by workers' involvement in the peace movement, which played an inestimable role in helping to establish trade unions as a standard feature of the nation's political system, despite considerable resistance from the political and economic establishments.

Sōhyō's leadership had to contend with three major considerations in order to organize an effective movement. First, they had to revise the elitist, top-down approach used by Sanbetsu officials in the late 1940s, so as not to cause unnecessary divisions within their own ranks. Second, union leaders had to prod ordinary workers out of their 'feudalistic and passive' mentality so that they would learn to assert their rights and take part in the labour movement in a more pro-active manner. Third, senior union officials had to devise an effective way to harness the activism of grassroots radicals in advancing the labour movement. Use of the mass line approach proved quite effective in addressing the three issues.

The growth of worker activism, however, gave rise to continuous disputes as to what extent the labour movement should rely on grassroots initiative, as well as to the degree to which the workers' struggle should be allowed to overstep the traditional bounds of union activity.

The Mindō leaders, while appreciating the usefulness of rank-and-file activism, demonstrated shrewd realism. Mindō officials, in contrast to Takano and other union radicals, believed that radicalism at the grassroots level could never be a prime mover for the labour movement, and that the bottom-up approach relying mainly on grassroots activists would be impracticable. When grassroots activism acquired a life of its own and went beyond the Mindō leadership's control during the *Anpo Tōsō*, it prompted the leaders to push the radical genie back in the bottle. Thus the *Anpo* ended with a serious clash between conservatism at the leadership level and radicalism at the grassroots level, a phenomenon that commonly hampers many social movements. The rift between lower-ranking activists and the Sōhyō leadership spelled an end to the heyday of the union peace movement based on the mass line approach. The top-down structure of labour organizations, though less pronounced than in the days of the Sanbetsu leadership, remained a significant feature of the labour movement, and came to the fore again following the protest against the security treaty.

With the Mindō officials reverting to their moderate approach, the forces that had pushed for externalization of the labour movement were reined in, thereby narrowing the reach of the political activities that unions took up, as well as the ideological dimensions of the workers' struggle that had become both nationwide and international.

During the whole post-war period up to 1960, no peace campaigns were conducted by organized labour without union theoreticians linking them to economic issues facing workers. A determination to fight tough economic battles, and the left-wing stance on peace issues, were two indivisible elements of organized labour's overall policy. This often made it difficult to tell whether workers' actions were motivated by their genuine yearning for peace or by their economic grievances, and most workers did not make any conscious effort to distinguish the two. While almost all labour disputes in those days were described as a 'workers' fight for peace', peace often had a merely symbolic meaning in many of the struggles, and receded at times into the distant background, to have only minimal relevance to actual issues facing workers at the height of fierce industrial action.

While the righteous anger of workers toward their antagonists was more often than not the predominant element of organized labour's attitude to peace, unions failed to explore key issues of war prevention. While Sōhyō unionists criticized the JSP policy on peace, which they argued focused primarily on diplomatic and security issues, the labour federation lacked viable visions on these vitally important policy issues, except for talking about cooperation with the socialist and developing nations in broad terms. Unionists never made it clear, for example, whether at least some measures to ensure self-defence were necessary, after it became apparent that the United Nations would be unable to guarantee the security of Japan as the JSP policy-makers had hoped.

Leftist workers' optimistic hope for world peace was based on their reading of the international situation, which appeared to show signs of rapprochement, and on the rapid pace of industrial growth and development of leading-edge space/military technology in the communist camp. The way workers supported their arguments about the prospects for peace with the on-going developments in the international arena points to a pacifistic attitude, to use Martin Ceadel's term. The way leftist workers either explicitly or implicitly condoned an arms build-up or use of force by socialist countries or developing nations struggling for their independence, also contradicted their professed support for the war-renouncing Constitution. It is also not clear whether workers regarded the Constitution primarily as an effective weapon that would help them to counter the policy actions of government and corporate management, or whether they aspired to practise the pacifist ideals it stipulated.

Organized labour also lacked the ideological flexibility and resourcefulness necessary to refashion guiding principles for their labour/peace movement that would match the changing economic times and the changing attitudes to work.

Shortly after the war, union leaders had to modernize the attitude of ordinary workers in order to turn them into effective actors in trade unionism. They thereby sought to narrow the gap between intellectual unionists and the less 'enlightened' rank and file. The inexorable pace of modernization in Japanese society in later years, however, pushed the class-warfare-based worldview of senior union officials and activists out of sync again with the sentiments of average workers. Amid the rising standard of living, workers acquired an increasingly modern and rational outlook as they grew accustomed to the accoutrements of a newly industrializing society. The modernity that union leaders had hoped would help instil class consciousness in rank-and-file workers, promoted an almost effortless adaptation to the growing prosperity of a capitalist economy, and ironically gave rise to a new generation of modern men with less affinity for the combative ethos of the Sōhyō-style labour movement.

Women, after having their abilities tested to the utmost in contending with great hardships during the war and its immediate aftermath, had to learn to grow up fast in a post-war world premised on a completely new set of principles. Any conscious efforts women made either to think about peace issues or seek peace through direct action went hand-in-hand with their growth as members of the new post-war society. The process led to the realization that peace had wide-ranging implications for every facet of their personal existence. That prompted ordinary women to take a holistic approach to peace issues, in a way that would address the political, economic, social and moral aspects of their personal lives.

Women began the process of introspection by questioning whether the old official ideology that so shattered the lives of individuals in pursuit of achieving the state's goals could be justified. The process of examining and deconstructing the old morality in search of new values led women to believe that the spontaneous efforts of individuals to attain a reasonably decent standard of living for their families, which in itself was devoid of any morality, was a rightful cause to fight for. The lives of humble people, regardless of their worth to the larger society, gained in importance, and efforts to improve them became a worthy cause in itself. And this enabled ordinary women to play up their status as mothers or housewives in order to assert their rights.

Ordinary women considered the issue of peace in terms of things that directly concerned their daily lives, and accorded paramount importance to people's personal needs in advancing arguments over war and peace. This kind of down-to-earth popular wisdom, which could be termed people-first pacifism, or *seikatsu heiwa shugi*, restored a significant degree of sanity and a humane quality to the nation's thinking. The wartime policy that legitimized total sacrifice at the personal level for the cause of the state eventually proved bankrupt.

While the process helped women to deepen their understanding of the basic human rights aspect of the new post-war peace discourse, the women's peace movement also involved a fight against the general conservatism of early post-war society and their own attitudes. Most housewives in the early post-war days believed that the act of taking to the streets to press political issues challenged the generally accepted notion of propriety. As they backed up their case for direct action with what they argued to be the legitimacy of satisfying people's personal needs, however, female peace campaigners succeeded in having the acceptability of engaging in peace activities enhanced in the eyes of the general public.

The issue over feminism was also of great importance, particularly for underprivileged women living mainly in rural areas. Their struggle to improve their status, however, was seldom linked to the peace movement.

Middle-class housewives in urban and suburban areas, who were more privileged in terms of the rights they enjoyed, paradoxically showed considerable reluctance to try further to emancipate themselves, and were fearful of the consequences that would result from any attempt to break with the old role model of housewife. Thus their peace movement tended to lack any vision for a qualitatively different new world as far as their own condition was concerned. Since their actions were characterized by timidity, through which they avoided upsetting the existing system excessively, activist housewives did not possess the daring of activist workers, many of whom, in their preoccupation with the advancement of their cause, cared little about whether they would be able to make a living or not.

But the need to defy public criticism in order vocally to call for peace, and the painful memories of the wartime past, for which they held themselves partly responsible, made middle-class women realize that it was necessary for them to break the mould of their accustomed and somewhat comfortable existence as traditional housewives. Thus the women's peace movement was accompanied by their efforts to outgrow their status as subordinate spouses in order to become independent human beings. Through such a process, many ordinary housewives unwittingly conducted a feminist movement, although theirs differed from the kinds of proactive campaign staged by later feminists, whose chief aim was the more radical equalization of gender roles.

Housewives who dared not speak out at large gatherings and did not know how to assert their rights in public, formed small groups in which they were able freely to express their views on an equal footing with other women. Such a method of organizing informal activities served as an equalizer of relationships. These activities also helped to enhance the liberties of ordinary women and counter the stifling authoritarian atmosphere of the pre-war establishment.

Housewives, who had just awoken to a new set of post-war values and were struggling to wean themselves from the morality of wartime Japan, continued to be the leading actors in the women's peace movement throughout the first fifteen post-war years. The discourse of women's peace campaigns, therefore, remained largely unchanged during this period, after which the peace movement was taken over in later years by younger generations of women, who laid increased emphasis on the feminist aspect of peace activities.

On the other hand, the very simplicity of their ideas about peace made them impervious to shifts in ideological trends, which contrasts with the peace thought of organized labour. Although their views tended to be naive and their perspectives were narrowly circumscribed by their immediate surroundings, women's ideas on peace relied little on the ideology of great thinkers, unlike unionists' views, which were borrowed heavily from Marxist orthodoxy, and this also helped to enhance the durability of ordinary women's peace thought over the years. The views of unionists, whose ideological reach extended as far as China, the Soviet Union, the rest of Asia and Africa, ironically proved vulnerable to the vagaries of international trends.

The focus on existential issues at a personal level, however, often prevented women from paying much attention to the international aspect of peace issues. Women, who had to deal with harsher conditions in terms of their standard of living and the narrow, feudalistic attitude of their relatives and acquaintances, tended to pay attention more to the flaws of the domestic system, and they equated peace with the desirable condition in which they aspired to live. Many others also did not think through the complex implications of taking a stand against all wars or embracing the peace Constitution, complete with its ban on Japan's possession of armed forces. In fact, the pervasive attitude of women as a whole might be called 'negative pacifism'. Their abhorrence of war and total refusal to go through any similar kind of calamity again points to their retreatist attitude that sought to just wish away any more war. In so doing, they refused to confront the realities of the prevailing international situation, where by all appearances it was still impossible completely to banish war. Their overall attitude therefore was fraught with ambiguities and contradictions. The bulk of women's support for the peace Constitution, which was consistently stronger in opinion polls than that demonstrated by men, was accounted for by this kind of inchoate mass of not-so-principled pacifist moods.

Such failings aside, however, Japan had never seen so many housewives cut such prominent figures in politics since the Rice Riot of 1918, when ordinary women began protesting against rice shortages in spontaneous reaction to a direct threat to their lives. In the early post-war years, the most naive sector of the population re-emerged on the political scene in such massive numbers that the phenomenal people-power demonstrated in the anti-nuclear movement, for example, led intellectuals like Yasui Kaoru to pin their hopes on people's raw energy fuelled by their desire to improve their own well-being as well as the world around them.[1] Even women acting primarily out of self-love in voicing their anti-war sentiment appeared to herald the advent of a new era based on a new set of principles, and many peace activists saw in such an attitude an antithesis which they hoped would counter what the wartime regime had stood for, and thereby promote peace. This served further to augment the intellectual discourse that casts in an idealized light the values derived from the mundane experiences of common men and women.[2]

A comparison of organized labour with female activists shows that the climate surrounding the union peace movement proved much tougher. Membership of a large labour organization inevitably limited individual workers' leeway for independent action. The workings of a top-heavy labour organization, in which the leadership wielded considerable clout, did not allow the rank-and-file the kind of spontaneity demonstrated by members of women's peace groups with 'bottom-heavy' structures.

The prestige of socialist ideology, which was expounded in a highly doctrinaire manner, held considerable sway over workers, thereby stifling ideological flexibility at the grassroots. The cut-and-dried Marxist rhetoric mouthed by unionists suggests that whatever ideological differences they had among themselves were mainly about whether or not they should organize more radical or moderate direct action. Unionists also had to expend substantial energy on economic struggles as well as on infighting within union circles. The challenges workers faced in their confrontation with corporate management and the government were exponentially harsher than anything middle-class housewives experienced in the course of their peace activities.

Against this backdrop, any outlook individual workers might have developed on peace issues tended to be subsumed under the fiery but impersonal rhetoric employed by labour organizations to advance their movement. As a result, unions' arguments on peace tended to lack any deep insight into war and peace as such. Any effects that were produced by workplace cultural activities, which served as a corrective to this tendency, were short-lived and appear to have influenced a rather limited sector of organized labour.

While mainly leftist groups of women collaborated with unionists during the *Anpo Tōsō*, the joining of forces of the two appears to have produced little fresh insight into peace issues. Since organized labour had failed to create a new core of universal peace thought, the simple ideas developed by women became dominant in the nation's peace discourse.

Ordinary women, who were less blinkered by ideological dogma, were the ultimate empiricists. And the moral they drew from their own experience of the war was that human life is sacred, an idea that was nothing new in the history of peace movements abroad, but was quite novel in Japan considering the moral discourse of total self-sacrifice that had enjoyed widespread currency until the end of the war. This kernel of thought helped to create a discourse more universally shared by ordinary Japanese than any other political ideology.

This humanitarian strand of peace thought became more cosmopolitan in later years, in contrast to the nationalist discourse of peace campaigners in the early post-war years. The new generation of activists tried to work out ideas that would hold out a universal appeal to both men and women as citizens and across borders. That created more room for collaboration between male workers and female activists. When these two groupings joined forces it paved the way for the flourishing of the anti-Vietnam War movement, in which a large number of ordinary Japanese conducted a campaign premised on a broad consensus, opposing killings by both Americans and Vietnamese from a humanitarian standpoint.

As many unions withdrew from the peace movement, peace as viewed by workers was transformed from an issue to be contested through a mass organ into a matter of individual belief. As a result, citizen's groups began playing an increasingly prominent role in the peace movement from the mid-1960s.

The attitude of women and workers, who professed their belief in the peace Constitution in the period covered by this book, was characterized, however, by a fundamental contradiction, because pacifism was adopted as the policy of the state.

Most Western pacifists embraced war resistance because they were inspired by their Protestant or libertarian tradition, and decided to take no part in war in the belief such an act would be in fundamental conflict with their religious belief or political ideology, which objected to any act of coercion by the state that would violate the civil rights of individuals. Their dissident stance inevitably clashed with state interests, and they had to endure considerable persecution until they finally persuaded their governments to institutionalize conscientious objection.

In contrast, few Japanese believed in absolute pacifism as something they would practise as individuals, despite their support for the pacifist Constitution. Since renunciation of war was written into law by the authorities, many Japanese tended to take it for granted that Japan would never engage in a war and they, except for a minority of committed believers, absolved themselves of the need to consider whether they as individuals would refuse to take arms in the face of an external military threat. The attitude of the general public in this regard was quite complacent, although the moral implications inherent in the spirit of the Constitution would call on believers in pacifism to make that tough choice in the event of a major crisis. This explains why the ideas of conscientious objection, or Gandhian pacifism, which calls for non-violent resistance in the face of violent acts committed by others, had so few supporters among the Japanese; the tiny minority who subscribed to absolute pacifism were mainly adherents of religions such as Christianity and Buddhism. Most other active supporters of the Constitution were pacificists as defined by Ceadel, because they were unable to make a convincing case for a national security system that did not rely on military force.

Very often in the context of Japan's peace movement in the early post-war years, war resistance was less a matter of defending a personal moral belief than an act of collective advocacy calling on the government to oppose nuclear weapons and rearmament, not to sign partial peace- or Japan-US security treaties, or to drop other policy measures that activists considered to be inimical to peace. As has been seen in the previous chapters, both unionists and women organized their peace movements as collective campaigns, more often than not calling on the government to meet their personal needs by implementing or rejecting certain policy measures.

This collective action taken by a vast number of people at the grassroots, however, had a significant impact on democratic practices in post-war Japan, as well as on ordinary people's attitude to democracy. And the legitimacy of taking such action was backed up by post-war reforms that established peace and democracy as unassailable concepts in the nation's popular discourse.

Peace and democracy, to use the phrase of historian John Dower, became the great mantra of post-war Japan.[3] The new ideals, both because of the authoritativeness of the way SCAP decreed them from above and their compelling psychological attraction to the war-weary nation, were embraced by most Japanese as a slogan embodying what they hoped to be a much brighter and qualitatively more civilized new era.

General MacArthur, testifying before a US Senate committee after returning from Japan, compared the Germans to middle-aged men and the Japanese to twelve-year-old boys in terms of the two nations' scientific, artistic, religious and cultural achievements. MacArthur regarded the Japanese as an isolated and backward nation, who had learned for the first time after the war to appreciate, enjoy and practice 'freedom', a concept Americans are accustomed to from birth.

Indeed, many Japanese drank in the new ideas promoted by their new rulers with the voracious appetite of youth.

Ever since, occasions on which the Japanese used the word 'peace' ran the gamut from the sublime to the ridiculous. It was used to name streets, bridges, a cigarette brand, schools and companies, including a maker of pachinko pinball machines. The word 'peace' was so commonly and routinely used that the very ubiquity of the word in Japan's post-war locution made it often sound quite banal, and its use often became sloganeering largely devoid of any fresh or deep meaning.

In the first fifteen post-war years, when people faced numerous problems on various fronts, peace meant many things, as has been argued at various points in this book. When people formed peace movements, peace was not the sole issue they contested. Their movements were also linked to issues such as the ruling classes' oppression of the working class, inflation, social security, the underprivileged status of women, children's education and the democratic parliamentary process. The actual problems ordinary Japanese faced in their daily lives mostly concerned personal issues, which were far smaller than the big questions of war and peace. But peace was perceived to be an ideal condition of one's life that would result when the microcosm of people's own 'small' problems had been resolved. So working for peace was the same as working to address all problems large and small related to individuals' personal concerns.

Just as the legitimacy of striving for peace was sanctioned by the peace Constitution, tackling personal problems also became a legitimate cause in itself under Japan's post-war system. And this effected a systemic change in Japan's political environment.

The political scientist C. Douglas Lummis has pointed out the revolutionary implications of Japan adopting the new Constitution after its surrender. He says the Constitution institutionalized a radical transfer of power from the emperor and the state to the people, and denied the state the right to build and use military power – something generally considered a natural right of a sovereign state. Seen as an event in Japan's political history, therefore, the Constitution represented a revolutionary change in its national polity.[4]

As Lummis points out, whether in the history of the US, France, Russia or China, the enforcement of as revolutionary a constitution had been accompanied by enormous bloodshed. It should be noted, however, that during World War II there was no organized resistance against the wartime government in Japan that can be compared to the failed revolt of German military officers against the Nazi regime, or the resistance movements in France and Italy. The Japanese by contrast had the new Constitution forced on them by outsiders and had not fought on their own to win radically enhanced rights for the people.

Even after the catastrophic end of the war, in which people's loyalty to the emperor and the state was repaid with the loss of their loved ones and livelihoods, people were still wedded to the old ways. This is indicated by surveys prior to the promulgation of the Constitution that suggest people's main concern regarding constitutional issues was what would become of the emperor.[5] Many Japanese needed prodding by outsiders to accept the modern democratic institutions provided by the Constitution.

After SCAP withdrew its earlier support for popular initiatives in democratizing the political system amid the so-called 'reverse course' from the late 1940s, Japanese activists were on their own to defend the post-war democratic and pacifist principles. Subsequently, peace and other social movements were organized largely to protest against the actions of the Japanese government and the US, both of which now appeared bent on undoing many of the post-war reforms they themselves had introduced.

Most Japanese, however, were not heroes who had been able to take a lone stand against Japan's wartime policy, or who had the courage to practise absolute pacifism in the cause of peace. Those who took part in post-war peace and pro-democracy movements often tended to be guarding the fruits of post-war democratic reform and the improved conditions of life, rather than trying to make vigorous strides in democratization and halt Japan's steady military build-up.

The post-war institutional reforms, however, had created a legal system that legitimized and accorded great value to people's concerns of this kind. The preamble to the Constitution states, 'We, the Japanese people [are] resolved that never again shall we be visited with the horrors of war through the action of government'. Whether or not they were aware of what the preamble said, people believed that they had the right to be spared any war waged by governments. Article 9 was a welcome guarantee that forbade their own government from once again going to war. The institutional guarantee, as well as the official pacifist tenet the nation had adopted shortly after the war, were believed to have sanctioned people's peace activities, and that emboldened countless Japanese anti-heroes, who had been cowed into obedience by the wartime government, to call for peace as their legitimate and inalienable right.

Since their peace activities encompassed other efforts to redress the feudal remnants that still inhibited the democratization of Japanese society, the act of calling on the government to work for peace served as a great equalizer, transforming the relationship between individuals and the state, between men and women, between employers and employees and between parents and children. In the process, the pendulum had swung from the 'big' issues of the state to the 'small' issues of individuals. The people broke with the heroic discourse of the wartime moral code to embrace the discourse of the weak and humble, who could never become heroes. Amid such a post-war climate, the imperial ideology, whose advocates invoked the good of the state to advance their arguments, lost its former rallying power.

Since the peace movement was aimed at more firmly institutionalizing the pacifist and democratic post-war tenets, the active process did much to democratize and modernize the outlook of ordinary Japanese. In order to assert their right to peace or press other demands, many Japanese had to learn to break out of the pre-war mould of being loyal subjects, and to that end had to make conscious efforts to narrow the gap between their old attitudes and the new concepts introduced by SCAP such as civil rights. Since the peace movement involved a transition to a universal belief system based on basic human rights, its implications were far more multifaceted than those of peace activities staged in more developed nations, such as Britain's ban-the-bomb movement that took place in the same period.

In making conscious efforts to change their outlook, many activists learned that a legal framework guaranteeing democracy that was put in place by outsiders was not sufficient to ensure democracy, and that a certain level of political activism at the grassroots, namely their own involvement, was indispensable to promote a vibrant democratic political process. Of all social movements organized in the early post-war years, the peace movement was mounted on the largest scale, and other grassroots activities, even when not directly related to any peace issue, were conducted more or less in the name of peace. These activities all served as an important experience through which people learned for the first time what it actually meant to practise democracy.

From 1950, when the Korean War broke out, the pacifist policy premised on Article 9 came under fierce attack from the Washington-Tokyo alliance pursuing Cold War policies, and from right-wing conservatives who sought to scrap civil rights provisions as well. Popular support for Article 9, following the test of such an unfavourable political climate, grew even stronger. After losing their official backing, pacifist post-war tenets were refashioned by ordinary people in the course of the political struggles in the 1950s, as they embraced peace as the nation's motto, of their own accord and in defiance of the conservative government.

Issues over military bases, Japan's peace treaty with its former enemies and the *Anpo Tōsō* raised the deep concern of a relatively limited sector of the populace. According to protest organizers, some 330,000 demonstrators surrounded the parliament building at the height of the *Anpo*, and that is the largest number ever mustered by any popular movement in post-war Japan. The figure is quite modest compared with the turnouts of demonstrators reported in Europe during the anti-nuclear movement in the early 1980s, or during the US-led war against Iraq in 2003. After peaking during the *Anpo* of 1960, citizens' participation in anti-war demonstrations continued to decline in Japan, except for another resurgence of popular activism during the Vietnam War. If the size of peace rallies and demonstrations held in Japan is any guide, *engagement* on the part of the nation's citizenry, which would be vital for the nurturing of a vibrant civil society, apparently has failed to become part of Japan's political tradition to the extent seen in Europe, or in South Korea, where grassroots activism became strong in response to the country's repressive military dictatorship.

Still, the socio-political dynamics of the 1950s in Japan, which were created by the active peace and pro-Constitution campaigns of intellectuals and other activists combating the often reactionary policies of the conservative government, appear to have helped to channel the nameless anti-war feelings of ordinary Japanese citizens into support for Article 9, which became the symbol of their pacifist credo. From then on, support for Article 9 continued to climb, and the war-renouncing clause won approval ratings of 70–90 per cent in public opinion polls taken from the 1960s to the 1980s.[6]

The bulk of the popular support for pacifist government policy did not necessarily manifest itself in vigorous political activism, but people's anti-war sentiment, often inarticulate but still momentous, forced the hand of successive post-war governments and compelled them to change the way they dealt with the people. Japan's political leadership came to realize that it was no longer able to act in an authoritarian manner. That made it impossible to revise the Constitution against the will of a majority of the people, even though the ruling party continued to profess its aim of constitutional amendment.

Although conservative governments managed to conclude a partial peace treaty and the Japan-US security treaty, as well as establishing the Self-Defence Forces (SDF), widespread pacifist public sentiment (together with the opposition parties that exploited it) managed to win significant concessions from the conservatives: the government decided not to exercise rights to collective security activities in 1954, pledged not to send the SDF abroad also in 1954, adopted the three nuclear principles not to manufacture, acquire or admit onto Japan's soil nuclear weapons in 1967, and banned arms exports in 1976. Since the SDF was barred from military activities other than the defence of Japan, that limited the type of weaponry the government could acquire, as well as the amount of money it could spend on military procurement.

Because the Constitution so restricted its policy options, Japan, whenever it tried to achieve foreign policy objectives, had to focus its efforts on economic initiatives such as overseas assistance projects. Japan as a result has been unable to engage in any military campaigns abroad, extend military support to other countries or export arms, unlike all the other members of the Group of Seven major industrialized nations. Japan consequently created a new paradigm of a major player in the world whose economic prowess has not translated into status as a military power, and which seeks to attain its foreign policy objectives through non-military means. The public's pacifist sentiment played an important role in causing this to happen.

The conservative governments would not have granted all these concessions to the pacifist camp so easily if they had not been compelled to do so after an intense tug-of-war with the opposition. The intense wrangling between the conservative establishment, which was largely hostile to the popular peace discourse, and their opponents was the very factor that provided the tensions between the government and the people which would be indispensable to maintain the vibrant political process.

The realities of the Cold War, however, put the nation's political system seriously at odds with Article 9.

The Cold War in particular had a highly divisive effect on the nation's security debate. The very presence of SDF and US armed forces on the country's soil, which negates Article 9, made Japan's pledge to pacifism as a national policy doubtful in the eyes of both domestic and foreign observers. Japan's foreign policy, which seldom challenged US policy on security matters, together with its steady military build-up, firmly created two mutually incompatible spheres on Japan's political scene. Advocates of one sphere included military/defence pragmatists, nationalists who wanted to see Japan develop into a military power as befitted its economic clout, and a number of ultra-nationalists who steadfastly refused to admit any wrongdoing in Japan's wartime past. Many in this group played the anti-communism card with a view to advancing their conservative agenda and/or countering the democratic/pacifist discourse created by the post-war reforms. The other sphere was dominated by committed pacifist liberals or leftists. In the face of intransigence on the part of the conservatives, the pacifist camp stuck to its guns and became as uncompromising as its opponents. The irreconcilable nature of the rivalry between the two camps made any political dialogue almost impossible, and made national thinking on war and peace issues appear schizophrenic.

Besides the Cold War, the desire to put people's personal needs first, which was predominant in the popular peace discourse, gave rise to a rather unprincipled rationalization of security matters. The SDF had been considered necessary by pluralities or majorities of the Japanese ever since they were formed in 1954, and except for a very brief period during the *Anpo Tōsō*, those supportive of the Japan-US security treaty continued to outnumber those against the bilateral treaty.[7] Public opinion polls show the numbers of those opposing Japan's nuclear armament rising from 62 per cent in 1955 to more than 80 per cent in the 1980s, while those supporting nuclear armament declined from 23 per cent to around 10 per cent during the same period.[8] All the while Japan remained beholden to the military agreement with the US, whose policy options included massive nuclear retaliation.

Thus the international relations specialist Kōsaka Masataka noted the 'hypocrisy' of the Japanese supporting the mutually irreconcilable propositions,[9] and C. Douglas Lummis detected on the part of the Japanese public 'shrewd Realpolitik, namely, an implicit preference for an arrangement in which the fighting would be done by someone else'.[10]

The desire to prevent the government or the military from infringing upon civil rights as in the days of imperial Japan, and to enjoy a sense of security at the same time prompted many Japanese to cling to the SDF and the Japan-US military alliance as well as the Constitution. This tendency to seek to have one's cake and eat it, too, regarding security matters was also a product of the popular peace discourse that prioritized people's personal needs. Most Japanese, who expressed support for Article 9, thereby rationalized or fudged about the conflict between the imperatives of national security and the Constitution.

The popular attitude towards peace in Japan has consisted either of people's moral faith in the nation's new motto for the post-war world, or a pacifist mood of rather indeterminate nature. While committed activists never doubted their belief in absolute pacifism, the level of commitment on a nationwide scale was far more diluted, because the peace Constitution was perceived by most Japanese as a given, allowing people to go about their business of making a living in peace.

Since the Japanese in effect fell back on conventional security measures backed up by force when it came to the nation's defence, their mind-set that sought a guarantee for the safety of the nation in armed security made popular response to any serious international dispute, such as territorial conflicts with neighbouring countries, not so dissimilar to the response of peoples in nations that did not have a Constitution as pacifist as Japan's. While the Japanese did not doubt themselves to be a peace-loving nation, whether or not they were actually more peaceful than other peoples of the world is debatable, considering the way intense nationalist animosity still flares up among many Japanese whenever territorial disputes arise with its neighbours such as Russia, China and South Korea. The recent revelations about the abduction of Japanese citizens by North Korean operatives, and Pyongyang's nuclear weapons development programme, have also given rise to an alarming level of xenophobia. Such tendencies suggest that the

Japanese could become as combative at least in a war of words as any people in the world.

Another important aspect of peace that was often neglected in the people's pacifist discourse was reconciliation with Japan's former enemies and its responsibility for the war.

Amid the authoritarian and repressive pre-war and wartime political tradition, many Japanese had tended passively to follow the government's war policies, and did not believe they had played an active part in causing the war. The Far East Military Tribunal also heaped blame for the war on Japan's political and military leadership and exonerated ordinary Japanese from any responsibility. While SCAP subsequently ceased to press the issue of war responsibility, the Japanese government never clarified its stand on Japan's war crimes in an unequivocal way. Any official gestures, such as a statement of formal apology towards the Japanese people or other countries, or abdication by the emperor, could have made it clear where the government stood regarding Japan's conduct during the war. In the absence of such action on the part of the government, no normative discourse regarding war responsibility was created at the grassroots level. While it was natural for people to feel sympathetic to foreign victims of the war, it was also all too human to be in denial about the war crimes issue. In the absence of a clear moral norm about the issue, these differing natural impulses of ordinary Japanese were left to take their own courses. Victim consciousness as a result gained ascendancy among the Japanese over a sense of remorse about their own conduct.

The Bikini H-bomb test that claimed the lives of Japanese fishermen was called the 'third nuclear bombing of Japan'. There was initially an outpouring of indignation at what people perceived as the unjust suffering the Japanese were being put through again, which was later sublimated into a moral crusade to work for a world free of nuclear weapons. Most people failed to interpret the atomic bombings of Hiroshima and Nagasaki as the culmination of a conflagration that the Japanese themselves had started.

Leftists, meanwhile, did not hide their rage at seeing US military bases on their soil, and denounced 'US colonialism'. But it is doubtful whether they would have been able to seethe with righteous anger the way they did if they had considered the far greater hardship that Japan had caused peoples in the lands it had occupied.

As has been seen, peace activists were largely preoccupied with how to defend their lives and livelihoods as well as the need to eliminate seeds of war on the domestic scene, such as the undemocratic actions of government and corporate management. They as well as progressive/leftist intellectuals were engrossed with their work to create a much better society in the wake of the war.

As Yoon Keun Cha, a Korean historian residing in Japan, points out, while the Japanese responded enthusiastically to universal concepts and ideals such as liberty, equality and human rights and their outlook became imbued with fresh moral zeal, their moral compass did not extend much beyond the country's borders.[11]

It was when Japan's later economic boom began to alleviate people's harsh living conditions that the grassroots peace movement became less of a collective advocacy aimed at advancing people's own interests. During the anti-Vietnam War movement that began in the mid-1960s, activists started to engage in a peace campaign that was not directly related to their personal condition. Only when the need to establish democracy on the domestic political scene became less urgent, and their own economic problems less pressing, did people start to think more deeply about the moral implications of being citizens of a country that extended active support to the US war effort in Vietnam. Only then did more people begin to consider how to come to grips with the ongoing war as individuals also, because an increasing number of workers, who were quitting the old mass organizations of the left, began acting in their capacities as individual citizens.

For both unionists and women in the early post-war period, the peace movement was about finding their place in a new post-war world. Even after modern labour legislation was enacted following the end of the war, unionists still had to put up a resolute fight to establish the labour movement as a fixture in Japan's economic and political system, and thereby win more respect for workers' rights from the government and corporate management. Women had to learn what it took to become independent human beings enjoying equal status with men, and hence fulfil their role as fully enfranchized, autonomous members of society. In the face of the struggle to more firmly institutionalize the nation's fledgling democracy while meeting their personal needs at the same time, they were unable to make a clear distinction between matters of peace as such and various democratic, economic and other issues, which they linked either directly or indirectly to peace. Their peace activities as a result were conditioned very much by the transition from the wartime system, in which both workers and women struggled to adapt and live up to new post-war institutions. It was a phase Japanese peace activists later passed through.

A singular discourse of peace, however, was born from the formative post-war years through the *Anpo Tōsō* and continued to persist through later years.

On the whole, human frailty, which appears to resonate with their timid quiescence during the war, is the most salient trait that characterizes the writings of ordinary Japanese in the early post-war years. In such writings, they tearfully lamented the horrors of the war they had experienced and sighed over their current economic hardship and personal weaknesses that added to the difficulty of taking on the various challenges of their lives.[12] With the cause of wartime Japan discredited by its catastrophic defeat, the war left in its wake nothing in people's minds but an unprecedented proportion of human misery. The moral drawn from such an experience was that war should be avoided by all means, because it is simply unjust to make anyone go through such great suffering.

This stands in stark contrast to the moral drawn from the war by the victorious Allied nations, which concluded that the war was worthwhile and that future generations should follow the example of those heroes who fought the war, even at the cost of great human suffering. Countless World War II documentaries and feature films, American and British, chronicle the enduring hardships of their countrymen and conclude their accounts on a celebratory note, exalting their deeds of courage and perseverance. They thereby produced a quite different interpretation of the war. In a victorious country, the glory of the nation's 'heroic fight to defend civilization' tends to eclipse the human suffering and relegates the lingering trauma that afflicts its own people to the edge of collective memory. The festive tale of a nation's valour requited with the successful outcome of the fighting also deflects public attention away from the human suffering inflicted on the other side.

The ordinary Japanese showed little interest in wartime heroics, and opted to uphold the right of frail human beings to live in peace.

It must be noted, however, that despite numerous contradictions and ambiguities about their principles regarding their objection to war, there is an undeniable moral bent to the popular pacifism of the early post-war years. The moral discourse radically changed between the wartime and post-war periods because people's dedication to the wartime cause was betrayed and outraged by the tragic consequences of the war. The reservoir of popular sensibilities, which was amenable to some kind of moral tenet, had been fostered under the strict authoritarian mores of imperial Japan. And this reservoir of morality continued to persist, even after the bankruptcy of the ethical code prescribed by the wartime government, and sought redemption in a new ideal.

Peace was an apt word to summarize the nation's new post-war ideal. The ideal crystallized from the inchoate feelings of the people, many of whom would have been still too distraught or preoccupied with their hand-to-mouth existence to know how to describe their sentiments clearly had SCAP not supplied the new catchword. The notion of peace held a powerful appeal for ordinary people because, among other things, of the regenerative imagery it conjured. One war widow wrote on 15 August 1963:

> As a member of a war-bereaved family, I will never forget how foolish it was to have fought that war and how tremendous a sacrifice we were forced to make in vain. But I intend to defend the Japanese Constitution which we have earned through that sacrifice, even at risk to my own life. ... Its Article 9, in particular, states the very thing that we had cried out for during the war years. It is like a field poppy that suddenly blooms one night on soil that has absorbed a river of blood shed in vain. Article 9 embodies the flowering of the souls of those who died worrying about the fate of their country and their relatives. If there is anything we can do to console those souls, it is to defend Article 9.[13]

Peace turned into a new faith that the people adopted with a sense of contrition and a vow to redeem themselves by striving never to go to war again. The unprecedented intensity of moral fervour that people demonstrated in the early post-war years produced an effect that might deserve to be called the rebirth of a nation.

Appendix I
The Constitution of Japan

Promulgated on 3 November 1946; effective as of 3 May 1947

Preamble

We, the Japanese people, acting through our duly elected representatives in the National Diet, determined that we shall secure for ourselves and our posterity the fruits of peaceful cooperation with all nations and the blessings of liberty throughout this land, and resolved that never again shall we be visited with the horrors of war through the action of government, do proclaim that sovereign power resides with the people and do firmly establish this Constitution. Government is a sacred trust of the people, the authority for which is derived from the people, the powers of which are exercised by the representatives of the people, and the benefits of which are enjoyed by the people. This is a universal principle of mankind upon which this Constitution is founded. We reject and revoke all constitutions, laws, ordinances, and rescripts in conflict herewith.

We, the Japanese people, desire peace for all time and are deeply conscious of the high ideals controlling human relationships, and we have determined to preserve our security and existence, trusting in the justice and faith of the peace-loving peoples of the world. We desire to occupy an honoured place in an international society striving for the preservation of peace, and the banishment of tyranny and slavery, oppression and intolerance for all time from the earth. We recognize that all peoples of the world have the right to live in peace, free from fear and want.

We believe that no nation is responsible to itself alone, but that laws of political morality are universal; and that obedience to such laws is incumbent upon all nations who would sustain their own sovereignty and justify their sovereign relationship with other nations.

We, the Japanese people, pledge our national honour to accomplish these high ideals and purposes with all our resources.

Chapter II. Renunciation of war

Article 9

Aspiring sincerely to an international peace based on justice and order, the Japanese people forever renounce war as a sovereign right of the nation and the threat or use of force as means of settling international disputes.

In order to accomplish the aim of the preceding paragraph, land, sea, and air forces, as well as other war potential, will never be maintained. The right of belligerency of the state will not be recognized.

Appendix II
The Third Peace Declaration by Women of an Unarmed Japan (abridged)

1. Japan has rediscovered at the price of phenomenal sacrifices made through the war the idealism of a war-renouncing and unarmed nation dedicated to absolute pacifism, which is codified by the Constitution. This is the identity of the new Japan, its goal and its moral underpinning. But if we can not live up to this idealism, even if we avert foreign aggression by not practising this idealism, we will lose the meaning of the nation's existence and suffer moral decay.
2. For the sake of world peace, Japan and all of Asia should belong to neither the US nor Soviet bloc but should form a neutral third force. ... Although the third force that exists in Asia today [*author's note*: this means countries such as India, Pakistan and Burma] is still quite weak, its strength lies in its act of doing the right thing. There is no alternative for Japan but to join the third force after signing a peace treaty if it is to work for Asia's independence and world peace. If Asian nations cooperate to strengthen the third force, it will help resolve crises that emerge both for Asia and the whole world. A great task of humankind has been assigned to Asia.
3. It is clear that Japan should pay compensation for the damage it has caused the Asian nations it invaded, and lack of economic means should not be used as an excuse for not doing so. Although we are extremely poor, we should pay reparations as an act of atonement.
4. It goes without saying that the proposed Japan-US military agreement, which involves the continuing existence of a US military presence in Japan, use of military bases by the US and Japan's rearmament, would violate the peace Constitution. An anti-communist military accord, that presupposes Soviet invasion and justifies itself by the pretext of countering the threat such a contingency would pose, would heighten the tensions between the two adversarial camps in Japan and throughout the Far East region, and could ignite another war. The history of humankind demonstrates that an attempt to preserve peace through armament will eventually pave the way for another war. We do not fear a so-called military vacuum. We believe that the human spirit emanating from truth is mightier than 10 million troops or any state-of-the-art

Appendix II: The Third Peace Declaration 225

weapon. We earnestly desire that peace and security should be preserved through efforts to transform the United Nations, which embodies the conscience of the world, into a better organization for world peace.

5 The phrase Japan-US economic cooperation sounds pleasant and promising. But if it means that Japan will collaborate with the US to assist its global policy and vast military expansion, the meaning of the phrase is essentially military, which darkens our hearts because then we can not hope for the development of Japan's peacetime industry, prosperity, resumption of trade with Asian nations and a rise in our living standard.

We are not politicians, diplomats or businesspeople. Such people might think our ideas and desires are unrealistic. But people who view things only from their professional standpoint tend to lose sight of humanism. We, as women and mothers, who protect the invaluable lives of people, hope to think and act from the standpoint of humanism.

Signed on 15 August 1951 by Jōdai Tano, Ichikawa Fusae, Fujita Taki, Hiratsuka Raichō, Hirabayashi Taiko, Nogami Yaeko, Gauntlett Tsuneko, Kamichika Ichiko and others.

Notes

Abbreviations

1 The official English name of the Nihon Shakaitō was the Social Democratic Party of Japan. The politicians who formed the Nihon Shakaitō after the war represented a wide spectrum of leftist thought, including Marxists and social democrats. Because of their ideological differences, they immediately began bickering over what to name their new party, but later agreed to compromise by calling the party Nihon Shakaitō – which translates as the 'Japanese Socialist Party' – and adopting as its English appellation the 'Social Democratic Party of Japan'. I have used the name 'Japanese Socialist Party' (JSP) in this book because it better reflects the ideological orientation of the party, in which the Marxists were ascendant over their social democratic colleagues.

Introduction

1 According to a telephone interview conducted on 1,500 people by *The Asahi Shimbun* in early November 1990, 78 per cent said 'no' when asked whether the SDF should be dispatched abroad at a time of international conflict. Only 15 per cent responded 'yes'. Cited in Sasaki Yoshitaka, *Umi o Wataru Jieitai: PKO Rippō to Seiji Kenryoku* [The Overseas Dispatch of the Self-Defense Forces: The International Peacekeeping Legislation and the Political Establishment], Tokyo: Iwanami Shoten, 1991, p. 49.
2 Hisae Masahiko, *Kyūten Ichiichi to Nihon Gaikō* [The September 11 Terrorist Attacks and Japanese Diplomacy], Tokyo: Kōdansha, 2002, pp. 52–5.
3 The Tokugawa shogunate banned intercourse with the outside world from the 1630s onward except for commercial trade with the Dutch, the Chinese, the Koreans and the Ryukyuans. The ban was lifted in 1854.
4 Fujii Tadatoshi, *Heitachi no Sensō* [Soldiers' Wars], Tokyo: Asahi Shimbunsha, 2000, pp. 8–9.
5 Ōe Shinobu, *Sensō to Minshū no Shakaishi* [The Social History of Japan's Wars and People], Tokyo: Tokuma Shoten, 1979, pp. 76–8; and Ōe, *Nichiro Sensō to Nihon Guntai* [The Russo-Japanese War and the Japanese Military], Tokyo: Rippū Shobō, 1987, p. 157.
6 Ishida Takeshi, *Nihon no Seiji to Kotoba* [Language in Japanese Politics], 2 vols, Tokyo: Tokyo University Press, 1989, i, pp. 42–65.
7 Ōe, *Nichiro Sensō to Nihon Guntai*, pp. 27–8; and Herbert P. Bix, *Hirohito and the Making of Modern Japan*, New York: HarperCollins, 2000, pp. 52–3.
8 Tahara Sōichirō, *Nihon no Sensō* [Japan's Wars], Tokyo: Shōgakukan, 2000, pp. 215 and 485–6; and Ōe, *Nichiro Sensō to Nihon Guntai*, pp. 158–9.

9 Fujiwara Akira, *Shiryō Nihonshi: Guntainai no Hansen Undō* [Primary Materials on Japanese History: Anti-war Activities within the Military], 13 vols, Tokyo: Ōtsuki Shoten, 1980, i, pp. 7–70, 86–90, 200, 207, 216, 337–46, 339, 349–50.
10 Yui Masaomi, '1940nendai no Nihon [Japan in the 1940s]', in Asao Naohiro, Amino Yoshihiko, Ishii Susumu, Kano Masanao, Hayakawa Shōhachi and Yasumaru Yoshio (eds) *Nihon Tsūshi: Kindai 4* [The Complete History of Japan: the Modern Era], 21 vols, Tokyo: Iwanami Shoten, 1995, xix, pp. 6–8.
11 Ōe, *Nichiro Sensō to Nihon Guntai*, p. 161; and Miyamoto Yuriko, 'Watashitachi wa Heiwa o Tebanasanai [We Will Never Give Up Peace]', *Fujin Minshu Shimbun*, 12 August 1948.
12 An account by Okabe Itsuko on the NHK Educational TV programme aired on 15 August 2000; and Asahi Shimbun Tēma Danwashitsu (ed.) *Nihonjin no Sensō* [Wars As Experienced by the Japanese], Tokyo: Heibonsha, 1988, pp. 240–1.
13 No official records are available on conscientious objectors, who refused to fight in Japan's past wars. Kitamikado Jirō, for example, who had visited Manchuria and witnessed the Japanese army's brutalities against the Chinese there, refused to join the army when he was called up in 1938 on the grounds that an act of killing could not be justified whatever the reason. Though he had braced himself for his possible execution, he was given a non-combatant assignment apparently because the army considered him to be out of his mind. See Yoshida Ryōko, 'Chōhei Kihi: Korosaretemo Iikara Korosumaito Omotta [Draft Dodging: I Was Determined not to Kill even if I Got Killed]', in *Shūkan Kinyōbi*, 9 August 2002, p. 15; and Motoki Yamamura, *Sensō Kyohi: 11nin no Nihonjin* [Non-cooperation with War: The Cases of Eleven Japanese], Tokyo: Shōbunsha, 1987, for other examples of individual soldiers' non-cooperation during World War II.
14 The historian Irokawa Daikichi, who was a university student during the war, argues judging from his experience, that probably only about 10 per cent of the people who stayed in Japan during the fighting, or seven or eight million people, genuinely believed in the country's war aims and made tireless efforts in the spirit of *jinchū hōkoku* (to demonstrate utmost loyalty in service of the country). He argues that such activists were mostly in the middle class and that there were very few such people in the upper and lower classes. Among those who demonstrated enthusiastic support for the war effort of their own accord, Irokawa cites middle-ranking municipal officials, some primary and secondary school teachers, Shinto priests and senior officials of associations of war veterans and reservists, caretakers of patriotic women's and youth groups, the heads of neighbourhood associations, military and regular police officers, lower-ranking officials of plants producing weapons and matériel, some salaried workers, craftsmen and farmers and a great many schoolchildren indoctrinated with wartime propaganda. According to Irokawa, most others passively fell into line at the instance of activists, and others just went along with the prevailing political winds. Irokawa, who was mobilized with his fellow students to perform farm work in rural areas around 1943, also said he was struck by the widespread war-weariness or even indifference to the war among farmers. See Irokawa Daikichi, *Kindai Nihon no Sensō* [Wars in Modern Japan], Tokyo: Iwanami Shoten, 1998, pp. 71–2.

The political thinker Maruyama Masao, in a similar, rather impressionistic manner, recalled that certain sectors of the middle class gave active support to Japan's pre-war and wartime 'fascism'. Among such people were small factory owners, foremen at factories in urban areas, general contractors, shop owners, chiefs of construction crews, small landowners, landed farmers, schoolteachers, municipal officials, low-ranking bureaucrats, and Buddhist and Shinto priests. Maruyama said other members of the middle class, including urban, white-collar workers, journalists and intellectuals, were far less supportive and many disliked

fascism. See Maruyama Masao, *Gendai Seiji no Shisō to Kōdō* [Thoughts and Actions in Modern Politics], Tokyo: Miraisha, 1960, pp. 63–4.
15 Hirokawa Tadahide, 'Kokumin no Haisen Taiken [The People's Experience of the Defeat]', in Fujiwara Akira and Imai Seiichi (eds) *Jūgonen Sensōshi* [The History of the 15-year War], 4 vols, Tokyo: Aoki Shoten, 1989, iv, p. 51.
16 Public opinion surveys show nearly 70 per cent thought shortly before Japan's surrender that the war was not winnable and that about the same percentage did not want to continue fighting any more. See Yoshimi Yoshiaki, *Kusanone no Fashizumu* [Grassroots Fascism], Tokyo: Tokyo University Press, 1987, p. 250.
17 SCAP stands for Supreme Commander for the Allied Powers and also means the occupation authorities.
18 Sodei Rinjirō, *Haikei Makkāsāsama* [Dear General MacArthur], Tokyo: Ōtsuki Shoten, 1985, p. 9.
19 Hidaka Rokurō, 'Taishūron no Shūhen [The Background of the Debate on Ordinary People]', *Minwa*, March 1959, pp. 4–6.
20 Naramoto Tatsuya, 'Nihon ni okeru Sākuru Katsudō no Hatten [The Development of Informal Group Activities in Japan]', *Chisei*, November 1955, pp. 38–9.
21 Sagawa Michio, 'Seikatsu Kiroku Undō no Keifu to Sono Konnichi no Mondai [The History of the Movement To Record Personal Histories and Its Current Problems]', *Gekkan Shakai Kyōiku*, September 1959, p. 13.
22 In 1954 a great public outcry was triggered when twenty-three Japanese fishermen were exposed to massive radiation from a US hydrogen bomb test on Bikini Atoll. The death of some of the fishermen and a widespread food scare over contaminated tuna led to a groundswell of anti-nuclear activities that claimed to have collected over 20 million signatures calling for a nuclear weapons ban between August and December 1954.
23 According to Ikeda Shintarō, for example, the outpouring of popular anti-nuclear sentiment and support for diplomatic neutrality following the Bikini test prompted US Secretary of State John Foster Dulles to reconsider his often high-handed approach to pressure Japan to step up rearmament. President Dwight Eisenhower's administration subsequently decided in April 1955 not to demand that Japan should further build up its forces at the risk of jeopardizing its political and economic stability.

The political scientist Watanabe Osamu argued that already in the early 1950s, Japanese conservative politicians had to take into account the public's strong anti-war sentiment in devising their electoral strategies. The Kaishintō party, which was formed in 1952 by conservatives opposed to Prime Minister Yoshida Shigeru's government, tried to appeal to the nationalistic sentiment of the people, who had grown weary of US occupation, by calling for an 'independent' foreign policy and the establishment of self-defence forces, which it argued necessitated a revision of the Constitution. But Kaishintō politicians learned to their chagrin that their ideas were quite unpopular among voters who nursed anti-war and anti-military feelings that were much stronger than their sense of nationalism. Though it quickly toned down its policy goals of a military build-up and constitutional amendment, the party suffered successive setbacks in October 1952 and April 1953 lower house elections. Watanabe argued that through their repeated election defeats and contact with their constituencies, conservatives learned that an open commitment to constitutional amendment was a good way to lose elections. Watanabe also noted that a majority of the news media, which supported constitutional amendment until the early 1950s, became cautious about it during the mid-1950s as the press became wary of the way the conservative government tried to revise the Constitution without securing public consensus on the issue. Watanabe argued that the media also caught on to the growing public support for the Constitution and tried to strike a balance between the government and public opinion, the resulting effect of which was to help further boost popular support for Article 9. See Ikeda Shintarō, 'Chūritsu Shugi to Yoshida no Makki Gaikō [A Neutral Policy and Japan's Diplomacy in the Final Days of the Yoshida Government]', in Toyoshita Narahiko (ed.) *Anpo Jōyaku no Ronri: Sono Seisei To Tenkai* [The Logic of the Japan-US Security Treaty: Its Beginning and Development], Tokyo: Kashiwa Shobō, 1999, pp. 164–83; and Watanabe Osamu, *Nihonkoku Kenpō Kaiseishi* [The History of Japanese Constitutional Amendment], Tokyo: Nihon Hyōronsha, 1987, pp. 233–332, 473–7.

It should also be noted that the 1959–60 protest movement against revision of the Japan-US security treaty (*Anpo Tōsō*) claimed only the life of one protester, but the death of the young girl sent shock waves throughout the nation and added to the furore among the activists who were already seething with anti-government sentiment. Amid such a combustible atmosphere, the strength of the anti-war and anti-military sentiment of the public was such that it deterred the Defence Agency from using force against the protesters. This stands in sharp contrast to the wartime era, when the Japanese felt powerless to resist a government that had let over 3 million of their countrymen die.

24 Martin Ceadel, *The Origins of War Prevention: The British Peace Movement and International Relations, 1730–1854*, Oxford: Clarendon Press, 1996, p. 41.
25 April Carter, *Peace Movements: International Protest and World Politics since 1945*, London: Longman, 1992, p. 4; and Michael Howard, *War and the Liberal Conscience*, Oxford: Oxford University Press, 1978, p. 36.
26 Charles Chatfield, *For Peace and Justice: Pacifism in America 1914–1941*, Knoxville: University of Tennessee Press, 1971, p. 341.
27 Martin Ceadel, *Pacifism in Britain*, Oxford: Clarendon Press, 1980, p. 13.
28 *Ibid.*, pp. 3–5. Ceadel, who uses the term pacificism following A. J. P. Taylor's usage, admits the distinction between pacifism and pacificism is somewhat contrived and says he uses the word pacificism partly because there is no other term that can more conveniently be used to describe the non-pacifist strand of objection to war within the peace movement.
29 *Ibid.*, pp. 4–5.
30 Cited in Ishida Takeshi, *Nihon no Seiji to Kotoba*, p. 8.
31 *Ibid.*, p. 9.
32 Ceadel, *Pacifism in Britain*, p. 5.
33 Fujiwara Osamu, 'Sensō to Heiwa o Meguru Shisō no Shoruikei [Types of Thought Concerning War and Peace]', *Tokyo Keizai Daigaku Kaishi*, November 1992, p. 33.
34 See *ibid.*, p. 54. Shortly after the formation of the Police Reserve, the forerunner to the SDF, in 1950, 53.8 per cent of the public polled by *The Asahi Shimbun* said Japan should possess a military. People sharing this view continued to outnumber those who opposed a military, until the establishment of the SDF in 1954. *Asahi Shimbun*, 15 November 1950 and 16 May 1954.
35 In January 1960, the Japanese and US governments signed a revised bilateral security treaty that, in contrast to the earlier treaty that was put into effect in 1952, pledged the US to defend Japan and called for the two countries further to build up their defence capabilities. Opponents of the revised treaty contended that it would inexorably subjugate Japan to the US military strategy in East Asia and increase the chances of Japan becoming embroiled in another war. The way the ruling Liberal Democratic Party forced bills on the treaty revision through the lower house of the parliament on 19 May 1960 aroused widespread public anger and triggered the nation's largest popular protest that saw over 300,000

demonstrators gather around the parliament building on a single day at its height, according to leftist claims. Although the treaty revision was passed in June of the same year, then Prime Minister Kishi Nobusuke resigned in view of overwhelming public sentiment against him and also because some factions within the LDP turned against him.
36 Wada Haruki, 'Sengo Nihon Heiwa Shugi no Genten [The Origins of Japan's Post-war Pacificism]', in *Shisō*, December 2002, pp. 5–26.
37 See Carol McClurg Mueller, 'Building Social Movement Theory', in Aldon D. Morris and Carol McClurg Mueller (eds) *Frontiers in Social Movement Theory*, New Haven and London: Yale University Press, 1992, p. 5; Thomas R. Rochon, *Mobilizing For Peace: The Antinuclear Movements in Western Europe*, Princeton: Princeton University Press, 1988, p. 212; and Wesley Sasaki-Uemura, *Organizing the Spontaneous: Citizen Protest in Postwar Japan*, Honolulu: University of Hawaii Press, 2001, pp. 12–4.
38 See Rochon, *The Antinuclear Movements in Western Europe*, xvii, pp. 14–17.
39 NHK Hōsō Seron Chōsajo (ed.) *Zusetsu Sengo Seronshi* [The Illustrated History of Post-War Public Opinion], Tokyo: Nihon Hōsō Shuppan Kyōkai, 1975, p. 175.
40 Takabatake Michitoshi, 'Rokujūnen Anpo no Seishinshi [The History of Ideas Concerning the 1960 *Anpo*]', in Tetsuo Najita, Maeda Ai and Kamishima Jirō (eds) *Sengo Nihon no Seishinshi* [The Post-War History of Ideas in Japan], Tokyo: Iwanami Shoten, 1988, pp. 70–1.
41 Ōkōchi Kazuo, 'Sōhyō Ron [Opinions about Sōhyō]', *Sekai*, September 1955, pp. 63–73.
42 Shimizu Shinzō, *Nihon no Shakai Minshushugi* [Social Democracy in Japan], Tokyo: Iwanami, 1961, p. 29.
43 Interview with Higuchi Tokuzō, 26 May 1999; and with Negami Masayuki, 8 August 1999.
44 Ōkōchi Kazuo (ed.) *Nihon no Rōdō Kumiai* [Japanese Labour Unions], Tokyo: Tōyō Keizai Shimpōsha, 1954, p. 11.
45 For example, see Fujin Minshu Kurabu Nijūnenshi Hensan Iinkai (ed.) *Kōro Nijūnen: Fujin Minshu Kurabu no Kiroku* [A 20-year Voyage: The Records of the Women's Democratic Club], Tokyo: the Women's Democratic Club, 1967, pp. 67–8; Itō Yasuko, *Sengo Nihon Joseishi* [Post-war History of Japanese Women], Tokyo: Ōtsuki Shoten, 1974, p. 77; and Fujin Minshu Club (Saiken) (ed.) *Asu o Hiraku* [Paving the Way for Tomorrow], Tokyo: Fujin Minshu Club (Saiken), 2000, p. 43.
46 Frank Parkin, *Middle Class Radicalism: The Social Bases of the British Campaign for Nuclear Disarmament*, Manchester: Manchester University Press, 1968, p. 2.
47 *Ibid.*, p. 3.
48 Sasaki-Uemura, *Organizing the Spontaneous*, p. 13.
49 Fujiwara Osamu, *Gensuibaku Kinshi Undō no Seiritsu: Sengo Nihon Heiwa Undō no Genzō* [The Formation of the Anti-Nuclear Movement: The Origins of the Japanese Post-war Peace Movement], Yokohama: Meiji Gakuin Kokusai Heiwa Kenkyūjo, 1991.
50 See, for example, Nihon Heiwa Iinkai (ed.) *Heiwa Undō Nijūnen Undōshi* [The 20-year History of the Peace Movement], Tokyo: Ōtsuki Shoten, 1969; and Kumakura Hiroyasu, *Sengo Heiwa Undōshi* [The History of the Post-war Peace Movement], Tokyo: Ōtsuki Shoten, 1959.
51 See, for example, Hiroko Storm, 'Japanese Women and the Peace Movement in the 1950s: Opposition to Nuclear Testing', *Asian Profile*, Hong Kong, vol. 26, no. 1, February 1998, pp. 17–28; Yamaya Shinko, 'Women and the Peace Movement', *Peace Research in Japan*, Tokyo, 1976, pp. 72–7; and Shishido Yutaka, 'The Peace Movement of Post-war Japanese Christians', *Japan Christian Quarterly*, Tokyo, vol. 51, no. 4, fall 1985, pp. 215–24.
52 See, for example, Ōkōchi Kazuo and Matsuo Hiroshi, *Nihon Rōdō Kumiai Monogatari* [The Story of Japanese Labour Unions], Tokyo: Chikuma Shobō,

1969; Murakami Kanji, *Sōhyō Monogatari* [The Story of Sōhyō], Tokyo: Nihon Hyōronsha, 1960; Itō Yasuko, *Sengo Nihon Joseishi* [The Post-war History of Japanese Women], Tokyo: Ōtsuki Shoten, 1969; and Nagahara Kazuko and Yoneda Sayoko, *Onna no Shōwashi* [The History of Women in the Showa Era], Tokyo: Yūhikaku, 1966.
53 See, for example, Nihon Hahaoya Taikai Jūnenshi Hensan Iinkai (ed.) *Hahaoya Undō Jūnen no Ayumi* [The 10-year History of the Mothers' Movement], Tokyo: Nihon Hahaoya Taikai Renrakukai, 1966; Fujin Minshu Kurabu Nijūnenshi Hensan Iinkai (ed.) *Kōro Nijūnen: Fujin Minshu Kurabu no Kiroku* [A 20-year Voyage: The Records of the Women's Democratic Club], Tokyo: The Women's Democratic Club, 1967; and Nikkyōso Fujinbu (ed.) *Nikkyōso Fujinbu Sanjūnenshi* [The 30-year History of Nikkyōso's Women's Section], Tokyo: Rōdō Kyōiku Centre, 1977.
54 Andrew Gordon, 'Contests for the Workplace', in Andrew Gordon (ed.) *Postwar Japan as History*, California, University of California Press, 1993, pp. 373–94; and Andrew Gordon, *The Wages of Affluence: Labor and Management in Postwar Japan*, Cambridge, Harvard University Press, 1998.
55 Ōtake Hideo, *Sengo Nihon no Ideology Tairitsu* [Ideological Conflicts in Post-war Japan], Kyoto: Sanichi Shobō, 1996, pp. 236–40.
56 George R. Packard III, *Protest in Tokyo: The Security Treaty Crisis of 1960*, Princeton: Princeton University Press, 1966, vi–vii.
57 To cite a few examples of such works besides Packard's book, Takabatake Michitoshi, 'Rokujūnen Anpo no Seishinshi [The History of Ideas Concerning the 1960 *Anpo*]', in Tetsuo Najita, Maeda Ai and Kamishima Jirō (eds) *Sengo Nihon no Seishinshi* [The Post-war History of Ideas in Japan], Tokyo: Iwanami Shoten, 1988, pp. 70–1; and Minaguchi Kōzō, *Anpo Tōsōshi* [The History of the *Anpo Tōsō*], Tokyo: Shakai Shinpō, 1968.
58 In all instances except for one each in Chapters 5 and 6, the Tokyo edition of *The Asahi Shimbun* was used in this book.

1 Early years

1 Shin Sanbetsu Nijūnenshi Hensan Iinkai (ed.) *Shin Sanbetsu no Nijūnen* [The 20-year History of Shin Sanbetsu], 2 vols, Tokyo: Shin Sanbetsu, 1969, i, p. 4.
2 Hōsei University Ōhara Shakai Mondai Kenkyūsho (ed.) *Shōgen: Sanbetsu Kaigi no Tanjō* [Witness Accounts of the Beginning of Sanbetsu Kaigi], Tokyo: Sōgō Rōdō Kenkyūsho, 1996, p. 211.
3 Sumiya Mikio, 'Rōdō Undō ni okeru Shinri to Ronri [The Psychology and Logic of the Labour Movement]', in Itō Sei *et al.* (eds) *Kindai Nihon Shisōshi Kōza* [Modern Japanese Intellectual History], 15 vols, Tokyo: Chikuma Shobō, 1960, v, p.188.
4 *Ibid.*
5 Negami Masayuki, *Kokutetsu Rōdō Kumiai Undō no Ichiyoku o Ninatte* [Supporting the National Railway Workers' Union], unpublished writing. Interview with Negami on 8 August 1999. Sumiya Mikio, 'Gijutsu Kakushin to Keiei Kazoku Shugi [Technological Innovation and a Paternalistic Management System]', *Chūō Kōron*, May 1961, p. 91.
6 Ishikawa Akihiro, *Shakai Hendō to Rōdōsha Ishiki* [Social Change and Workers' Attitudes], Tokyo: Nihon Rōdō Kyōkai, 1975, pp. 13–15; and Hidaka Rokurō, *Gendai Ideology* [Modern Ideology], Tokyo: Keisō Shobō, 1960, p. 322.
7 Funabashi Naomichi, 'Rōdō Kumiai Soshiki no Tokushitsu [Characteristics of Labour Unions]', in Ōkōchi Kazuo (ed.) *Nihon no Rōdō Kumiai* [Japanese Labour Unions], Tokyo: Tōyō Keizai Shimpōsha, 1954, p. 26; Ōkōchi Kazuo, *Sengo Nihon no Rōdō Undō* [The Labour Movement in Post-war Japan],

232 Notes

Tokyo: Iwanami Shoten, 1955, pp. 8–9; and Takahashi Masanori, *Rōdō Kumiai to Shakai Shugi* [Labour Unions and Socialism], Tokyo: Sangyō Keizai Kenkyū Kyōkai, 1990, p. 58.

8 Ōkōchi, *Sengo Nihon no Rōdō Undō*, pp. 10, 11, 22.
9 *Ibid.*, p. 65.
10 Interview with Ōtsuka Masatatsu on 22 October 1999.
11 Hōsei University Ōhara Shakai Mondai Kenkyūsho (ed.) *Shōgen: Sanbetsu Kaigi no Tanjō*, p. 46.
12 Hirasawa Eiichi, *Sōgiya* [Labour Dispute Handlers], Tokyo: Ronsōsha, 1982, pp. 21–3.
13 Monogatari Sengo Rōdō Undōshi Kankō Iinkai (ed.) *Monogatari Sengo Rōdō Undōshi* [The History of Post-war Labour Movement], 10 vols, Tokyo: Kyōiku Bunka Kyōkai, 1998, iii, p. 71.
14 Interview with Higuchi Tokuzō on 26 May 1999. Ōkubo Kazushi, *Kaze Wa Cuba Kara Fuitekuru* [Winds Blow from Cuba], Tokyo: Dōjidaisha, 1998, p. 158. Higuchi was born in 1928 and graduated from Yokohama High School of Commerce after the war. He became a political activist around 1947 and served at the Horikawachō union secretariat of Toshiba Corporation in 1948. As a member of the JCP, he was involved in the labour movement in the Tokyo-Yokohama area, but was later expelled from the party.
15 *Ibid.*
16 Higuchi interview.
17 Ōtsuka Masatatsu, *Watashi no Sengo* [My Post-war Life], unpublished writing, pp. 8–9. Ōtsuka was born in 1926 and served in the army in Kyushu. He later majored in theology at Nihon University and in philosophy at Hosei University. He was actively involved in the Sunagawa anti-military base campaign and the *Anpo Tōsō* as a secretary of a regional postal union (*Zentei*) branch.
18 Takeuchi Motohiro, *Watashi no Sengoshi: Kakenuketa Seishun* [My Post-war History: Tumultuous Days of My Youth], unpublished writing, pp. 10, 11, 21, 22. Interview with Takeuchi on 23 April 2000. Takeuchi was born in 1932 and majored in commerce and economics at the junior college of Nihon University. He later helped organize the Sunagawa anti-military base campaign and the *Anpo* protest as secretary of the Tokyo Local Council of Trade Unions. He was a JCP member for most of the 1950s through the early 1960s.
19 Uchiyama Mitsuo, *Shokuba no Rōdō Undō* [Workplace-based Labour Movements], Tokyo: Rōdō Junpōsha, 1970, p. 329.
20 Tsurumi Kazuko, *Social Change and the Individual*, Princeton: Princeton University Press, 1970, p. 99.
21 See, for example, the account of Tatsu Ishimota in 'Hamakaze yo Kibō o Nosete' Shuppan Iinkai (ed.) *Hamakaze yo Kibō o Nosete* [A Sea Breeze That Brings Us Hope], Yokohama: 'Hamakaze yo Kibō o Nosete' Shuppan Iinkai, 2000, pp. 80–1; Higuchi and Takeuchi interviews.
22 Takada Yoshitoshi, 'Kōdō no Imi no Hakkutsu [Delving into the Meanings of Actions]', *Shisō no Kagaku*, August 1959, p. 29. Higuchi and Takeuchi interviews.
23 Takada, 'Kōdō no Imi no Hakkutsu', pp. 26–8.
24 Ishii Heiji, *Watashi no Zentei Yonjūnenshi* [My 40 Years at Zentei], Tokyo: Zentei Fukushi Centre, 1993, p. 183.
25 *Rōdō Sensen*, 11 May 1948. *Rōdō Sensen* was a newspaper published by Sanbetsu.
26 *Rōdō Sensen*, 11 August 1948.
27 Higuchi and Ōtsuka interviews.

28 Higuchi Tokuzō, *Meshi to Tamashii to Sōgo Fujo* [Food, the Soul and Mutual Help], unpublished paper, 2001, p. 14. Higuchi interview.
29 Yamada Yoshimi, '1970 Nen to Nihon Kyōsantō [The Year 1970 and the Japanese Communist Party]', *Keizai Hyōron*, extra edn, December 1964, p. 78.
30 Ōtsuka interview. Ōtsuka left the JCP after criticizing the leadership for 'excessively politicizing the labour movement'.
31 Sumiya Mikio, 'Rōdō Undō niokeru Hiyaku to Hatten [Development of the Labour Movement]', in Oka Yoshitake (ed.) *Gendai Nihon no Seiji Katei* [The Political Process in Modern Japan], Tokyo: Iwanami Shoten, 1958, p. 413.
32 Hirasawa, *Sōgiya*, p. 41.
33 *Ibid.*, pp. 26–9, 31.
34 *Ibid.*, p. 40.
35 The acronym GHQ, which stands for the general headquarters of SCAP, is used to mean the US occupation authorities.
36 When mainly public-sector unions had been demanding substantial wage hikes from late 1946, then Prime Minister Yoshida Shigeru infuriated organized labour on 1 January 1947 by calling it 'an insolent rabble [*futei no yakara*]'. Subsequently, unions, under the leadership of the JCP, set about organizing a highly politicized movement aimed at replacing the Yoshida government with a 'people's government [*jinmin seifu*]'. To this end, public unions scheduled their 'general' strike for 1 February but the plan was abandoned at the last minute on 31 January at the behest of General MacArthur.
37 *Rōdō Sensen*, 12 May 1950.
38 *Rōdō Sensen*, 19 June 1950.
39 *Rōdō Sensen*, 26 April 1948.
40 *Zentei Shimbun*, 17 June 1949.
41 *Rōdō Sensen*, 8 May 1950.
42 *Ibid.*
43 Shimizu Shinzō, *Sengo Kakushin Seiryoku* [Post-war Reformist Forces], Tokyo: Aoki Shoten, 1966, p. 139.
44 In the so-called Shimoyama incident, Shimoyama Sadanori, the head of the National Railway Authority, who announced the decision to dismiss 95,000 railway staff on 1 July 1949, went missing on the fifth of the same month and was found dead the following day on the railroad tracks in Tokyo's Adachi Ward. It is still not known whether Shimoyama committed suicide or was murdered. On the night of 15 July of the same year, an unmanned train in a train yard at Mitaka, Tokyo suddenly began running and crashed into nearby shops, killing six. This is known as the Mitaka incident. In another event on 17 August of the same year, known by the place-name Matsukawa, near which it happened, a train derailed, resulting in the death of three people. The derailment was caused by faulty rail tracks, which were found to have been tampered with. The government held communists responsible for each of these three cases.
45 Negami interview. Negami, who was born in 1920, left the middle school under Japan's old school system before completing his course. He took charge of workers' cultural activities as an official of the National Railway Workers' Union. He was a member of the Kakushin Dōshikai (the Association of Reformers) called Kakudō for short. The group was affiliated with the Rōnō Party, which was founded in 1948 by Kuroda Hisao, Kimura Kihachirō and others in hopes that it would form a united front by bringing together the right and left wings of the JSP with the JCP. Negami was a member of the party until it was disbanded in 1957 to merge with the JSP.
46 Ōkōchi, *Sengo Nihon no Rōdō Undō*, pp. 39–41.
47 Iida Hichizō in a 28 May 1997 broadcast of NHK Education Television. Iida was arrested with his communist colleagues on suspicion of involvement in the Mitaka incident of 1949.

48 A massive firing of communist workers and labour activists, who were considered communist sympathizers, was conducted mainly by private companies at the behest of SCAP in 1950. According to a Labour Ministry survey conducted as of December 1950 and the National Personnel Authority data of November 1950, a total of 10,972 workers were dismissed from private firms and 1,177 lost their jobs at government agencies. See Monogatari Sengo Rōdō Undōshi Kankō Iinkai (ed.) *Monogatari Sengo Rōdō Undōshi*, iii, p.87.
49 Kokubun Ichitarō, 'Heiwa Undō [The Peace Movement]', in Takeuchi Yoshimi (ed.) *Sengo no Minshū Undō* [Popular Movements in the Post-war Era], Tokyo: Aoki Shoten, 1956, pp. 125–7.
50 *Rōdō Sensen*, 6 April 1948.
51 *Rōdō Sensen*, 26 April 1948.
52 Takahashi Hikohiro, 'Kokumin Ishiki no Henka to Shakai Undō [Change In Public Opinion and Social Movements]', in Rekishigaku Kenkyūkai and Nihonshi Kenkyūkai (eds) *Kōza Nihon Rekishi II: Gendai 1* [Lecture Series in Japanese History: Recent History 1], Tokyo: Tokyo University Press, 1985, pp. 138–9.
53 See *Sekai Heiwa*, *Jiyū no Koe* and *Kōwa Shimbun*. *Sekai Heiwa* was published by a JCP-affiliated peace organization called Heiwa Yōgo Nihon Iinkai, *Jiyū no Koe* by Genron Danatsu Hantai Dōmei, a group of workers dismissed during the Red Purge and *Kōwa Shimbun* by Zenmen Kōwa Aikoku Undō Kyōgikai, a peace group comprising the JSP, the Rōnō party, the JCP and various groups involved in social movements.
54 According to Ōtsuka Masatatsu, the JCP in the late 1940s never conducted the kind of thorough education needed to awaken workers to 'class consciousness' and thereby encourage more rank-and-file commitment to the labour movement. The view is echoed by a JCP member, who said the party had not conducted systematic education to inculcate class consciousness in workers and had thus been unable to fight the Red Purge effectively. See Kobayashi Shigeru, 'Red Purge Hantai Tōsō ni tsuite [About the Protest against the Red Purge]', *Zenei*, December 1959, p. 88. Ōta Kaoru, chairman of Sōhyō from 1958 to 1966, also said if Sanbetsu had cultivated closer ties with rank-and-file workers, its precipitous demise might have been prevented. Ōta Kaoru, *Tatakai no Nakade* [Amidst the Struggle], Tokyo: Aoki Shoten, 1971, p. 55.

2 The Korean War and the peace treaty

1 Interview with Hino Saburō on 22 September 1999. Hino, who was born in 1932, began working for the National Railways after graduating from high school. He became actively involved in the labour movement after the Red Purge and led the railway union's choral singing activities. He says he joined the JCP in 1950 shortly after SCAP began cracking down on communists with the aim of salvaging the battered party. See also Hino Saburō, 'Waga Seishun Jidai, Gyakkyō o Kirihiraku [The Days of My Youth: Overcoming Adversity]', in 'Hamakaze yo Kibō o Nosete' Shuppan Iinkai (ed.) *Hamakaze yo Kibō o Nosete* [A Sea Breeze That Brings Us Hope], Yokohama: 'Hamakaze yo Kibō o Nosete' Shuppan Iinkai, 2000, pp. 356–7.
2 *Jiyū no Koe*, 15 October 1950.
3 Kokutetsu Rōdō Kumiai, *1951 Nendo Tōsō Hōshinsho* [The Policy for Fiscal 1951 Struggles], pp. 82–3. Negami interview.
4 Hino interview. For further details about the National Railway's cooperation with the US war effort during the Korean War, see Yamazaki Shizuo, *Shijitsu de Kataru Chōsen Sensō Kyōryoku no Zenyō* [Historical Facts about Japan's Cooperation with the Korean War], Tokyo: Hon no Izumisha, 1998.

5 *Kokutetsu Shimbun*, 14 August 1952; and Shisō no Kagaku Kenkyūkai, *Kyōdō Kenkyū: Shūdan: Sākuru no Sengo Shisōshi* [Joint Research on Groups: The Postwar Intellectual History of Social Circles], Tokyo: Heibonsha, 1976, pp. 185–207; Hino Saburō, 'Waga Seishun Jidai, Gyakkyō o Kirihiraku', pp. 358–9. Hino interview.
6 Saitō Kisaku, 'Kokutetsu Rōdōsha wa Heiwa to Tōitsu ni Susumu [National Railway Workers' Progress toward Peace and Unity]', *Zenei*, no. 53, 1950, p. 69; and Ashigara Sadayuki, *Tetsuro no Hibiki* [The Sound of the Rails], Tokyo: Rironsha, 1954, p. 135. *Zenei* also reports that the National Railway Workers' Union voted down cooperation with the United Nations, or support of the war effort, by 335 votes to 89 in defiance of centre-right leaders of Kokurō, railway managers and plainclothes policemen who also attended the convention. But this is at variance with the report in the 17 October 1950 issue of *The Asahi Shimbun*, which says that a significant number of delegates argued that the union should more clearly express its support for the UN. According to *The Asahi Shimbun*, many unionists also said that it was difficult to put into action the policy the union had adopted earlier to promote the peace movement. The *Zenei* report of the Kokurō unionists opposing support for the UN is also denied by Negami Masayuki, a senior union official who attended the Matsue convention. Negami says that workers would have faced a trial by the occupation forces if they had openly opposed cooperation with the war effort. But both Negami and Hino Saburō agree that working conditions had become so harsh immediately after the outbreak of the Korean War that many workers found them almost life-threatening.
7 Interview with Seto Sadao on 20 March 2000. Seto was born in 1927 and studied for a year at today's equivalent of high school under Japan's old school system. He was then employed by the National Railways and served as the head of a Kokurō branch in Chigasaki, Kanagawa from the 1950s. He joined the JCP in 1952.
8 *Kokutetsu Bunka*, 20 June 1953, pp. 32–4.
9 Ashigara, *Tetsuro no Hibiki*, p. 108.
10 Ōkōchi Kazuo and Matsuo Hiroshi, *Nihon Rōdō Kumiai Monogatari* [The Story of Japanese Labour Unions], Tokyo: Chikuma Shobō, 1969 ii, pp. 9–10.
11 Monogatari Sengo Rōdō Undōshi Kankō Iinkai (ed.) *Monogatari Sengo Rōdō Udōshi* [The History of Post-war Labour Movement], 10 vols, Tokyo: Kyōiku Bunka Kyōkai, 1998, iii, p. 81; and Ministry of Labour, *Shōwa Nijūkunen Rōdō Keizai no Bunseki* [Analysis of the Labour Economy in 1954], p. 223.
12 *Sōhyō*, 3 April 1953.
13 Takaragi Fumihiko, 'Ōta-san no Omoide ni Kanrenshite [Memories of Mr Ōta]', *Shinpo to Kaikaku*, February 1999, p. 31; and *Zentei Shimbun*, 1 June 1949.
14 *Shin Sanbetsu*, 10 February 1985. Interview with Mito Nobuto on 10 October 1999.
15 *Ibid.*
16 Hosoya Matsuta, 'Takano-Hosoya Line no Koro [The Days of the Takano-Hosoya Axis]', p. 105. The photocopied transcript of the interview with Hosoya Matsuta, which was conducted by Shimizu Shinzō, Nakajima Masamichi and Tatsui Yōji, was found in the Takano Minoru collection at Shinshū University. It is not known what publication carried the interview except that it was published in conjunction with the release of the third volume of *Takano Minoru Chosakushū* by the publisher Tsuge Shobō.
17 Shin Sanbetsu (ed.) *Zoku Shin Sanbetsu no Nijūnen* [The 20-year History of Shin Sanbetsu: Sequel], Tokyo: Atlas Network, 1988, p. 268.
18 Abe Yoshishige, Ōuchi Hyōe, Nishina Yoshio *et al.*, 'Sensō to Heiwa ni Kansuru Nihon no Kagakusha no Seimei [A Japanese Scientists' Statement on War and

Peace]', *Sekai*, March 1949, pp 6–9; Heiwa Mondai Danwakai, 'Kōwa Mondai ni tsuite no Heiwa Mondai Danwakai Seimei [A Heiwa Mondai Danwakai's Statement on the Issue of the Peace Treaty]', *Sekai*, March 1950, pp. 60–4; and Heiwa Mondai Danwakai, 'Mitabi Heiwa ni tsuite [For the Third Time on Peace]', *Sekai*, December 1950, pp. 21–52.
19 Mito interview on 10 October 1999. Mito was born in 1914 and graduated from Hiroshima commercial school. He became a labour activist in the pre-war days and joined the JCP in 1931. He was arrested in 1934 on charges of violation of the Peace Preservation Law. He left the JCP after the war's end when he defected from Sanbetsu to found Sanbetsu Mindō in 1948, and joined the JSP at the time of the peace treaty debate around 1950.
20 Shin Sanbetsu Nijūnenshi Hensan Iinkai (ed.) *Shin Sanbetsu no Nijūnen* [The 20-year History of Shin Sanbetsu], 2 vols, Tokyo: Shin Sanbetsu, 1969, i, p. 341.
21 *Ibid.*, pp. 196, 199, 204.
22 *Ibid.*
23 Mito interview.
24 Shin Sanbetsu (ed.) *Zoku Shin Sanbetsu*, pp. 28–9.
25 Shin Sanbetsu, 10 February 1985.
26 Shin Sanbetsu (ed.) *Shin Sanbetsu no Nijūnen*, i, pp. 161 and 170.
27 Ministry of Labour (ed.) *Shiryō Rōdō Undōshi* [Materials on the History of the Labour Movement], 1951, p. 248.
28 Shiota Shōbei, 'Rōdō Kumiai to Seiji [Labour Unions and Politics]', in Ōkōchi Kazuo (ed.) *Nihon no Rōdō Kumiai* [Japanese Labour Unions], Tokyo: Tōyō Keizai Shinpōsha, 1954, p. 90; and *Asahi Shimbun*, 16 July 1952.
29 Ministry of Labour (ed.) *Shiryō Rōdō Undōshi*, 1951, p. 249.
30 *Ibid.*, p. 250.
31 Shin Sanbetsu, *Shin Sanbetsu no Nijūnen*, i, pp. 344–5; and Shitetsu Sōren Nijūnenshi Hensan Iinkai (ed.) *Shitetsu Sōren Nijūnenshi Shiryōhen* [Appendix to the 20-year History of the General Federation of Private Railway Workers' Unions of Japan], Tokyo: Rōdō Junpōsha, 1969, p. 360.
32 *Asahi Shimbun*, 5 July 1952 and 23 January 1953.
33 Takashima Kikuo, *Sengo Rōdō Undōshi Ron* [A Critique of the History of the Post-war Labour Movement], Tokyo: Tsuge Shobō, 1977, p. 85.
34 Within Kokurō, too, some unionists argued that joining Sōhyō would go against the principles of the working class because the labour organization was guided by the enemy class and was supporting the reactionary and warmongering policies of Prime Minister Yoshida Shigeru's government. But Kokurō eventually voted to join Sōhyō by 262 votes to 156. See Kokutetsu Rōdō Kumiai (ed.) *Kokutetsu Rōdō Kumiai Nijūnenshi* [The 20-year History of the National Railway Union], Tokyo: Rōdō Junpōsha, 1960, p. 440.
35 Shimizu Shinzō, *Sengo Kakushin no Hanhikage* [Semidarkness in the Post-war Reform Movement], Tokyo: Nihon Keizai Hyōronsha, 1995, p. 115.
36 Cited in Ariga Sōkichi, *Kokutetsu Minshuka e no Michi* [The Road to Democratization of the Japanese National Railway], Tokyo: Tetsurō Yūai Kaigi, 1989, p. 134. The 'chicken to duck' metaphor is generally attributed to Takano Minoru. Another account attributes the metaphor to a Japanese interpreter, who was told by a SCAP official, 'Sōhyō should join the ICFTU unless it wants to become a lame duck', and failed to understand the meaning of the phrase 'lame duck'.
37 Material for the Sōhyō's second annual conference, 1951, p. 10.
38 Takano Minoru Chosakushū Henshū Iinkai (ed.) *Takano Minoru Chosakushū* [A Collection of Writings by Takano Minoru], 5 vols, Tokyo: Tsuge Shobō, 1976, i, pp. 11–12.
39 Interview with Andō Jinbei on 1 September 1997. Andō joined the JCP in 1948 and was expelled from the University of Tokyo in 1950 because of his left-wing

political activities as a key member of the All Japan Federation of Student Unions (Zengakuren). A lifelong political activist, he briefly worked for Sōhyō in the mid-1950s.

40 Hino interview. Hino was found by the national railway company to be a communist although he had kept secret his JCP membership ever since he joined the party in 1950. He says that nearly cost him his job, but that he was able to continue working for the national railways because the occupation ended in 1952. The journalist Kobayashi Tomie, who was not a member of the JCP, was dismissed from her newspaper company during the Red Purge because her union activities made her suspect in the eyes of managers. Kobayashi says she felt a sense of powerlessness in those days in the face of the so-called Potsdam directives SCAP imposed in disregard of labour legislation protecting workers' rights. Interview with Kobayashi on 4 April 2002. Kobayashi was born in 1916 and graduated from women's high school. She was formerly a reporter on the *Mainichi Shimbun*.

41 Ōtake Hideo, *Sengo Nihon no Ideology Tairitsu* [Ideological Conflicts in Post-war Japan], Kyoto: Sanichi Shobō, 1996, p. 213.

42 Shimizu Shinzō, 'Sōhyō Sanjūnen no Balance Sheet [The Balance Sheet for the 30-year History of Sōhyō]', in Shimizu Shinzō (ed.) *Sengo Rōdō Kumiai Undōshi Ron* [Critiques of the Post-war History of the Labour Movement], Tokyo: Nihon Hyōronsha, 1982, p. 333.

43 Takashima, *Sengo Rōdō Undōshi Ron*, p. 111.

44 Zenkoku Kinzoku Rōdō Kumiai (ed.) *Zenkoku Kinzoku 30 Nenshi* [The 30-year History of the National Trade Union of Metal and Engineering Workers], Tokyo: Rōdō Junpōsha, 1977, pp. 357–60.

45 Shioda Shōbei, 'Rōdō Kumiai to Seiji [Labour Unions and Politics]', in Ōkōchi Kazuo (ed.) *Nihon no Rōdō Kumiai* [Japanese Labour Unions], Tokyo, Tōyō Keizai Shinpōsha, 1954, p. 64.

46 While most interviewees contacted by the author say the mood among ordinary workers was ripe for the adoption of the peace principles, the limited number of opinion polls available makes it difficult to gauge the extent of support ordinary workers expressed for the new union policy toward peace issues. A survey conducted by Tokyo Chikyō, a grouping of unions in the Tokyo area, showed an overwhelming majority of workers were supportive of a comprehensive peace treaty and opposed rearmament. They expressed their views on condition of anonymity because most were afraid of making their opinions known. See *Kōwa Shimbun*, 22 May 1951. Surveys conducted by Zentei in two small provincial towns suggest that anti-war sentiment was widely shared even by those living far from Tokyo. At the postal union's Nagano chapter in charge of postal savings, 667 workers (85 per cent) supported a comprehensive peace treaty while 117 (15 per cent) favoured a partial treaty. With regard to rearmament, 668 (84.7 per cent) were against and 92 (11.6 per cent) approved an armed build-up, with 28 (3.7 per cent) saying 'don't know'. In Shimane, of 558 respondents, 377 supported a comprehensive peace treaty and 159 called for a partial peace treaty. A total of 422 opposed rearmament, with 129 in favour. See *Zentei Shimbun*, 14 February 1951. The 11 March 1951 issue of *Asahi Shimbun* also notes that the JSP's three peace principles generally enjoyed wide support among rank-and-file workers of various unions.

47 *Kōwa Shimbun*, 16 October 1951.

48 *Kokutetsu Shimbun*, 30 January 1951.

49 *Ibid.*, 5 February 1951.

50 Negami Masayuki, *Kokutetsu Rōdō Kumiai Undō no Ichiyoku o Ninatte* [Supporting the National Railway Workers' Union], unpublished writing, p. 104. Interview with Negami on 2 September 1999.

51 Kokutetsu Rōdō Kumiai, *1951 Nendo Tōsō Hōshinsho*, pp. 25–41.
52 *Ibid.*, pp. 42–59.
53 Ariga, *Kokutetsu Minshuka*, p. 163.
54 Kokutetsu Rōdō Kumiai, *1951 Nendo Tōsō Hōshinsho*, p. 88.
55 *Kōwa Shimbun*, 19 June 1952. Labour unions opposed the Anti-Subversive Activities Law, enacted in July 1952 to punish violent acts of sedition, in the belief that it was targeted at the labour movement.
56 Kokutetsu Rōdō Kumiai, *Kokutetsu Rōdō Kumiai Nijūnenshi*, pp. 550–4; and Kokutetsu Rōdō Kumiai Shizuoka Chihō Honbu (ed.) *Kokurō Shizuoka Sanjūnenshi* [The 30-year History of the National Railway Union's Shizuoka Chapter], Shizuoka: Kokutetsu Rōdō Kumiai Shizuoka Chihō Honbu, 1983, p. 49.
57 Zenkoku Kinzoku (ed.) *Zenkoku Kinzoku Sanjūnenshi*, p. 358; and Ōsawa Kiyoshi, 'Nikkō Akabane no Tōsō Kiroku [Records of the Struggle at Nippon Steel's Akabane Plant]', *Shakai Shugi*, March 1953, pp. 60–3.
58 *Kōwa Shimbun*, 19 June 1952.
59 Ministry of Labour (ed.) *Shiryō Rōdō Undōshi*, 1951, pp. 258–65.
60 Iwai Akira, a key Kokurō official who was a member of the Rōdōsha Dōshikai, said the idea for the pacifist policy came from the youth section of the JSP, which suggests the original idea, indeed, came from Shin Sanbetsu as Mito claims. See Iwai Akira, *Sōhyō to tomoni* [With Sōhyō], Tokyo: Yomiuri Shimbunsha, 1971, p. 57.
61 Shimizu Shinzō, *Sengo Kakushin Seiryoku* [The Post-war Reformist Force], Tokyo: Aoki Shoten, 1966, p. 175.
62 Shimizu, *Nihon no Shakai Minshushugi* [Social Democracy in Japan], Tokyo: Iwanami, 1961, p. 52.
63 Takashima Kikuo, *Sengo Rōdō Undōshi Ron*, pp. 79–80.
64 The other two unions that left Sōhyō were the Japanese Broadcasting Labour Union and the National Cinema and Theatre Workers' Union.
65 Shioda Shōbei, 'Rōdō Kumiai to Seiji', in Ōkōchi (ed.) *Nihon no Rōdō Kumiai*, pp. 89–90; *Sōhyō*, 14 September 1951; and *Asahi Shimbun*, 13 July 1952.
66 *Sōhyō*, 5 September 1950. According to Ōta Kaoru, Kaiin probably wanted to join the ICFTU because Japanese ships were barred from entering Soviet and Chinese territorial waters and had to put into ports of capitalist nations. See Ōta Kaoru, *Hibike Rappa* [Sound the Trumpet], Tokyo: Nihon Keizai Shimbun, 1974, p. 87.

3 The Takano years

1 Takano Minoru Chosakushū Hensan Iinkai (ed.) *Takano Minoru Chosakushū* [A Collection of Writings by Takano Minoru], 5 vols, Tokyo: Tsuge Shobō, 1976, ii, pp. 360 and 365.
2 Takashima Kikuo, *Sengo Rōdō Undōshi Ron* [A Critique of the History of the Post-war Labour Movement], Tokyo: Tsuge Shobō, 1977, p. 267: and Shimizu Shinzō, *Nihon no Shakai Minshu Shugi* [Social Democracy in Japan], Tokyo: Iwanami Shoten, 1961, p. 52.
3 Takashima Kikuo, 'Takano san ni okeru Rōdō Undō to Tō [The Labour Movement and Political Parties for Mr Takano]', in Inomata Tsunao Chosaku Ikō Kankō Kai (ed.) *Ichi Kaikyū Senshi no Bohyō* [The Tombstone of a Class Warrior], Tokyo: Inomata Tsunao Chosaku Ikō Kankō Kai, 1975, p. 4.
4 *Ibid.*, p. 5. Shimizu, *Sengo Kakushin no Hanhikage* [Semidarkness in the Post-war Reform Movement], Tokyo: Nihon Keizai Hyōronsha, 1995, p. 430.
5 Takano Minoru Chosakushū Hensan Iinkai, *Takano Minoru Chosakushū*, ii, p. 550.

Notes 239

6 Shimizu, *Sengo Kakushin no Hanhikage*, p. 126. Yamaguchi Kenji, former head of the JSP's youth section, however, quotes Takano as saying that the platform, which served as a basis for the JCP's switch to violent guerrilla tactics, was drawn up in China and therefore was out of touch with the realities in Japan. Takano is said to have stated that though the platform would be of little use, it would be important in promoting cooperation with China. The episode suggests that Takano was something of a wily tactician with a convoluted mind. See Shimizu Shinzō no Omoide Kankō Iinkai (ed.) *Kunshiran no Hanakage ni* [Under the Shadow of a Kaffir Lily], Tokyo: Heigensha, 1997, p. 117.
7 The Socialism Association was established by the centre-left groups of Sōhyō and the JSP to promote socialist thought and devise socialist theories for Sōhyō's actions.
8 In contrast to the Rōnō school's one-stage revolution thesis, the so-called Kōza school, whose view was espoused by the JCP, held that a nationalist bourgeois revolution should take place first, to be followed by a socialist revolution led by the proletariat.
9 Inomata Tsunao Chosaku Ikō Kankō Kai (ed.) *Ichi Kaikyū Senshi no Bohyō*, p. 5.
10 *Ibid.*, p. 26. Takano Minoru Chosakushū Henshū Iinkai (ed.) *Takano Minoru Chosakushū*, i, Appendix p. 5.
11 *Shūkan Rōdō Jōhō*, 16 February 1955. Takashima Kikuo also echoes this point, saying, 'One of the most important things I learned from Mr Takano was that individual workers' initiative counted more in the labour movement than any tactic or strategy'. See Takashima, *Sengo Rōdō Undōshi Ron*, p. 3.
12 Takashima, *Sengo Rōdō Undōshi Ron*, p. 267.
13 *Shūkan Rōdō Jōhō*, 23 February 1955, p. 9.
14 *Tokyo Chihyō*, 10 October 1957, p. 11.
15 *Asahi Shimbun*, 19 January 1955, morning edn.
16 *Sōhyō*, 17 July 1953.
17 Interview with Yoshioka Tokuji, former head of the All Japan Harbour Workers' Union, on 26 August 1999. Yoshioka Tokuji, *Minato no Undō Yonjūnen* [The 40-year History of the Port Workers' Labour Movement], Tokyo: Kasahara Shoten, 1991, p. 180.
18 Cited in Taguchi Fukuji, 'Sōhyō ni Okeru Leadership [Leadership in Sōhyō]', in Itō Sei *et al.* (ed.) *Kindai Nihon Shisōshi Kōza* [Modern Japanese Intellectual History], 15 vols, Tokyo: Chikuma Shobō, 1960, v, p. 353.
19 The view is echoed by Seto Sadao, a JCP activist, who said he took heart from the emergence of Takano as a Sōhyō leader. Yoshioka was born in 1917. He is a graduate of primary school under the pre-war school system. He began working for a port contractor in Kyushu in 1946 after serving in the military for over eight years. He was a JSP member during the period covered by this book, whereas Seto has remained a JCP member ever since. Yoshioka and Seto interviews.
20 Monogatari Sengo Rōdō Undōshi Kankō Iinkai (ed.) *Sengo Rōdō Undōshi* [The History of the Post-war Labour Movement], 10 vols, Tokyo: Kyōiku Bunka Kyōkai, 1998, iv, pp. 111–2.
21 *Shūkan Asahi*, 12 July 1953, p. 10. Though the Soviet Union and China began making peace overtures after the death of Stalin in March 1953, Dulles was opposed to ending the war. Churchill, however, criticized Dulles's preference for escalating the war.
22 Ōta, *Tatakaino Nakade* [Amidst the Struggle], Tokyo: Aoki Shoten, 1971, p. 77.
23 Takaragi Fumihiko, 'Shin no Leader de atta Ōta Kaoru San [Mr Ōta Kaoru, a True Leader]', *Shinpo to Kaikaku*, December 1998, p. 14.
24 Ōta, *Hibike Rappa* [Sound the Trumpet], Tokyo: Nihon Keizai Shimbun, 1974, p. 91.

240 *Notes*

25 Among those who visited the Soviet Union and China in the early 1950s were Hoashi Kei, an official of the Japanese Association of Corporate Executives; Miyakoshi Kisuke, a member of conservative political party Kaishintō; and Kōra Tomi, an upper house member of the Democratic Party, who defied government warnings against her trip to the communist bloc. They significantly influenced public opinion with their rosy views of the socialist nations. See *Sekai Heiwa*, 15 July 1952; *Kōwa Shimbun*, 10 July 1952 and 24 July 1952.

26 The five basic principles articulated by Nehru and Chou and ratified at the 1955 Bandung Conference of non-aligned nations are: (1) mutual respect for each other's territorial integrity and sovereignty; (2) mutual non-aggression; (3) mutual non-interference in each other's internal affairs; (4) equality and mutual benefit; and (5) peaceful co-existence.

27 Kojima Tomoyuki, *Chūgoku Seiji To Taishū Rosen* [Chinese Politics and the Mass Line], Tokyo: Keiō Tsūshin Kabushiki Kaisha, 1985, pp. 8–11.

28 Cited in *Zentei Jihō*, April 1959, pp. 20–1.

29 Cited in Taguchi Fukuji, 'Sōhyō ni Okeru Leadership', pp. 353–4.

30 *Ibid.*, p. 355.

31 *Shūkan Asahi*, 12 July 1953, p. 10.

32 Sōhyō, however, did not send delegates to the WFTU convention. See Inumaru Giichi, Tsujioka Seijin and Hirano Yoshimasa, *Sengo Nihon Rōdō Undōshi* [The History of the Post-war Labour Movement in Japan], Tokyo: Gakushū no Tomo Sha, 1989, pp. 210–12.

33 When he was a senior official of Sōdōmei in February 1946, Takano negotiated with the JCP leader Tokuda Kyūichi to unite JCP-affiliated and non-JCP unions. But the 'united front' of the labour union never materialized because the talks between the two camps collapsed about a month later.

34 The JCP adopted a new platform in 1951 that was premised on the view that Japan was under the complete domination of the US. This served as a basis for the JCP's switch to violent guerrilla tactics aimed at sabotaging support services in Japan for the US war effort in Korea. Communists organized what they called 'a struggle for resistance and self-defence' in both urban and rural areas, on the grounds that they had no choice but to use force to counter the dominance of the armed 'reactionary' US and Japanese forces. They formed militia units and constructed bases in the countryside, inspired by the tactics of the Chinese Liberation Army, which had successfully overthrown the Kuomintang government.

35 Shimizu, *Sengo Kakushin no Hanhikage*, p. 103; and Higuchi Tokuzō, *Uyoku 'Rōsen Tōitsu' Hantai* [Opposition to the Right-wing 'United Labour Front'], Tokyo: Tsuge Shobō, 1981, pp. 52–3.

36 Higuchi Tokuzō, *Uyoku 'Rōsen Tōitsu' Hantai*, pp. 109–10.

37 Shimizu Shinzō no Omoide Kankō Iinkai (ed.) *Kunshiran no Hanakage ni*, pp. 100–1.

38 Among such critics was Hosoya Matsuta, who led the Mindō movement in the late 1940s and became a leader of Shin Sanbetsu. *Shūkan Asahi*, 12 July 1953, p. 5.

39 *Ibid.*

40 Hosoya, 'Takano-Hosoya Line no Koro', p. 118.

41 Higuchi Tokuzō, *Uyoku 'Rōsen Tōitsu' Hantai'*, p. 112.

42 *Shakai Times*, 13 July 1953. *Asahi Shimbun*, 12 July 1953 and 31 August 1957.

43 Sone Eki put forward an original proposal for the three peace principles in November 1949, which was adopted by the party leadership after being modified. See Gekkan Shakaitō Henshūbu (ed.) *Nihon Shakaitō no Sanjūnen* [The 30-year History of the Social Democratic Party of Japan], Tokyo: Nihon Shakaitō Chūō Honbu Kikanshikyoku, 1976, pp. 121–4.

44 *Sōhyō*, 7 December 1951.
45 Takagi Ikurō (ed.) *Shimizu Shinzō Chosakushū* [A Collection of Writings by Shimizu Shinzō], Tokyo: Nihon Keizai Hyōronsha, 1999, pp. 85–103.
46 Shimizu, *Sengo Kakushin Seiryoku*, [The Post-war Reformist Force], Tokyo: Aoki Shoten, 1966, pp. 190–1.
47 Takano Minoru, 'Kyūgoku Sensen eno Hossoku [The Beginning of the Popular Front to Rescue the Nation]', *Shakai Shugi*, November 1953, pp. 4–5; and *Asahi Shimbun*, 12 December 1953, morning edn.
48 Though most informal group activities appear to have spread among workers following the end of the occupation, Sagawa Michio recalled that they began in earnest in 1951. See Sagawa Michio, 'Seikatsu Kiroku Undō no Keifu to Sono Konnichi no Mondaiten [The History of the Movement to Record Daily Lives and its Current Problems]', in *Gekkan Shakai Kyōiku*, September 1959, p. 13.
49 Negami interview.
50 Hino Saburō, *Rail yo Takarakani Utae* [Railway, Sing Out Loud], Tokyo: Kōyō Shuppansha, 1988, p. 123.
51 Takada Yoshitoshi, 'Sākuru Undō no Teitai o Yaburu [In Order To Revive Group Activities]', in *Shisō no Kagaku*, July 1959, p. 21; and Sagawa, 'Seikatsu Kiroku Undō no Keifu', p. 13.
52 Sagawa, 'Seikatsu Kiroku Undō no Keifu', p. 14.
53 Hino, *Rail yo Takarakani Utae*, p.51.
54 Sagawa, 'Seikatsu Kiroku Undō no Keifu', p. 13: and Kido Noboru (ed.) *Shi to Jōkyō: Gekidō no Gojū Nendai* [Poems and the Situation: The Turbulent '50s], Tokyo: Bungaku Dōjin Menokai, 1992, pp. 90–1.
55 Kawamura Yasuo, *Sokoku no Nakani Ikoku ga Aru*, quoted in Kido (ed.) *Shi to Jōkyō*, pp. 90–1.
56 Kido (ed.) *Shi to Jōkyō*, pp. 91–3. See also poems in Rironsha (ed.) *Keihin no Niji: Rōdōsha no Kaihō Shishū* [The Rainbow of Keihin: Workers' Poems for the Liberation of the Nation], Tokyo: Rironsha, 1952; and Tsuboi Shigeharu and Onchi Terutake (eds) *Nihon Kaihō Shishū* [Poems for the Liberation of Japan], Tokyo: Iizuka Shoten, 1950.
57 Takada, 'Kōdō no Imi no Hakkutsu [Delving into the Meanings of Actions]', *Shisō no Kagaku*, August 1959, pp. 29–30.
58 Tsurumi Kazuko, 'Ōrakana Doryoku o [Laid-Back Efforts]', *Sōhyō*, 1 January 1956.
59 *Zendentsū Bunka*, no. 10, 1956, p. 17.
60 Kido Noboru (ed.) *Shi to Jōkyō*, p. 113.
61 *Zendentsū Bunka*, no. 5, 1955, p. 16; and *Gekkan Sōhyō*, November 1957, p. 40.
62 Naramoto Tatsuya, 'Nihon ni Okeru Circle Katsudō no Hatten [Development of Society Activities in Japan]', *Chisei*, November 1955, p. 37; and *Zentei Bunka*, no. 6, (1954), p. 14.
63 Negami interview.
64 Seto interview.
65 Sakizaki Kaneaki, Circle Katsudō Nyūmon [An Introduction to Social Activities], Kyoto: Sanichi Shobō, 1957, p. 50.
66 Hino, *Rail yo Takarakani Utae*, p. 114.
67 *Utagoe Shimbun*, 15 July 1958.
68 Hino, *Rail yo Takarakani Utae*, p. 31.
69 *Chisei*, November 1955, pp. 52–3.
70 Yoshioka interview. The view is echoed by other workers in 'Rōdō Kōza Hatten no Tameni [To Promote Learning of Workers]', in *Zentei Bunka*, no. 5, 1954, pp. 38–9.
71 *Zentei Bunka*, September 1955, p. 27; and Seki Akiko, *Utagoe ni Miserarete* [Enchanted by Singing], Tokyo: Ongaku Centre, 1971, pp. 81 and 107.

72 'Utagoe wa Ryōgen no Hi no Gotoku [Choral Singing Spreads Like Wildfire]', in *Zendentsū Bunka*, no. 5, 1955, p. 12.
73 Ōtsuka interview.
74 Ōtsuka and Hino interviews. Hino, *Rail yo Takarakani Utae*, p. 85; and Fujiwara Akira (ed.) *Nihon Minshū No Rekishi: Minshū no Jidai e* [The History of the Japanese People: To the Age of the People], 11 vols, Tokyo: Sanseidō, 1976, xi, pp. 16–21. But caution should be exercised in estimating the impact this type of activism had on the labour movement, because the degree of the popularity of cultural activities appears to have varied widely from one union to another. Unions with thriving society activities included those of coal miners, national railwaymen, synthetic chemicals, steel, telecommunications and postal workers.
75 Hino interview.
76 Naramoto Tatsuya, 'Nihon ni okeru Circle Katsudō no Hatten', *Chisei*, November 1955, p. 39.
77 Fukuda Reizō, 'Circle to Rōdō Kumiai [Workers' Societies and Labour Unions]', *Chisei*, November 1955, pp. 41–2; and *Zentei Bunka*, no. 6, 1954, p. 15.
78 Interview with Fukuda Reizō on 10 November 1999. Fukuda Reizō, 'Circle to Rōdō Kumiai', *Chisei*, November 1955, p. 42. Fukuda was born in 1923 and majored in French at Osaka University of Foreign Studies. He served in the military on Sumatra Island during the war. He began working for the national railway company in 1949. He had no party affiliation until he joined the JCP around 1960 and was expelled by the party in 1964.
79 Hino, *Rail yo Takarakani Utae*, pp. 33 and 121.
80 *Zentei Shimbun*, January 1960.
81 *Kokumin Bunka*, 25 March 1995, p. 14; 25 April 1995, p. 14.
82 For more details about the *Uchinada* campaign, see Chapter 5.
83 Shinofuji Mitsuyuki, 'Shokuba Tōsō no Rekishiteki Keifu to Sōkatsu [The History of Workplace Struggles]', *Gekkan Rōdō Kumiai*, February 1980, pp. 15–16.
84 Interview with Yokoi Kameo on 30 September 1999. Yokoi Kameo, 'Entenka 56 Nichi o Kōshin shite [A 56-day March Under the Blazing Sun]', *Heiwa Nihon*, September 1959, p. 28. Yokoi Kameo was born in 1909 and died in 2001. He dropped out of a technical school after finishing elementary school in 1917. He subsequently worked as a mechanic and joined the JCP in 1927. He fought in Manchuria and the Philippines during the war, after which he resumed his activities as a labour activist.
85 Higuchi interview.
86 Shinofuji, 'Shokuba Tōsō', pp. 13–14.

4 The labour movement under Mindō leadership and the *Anpo Tōsō*

1 Inomata Tsunao Chosaku Ikō Kankō Kai (ed.) *Ichi Kaikyū Senshi no Bohyō* [The Tombstone of a Class Warrior], Tokyo: Inomata Tsunao Chosaku Ikō Kankō Kai, 1975, p. 11.
2 Ōta Kaoru, *Tatakai no Nakade* [Amidst the Struggle], Tokyo: Aoki Shoten, 1971, pp. 78 and 95.
3 Intellectuals outside organized labour considered it vital to enlist Sōhyō's organizational prowess in their peace and other campaigns, such as those to resist government attempts to control education and the mass media. They published with Takano, for example, a magazine called *Kokumin* [The Nation] in the mid-1950s to promote popular solidarity to resist the power structure both within and outside Japan. See also *Kokumin Bunka*, 25 February 1995, p. 16; 25 April 1995, p. 14; Yamabe Yoshihide, 'Shakaishugi Kyōkai Bunretsu no Koro [When the Japan Socialist Association Split Up]', in Shimizu Shinzō shi no Omoide Kankō Iinkai (ed.)

Kunshiran no Hanakage ni [Under the Shadow of a Kaffir Lily], Tokyo: Heigensha, 1997, p. 126; and Shimizu Shinzō, *Sengo Kakushin no Hanhikage* [Semidarkness in the Post-war Reform Movement], Tokyo: Nihon Keizai Hyōronsha, 1995, p. 430.

4 About 3,000 trade unionists went to the scene of the land survey aimed at the military airfield expansion on 4 November 1955, and some 4,000 protestors, including local residents, workers and students, gathered on 14 October 1956 to oppose another survey, according to Miyaoka Masao, the deputy head of the alliance opposing expansion of the Sunagawa base. The Labour Unions' Council in Support of Sunagawa Residents (Sunagawa Shien Rōso Kyōgikai) is reported to have decided to mobilize 5,000 workers a day after the government announcement in August 1956 of another land survey scheduled for 1–16 October. See Miyaoka Masao, *Sunagawa Tōsō no Kiroku* [The Records of the Sunagawa Struggle], Tokyo: Sanichi Shobō, 1970, pp. 212 and 215; and Hoshi Kiichi (ed.) *Shashinshū: Sunagawa Tōsō no Kiroku* [The Photo Collection of the Sunagawa Struggle], Tokyo: Keyaki Shuppan, 1996, p. 58.
5 *Sōhyō*, 11 October 1956.
6 'Zenshinsuru Tōitsu Sensen no Kadai [Progress of the United Front and Its Challenges]', *Zenei*, January 1959, p. 48.
7 Watanabe Tōru, 'Rōdō Undō [The Labour Movement]', in Takeuchi Yoshimi (ed.) *Sengo no Minshū Undō* [Popular Movements in the Post-war Era], Tokyo: Aoki Shoten, 1956, p. 110; and Takeuchi interview.
8 Iwai Akira, *Sōhyō to tomoni* [With Sōhyō], Tokyo: Yomiuri Shimbunsha, 1971, pp. 36–7; and Ōta, *Tatakai no Nakade*, pp. 94–5.
9 Ōta Kaoru, *Gendai no Rōdō Undō* [Today's Labour Movement], Tokyo: Rōdō Junpōsha, 1964, p. 206.
10 Ōta, *Tatakai no Nakade*, p. 233.
11 Nihon Rōdō Kumiai Sōhyō Gikai, *Sōhyō Jūnenshi* [The 10-year History of Sōhyō], Tokyo: Rōdō Junpōsha, 1964, p. 638; and *Asahi Shimbun*, 10 July 1954, morning edn, and 16 July 1954, morning edn.
12 Takano Minoru, 'Sōhyō Taikai o Mamore [Defend the Sōhyō Convention]', *Shūkan Rōdō Jōhō*, 19 August 1959, p. 3.
13 *Kokumin*, October 1955, p. 16.
14 *Ibid.*
15 Higuchi interview.
16 *Heiwa Nihon*, 1–15 September 1958, p. 11.
17 Nihon Rōdō Kumiai Sōhyō Gikai, *Sōhyō Jūnenshi*, pp. 201–2.
18 Higuchi Tokuzō, 'Akai Kakumei to Shiroi Kakumei [A Red Revolution and a White Revolution]', *Asu o Hiraku Tsūshin*, 1 April 2000, p. 9.
19 Takeuchi interview.
20 Takashima Kikuo, 'Kabu karano Tatakai o Jūshi Shita Haga San [Mr Haga Who Put Priority on Struggles From Below]', in Haga Tamishige San o Shinobu Kai (ed.) *Haga Tamishige San o Shinobu* [In Memory of Mr Haga Tamishige], Saitama: Haga Tamishige San o Shinobu Kai, 1996, pp. 74–5; and *Asahi Shimbun*, 25 October 1955, morning edn.
21 Takeuchi interview.
22 Yamada Yoshimi, '1970 Nen to Nihon Kyōsantō [The Year 1970 and the Japanese Communist Party]', *Keizai Hyōron*, extra edn, December 1964, p. 78. Yamada Yoshimi is a pseudonym used by Takeuchi Motohiro. Koyama Hirotake, *Sengo Nihon Kyōsantōshi* [The Post-war History of the Japanese Communist Party], Tokyo: Haga Shoten, 1972, p. 224.
23 Shimizu, *Sengo Kakushin Seiryoku* [The Post-war Reformist Force], Tokyo: Aoki Shoten, 1966, p. 206.
24 The suspects, who were alleged to have been involved in the Matsukawa incident of 1949, aroused considerable sympathy among workers because many activists

had numerous terrifying confrontations with the police through their union activities and feared active involvement in union affairs could lead to their arrest and even imposition of the death penalty.
25 Takeuchi interview.
26 Takeuchi and Higuchi interviews.
27 *Zenei*, February 1959, p. 91.
28 *Zenei*, May 1959, p. 78.
29 *Zenei*, October 1958, p. 61 and May 1959, p. 77. According to Takeuchi Motohiro's analysis, the number of JCP members working at factories increased 211 per cent over two years through 1 February 1961. See Yamada Yoshimi, '1970 Nen to Nihon Kyōsantō', p. 77.
30 'Shakaitō no Rōdōsha Tōin wa Nani o Nasubekika [What Should JSP Workers Do?]', *Shakai Shugi*, April 1957, p. 37.
31 Matsushita Keiichi and Shimizu Shinzō noted that communists tended to be more active than JSP members in local joint groups. See *Fujin no Koe*, November 1960, p. 24; and Shimizu Shinzō, 'Anpo Tōsō Sōkatsu no Ichidanmen [One Aspect of the Analysis of the *Anpo Tōsō*]', *Gekkan Shakaitō*, August 1960, p. 25.
32 Kōda Yoshimi, 'Sōhyō Hanshuryūha no Undō Rosen [The Policies of Sōhyō's Non-Mainstream Groups]', *Gekkan Rōdō Mondai*, October 1962, p. 15. Kōda Yoshimi is Takeuchi Motohiro's pseudonym.
33 Takashima, *Sengo Rōdō Undōshiron* [A Critique of the History of the Post-war Labour Movement], Tokyo: Tsuge Shobō, 1977, p. 269.
34 *Asahi Shimbun*, 19 January 1955, morning edn, 18 July 1955, morning edn, 26 July 1955, morning edn. Ōta Kaoru also noted that the JCP's self-criticism of 1955 and increased contacts with the WFTU helped to endear Sōhyō officials to the communist bloc. See Ōta Kaoru, 'Seitō to Rōdō Undō [Political Parties and the Labour Movement]', *Shakai Shugi*, October 1955, p. 26.
35 Nihon Rōdō Kumiai Sōhyō Gikai, *Sōhyō Wa Kaku Tatakau* [Thus Will Sōhyō Fight], 1956, pp. 58–9.
36 Zengakuren, or the All Japan Federation of Student Unions, was the student body aligned with the JCP.
37 The international relations specialist Sekine Katsuhiko noted many Japanese were still at a loss in early 1957 about what to make of the events in Hungary due to the lack of information available and differing views expressed in newspapers. He also noted that many, especially those with 'progressive' views, tended to attribute the Hungarian events to a plot systematically devised by anti-revolutionary elements. See Sekine Katsuhiko, 'Hangaria Mondai ni tsuite [About the Issue of Hungary]', *Shakai Shugi*, March 1957, pp. 35 and 37.
38 Koyama, *Sengo Nihon Kyōsantōshi*, pp. 208–11, 216–17 and 220–2.
39 *Sōhyō*, 8 November 1956; *Shakai Times*, 13 November 1956.
40 Nihon Rōdō Kumiai Sōhyō Gikai, *Sōhyō Wa Kaku, Tatakau*, 1957, p. 70.
41 Sōhyō's draft policy on the protest movement against the Police Duties Law, 24 October 1958, p. 1; and *Sōhyō*, 10 April 1959.
42 Material for the 15th Sōhyō extraordinary convention I, *Jōsei ni tsuiteno Nisan No Tokuchō* [A Few Characteristics of the Current Situation], 1959, p. A7.
43 The Sino-Soviet conflict that became apparent in 1960 was hardly discussed during the security treaty crisis. Leftist commentators attributed it either to US propaganda or argued that most of the talks about the disputes between China and the Soviet Union were based on unconfirmed information and speculation. See Minaguchi Kōzō, *Anpo Tōsōshi* [The History of the *Anpo Tōsō*], Tokyo: Shakai Shinpō, 1968, p. 102; Nakagawa Nobuo, 'Chūso no Ronsō [Debates between China and the Soviet Union]', *Gekkan Shakai Kyōiku*, October 1960, p. 50; and *Nihon to Chūgoku*, 21 September 1960.
44 The records of the 12th regular Sōhyō convention, 26 August 1959, p. 43.

45 The minutes of Sōhyō's 10th regular convention on 21 July 1958, pp. 32–3; and *Sōhyō*, 16 January 1959.
46 Koana Hisaji, 'Heiwa no Mondai wa Dō Kangaetara Yoinoka [What We Should Make of Issues over Peace]', *Zentei Bunka*, August 1959, pp. 25–6.
47 Minaguchi Kōzō, *Anpo Tōsōshi*, pp. 101–2; and 'Lockheed, Baishō to Kuroi Jettoki [Lockheed, Reparations and the Black Jet Aircraft]', *Chūō Kōron*, February 1960, p. 124.
48 Sōhyō's draft policy on the protest movement against the Police Duties Law, 24 October 1958, p. 3; and Nihon Rōdō Kumiai Sōhyō Gikai, *Sōhyō Wa Kaku Tatakau*, 1956, p. 91.
49 *Sōhyō*, 11 October 1956; and *Yomiuri Shimbun*, 25 October 1956, evening edn.
50 Hoshi Kiichi (ed.) *Shashinshū: Sunagawa Tōsō no Kiroku*, pp. 32, 58–9, 78–85 and 90.
51 *Zenei*, October 1957, p. 71; *Heiwa Shimbun*, 14 October 1956; and *Akahata*, 9 October 1956.
52 Tokyo Chihō Rōdō Kumiai Hyōgikai (ed.) *Sengo Tokyo Rōdō Undōshi* [The History of the Labour Movement in Post-war Tokyo], Tokyo: Rōdō Junpōsha, 1980, p. 1153.
53 *Tokyo Chihyō*, 1 July 1957, p. 3; and Takashima, *Sengo Rōdō Undōshiron*, p. 163.
54 Takeuchi Motohiro, *Watashi no Sengoshi: Kakenuketa Seishun* [My Post-war History: Tumultuous Days of My Youth], unpublished writing, p. 41.
55 Zenkoku Kinzoku, *Sōgi no Tokuchō to Zenkokuno Kinzoku Rōdōsha Shokun e no Uttae* [The Characteristics of Labour Disputes and an Appeal to All Metal Workers of Japan], July 1959, p. 1; Tokyo Chihyō Rōdō Kumiai Hyōgikai, *Tokyo Chihyō no Genjō to Saikin no Omona Tatakai nitsuite* [The Current State of Tokyo Chihyō and Recent Major Labour Disputes], 1960; *Sōhyō*, 11 September 1959; Zenkoku Kinzoku Rōdō Kumiai (ed.) *Zenkoku Kinzoku 30 Nenshi* [The 30-year History of the National Trade Union of Metal and Engineering Workers], Tokyo: Rōdō Junpōsha, 1977, p. 373; and Sōhyō's draft policy on the protest movement against the Police Duties Law, 24 October 1958, p. 6.
56 Zenkoku Kinzoku, *Sōgi no Tokuchō to Zenkokuno Kinzoku Rōdōsha Shokun e no Uttae*, p. 2; Yamada Shinzaburō, 'Chūshō Kigyō Rōdōsha no Soshiki to Tatakai [The Unionization and Struggle of Workers at Smaller Firms]', *Zenei*, December 1957, p. 110; Kimura Saburō, 'Kyōbōka suru Danatsu Seisaku to Tatakau Tameni [Fighting Worsening Repression]', *Zenei*, December 1959, pp. 65–6; and Tokyo Chihyō, *Tokyo Chihyō no Genjō*.
57 Tokyo Chihyō, *Tokyo Chihyō no Genjō*.
58 Congress members included among others Tokyo Chihyō, the Tokyo chapters of the JSP, the JCP, Zengakuren, anti-nuclear groups, the Alliance to Preserve the Constitution, and the Mothers Congress, commercial associations, anti-military base groups, youth groups, health and welfare lobbies, a doctors' society, a patients' association, a group working for the return of Okinawa to Japan, Japan-Soviet, Japan-China and Japan-North Korea fraternal associations and federations of cooperatives.
59 *Tokyo Chihyō*, 1 July 1957. As an increased number of unions looked up to Tokyo Chihyō for leadership, its membership expanded from 150,000 in 1950 to 350,000 in 1960.
60 Tsumura Takashi, 'Takano Minoru to Inomata Kenkyū Kankō Undō', in Inomata Tsunao Chosaku Ikō Kankō Kai (ed.) *Ichi Kaikyū Senshi no Bohyō*, p. 15.
61 Takano Minoru, 'Vittorio Apīru to Nihon no Rōdō Undō [The Vittorio Appeal and Japan's Labour Movement]', *Rōdō Jōhō Tsūshin*, 18 April 1956, Appendix p. 10.

62 Inumaru Giichi, Tsujioka Seijin and Hirano Yoshimasa, *Sengo Nihon Rōdō Undōshi* [The History of the Post-war Labour Movement in Japan], Tokyo: Gakushū no Tomo Sha, 1989, p. 211.
63 Takeuchi interview.
64 Tokyo Chihyō, *Tokyo Chihyō no Genjō*; and Tokyo Chihō Rōdō Kumiai Hyōgikai (ed.) *Sengo Tokyo Rōdō Undōshi*, pp. 642–6, 1156.
65 Minaguchi Kōzō, who led the National Congress To Block the Revision of the Japan-US Security Treaty, also noted that members of regional groups applauded far more enthusiastically than the national union leadership when workers and students stormed onto the parliament grounds during the *Anpo Tōsō*. See Minaguchi, *Anpo Tōsōshi*, p. 60. Shin Sanbetsu, which refused to cooperate with the JCP and therefore did not join the National Congress, also faced vocal criticism from its unionist membership based in provincial areas. Local affiliates opposed Shin Sanbetsu's instruction not to join the National Congress, and its historians note that the gap between Shin Sanbetsu headquarters and affiliated unions in provincial areas never widened as much as during the *Anpo Tōsō*. See Shin Sanbetsu Nijūnenshi Hensan Iinkai (ed.) *Shin Sanbetsu no Nijūnen* [The 20-year History of Shin Sanbetsu], 2 vols, Tokyo: Shin Sanbetsu, 1969, i, pp. 546–9.
66 Kyodo Printing Co. Union, *Kyōdō Insatsu Rōso no Taikai o Seikō Saseru Tameni* [To Ensure the Success of the Kyodo Printing Co. Union's Annual Convention], 1959, pp. 3–4.
67 Takeuchi, *Watashi no Sengoshi*, p. 65.
68 The National Congress planned monthly direct actions by union and other member groups to oppose the treaty. Sōhyō played a dominant role in the planning.
69 Takeuchi, *Watashi no Sengoshi*, p. 74.
70 *Ibid.*, p. 79.
71 Takeuchi, *Watashi no Sengoshi*, p. 88.
72 Shinobu Seizaburō, *Anpo Tōsōshi* [The History of the *Anpo Tōsō*], Tokyo: Sekai Shoin, 1961, pp. 216–17; and Koyama, *Sengo Nihon Kyōsantōshi*, pp. 257–8.
73 Nakamura Kenji, *Shakai Shugi Kyōkai o Kiru* [In Criticism of the Japanese Socialism Association], Tokyo: Nisshin Hōdō, 1977, pp. 132–3.
74 Nihon Rōdō Kumiai Sōhyō Gikai, *Sōhyō wa Kakutatakau*, 1958, p. 131; Iwai Akira, 'Sōhyō no Shin Undō Hōshinan nitsuite [About the New Policy Proposals of Sōhyō]', *Shakai Shugi*, July 1958, p. 37; and Ōta Kaoru and Iwai Akira, 'Rōdō Undō no Atarashii Tenkai ni tsuite [About New Developments in the Labour Movement]', *Shakai Shugi*, January 1959, p. 5.
75 Ōta Kaoru, 'Seitō to Rōdō Undō [Political Parties and the Labour Movement]', *Shakai Shugi*, October 1955, p. 27.
76 *Sōhyō*, 3 July 1959.
77 Ōta Kaoru, 'Nihonteki Kumiai Shugi [Japanese Trade Unionism]', *Shakai Shugi*, March 1960, pp. 25–40.
78 The workings of regional groups described here again rely on the author's interview with Takeuchi due to the dearth of material detailing the activities of grassroots activists. But the results of questionnaire surveys of unionists who organized regional activities, which are given in *Shakai Shugi* magazine, also provide information, albeit limited, about developments in regional cities. See 'Rōdō Kumiai no Chihō Rengō Soshiki ni tsuite [About Labour Unions' Regional Federations]', *Shakai Shugi*, May 1959, pp. 7–16 and July 1959, pp. 14–20.
79 Takeuchi. *Watashi no Sengoshi*, p. 90.
80 Iwai recalled it was the JCP, which showed the greatest eagerness to keep the direct action during the *Anpo Tōsō* as orderly as possible. See *Sōhyō*, 15 July

1960. The JCP's insistence on orderly action appears to have been motivated partly by the bad blood between the party and Zengakuren. The party insisted on moderation to oppose the radical actions of the student group. Considerably weakened by and still smarting from the devastating crackdown in the early 1950s, the JCP was able to muster a limited number of demonstrators. The party was also in the midst of a vigorous drive to boost its membership, so the need to preserve its battered apparatus and win more members apparently compelled the JCP to moderate its action.

81 Minaguchi Kōzō, who led the National Congress, noted the presence of political parties tended to be quite limited within grassroots local groups, so many leaders of such groups had no party affiliation and tended to become readily critical of the central leadership of the *Anpo Tōsō*. See Minaguchi Kōzō, 'Anpo Tōsō eno Hitotsu no Hansei [Self-criticism about the *Anpo Tōsō*]', *Gekkan Shakaitō*, August 1960, p. 12. Shimizu Shinzō also said that activists who were not affiliated with any political party outnumbered members of the JSP and the JCP in regional groups. See Shimizu, 'Anpo Tōsō Sōkatsu no Ichidanmen', *Gekkan Shakaitō*, August 1960, p. 27.

82 Takeuchi, *Watashi no Sengoshi*, p. 89.

83 One Kokurō worker said most of his colleagues shared his feeling that although the *Anpo Tōsō* would never lead to a revolution, it was worth putting up a fight just for the million-to-one chance that such a thing would happen. *Shūkan Rōdō Jōhō*, 5 Oct. 1960, p. 10.

84 Takeuchi interview; and Koyama, *Sengo Nihon Kyōsantōshi*, p. 263.

85 Takeuchi interview. The Tokyo Congress began disintegrating immediately after the *Anpo Tōsō* and never regained its former strength. The discontent that grew among communist activists during the *Anpo Tōsō* led many of them to leave the JCP in the late 1960s. See Koyama, *Sengo Nihon Kyōsantōshi*, pp. 250–6 and 263.

86 *Sōhyō*, 15 July 1960.

87 *Sōhyō*, 5 August 1960.

88 Ōta, *Gendai no Rōdō Undō*, p. 144; and Ōtsubo Yasuo, 'Watashino Keiaishita Ōta Kaoru San no Seikyo o Itamu [Mourning the Passing of Mr Ōta Kaoru Whom I Respected and Loved]', *Shinpo to Kaikaku*, December 1998, p. 7.

89 The years from 1959 through 1961 saw a sharp rise in the number of labour disputes and steep wage rises for major unions. See Takashima, *Sengo Rōdō Undōshiron*, pp. 112–13; and Hidaka Rokurō and Shimizu Shinzō, 'Kokumin Taiken wa Ikiteiru [The People's Experience Lives On]', *Sekai*, July 1961, pp. 45–7.

90 Takeuchi interview; and *Fujin Minshu Shimbun*, 3 July 1960.

91 *Gekkan Sōhyō*, June 1960, pp. 12–16; and July 1960, pp. 36–8.

92 Ōta, *Hibike Rappa* [Sound the Trumpet], Tokyo: Nihon Keizai Shimbun, 1974, p. 152. Ōta, *Tatakai no nakade*, pp. 163 and 165.

93 Takagi Ikurō (ed.) *Shimizu Shinzō Chosakushū* [A Collection of Writings by Shimizu Shinzō], Tokyo: Nihon Keizai Hyōronsha, 1999, pp. 237–8; Ōta Kaoru, *Gendai no Rōdō Undō*, pp. 87, 97, 169; and *Shūkan Rōdō Jōhō*, 25 February 1960, p. 11.

94 *Gekkan Rōdō Mondai*, August 1960, p. 30.

95 Ishihara Shinzō, 'Rōdō Undō to Sengo Sedai [The Labour Movement and Post-war Generations]', *Shisō*, July 1959, pp. 29–38.

96 'Josei no Atarashii Mebae [New Trends among Women]', *Fujin Kōron*, December 1956, pp. 248–9; and *Zendentsū Bunka*, no. 20, 1958, pp. 2–4.

97 Takada Yoshitoshi, 'Henkaku no Rinen ni Dō Chikazukuka [How to Deal with the Concept of Reform]', *Bungaku*, October 1959, pp. 112–13.

98 Kamisaka Fuyuko, 'Tokkō deatta Chichi to Watashi [My Father Who Was in the Thought Police and Me]', *Fujin Kōron*, August 1960, pp. 116–17.

248 *Notes*

99 Takada Yoshitoshi, 'Kōdō no Imi no Hakkutsu [Delving into the Meanings of Actions]', *Shisō no Kagaku*, August 1959, p. 30.
100 Takada Yoshitoshi, 'Henkaku no Rinen ni Dō Chikazukuka', pp. 111–12.
101 *Ibid*.; and Ōkōchi Kazuo, 'Taishū Undō no Gōrisei to Higōrisei [The Rationality and Irrationality of Mass Movements]', *Chūō Kōron*, May 1961, p. 45.
102 Takada, 'Kōdō no Imi no Hakkutsu', p. 26.
103 Ishihara, 'Rōdō Undō to Sengo Sedai', p. 38.
104 *Jichi Shimbun*, 2 March 1959; and Kido Noboru (ed.) *Shi to Jōkyō: Gekidō no Gojū Nendai* [Poems and the Situation: The Turbulent '50s], Tokyo: Bungaku Dōjin Menokai, 1992, p. 157.
105 Kido, *Shi to Jōkyō*, pp. 143–5.
106 Takada Yoshitoshi, 'Sākuru Undō no Teitai o Yaburu [In Order To Revive Group Activities]', *Shisō no Kagaku*, July 1959, p. 20–3.
107 Takagi (ed.) *Shimizu Shinzō Chosakushū*, p. 207.
108 Shinobu, *Anpo Tōsōshi*, p. 584.
109 Shimizu, *Sengo Kakushin no Hanhikage*, p. 203.
110 Nihon Rōdō Kumiai Sōhyō Gikai, *Anpo Tōsō ni tsuiteno Ishiki Chōsa Chūkan Hōkoku* [Interim Report on the Opinion Poll Concerning the *Anpo Tōsō*], 23 November 1960. The poll was conducted in the greater Tokyo area with about 1,000 questionnaires distributed to each industrial union federation polled. The survey also incorporates the results of interviews with rank-and-file workers. Respondents were asked to select multiple answers to the questions.
111 Higuchi Tokuzō, 'Kakumei Senryaku to Kakumei Moral [The Strategy and the Morals of Revolutionaries]', in Watanabe Ichie, Shiokawa Yoshinobu and Ōyabu Ryūsuke (eds) *Shinsayoku Undō Yonjūnen no Hikari To Kage* [Light and Shadow of the 40-year New Leftist Movement], Tokyo: Shinsensha, 1999, pp. 203–4.
112 Takagi (ed.) *Shimizu Shinzō Chosakushū*, p. 226.
113 Inomata Tsunao Chosaku Ikō Kankō Kai (ed.) *Ichi Kaikyū Senshi no Bohyō*, p. 38.

5 Elements of the peace activities of organized labour

1 The minutes of the international convention for anti-nuclear bomb campaigns (Gensuikin), 13 August 1957, p. 2.
2 *Sōhyō*, 15 September 1955 and 11 October 1956; *Tokyo Shimbun*, 10 October 1956, evening edn; *Yomiuri Shimbun*, 25 October 1956, evening edn; *Kinzoku Rōdōsha*, 2 and 23 October 1956; and *Heiwa Shimbun*, 28 October 1956.
3 Among those who volunteered their services in local communities, telecommunications workers offered to repair radios, Tōbu railway workers visited small villages to show educational slides, and local public servants organized talks with farmers. But such initiatives tended to be few in number, according to observers. See Itō Sanji, 'Rōdōsha ga Susumeru Nōson no Chiiki Katsudō [Community Activities Conducted by Workers in Rural Areas]', *Gekkan Shakai Kyōiku*, October 1959, p. 32.
4 *Sōhyō*, 15 July 1960.
5 *Kokumin Bunka*, 31 August 1960, p. 2; Mori Naohiro, *Kazoku Gurumi, Machi Gurumi* [Struggles Involving Workers' Families and Communities], Kyoto: Sanichi Shobō, 1958, pp. 4, 59, 62, 64; and *Heiwa*, January 1954, pp. 20 and 26.
6 Such a view was often expressed by both ordinary workers and even economists. One academic argued that there would be no peace unless workers fought to win a raise, saying that the growth of workers' purchasing power would be vitally

important for the development of peacetime industry. *Zendentsū Bunka*, no. 24, 1958, p. 17.
7 Mori Naohiro, 'Soshikijin Keisei no Kadai [Problems Regarding the Education of Members of an Organization]', in Gendai no Hakken Henshū Iinkai (ed.) *Gendai no Hakken* [The Discovery of Modernity], 12 vols, Tokyo: Shunjūsha, 1960, xii, p. 60; and Uchiyama Mitsuo, *Shokuba Tōsō Shokuba Orugu* [Workplace Struggles and Organization of Workplace Activities], Tokyo: Rōdō Hōritsu Junpōsha, 1959, p. 232.
8 Negami and Ōtsuka interviews.
9 Toshiba Rōren Jūnenshi Hensan Iinkai (ed.) *Kumiai Undōshi* [The History of the Union], Kanagawa: Toshiba Rōdō Kumiai Rengōkai, 1964, pp. 399–400, 459–61.
10 Kitagawa Ryūkichi, Nakabayashi Kenjirō, Sasaki Hiroshi, Masujima Hiroshi, Satō Takeji and Matsushita Keiichi, 'Sōhyō to Zenrō [Sōhyō and Zenrō]', *Chūō Kōron*, April 1960, p. 115.
11 Koyama Hirotake, *Sengo Nihon Kyōsantōshi* [The Post-war History of the Japanese Communist Party], Tokyo: Haga Shoten, 1972, p. 263.
12 *Heiwa Shimbun*, 16 December 1956.
13 *Heiwa Shimbun*, 1 January 1957.
14 *Heiwa Shimbun*, 16 December 1956: and 'Shokuba no Nakano Heiwa Soshiki [A Peace Group Within a Workplace]', *Heiwa Nihon*, May 1957, pp. 18–21.
15 *Shūkan Rōdō Jōhō*, 11 May 1955.
16 Matsumiya Yoshio, 'Yusuburareta Kokurō Taikai [The Disturbance during the Kokurō Convention]', *Gekkan Rōdō Mondai*, October 1960, p. 42.
17 Describing the mood among Kokurō workers, Ōta Kaoru said

> The national railway union struck because if that was what the whole nation wished, they were ready to lead the nation in the protest at the risk of suffering wage cuts and dismissals. They struck in the belief that if the government punished them, then the people would defend them.
> (See *Asahi Shimbun*, 5 June 1960, morning edn)

18 Negami, *Kokutetsu Rōdō Kumiai Undō no Ichiyoku o Ninatte* [Supporting the National Railway Workers' Union], unpublished writing, p. 111: and *Zenei*, February 1959, p. 85.
19 'Hijōkin Honmuka Tōsō o Tenbō Suru [Planning for the Struggle to Win Permanent Staff Status for Contract Workers]', *Zentei Jihō*, September 1960, p. 16; *Zentei Jihō*, May 1960, pp. 51–2; and *Zentei Shimbun*, 24 August 1960.
20 The Nissan union, for example, had won its say in the company's decision-making over matters regarding personnel appointments and work conditions. Ōkōchi (ed.) *Nihon no Rōdō Kumiai* [Japanese Labour Unions], Tokyo: Tōyō Keizai Shimpōsha, 1954, p. 69; and Kumagai Tokuichi and Saga Ichirō, *Nissan Sōgi 1953* [The 1953 Labour Dispute at Nissan Motor], Tokyo: Satsukisha, 1983, pp. 87, 167–9, 182–3.
21 *Kōwa Shimbun*, 14 August 1951.
22 Autoworkers' unions ignored labour ministry officials' threats of punishment and got management to grant a paid holiday on the day of the peace rally. See *Kōwa Shimbun*, 15 September 1951.
23 Hokuriku Tetsudō Rōdō Kumiaishi Hensan Iinkai (ed.) *Hokuriku Tetsudō Rōdō Kumiai Gojūnenshi* [The 50-year History of the Hokuriku Railway Union], Tokyo: Rōdō Kyōiku Centre, 1996, p. 34.
24 Uchiyama Mitsuo, *Kanbu Tōsō kara Taishū Tōsō e* [From Leaders' Struggle to Rank-and-file Workers' Struggle], Osaka: Rōdō Hōritsu Junpōsha, 1954, pp. 6–7.

25 *Ibid.*, p. 14.
26 *Ibid.*, pp. 36–7; Hokuriku Tetsudō Rōdō Kumiaishi Hensan Iinkai (ed.) *Hokuriku Tetsudō Rōdō Kumiai Gojūnenshi*, p. 67; Mori Naohiro, *Kanazawa ni Ikite* [Life in Kanazawa], Kanazawa: Mori Naohiro, 1985, p. 232.
27 Ōtake, *Sengo Nihon no Ideology Tairitsu* [Ideological Conflicts in Post-war Japan], Kyoto: Sanichi Shobō, 1996, pp. 234–5.
28 Both Iwai and Ōta noted that most Sōhyō unions, except for a handful of those at chemical and mining companies, were unable to stage a strike to demand a raise in the springtime wage negotiations of 1960 during the *Anpo Tōsō*, as they had been weakened on the economic front. But the fact that many workers resorted to direct action to oppose the security treaty at the risk of punishment by management, serves as an indication of how committed they were to the *Anpo Tōsō* and raises the question of whether they would take a risk to that extent just to vent frustration caused by their unsuccessful economic struggles. See Iwai Akira, *Ippan Keika Hōkoku* [A Report on Past Events] at the 15th Sōhyō regular convention, 31 July 1960, p. 35; and *Asahi Shimbun*, 5 June 1960, morning edn.

The numbers of and types of public corporation employees punished for their roles in the *Anpo Tōsō* are indicated in Table 5.1 below:

Table 5.1 Disciplinary actions taken against participants in the *Anpo Tōsō*

	Kokurō	*Zentei*	*Telecommunic-ations unions*	*Public tobacco and salt corporation unions*
Dismissals	13	—	—	—
Suspensions	151	187	37	26
Wage cuts	134	221	141	249
Reprimands	343	100	585	1,394
Warnings	630	11,900	1,394	—

Source: Momii Tsuneyoshi, 'Kankōrō to Futō Rōdō Kōi Seido [Public-Sector Unions and Their System of Unfair Employment Practices]', *Gekkan Rōdō Mondai*, October 1960, p. 20. Based on newspaper reports.

29 *Gekkan Sōhyō*, June 1960, p. 16.
30 Akiyama Minoru, 'Heiwa Undō no Rosen [The Policy for the Peace Movement]', *Zentei Jihō*, July 1959, p. 58; *Gekkan Rōdō Mondai*, August 1960, p. 30–1; and *Zenei*, October 1957, p. 71. Takashima Kikuo noted that delegates from Zenkoku Kinzoku, Nikkyōso and the Japanese Federation of Iron and Steel Workers' Unions, who had been emboldened through their experience in the Sunagawa campaign, managed to get Sōhyō to incorporate their demands regarding minimum wages and opposition against the productivity improvement movement into the Sōhyō policy platform in 1956. See Takashima Kikuo, *Sengo Rōdō Undōshiron* [A Critique of the History of the Post-war Labour Movement], Tokyo: Tsuge Shobō, 1977, p. 162.
31 *Shūkan Rōdō Jōhō*, August 1960, p. 3.
32 *Shūkan Rōdō Jōhō*, 9 December 1959, p. 13; 13 January 1960, p. 21; 27 January 1960, p. 3; and 3 August 1960, p. 22.
33 Shinobu Seizaburō, *Anpo Tōsōshi* [The History of the *Anpo Tōsō*], Tokyo: Sekai Shoin, 1961, p. 7; Zenkoku Kinzoku Rōdō Kumiai (ed.) *Zenkoku Kinzoku 30 Nenshi* [The 30-year History of the National Trade Union of Metal and

Engineering Workers], Tokyo: Rōdō Junpōsha, 1977, p. 374; the unpublished 1 July 1960 edn of the *Tokyo Chihyō*; and Hirasawa, *Sōgiya* [Labour Dispute Handlers], Tokyo: Ronsōsha, 1982, p. 155.
34 Takagi Ikurō (ed.) *Shimizu Shinzō Chosakushū* [A Collection of Writings by Shimizu Shinzō], Tokyo: Nihon Keizai Hyōronsha, 1999, p. 208.
35 *Shūkan Rōdō Jōhō*, 27 January 1960, p. 3.
36 Takeuchi interview.
37 Fujimoto Takeshi and Shimoyama Fusao, 'Nihon No Rōdōsha no Keizaiteki Jōtai [The Economic Condition of Japanese Workers]', *Keizai Hyōron*, April 1961, pp. 33–44.
38 *Asahi Shimbun*, 5 June 1960, morning edn.
39 Ōkōchi Kazuo, 'Taishū Undō no Gōrisei to Higōrisei [The Rationality and Irrationality of Mass Movements]', *Chūō Kōron*, May 1961, pp. 44–5.
40 *Heiwa*, February 1953, p. 60.
41 Higuchi Tokuzō, *Nihon Rōdō Undō: Rekishi to Kyōkun* [Japan's Labour Movement: Its History and Lessons], Tokyo: Daisan Shokan, 1990, p. 188.
42 Zennihon Kōwan Rōdō Kumiai (ed.) *Zenkōwan Undōshi* [The History of the All Japan Harbour Workers' Union], 2 vols, Tokyo: Rōdō Junpōsha, 1972, i, p. 123; *Kōwa Shimbun*, 15 April 1951; and *Rōdō Sensen*, 10 July 1950.
43 *Kōwa Shimbun*, 3 July 1952.
44 *Sōhyō*, 3 April 1953. Kokurō's Negami claims workers at his union chapter in Shizuoka Prefecture engaged in an active peace campaign toward the end of the Korean War primarily out of humanitarian concern for the Koreans. But such peace activities appear to have become possible only after the end of the US occupation. Negami interview.
45 Zennihon Kōwan Rōdō Kumiai (ed.) *Zenkōwan Undōshi*, i, p. 125; and Yoshioka interview.
46 Zennihon Kōwan Rōdō Kumiai (ed.) *Zenkōwan Undōshi*, i, p. 100; and *Zenei*, no. 59, 1951, p. 22.
47 Hayashi Eidai, *Kaikyō no Onnatachi* [Women of the Straits], Fukuoka: Ashi Shobō, 1983, pp. 199, 200–6. Although US Department of Defense data suggests that the death rate for African-Americans during the Korean War was proportionate to their representation in the troops at 8 per cent, there have been eyewitness accounts and widespread rumours about a disproportionately high number of black corpses unloaded at ports in the Kita Kyushu district. Ishikawa Masaharu, one of the stevedores who engaged in the acts of vandalism against weapons being shipped to Korea, says he began seeing a large number of corpses at the port of Moji in early 1951, and was furious because while white bodies were stored in caskets, those of African-Americans had been put in crude hemp bags. Rumours in those days had it that black soldiers were the first to go to the front line where the fighting was at its fiercest, and that their casualties therefore were much higher than those of white servicemen. The issue was taken up in one of the novels written by the popular novelist Matsumoto Seichō. Comments made by one character in the novel suggest that some Japanese, who felt wronged by what they perceived as the racial prejudice of American occupiers, believed it natural that the white Americans treated black soldiers as harshly. It is probable that far more black than white corpses arrived in the northern Kyushu area in the early months of the Korean War before the black and white units were later integrated during the war. Eyewitness accounts also abound about all-black units that arrived in Kokura, Kyushu in July 1950, shortly after the outbreak of the war. The black soldiers rioted in desperation before being sent to Korea, and are said to have engaged in extensive theft and rape. It is possible that large contingents of black soldiers were assembled mainly in and around Kokura, while white soldiers left for Korea from other embarkation points shortly after the

beginning of the fighting. The numbers of black soldiers and corpses arriving in northern Kyushu might have declined after black and white troops were integrated. See Matsumoto Seichō, *Kuroji no E* [A Picture against a Black Background], Tokyo: Kōbunsha, 1961, pp. 9–11, 36, 41–2, 53, 58–61; *Asahi Shimbun*, Seibu morning edn, 16 and 23 July 1975; *Asahi Shimbun*, Tokyo morning edn, 29 July 2003; and Fukuokaken Keisatsushi Hensan Iinkai (ed.) *Fukuokaken Keisatsushi: Shōwa Zenpen* [The History of the Fukuoka Prefecture Police: The First Volume for the Shōwa era], Fukuoka: Fukuokaken Keisatsu Honbu, 1980, pp. 848–52.

48 According to a survey by the Ministry of Labour's office in Hyogo Prefecture, the death toll among stevedores increased from nine in the first half of 1950 to thirteen in the second half, and the incidence of serious injuries rose from 714 to 1,094 during the same period. They were often forced to work for 24–36 hours at a time. Workers complained that they were frequently manhandled and would be sacked if they protested. See *Kōwa Shimbun*, 25 April 1951.

49 Zennihon Kōwan Rōdō Kumiai (ed.) *Zenkōwan Undōshi*, i, pp. 96–9.

50 *Ibid.*, p. 97.

51 *Kōwan Rōdō*, 21–23 June 1951 extra edn; and Yoshikawa interview. For details about the stevedores' protest against the Korean War, see also Yamazaki Shizuo, *Shijitsu de Kataru Chōsen Sensō Kyōryoku no Zenyō* [Historical Facts about Japan's Cooperation with the Korean War], Tokyo: Hon no Izumisha, 1998, pp. 107–10.

52 *Zenei*, no. 59, 1951, p. 22; Kōriyama Yoshie, *Nikoyon Saijiki* [The Diary of Day Labourers], Tokyo: Tsuge Shobō, 1983, p. 76; Nissan Rōdō Undōshi Hensan Iinkai (ed.) *Zenji Nissan Bunkai: Jidōsha Sangyō Rōdō Undōshi* [The Nissan Chapter of the Autoworkers' Union Federation: The History of Autoworkers' Unions], 3 vols, Tokyo: Nissan Rōdō Undōshi Hensan Iinkai, 1992, ii, p. 186; and Wada Haruki, *Chōsen Sensō* [The Korean War], Tokyo: Iwanami Shoten, 1995, pp. 126–7, 230–1.

53 Hirasawa, *Sōgiya*, pp. 67–8.

54 *Heiwa*, September 1953, p. 30. At its convention in November 1952, Shin Sanbetsu, noting the dilemma of workers engaged in production of military goods, tried to address the contradiction of conducting a peace movement while assisting in an arms build-up. The federation argued that isolated acts of sabotage would never develop into a widespread peace movement. In order to put up meaningful resistance, Shin Sanbetsu said, workers should conduct their wage battles across the boundaries of individual companies to fight rearmament and an economy that relied on military bases. See Shin Sanbetsu Nijūnenshi Hensan Iinkai (ed.) *Shin Sanbetsu no Nijūnen* [The 20-year History of Shin Sanbetsu], 2 vols, Tokyo: Shin Sanbetsu, 1969, i, p. 378. See also Kido Noboru (ed.) *Shi to Jōkyō: Gekidō no Gojū Nendai* [Poems and the Situation: The Turbulent '50s], Tokyo: Bungaku Dōjin Menokai, 1992, pp. 99–100.

55 *Asahi Shimbun*, 16 November 1952, morning edn.

56 Kohara Kaiko, 'Nikkyōso Fujinbu to Heiwa Undō [The Women's Section of Nikkyōso and the Peace Movement]', in Onnatachi no Genzai o Tou Kai (ed.) *Jūgoshi Nōto Sengohen: Chōsen Sensō to Gyaku Kōsu no Onnatachi* [Notes on the Post-war History of the Home Front: The Korean War and Women amid the Reverse Course], Tokyo: Impact Shuppankai, 1986, p. 59: and Tokyoto Kyōshokuin Kumiai (ed.) *Fudangi no mamano Shōgen* [Accounts of Things as They Were], Tokyo: Rōdō Junpōsha, 1963, p. 94.

57 *Asahi Shimbun*, 8 July 1952, morning edn.

58 Nissan Rōdō Undōshi Hensan Iinkai (ed.) *Zenji Nissan Bunkai: Jidōsha Sangyō Rōdō Undōshi*, ii, pp. 21, 142, 146, 173–5, 276.

59 *Ibid.*

60 Kumagai and Saga, *Nissan Sōgi 1953*, pp. 172–3.
61 *Asahi Shimbun*, 11 April 1953, morning edn.
62 Sōhyō, *Sōhyō wa Kaku Tatakau* [Thus Will Sōhyō Fight], 1952, p. 42.
63 See, for example, Kokutetsu Rōdō Kumiai Tokyo Chihō Honbu (ed.) *Kokutetsu Rōso Tokyo Chihō Honbu Nijūnen* [The 20-year History of the Tokyo Headquarters of the National Railway Union], Tokyo: Rōdō Junpōsha, 1961, p. 29.
64 Hōsei University Ōhara Shakai Mondai Kenkyūjo (ed.) *Shōgen Sanbetsu Kaigi no Tanjō* [Witness Accounts of the Birth of Sanbetsu], Tokyo: Sōgō Rōdō Kenkyūjo, 1996, p. 130.
65 *Ibid.*, pp. 45–6.
66 Ariyama Teruo, *Sengoshi no Nakano Kenpō to Journalism* [The Constitution and Journalism in Japan's Post-war History], Tokyo: Kashiwa Shobō, 1998, p. 37.
67 *Ōhara Shakai Mondai Kenkyūjo Zasshi*, May 1999, p. 67.
68 Sengo Rōdō Undōshi Kenkyūkai, 'Sengo Rōdō Undō no "Shinwa" o Minaosu [Reviewing the "Myth" about the Post-war Labour Movement]', *Sekai*, January 1999, pp. 289–90.
69 Ariyama, *Sengoshi no Nakano Kenpō to Journalism*, p. 20.
70 *Ibid.*, pp. 20, 126, 211, 222–53.
71 Takano Minoru Chosakushū Henshū Iinkai (ed.) *Takano Minoru Chosakushū* [A Collection of Writings by Takano Minoru], 5 vols, Tokyo: Tsuge Shobō, 1976, i, pp. 468–9.
72 *Sōhyō*, 17 August 1951.
73 While noting Japan's obligation to pay reparations, the peace treaty in effect exempted Japan from making payment and called on Japan to negotiate the matter on a bilateral basis when any country demanded compensation. Any reparations Japan agreed to pay were to be paid in the form of production, assistance to economic rehabilitation and other services.
74 *Sōhyō*, 17 August 1951.
75 *Sōhyō*, 24 August 1951.
76 *Sōhyō*, 12 November 1959.
77 Sōhyō, Materials for the 13th extraordinary meeting No. 1: *Jōsei ni tsuiteno Nisan no Tokuchō* [Several Characteristics of the Current Situation], 1959, B-8; and the records of the Sōhyō's 13th extraordinary meeting, p. 44. Takeuchi Motohiro of Tokyo Chihyō said that unionists were not entirely against paying reparations to the Southeast Asian countries, but that they were concerned that the reparations might serve to strengthen 'monopoly capital' instead of benefiting people. According to Takeuchi, the way politicians and companies in those days pushed for the reparations was far more direct and undisguised than the way Japan's official development aid (ODA), which was often used to enrich Japanese contractors, masqueraded as assistance for poor nations in later years. Takeuchi interview. See also 'Lockheed, Baishō to Kuroi Jettoki [Lockheed, Reparations and the Black Jet Aircraft]', *Chūō Kōron*, February 1960, p. 121.
78 *Nihon to Chūgoku*, 15 May 1953.
79 Yoshioka Tokuji, former head of the All Japan Harbour Workers' Union, said some local governments helped in the search for Chinese victims' bones and personal effects. It was in 1958 that the Health and Welfare Ministry and the Foreign Ministry presumably made their first offer to help the initiative to return the remains of the Chinese victims. But the leader of the initiative turned down the offer, saying his group could not accept their cooperation unless they expressed contrition for the victims of Japan's invasion of China in explicit terms. The vice-ministers of the two ministries declined comment on the matter. See also *Irei Jikkō Iinkai News*, 10 July 1958; and Yoshioka Tokuji, *Minato no*

254 *Notes*

       Undō Yonjūnen [The 40-year History of the Port Workers' Labour Movement], Tokyo: Kasahara Shoten, 1991, pp. 133–4.
80 The point was stressed also by the National Congress to Block the Revision of the Japan-US Security Treaty.
81 *Nihon to Chūgoku*, 1 April and 1 May 1960; and Nakamoto Takako, *Watashi no Anpo Tōsō Nikki* [My Diary of the *Anpo Tōsō*], Tokyo: Shinnihon Shuppansha, 1963, p. 128. Nakamoto noted that among the mourners was Ishibashi Tanzan (1884–1973), former LDP prime minister, who was outside the mainstream factions of his party.
82 *Nihon to Chūgoku*, 20 February 1950.
83 Interview with Uchiyama Mitsuo on 5 July 1999. Uchiyama, who was born in 1921, dropped out of Komazawa University. He joined the Hokuriku railway company in 1946 and led the anti-military base struggle of the Hokuriku Railway Union as its leader. He was a member of the Rōnō party. Takeuchi and Hino interviews.
84 Yokoi interview.
85 Yamaguchi Kenji, *Sengo Kakumei Mushuku* [A Wandering Post-war Revolutionary], unpublished writing, 2000, p. 7.

6 Prehistory and the early post-war years

1 Nagahara Kazuko, 'Josei Tōgo to Bosei [Organization of Women and Maternity]', in Wakita Haruko (ed.) *Bosei o Tou* [Studies of Maternity], Kyoto: Jinbun Shoin, 1985, p. 194.
2 The *ie* system is said to date back to the social practice of the medieval Kamakura era, whereby the male head of a household, *ie*, assumed substantial powers over other members of his family to preserve the family name and estate. The practice was later incorporated into Japan's civil code of 1898, which stated Japan's national polity was based on the *ie* system, thereby legally justifying severe restrictions on women's civil rights as compared with those of men.
3 Nagahara, 'Josei Tōgo to Bosei', pp. 195–205.
4 *Ibid.*
5 Sōka Gakkai Fujin Heiwa Iinkai (ed.) *Kappōgino Jūgo* [Aprons and the Home Front], Tokyo: Daisan Bunmeisha, 1987, pp. 49, 200, 205.
6 Fujii Tadatoshi, *Kokubō Fujinkai* [Women's Organization for National Defence], Tokyo: Iwanami Shoten, 1985, pp. 72–3 and 78–9.
7 Though it must be remembered that respondents in opinion polls taken after the end of the war tend to speak with the benefit of hindsight, a plurality or a majority of women said that although they were reluctant, they had no choice but to join Kokubō Fujinkai, according to an opinion survey conducted in November 1986 of 1,146 women in Osaka and other parts of the Kansai area, and another survey conducted of 279 women in 1983 by a volunteer group in Osaka Prefecture. See Sōka Gakkai Fujin Heiwa Iinkai (ed.) *Kappōgi no Jūgo*, pp. 190–1; and Kōjiya Mikiko, *Sensō o Ikita Onnatachi* [Women Who Experienced the War], Kyoto: Minerva Shobō, 1985, pp. 65–7.
8 Kanō Mikiyo, *Onnatachi no Jūgo* [Women's Home Front], Tokyo: Impact Shuppan, 1995, pp. 82–5.
9 *Fujin Kōron*, September 1953, p. 77.
10 *Ibid.*
11 Though the very small number of respondents suggests its accuracy as an indicator of the national mood is quite limited, an opinion survey the essay-writing society Seikatsu o Tsuzurukai conducted of its twenty-eight female members shows that twenty-two of them, even when the hardship caused by the war was at

its height in 1943–5, were not critical of the war. The poll result is indicative of the extent to which women had been inured to accepting the realities of their lives as they were. See Tsurumi Kazuko, *Seikatsu Kiroku Undō no Nakade* [Amid the Movement to Record Events in One's Life], Tokyo: Miraisha, 1963, pp. 161–5. See also Izuminokai Sensō Taikenki Hensan Iinkai (ed.) *Shufu no Sensō Taikenki* [Accounts of Housewives' Experiences of the War], Nagoya: Fūbaisha, 1965, pp. 58–9; and *Fujin to Kyōiku*, July 1959, p. 6.

12 Saotome Katsumoto, *Sensō o Kataritsugu* [Telling Younger Generations About the War], Tokyo: Iwanami Shoten, 1998, p. 219.
13 Aoki Yayoi, 'Watashi no Shittakoto [Things I Have Learned]', in Kusanomikai Dainana Group (ed.) *Sensō to Watashi* [The War and I], Tokyo: Kusanomikai Dainana Group, 1963, pp. 146–7.
14 Fujii, *Kokubō Fujinkai*, pp. 4–5.
15 Cited in Wakakuwa Midori, *Sensō ga Tsukuru Joseizō* [Wartime Images of Women], Tokyo: Chikuma Shobō, 1995, p. 104.
16 Higuchi Tokuzō, *Onko Chishin* [Learning Anew from Things Old], unpublished writing, 1992.
17 Hōsei Daigaku Ōhara Shakaimondai Kenkyūsho (ed.) *Shōgen Sanbetsu Kaigi no Tanjō* [Witness Accounts of the Birth of Sanbetsu Kaigi], Tokyo: Sōgō Rōdō Kenkyūsho, 1996, p. 36.
18 Tanaka Sumiko (ed.) *Josei Kaihō no Shisō to Kōdō: Sengohen* [Ideas Informing Women's Emancipation and Action Aimed at Their Realization: The Post-war Years], Tokyo: Jiji Tsūshinsha, 1975, p. 6.
19 Morita Fusako, 'Hitorini Natta Watashi [I Am By Myself Now]', *Sekai*, August 1959, p. 123; Nagahara Kazuko and Yoneda Sayoko, *Onna no Shōwashi* [Women's History of the Showa Era], Tokyo: Yūhikakusensho, 1986, pp. 154–5; and interviews with Kojima Senoko on 22 September 2000, and with Numabe Tamiko on 6 October 2000.
20 *Fujin Minshu Shimbun*, 17 October 1946.
21 Chino Yōichi, 'Chiiki Fujinkai [Regional Women's Organizations]', in *Asahi Journal* (ed.) *Onna no Sengoshi* [The Post-war History of Women], 3 vols, Tokyo: Asahi Shimbunsha, 1985, i, p. 120.
22 Itō Yasuko, *Sengo Nihon Joseishi* [The Post-war History of Japanese Women], Tokyo: Ōtsuki Shoten, 1974, p. 73.
23 *Fujin Minshu Shimbun*, 10 June 1948.
24 Morita Fusako, 'Hitorini Natta Watashi', p. 123. A similar view is expressed by a 40-year-old widow, who said:

> When the Constitution was promulgated, declaring total renunciation of war, we took great pride in it and vowed to protect it come what may. I managed to struggle desperately to protect my young children amid the chaos and economic hardship immediately after the war because of my firm belief that we could live in a society without war.
> (See *Asahi Shimbun*, 15 August 1952, evening edn)

25 Morita, 'Hitorini Natta Watashi', p. 124.
26 *Asahi Shimbun*, 20 November 1947.
27 *Fujin*, July 1947, p. 18.
28 *Ibid.*, p. 17.
29 *Fujin*, June 1948, p. 24.
30 *Fujin*, August 1948; and *Fujin Minshu Shimbun*, 12 August 1948.
31 *Fujin Minshu Shimbun*, 12 August 1948.

32 Maruoka Hideko, 'Heiwa no Botai [The Mother of Peace]', *Fujin*, August 1948, p. 7.
33 *Fujin Minshu Shimbun*, 12 August 1948.
34 *Nihon Fujin Shimbun*, 9 August 1948.
35 *Fujin Yūkensha*, 1 June 1948.
36 *Josei Shimbun*, 21 August 1949.
37 For example, see Fujin Minshu Kurabu Nijūnenshi Hensan Iinkai (ed.) *Kōro Nijūnen: Fujin Minshu Kurabu no Kiroku* [A 20-year Voyage: The Records of the Women's Democratic Club], Tokyo: the Women's Democratic Club, 1967, pp. 67–8.
38 Minpukyō was established in April 1948.
39 *Josei Kaizō*, December 1948, p. 17; and *Fujin Minshu Shimbun*, 29 July 1948.
40 *Nihon Fujin Shimbun*, 29 July 1948.
41 *Nihon Fujin Shimbun*, 19 August 1948. According to the 1 September 1948 issue of *Fujin Yūkensha*, the organ of the League of Women Voters, the conservatives' rally drew less than 1,000 participants instead of the 1,500 claimed by *The Nihon Fujin Shimbun*, another conservative paper.
42 *Nihon Fujin Shimbun*, 12 August 1949.
43 *Nihon Fujin Shimbun*, 19 August 1949.
44 *Nihon Fujin Shimbun*, 10 April 1950.
45 *Nihon Fujin Shimbun*, 21 April 1950.
46 *Ibid.*
47 *Nihon Fujin Shimbun*, 14 April and 21 April 1950.
48 *Nihon Fujin Shimbun*, 14 April 1950.
49 *Nihon Fujin Shimbun*, 24 June 1948; and *Fujin Yūkensha*, 1 August 1948.
50 *Josei Kaizō*, December 1948, p. 17.
51 Watanabe Michiko, *Atarashii Asa no Hibiki* [The Sound of a Fresh Morning], Tokyo: Domesu Shuppan, 1992, pp. 115–16.
52 *Nihon Fujin Shimbun*, 15 October 1948.
53 *Nihon Fujin Shimbun*, 21 April 1950.
54 *Nihon Fujin Shimbun*, 30 June 1950.
55 *Fujin Shimbun*, 26 October 1950.
56 *Ibid.*; and *Shufuren Dayori*, 1 August and 1 September 1950.
57 *Nihon Fujin Shimbun*, 30 June 1950.
58 Although the Press Code imposed by SCAP only lasted till October 1949, censorship or self-censorship by the media continued throughout the occupation. The JCP organ, *Akahata*, for example, was banned in July 1950, and the Red Purge carried out at around the same time was targeted at members of the press. When African-American soldiers rioted in the Kyushu city of Kokura in July 1950 shortly after the outbreak of the Korean War, the incident went unreported by the press because the media was unable to write about the US military except for things officially announced by the occupation forces. According to Professor Torigoe Shin of Seiwa College, some restrictions on free speech remained in effect even for a few years after the end of the occupation until around 1954. See *Asahi Shimbun*, Seibu morning edn, 23 July 1975. Torigoe Shin, 'Sengo Jidō Bungakushi no Kūhakuki: GHQ no Genron Tōsei o Kangaeru [A Lacuna of the Post-war History of Children's Stories: Reflection on the Controls of Free Speech by the GHQ]', Prange Bunkoten Kirokushū Henshū Iinkai (ed.) *Senryōki no Genron, Shuppan to Bunka: Prange Bunkoten Symposium no Kiroku* [Free Speech, Publishing and Culture During the Allied Occupation of Japan: The Records of the Prange Collection Symposium], Tokyo: Waseda and Ritsumeikan Universities: 2000, p. 28. See also Ariyama Teruo, *Sengoshi no Nakano Kenpō to Journalism* [The Constitution and Journalism in Japan's Post-war History], Tokyo: Kashiwa Shobō, 1998, pp.

219–63 for incidents of SCAP censorship of, and self-censorship by, the Japanese press during the Korean War.
59 Kudō Michiko, 'Keijō to Watashi [Keijō and I]', *Asahi Shimbun*, 1 July 1950.
60 *Asahi Shimbun*, 1 July 1950, morning edn.
61 *Nihon Fujin Shimbun*, 21 August 1950.
62 *Fujin Asahi*, October 1950, p. 36.
63 *Ibid.*
64 *Fujin Asahi*, December 1950, pp. 90 and 98.
65 *Josei Kaizō*, February 1951, p. 58.
66 Hiratsuka Raichō and Kushida Fuki (eds) *Warera Haha Nareba* [Because We Are Mothers], Tokyo: Seidōsha, 1951, p. 138.
67 *Fujin Yūkensha*, 1 August 1950.
68 *Fujin Minshu Shimbun*, 12 August 1950.
69 Tokyōso Fujinbu Nijūgonenshi Hensan Iinkai (ed.) *Honoo no Yōni: Tokyōso Fujinbu Nijūgonen no Ayumi* [Just Like a Flame: The 25-year History of the Women's Section of the Tokyo Teachers' Union], Tokyo: Tokyoto Kyōshokuin Kumiai Fujinbu, 1972, pp. 367–8.
70 Interview with Kondō Yūko on 27 April 2001. Kondō, who did not belong to any political party, estimates that communists made up about half the members of the club's local chapters. Kondō was born in 1926 and majored in Japanese literature at the Women's University of Japan.
71 *Nihon Fujin Shimbun*, 11 August 1950.
72 *Nihon Fujin Shimbun*, 25 and 28 August 1950.
73 *Nihon Fujin Shimbun*, 28 August 1950; and *Fujin Minshu Shimbun*, 26 November and 24 December 1950, 1 July 1951.
74 Shortly before the outbreak of the war, a commentator in the *Nihon Fujin Shimbun* deplored the wrangling that went on among politicians and academics over whether to conclude a comprehensive or partial peace treaty, and called their attitude unbecoming for a nation that had professed its commitment to peace. The commentator then went on to say, in an apparent effort to avoid politicizing the issue over peace, 'A glorious peace nation (*heiwa kokka*) can be firmly established only when people first establish a peaceful household and then try to spread the peace to neighbours, battlefields and the greater society'. See *Nihon Fujin Shimbun*, 22 May 1950.
75 Onnatachi no Genzai o Tou Kai (ed.) *Jūgoshi Nōto Sengohen: Chōsen Sensō Gyaku Kōsu no nakano Onnatachi* [Notes on the Post-war History of the Home Front: Women during the Korean War and the Reverse Course], Tokyo: Impact Shuppankai, 1986, pp. 20–1 and 72.
76 *Nihon Fujin Shimbun*, 23 October 1950.
77 Kobayashi Tomie and Yoneda Sayoko (eds) *Hiratsuka Raichō Hyōronshū* [Writings by Hiratsuka Raichō], Tokyo: Iwanami Shoten, 1987, pp. 281–2.
78 *Fujin Yūkensha*, 1 February 1951.
79 *Ibid.* See Appendix II.
80 *Josei Shimbun*, 11 July 1950.
81 Kanō Mikiyo, 'Nigai "Dokuritsu" [A Bitter Taste of "Independence"]', in Onnatachi no Genzai o Tou Kai (ed.) *Jūgoshi Nōto Sengohen: 'Dokuritsu Nihon' to Onnatachi* [Notes on the Post-war History of the Home Front: 'Independent Japan' and Women], Tokyo: Impact Shuppankai, 1987, pp. 6–26.
82 This point is repeated in the third statement in Appendix II.
83 *Josei Shimbun*, 21 November and 1 December 1948.
84 According to research by Yamaya Shinko, when Christian groups sent delegates on a visit to China in 1957, the main purpose was to apologize for the invasion of China by Japan, which suggests the Christians' peace activities were motivated to a significant extent by their sense of contrition towards foreign victims of Japan's

258 *Notes*

war. See Yamaya Shinko, 'Women and the Peace Movement', in *Peace Research in Japan*, 1976, p. 73.
85 *Ibid.*
86 *Josei Shimbun*, 11 July 1950.
87 *Shufu no Tomo*, July 1952, p. 62, and January 1953, p. 212.

7 The rise of a grassroots peace movement

1 In January 1948, SCAP demanded that labour unions abolish their youth and women's sections, as it feared the radicalization of young male and female unionists amid the escalating labour strife. As a result, women's sections at most unions were either abolished or recast into more politically innocuous bodies for women's affairs.
2 Kohara Kaiko, 'Nikkyōso Fujinbu to Heiwa Undō [The Women's Section of Nikkyōso and its Peace Movement]', in Onnatachi no Genzai o Tou Kai (ed.) *Jūgoshi Nōto Sengohen: Chōsen Sensō Gyaku Kōsu no Onnatachi* [Notes on the Post-war History of the Home Front: Women During the Korean War and the Reverse Course], Tokyo: Impact Shuppankai, 1986, p. 59; and interview with Hashiguchi Kazuko on 19 October 2000.
3 Hashiguchi interview; Nikkyōso Fujinbu (ed.) *Nikkyōso Fujinbu Sanjūnenshi* [The 30-year History of Nikkyōso's Women's Section], Tokyo: Rōdō Kyōiku Centre, 1977, pp. 232–3; and Uehara Senroku, *Rekishi Ishiki ni Tatsu Kyōiku* [Education Based on Historical Awareness], Tokyo: Kokudosha, 1958, pp. 60–2.
4 An annual research conference of women teachers was held three times from 1952 to 1954. Nikkyōso was unable to organize any further such national meetings due to a shortage of funds.
5 Hashiguchi interview on 5 July 2000. Hashiguchi was born in 1926 in Seoul. Upon finishing a girls' normal school, she began teaching at a primary school. She went to live in Japan after the war and taught at primary and middle schools in Kagoshima. She joined the full-time staff of Nikkyōso, and was appointed deputy head of the teachers' union in 1980. She was a JSP member.
6 According to the historian Fujime Yuki and the writer Gotō Tsutomu, the number of streetwalkers who served mainly US soldiers increased from an estimated 1,000 shortly before the Korean War to some 8,000 in October 1950 in Sasebo, a Kyushu city that became a major base for logistical support during the Korean War. The total number of such prostitutes across Japan rose from 50,000 in February 1951 to 125,000 by July of the same year, when the number of US troops stationed in Japan exceeded 200,000. In the process, cabarets, dance halls and dubious inns proliferated across Japan. While noting that it is impossible to make an accurate estimate of rapes committed by US soldiers, Fujime quotes newspaper reporters who discussed the issue in the late 1950s and gave an estimated figure of at least 30,000 women raped every year during the Allied occupation. See Fujime Yuki, 'Reisen Taisei Keiseiki no Beigun to Seibōryoku [The Sexual Violence of US Servicemen during the Formation of the Cold War System]', in 'Josei, Sensō, Jinken' Gakkai Gakkaishi Henshū Iinkai (ed.) *Josei Sensō Jinken* [Women, War, Human Rights], Shiga: Kōrosha, 1999, no. 2, pp. 118, 125 and 126; Hashiguchi interview; Nikkyōso Fujinbu (ed.) *Nikkyōso Fujinbu Sanjūnenshi*, pp. 235–7; and *Fujin Minshu Shimbun*, 9 September 1950.

It is widely believed that SCAP's tightened censorship and crackdowns swiftly brought peace activists to submission, and that the mere handful of those who dared to stage an anti-war protest was strictly limited to communists and other left-wingers. Bold actions initiated by some housewives, however, give rise to the question of whether an exaggerated myth had been created about the autocratic powers SCAP exercised to suppress peace activities.

Kansai Shufu Rengōkai (Kansai Shufuren), an Osaka-based association of housewives, initiated a vocal campaign against war toys and took to the streets, calling on the public not to buy such toys because they were inimical to any effort to foster a peace-loving attitude in children. The group managed to get teachers and department stores to back its campaign, which turned into a nationwide movement.

Besides opposing war toys, the group openly called for the signing of a comprehensive peace, and urged local factory owners and their employees to end production of military matériel, which was being shipped to Korea and Taiwan, and managed to persuade at least some of them to do so. Higa Masako, the leader of the association, did not hide her group's daring intention when she said

> We will call on 4,000 factory workers in this town today [not to produce any military supplies] with the aim of cultivating in them the same attitude as that of French workers, who threw themselves across the railway tracks to block the transport of military matériel.

Despite the general belief that any open activities criticizing the atomic bombings in Hiroshima and Nagasaki became possible only after the departure of the occupation forces, Kansai Shufuren held an exhibition on the atomic bombings in 1951, and some SCAP officials accepted the group's invitation to visit the exhibition. See Kansai Shufu Rengōkai (ed.) *Shōhisha Undō Sanjūnen: Kansai Shufuren No Ayumi* [Thirty Years of the Consumer Movement: The History of Kansai Shufuren], Osaka: Kansai Shufuren, 1976, pp. 46–56.

7 Nikkyōso Fujinbu (ed.) *Nikkyōso Fujinbu Sanjūnenshi*, pp. 239–40.
8 *Ibid.*, pp. 240, 310, 322.
9 *Kyōiku Shimbun*, 24 November 1959.
10 'Heiwa Kyōiku o Ikani Tenkaisuruka [How to Conduct Peace Education]', *Kyōiku Hyōron*, June 1952, p. 511.
11 Yamagishi Masae, a report to the Third Women Teachers' Research Conference on the activities of teachers in Niigata Prefecture, 1954, pp. 26–7; and Nihon Kyōshokuin Kumiai (ed.) *Daisanshū Nihon no Kyōiku: Daisankai Zenkoku Kyōiku Kenkyū Taikai Hōkoku* [Tertiary Education in Japan: Reports to the 3rd National Pedagogical Research Conference], Tokyo: Kokudosha, 1954, pp. 80–2, 84, 100–2, 108, 112, 136.
12 Nagasakiken Kyōshokuin Kumiai Fujinbu (ed.) *Ronbunshū* [A Collection of Essays], a report to the 1954 women teachers' research conference, pp. 27–8, 146, 152; Ōkubo Tsuyoko, *Nōson no Fujin ya Kodomo no Kaihō o Mezashite* [Aiming for the Emancipation of Women and Children in Rural Areas], a report on the activities in Fukui Prefecture to the 1954 Nikkyōso women teachers' research conference, p. 2; and Suematsu Hisako, *Heiwa Kakuho no Tame no Kyōiku Jissen* [Educational Activities Aimed At Promoting Peace], a report on activities in Fukuoka Prefecture to the 1954 women teachers' research conference, p. 1.
13 Ōkubo Tsuyoko, *Nōson no Fujinya Kodomo no Kaihō o Mezashite*, pp. 3–25; Nagasakiken Kyōshokuin Kumiai Fujinbu (ed.) *Ronbunshū*, pp. 26–7; Suzuki Mina, *Iwate, Shutoshite Nishi Iwai Chiku niokeru Seinen Fujin Teikei no Ayumi to Shomondai* [Cooperation with Youths and Women and Problems in Iwate Prefecture including the Nishi Iwai District], a report to the 1954 women teachers' research conference, pp. 1–8; Hasegawa Toyo *et al.* (eds) *Kihonteki Jinken o Dō Mamorinukuka* [How to Defend People's Basic Human Rights], a report on the activities in Yamagata Prefecture to the 1954 women teachers' research conference, pp. 17–23; Ōnishi Tsuyako, *Heiwa to Fujin Kaihō o Mezashiteno Fujin Kyōshi no Shimei* [Women Teachers' Mission To Achieve

Peace and Emancipate Women], a report on the activities in Okayama Prefecture to the 1954 women teachers' research conference, pp. 2–21; Ono Kiyoko, *Chiiki no Fujin o Taishō toshita Ie ni taisuru Ishiki Chōsa* [An Opinion Survey on Family Issues Conducted of Women in Local Communities], a report on the activities in Fukushima Prefecture to the 1954 women teachers' research conference, pp. 1–8; Tanaka Fuyuko, *Heiwa Kyōiku wa Ikani Suishin Subekika* [How To Conduct Peace Education], a report on activities in Kōchi Prefecture to the 1954 women teachers' research conference, p. 4; and Amakusa Toshi, *Chiiki niokeru Seinen Fujin tono Teikei nitsuite* [On Cooperation with Women and Youths in Local Communities], a report on activities in Miyazaki Prefecture to the 1954 women teachers' research conference, pp. 2–14.
14 Nihon Kyōshokuin Kumiai (ed.) *Daisanshū Nihon no Kyōiku*, p. 94; Amakusa Toshi, A Report to the No. 3 Women Teachers' National Research Conference on the Activities of the Miyazaki Prefecture Teachers' Union, 1954, pp. 11–12; and Ishikawaken Kyōshokuin Kumiai Fujinbu (ed.) A Report to the No. 3 Women Teachers' National Research Conference on the Activities of the Ishikawa Prefecture Teachers' Union, 1954.
15 'Heiwa Kyōiku o Ikani Tenkaisuruka', in *Kyōiku Hyōron*, June 1952, pp. 521–44; and Nagasakiken Kyōshokuin Kumiai Fujinbu (ed.) *Ronbunshū*, pp. 26–7.
16 Maruoka Hideko, *Aru Sengo Seishin* [Spirit of the Post-war Era], Tokyo: Hitotsubashi Shobō, 1969, p. 129.
17 Sakisaka Sachiko, 'Hahatachi to Teo Tsunagu Jokyōshi [Women Teachers Allying with Mothers]', *Fujin Asahi*, April 1955, pp. 64–72.
18 Teachers themselves admitted, however, that many of their colleagues showed little interest in the peace movement which, unlike other union activities, would generate no economic benefits, and feared their involvement in the peace movement would brand them as 'Reds'. See Ohara Kaiko, 'Nikkyōso Fujinbu to Heiwa Undō', pp. 60–1. Hashiguchi estimates that fewer than 10 per cent of Nikkyōso's women teachers were activist enough to organize their pupils' mothers outside school or engage in other community work. On the other hand, observers who attended Nikkyōso's pedagogical research conferences often expressed admiration for teachers, who showed considerable dedication in tackling educational issues, and were paying to attend such meetings despite their poverty, heavy workload and other numerous personal problems. The writer Ishikawa Tatsuzō, who did research in order to write a novel about Nikkyōso teachers in a provincial town, said that though Nikkyōso on the whole took a left-wing stand on political issues, very few teachers who attended their pedagogical research meetings were committed to left-wing issues because they had their hands full with educational problems and had little time to spare for political activities. See Ishikawa Tatsuzō, *Ningen no Kabe* [Human Walls], Tokyo: Shinchōsha, 1973, pp. 311 and 354; Maruoka, *Aru Sengo Seishin*, p. 40; and *Heiwa Fujin Shimbun*, 17 February 1956.
19 *Fujin Minshu Shimbun*, 9 December 1949.
20 *Kōwa Shimbun*, 9 October 1951.
21 *Kōwa Shimbun*, 25 April 1951; *Fujin Sensen*, 10 July 1951; *Shufu Shimbun*, 17 November 1950 and 30 June 1951; and *Heiwa Fujin Shimbun*, 11 and 18 February 1951.
22 *Fujin Minshu Shimbun*, 11 February 1951.
23 *Kōwa Shimbun*, 26 February 1953.
24 *Kōwa Shimbun*, 15 May 1951.
25 *Fujin Sensen*, 20 October 1951.
26 *Heiwa Fujin Shimbun*, 1 April and 20 May 1951.
27 Hashiguchi interview.
28 *Kyōiku Shimbun*, 2 February 1951.

29 *Asahi Shimbun*, 6 July 1950, morning edn.
30 *Nihon Fujin Shimbun*, 1 and 4 September and 29 December 1950.
31 There were some forty-four UNESCO groups across Japan in 1948, according to the 24 September 1948 issue of *Nihon Fujin Shimbun*.
32 *Ibid.*
33 *Asahi Shimbun*, 20 November 1949 and 22 November 1950; and *Unesco Nippon*, 21 June 1952, 21 October 1953 and 1 November 1953. Residents in some areas, however, appeared to have engaged in the UNESCO movement with great enthusiasm. One Nikkyōso member reported in November 1951 on young residents of Saga Prefecture actively conducting the UNESCO movement with a view to fighting the feudalistic social mores in their communities. See 'Heiwa Kyōiku o Ikani Tenkai Suruka', *Kyōiku Hyōron*, June 1952, p. 515. A UNESCO group in Nara Prefecture is said to have successfully worked with a local municipal assembly to block the government's attempt to set up a rest and relaxation centre for US soldiers in the area. See *Asahi Shimbun*, 24 July 1952, evening edn.
34 *Fujin Minshu Shimbun*, 12 August 1948.
35 Ogata Noboru, 'Fujin Shimbunron [On Women's Newspapers]', *Josei Kaizō*, March 1949, p. 14.
36 *Nihon Fujin Shimbun*, 17 February 1950.
37 *Asahi Shimbun*, 3 March 1952, morning edn.
38 *Ibid.*, 23 March 1952.
39 *Fujin to Kyōiku* February 1960, pp. 96–7.
40 *Asahi Shimbun*, 1 February 1952, morning edn, 7 February 1952, morning edn, 23 June 1952, morning edn, 11 July 1952, morning edn, 18 November 1952, morning edn, 29 December 1952, evening edn, and 1 April 1953, evening edn. See also *Fujin Asahi* (November 1952), pp. 51–2. In a survey of 1,352 working women of eighteen years old and above, and of 494 housewives in Tokyo, the Ministry of Labour's Women and Minors Bureau reports that of all political issues, the second-highest percentage of housewives said they were most concerned about Japan's rearmament, followed by those who said their primary concern was the possibility of another war breaking out. Table 7.3 below shows their response to the question asking them what political issue they were most concerned about.

Table 7.3 Women's degree of concern with political issues (expressed as a percentage)

	Working women	Housewives
Rearmament	31.9	23.8
Another war breaking out	30.3	43.7
The peace treaty and Japan's independence	14.3	13.2
International politics	13.1	8.6
Conflict in Korea	2.7	0.6
Problems concerning the JCP	1.0	2.0
Others	6.7	8.1

Source: Women and Minors Bureau of the Ministry of Labour, *Fujin wa Nani o Kangaete Iruka* [What Are Women Thinking About?], *Fujin Kankei Shiryō Series Chōsa Shiryō*, no. 10, July 1952.

262 *Notes*

With regard to rearmament, the women responded as shown in Table 7.4 below:

Table 7.4 Women supporting or opposing rearmament (expressed as a percentage)

	Working women	Housewives
Support rearmament	31.8	37.5
Oppose rearmament	59.4	51.0
Don't know	8.8	11.5

Source: Women and Minors Bureau of the Ministry of Labour, *Fujin wa Nani o Kangaete Iruka* [What Are Women Thinking About?], *Fujin Kankei Shiryō Series Chōsa Shiryō*, no. 10, July 1952.

Of those in favour of rearmament, the majority of both working women and housewives said it was natural for an independent country to possess armed forces, that there was no choice given the international situation, or that Japan could be attacked by a foreign country. Of those opposed, the majority said they hated war, that they did not want to get embroiled in another war or that they did not want to have their relatives join the military. By age group, a high percentage of housewives in their twenties and thirties was reported to be against rearmament, and a large number of housewives in their fifties were found to be in favour of rearmament. See the Women and Minors Bureau of the Ministry of Labour, *Fujin wa Nani o Kangaete Iruka* [What Are Women Thinking About?], *Fujin Kankei Shiryō Series Chōsa Shiryō*, no. 10, July 1952, pp. 16–18.

41 *Asahi Shimbun*, 15 August 1952, evening edn.
42 Nakano Miya, 'Fujin Daigishi [Female Legislators], *Asahi Shimbun*, 2 September 1952, evening edn.
43 Ōmura Ayako, 'Shinsō o Socchokuni [Frankly Tell Us the Truth]', *Asahi Shimbun*, 7 February 1952, morning edn.
44 *Ibid.*, 14 February 1953, morning edn. Poll results shown in the 5 October 1953 issue of *Mainichi Shimbun*, a nationwide paper like *Asahi Shimbun*, reveal 38.0 per cent of women favoured rearmament while 35.2 per cent were opposed. But the percentage of women favouring rearmament was much lower than that of men, which stood at 56.7 per cent. The results of an opinion poll published in the 17 December 1950 issue of the Nagoya-based newspaper *Fujin Shimbun* showed 75.9 per cent of 1,652 women polled opposed rearmament. Of those, 62.6 per cent said they wanted no more war or that they wanted to abide by the war-renouncing Constitution. A slightly higher percentage of unmarried young women opposed rearmament compared with housewives. On the other hand, the 10 February 1952 issue of the paper reports that women who had barely survived a perilous flight from Manchuria were vigorously calling for a stronger national defence capability.
45 *Asahi Shimbun*, 10 January 1951.
46 *Asahi Shimbun*, 11 February 1953, evening edn.
47 *Ibid.*
48 The sociologist Tsurumi Kazuko recalled that many Japanese in those days, whether they were unionists, residents of small villages or housewives, began to think that the democracy that was forced on them by the authorities was a fake. Tsurumi said that as everything on the economic, political and social fronts appeared to revert to the oppressive climate of the wartime past, their earlier enthusiasm for 'post-war' democratization had evaporated. See Tsurumi Kazuko, *Seikatsu Kiroku Undō no Nakade* [Amidst the Movement to Record One's Life], Tokyo: Miraisha, 1963, p. 87.

49 Muchaku Seikyō (ed.) *Yamabiko Gakkō* [School of Echoes in the Mountains], Tokyo: Seidōsha, 1951. Kokubun Ichitarō, *Atarashii Tsuzurikata Kyōshitsu* [New Essay-writing Class], Tokyo: Nihon Hyōronsha, 1951.
50 Muchaku Seikyō, *Yamabiko Gakkō*, pp. 292–3.
51 *Kokutetsu Bunka*, August 1956, p. 36.
52 Tsurumi Kazuko and Makise Kikue (eds) *Hikisakarete* [Torn between Duty and Emotion], Tokyo: Chikuma Shobō, 1959, pp. 211–17.
53 *Fujin Shidōsha*, June 1959, p. 105.
54 *Hikisakarete*, pp. 211–17.
55 Fujishima Udai, 'Nihon no Tomoshibi [Lights of Japan]', *Fujin Kōron*, January 1957, pp. 233–7.
56 *Ibid*.
57 *Ibid*.
58 Nihon Sakubun no Kai (ed.) *Seikatsu Tsuzurikata Jiten* [A Reference Book on Essays on One's Own Life], Tokyo: Meiji Tosho Shuppan, 1958, p. 442.
59 *Asahi Shimbun*, 4 November 1952, evening edn, 27 May 1953, evening edn, and 3 June 1953, evening edn.
60 Yoshikawa Aiko *Asahi Shimbun*, 18 May 1953, evening edn.
61 Sasaki Yai, 'Nōkanki o Furikaette [Looking Back on the Time I Took Off Farm Work]', *Asahi Shimbun*, 25 May 1953, evening edn.
62 The *Asahi Shimbun* began offering in 1952 a column titled *Hitotoki* [A Brief Moment] as a forum for ordinary women to express their views, and the *Mainichi Shimbun* started a similar section entitled *Women's' Feelings* in 1955. Magazine publishers and broadcasting companies also began organizing projects to provide a forum where women could voice their opinions, because they thought such projects were necessary to meet the needs of women who showed growing concern for a wide range of social and political issues. See Onnatachi no Genzai o Tou Kai (ed.) *Jūgoshi Nōto Sengohen: Mohaya Sengo dewa nai?* [Notes on the Post-war History of the Home Front: Is the Post-war Era Over?], Tokyo: Impact Shuppankai, 1988, p. 11; and Washio Chigiku, ' "Tōsho Fujin" Anpo Ni Yureru ["Mrs Letters to the Editor", Who Was Shaken by the *Anpo*]', in Onnatachi no Genzai o Tou Kai (ed.) *Jūgoshi Nōto Sengohen: Onnatachi no Rokujūnen Anpo* [Notes on the Post-war History of the Home Front: Women's 1960 *Anpo Tōsō*], Tokyo: Impact Shuppankai, 1990, pp. 72–3.
63 A group called Kusanomikai (Seeds of Grass) was formed in 1955 by women who contributed their writings to *Asahi Shimbun*, while those who wrote to *Mainichi Shimbun* set up the Wild Rose Society.
64 In a Miyagi Prefecture town called Shiraishi, some thirty such grassroots groups were reported in the mid-1950s, and they began corresponding with similar groups in Gifu Prefecture. In another small town, Chichibu, Saitama Prefecture, about twenty women's neighbours' associations banded together to form a federation that began actively to organize study sessions and take part in the democratization movement from the mid-1950s. See *Fujin Kōron*, June 1956, pp. 156–7; and *Heiwa Nihon*, 15 June 1957, pp. 16–19.
65 Tsutaka Masabumi, 'Fujin no Sākuru Katsudō [Women's Group Activities]', in Ogawa Tarō (ed.) *Shūdan Kyōiku Jissen Ron* [On Ways to Conduct Group Education], Tokyo: Meiji Tosho Shuppan, 1958, pp. 205–19; and Shigematsu Keiichi, 'Fujinkai Buchikowashi Ron [Women's Societies Should Be Broken Up]', *Fujin Kōron*, July 1959, pp. 122–7.
66 The Women and Minors Bureau of the Ministry of Labour, *Fujin no Genjō* [The Current Condition of Women], 11 August 1959, p. 93.
67 *Fujin Kōron*, June 1956, pp. 156–7.
68 Awata Yasuko, 'Shufu no Mezame to Chiisana Kōfuku [Housewives' Awakening and Small Happiness]', *Shisō*, October 1959, p. 130.

264 *Notes*

69 Onnatachi no Genzai o Tou Kai (ed.) *Jūgoshi Nōto Sengohen: Gojūgonen Taisei no Seiritsu to Onnatachi*, [Notes on the Post-war History of the Home Front: The Emergence of the 1955 System and Women], Tokyo: Impact Shuppankai, 1987, p. 56.
70 Tsurumi Kazuko, *Seikatsu Kiroku Undō no Nakade*, p. 192. See also Kobayashi Tsuneo, 'Kakemeguru Jidōsha Bunko to Dokushokai [Travelling Car Libraries and Reading Societies]', *Gekkan Shakai Kyōiku*, October 1960, p. 44; and *Shin Josei*, December 1954, photo pages and September 1955, pp. 92–3.
71 Fujiwara Osamu, *Gensuibaku Kinshi Undō no Seiritsu: Sengo Nihon Heiwa Undōno Genzō* [The Formation of the Anti-nuclear Movement: The origins of the Japanese Post-war Peace Movement], Yokohama: Meiji Gakuin Kokusai Heiwa Kenkyūjo, 1991, p. 44.
72 In Suginami Ward, Tokyo, which can be arguably called the epicentre of the anti-nuclear movement, women collected some 100,000 of a total 270,000 anti-nuclear signatures tallied. See *Asahi Shimbun*, 3 August 1954, evening edn.
73 *Asahi Shimbun*, 3 August 1954, evening edn.
74 The group was founded in 1952. Amid the economic hardship of the early post-war years, women were concerned literally about how to protect their children from the lingering effects of the last war such as disease and material shortages. Since the actual reality facing children belied various items of post-war legislation calling for the improvement of children's well-being, the group sought to bring the conditions in which children lived more into line with the goals stated by the laws. They tackled such issues as the effects of military bases on children, democratization of the way PTA activities were organized, and compilation of desirable teaching materials for children. Also on the society's agenda was rising delinquency among children who were neglected or harshly treated by their parents, who were too busy trying to make ends meet or who were traumatized themselves by the hardship they had endured during and after the war. Another key concern for the society was some 1 million children who had lost their fathers to the war.
75 Hashiguchi interview; and Yamagataken Taishoku Fujin Shokuin Renraku Kyōgikai (ed.) *Harukanaru Michi Naredo* [Though We Have a Long Way Ahead], Yamagata: Dewajikai Jimukyoku, 1984, p. 302.
76 Onnatachi no Genzai o Tou Kai (ed.) *Jūgoshi Nōto Sengohen: Gojūgonen Taisei no Seiritsu to Onnatachi*, p. 59; and Nihon Hahaoya Taikai Jūnenshi Hensan Iinkai (ed.) *Hahaoya Undō Jūnen no Ayumi* [The 10-year History of the Mothers' Movement], Tokyo: Nihon Hahaoya Taikai Renrakukai, 1966, p. 45.
77 Kominami Momoyo, 'Hibachi no Hi wa Moetsuzukete [The Fire in a Brazier Burns On]', in Iwasaki Kikue and Ōki Motoko (eds) *Kusanone no Hahatachi* [Mothers at the Grassroots], Tokyo: Domesu Shuppan, 1991, p. 106; and *Fujin Minshu Shimbun*, 16 March 1961.
78 Hiroshima Joseishi Kenkyūkai (ed.) *Hiroshima no Onnatachi* [Hiroshima Women], Tokyo: Domesu Shuppan, 1987, pp. 72–5; Daigo Fukuryūmaru Heiwa Kyōkai (ed.) *Bikini Suibaku Hisai Shiryōshū* [Materials on the Bikini Hydrogen Bomb Tests], Tokyo: Tokyo University Press, 1976), pp. 352–7, 480, 501; and interview with Saitō Tsuruko, November 1999. Saitō, who was born in 1909, became one of the most well known activist housewives after beginning her social studies under the tutelage of Yasui Kaoru in Suginami, Tokyo in the early 1950s.
79 Tsujimura Teruo, *Sengo Shinshū Joseishi* [The Post-war History of Shinshū Women], Nagano: Naganoken Renraku Fujinkai, 1966, p. 542.
80 At the 1958 National Mothers' Congress, the discussion forum dedicated to school education, in particular, attracted a huge audience as participants were concerned about the introduction of teacher work assessments and ethics classes at school, which they feared could further boost the government's

control over school education. See Shimada Tomiko, 'Hahaoya Undō eno Kitai [Expectations for the Mothers' Movement]', *Gekkan Shakai Kyōiku*, September 1958, p. 75.
81 In 1959, the Japanese PTA National Council tried to revise its rules in a way that would limit the number of women delegates, who tended to be sympathetic to the views of Nikkyōso teachers. See Hirayu Kazuhito, '1959 Nen Nihon PTA no Ugoki [The Activities of the National PTA Federation in 1959]', *Gekkan Shakai Kyōiku*, December 1959, pp. 34–5.
82 Under its slogan, 'Aim for the happiness of one's own family and society', members of Kusanomikai spent much of their time discussing social, political and domestic issues as well as children's education. See *Gekkan Shakai Kyōiku*, November 1959, p. 19; and Ishii Ayako, 'Kusanomikai e: Kininaru Seikaku no Aimaisa [The Puzzling Ambiguity of Kusanomikai]', *Gekkan Shakai Kyōiku*, August 1960, p. 94.
83 Interview with Numabe Tamiko on 6 October 2000.
84 Tatewaki Sadayo and Shimazu Chitose, 'Senzen Sengo no Fujin Undō o Megutte [On Women's Movements before and after the War]', *Rekishi Hyōron*, November 1966, pp. 16–17.
85 After the Mothers' Congress of Fukushima Prefecture decided to oppose the revision of the Japan-US security treaty in 1959, the LDP ordered its local chapters to get local governments and PTAs to end their financial support to local Mothers' Congresses. The LDP issued a similar instruction to its local bodies so as to cut off prefectural governments' subsidies to anti-nuclear campaigns. See Chino Yōichi (ed.) *Shiryō Shūsei Gendai Nihon Josei no Shutai Keisei* [A Collection of Materials on Formation of Women's Identity in Modern Japan], 3 vols, Tokyo: Domesu Shuppan, 1996, iii, p. 23. The LDP also tried to increase funding for housewives' classes organized by local authorities and regional women's organizations in an effort to pit them against the Mothers' Congress. See Saitō Shun, 'Fujin Dantai no Gakushū Katsudō Hihan [A Critique of Educational Activities by Women's Organizations]', *Gekkan Shakai Kyōiku*, November 1959, p. 16; and Inui Hatsuko, 'Shikarareta Hahaoya Taikai [The Mothers' Congress That Got a Scolding]', *Gekkan Shakai Kyōiku*, December 1959, p. 46.
86 According to mothers' movement organizers, the number of participants in the national congress continued to climb from 2,000 in 1955 to 4,000 in 1956, 7,000 in 1957, 10,000 in 1958, 12,000 in 1959 and to 13,900 in 1960. See Shimada Tomiko, 'Hahaoya Undō eno Kitai [Expectations for the Mothers' Movement]', *Gekkan Shakai Kyōiku*, September 1958, p. 95.
87 Arase Yutaka, 'Nihonjin no Kokka Ishiki [The Japanese View of the State]', *Shisō*, August 1960, p. 45. The furore over the *Anpo Tōsō* was such that even women in their seventies, who had watched nothing but soap operas on TV, were glued to the news and programmes on politics. One such woman is reported to have attended on her own the funeral of Kanba Michiko, an activist who died in a violent clash between students and police. See *Kokumin Bunka*, 31 July 1960, p. 20.
88 Tanaka Satoko, who later headed the national umbrella for regional women's organizations, recalled that when members of regional organizations saw a sea of red flags at the site of a nationwide anti-nuclear rally and tried to leave in disgust, Yamataka urged them to stay, saying a nuclear bomb, if it ever struck, would not distinguish between communists and non-communists. Interview with Tanaka Satoko on 21 November 2000. See also Zenkoku Chiiki Fujin Dantai Renraku Kyōgikai (ed.) *Zenchifuren Sanjūnen no Ayumi* [The 30-year History of the National Federation of Regional Women's Organizations], Tokyo: Zenkoku Chiiki Fujin Dantai Renraku Kyōgikai, 1986, p. 41.

89 The federation of regional groups claims it sent some 1,000 delegates from eighteen prefectures to the first annual international anti-nuclear rally convened in Hiroshima in 1955. See Zenkoku Chiiki Fujin Dantai Renraku Kyōgikai (ed.) *Zenchifuren Sanjūnen no Ayumi*, p. 41; *Fujin Jihō*, 1 September and 1 December 1956, 20 September and 1 December 1957; and Zenkoku Chiiki Fujin Dantai Renraku Kyōgikai (ed.) *Zenchifuren Jūnen no Ayumi* [The 10-year History of the National Federation of Regional Women's Organizations], Tokyo: Shōwa Shuppan Bunka, 1965, p. 80.
90 *Fujin Jihō*, 1 October 1958.
91 Tsujimura Teruo, *Sengo Shinshū Joseishi*, pp. 530–8.
92 *Fujin to Kyōiku*, February 1960, pp. 6, 19–20.
93 Saeki Yuki, 'Tadashiku Miyō [Let's See Things As They Are]', *Fujin to Kyōiku*, July 1959, pp. 50–1.
94 *Fujin Jihō*, 15 August 1959; and Zenkoku Chiiki Fujin Dantai Renraku Kyōgikai (ed.) *Zenchifuren Jūnen no Ayumi*, p. 107.
95 Tanaka Satoko interview; and Tanaka Satoko, 'Hibakugo Hanseiki no Joseitachi [Women Half a Century after the Atomic Bombings]', *Gunshuku Mondai Shiryō*, August 1994, pp. 33–4. Tanaka was born in 1925 and graduated from Jissen Technical Academy for Women. She began working for the Tokyo Federation of Regional Women's Organizations in 1949 and had no affiliation with any political party.
96 Zenkoku Chiiki Fujin Dantai Renraku Kyōgikai (ed.) *Zenchifuren Jūnen no Ayumi*, p. 111.
97 Zenkoku Chiiki Fujin Dantai Renraku Kyōgikai (ed.) *Zenchifuren Sanjūnen no Ayumi*, p. 44.
98 According to the historian Itō Yasuko's study, just over 50 per cent of the total of 7,000 participants at the 1957 National Mothers' Congress were housewives, whereas housewives and women from rural farming or fishing communities belonging to no particular organization made up only 15.6 per cent of the total of 1,894 women attending the Japanese Women's Convention (Nihon Fujin Taikai) of 1953, a similar gathering that discussed ways to protect children, and the right to defend one's life and peace. See Itō Yasuko, 'Sengo Kaikaku to Bosei [Post-war Reform and Maternity]', in Wakita Haruko (ed.) *Bosei o Tou* [Studies of Maternity], Kyoto: Jinbun Shoin, 1985, pp. 239 and 243.
99 Women and Minors Bureau of the Ministry of Labour, *Fujin no Genjō*, 11 August 1959, p. 91; and *Gekkan Shakai Kyōiku*, November 1959, p. 19.
100 Sekiya Ranko, 'Keishokuhō "Kaisei" o Meguru Fujinsō no Ugoki Nitsuite [Women's Activities against the Revision of the Police Duties Law]', *Shisō*, February 1959, pp. 36–43.
101 *Gekkan Shakai Kyōiku*, December 1957, p. 39.
102 Nihon Tōkei Kyōkai (ed.) *Nihon Chōki Tōkei Sōran* [National Statistics of Japan], 5 vols, Tokyo: Nihon Tōkei Kyōkai, 1988, i, p. 49, and ii, p. 34.
103 *Gekkan Shakai Kyōiku*, November 1959, pp. 18–20.
104 Sekiya, 'Keishokuhō "Kaisei" o Meguru Fujinsō no Ugoki Nitsuite', pp. 36–43.
105 Fujiwara Tei, 'Shicchi Kaifuku no Jidai [Time for Regaining Lost Ground]', *Fujin Kōron*, October 1959, p. 88.
106 Interview with Numabe Tamiko on 25 August 2003.
107 See Hozumi Sayo, 'Ippan Fujinsō no Shakai Ishiki [The Social Consciousness of Ordinary Women]', in Fukutake Tadashi (ed.) *Nihonjin no Shakai Ishiki* [The Social Consciousness of the Japanese], Kyoto: Sanichi Shobō, 1960, p. 266.
108 Itō, 'Sengo Kaikaku to Bosei', in *Bosei o Tou*, p. 243.
109 Ishigaki Ayako, 'Shufu to iu Daini Shokugyōron [Housewifery as a Second Occupation]', *Fujin Kōron*, February 1955, pp. 48–53.

110 According to a survey conducted by the Ministry of Education in March 1958, a total of some 3.86 million women attended 62,000 classes held across the country each year in the late 1950s. Similar classes organized by the Ministry of Education to educate women about democracy, the Constitution and the electoral process totalled 1,000 in 1945 and 1,060 in 1946. Cited in Shigematsu Keiichi, 'Fujin Gakkyū Imamade to Korekara [The Past and the Future of Fujin Gakkyū]', *Gekkan Shakai Kyōiku*, August 1960, pp. 20–4.
111 Farm cooperatives began setting up women's sections from around 1951 with a view to improving the economic and social standing of farm wives.
112 Hozumi, 'Ippan Fujinsō no Shakai Ishiki', p. 264.
113 Yamagataken Josei no Ayumi Hensan Iinkai (ed.) *Toki o Tsumugu Yamagata no Joseitachi* [Yamagata Women Record Their Times], Yamagata: Michinoku Shobō, 1995, p. 358.
114 Tsujimura Teruo, *Sengo Shinshū Joseishi*, p. 569; and Mitsui Tametomo, 'Fujin no Katsudō wa Kokomade Kiteiru [Advances in Women's Activities]', *Gekkan Shakai Kyōiku*, August 1960, p. 14.
115 Eda Tadashi, 'Wakazuma no Gakushū Katsudō wa Dou Hatten Shitaka [The Progress in Young Wives' Educational Activities]', *Gekkan Shakai Kyōiku*, November 1959, p. 40.
116 *Heiwa Fujin Shimbun*, 8 August 1958.
117 See, for example, *Asahi Shimbun*, 24 August 1959, evening edn; and Sakai Setsuko, 'Hahaoya Taikai o Hirakumade [How We Organized a Mothers' Congress]', *Gekkan Shakai Kyōiku*, July 1961, pp. 22–5.
118 Yamashiro Tomoe, *Minwa o Umu Hitobito* [People Who Create Folklore], Tokyo: Iwanami Shoten, 1958, pp. 66–7.
119 The congress held in Nagano Prefecture in 1961, for example, is said to have drawn an audience of some 5,000. See Tsujimura, *Sengo Shinshū Joseishi*, p. 536.
120 Hani Setsuko and Ogawa Toshio (eds) *Fujin no Gakushū Kyōiku* [Learning and Education for Women], Tokyo: Aki Shobō, 1970, pp. 105 and 113.
121 *Fujin to Nenshōsha*, June 1956, p. 21.
122 *Ibid.*
123 The name of the community mentioned is not known, but it appears to be a village in Nagano Prefecture. Hara Takeno, 'Katasumi no Kiroku [A Record of Small Things]', *Shisō*, July 1961, pp. 136–40.
124 *Ibid.*
125 Obara Tokushi, *Ishikoroni Kataru Hahatachi* [Mothers Who Talk to Pebbles], Tokyo: Miraisha, 1981.
126 *Ibid.*, pp. 24–6.
127 *Gekkan Shakai Kyōiku*, December 1957, pp. 98–9; Shijō Etsuko, 'Sanshirō Ningyō no Kai [The Society for Making Sanshiro Dolls]', *Gekkan Shakai Kyōiku*, February 1958, p. 54; *Gekkan Shakai Kyōiku*, March 1958, pp. 51–2; Onda Setsuko, 'Otto o Ugokashi Keiei o Ugokasu [Influencing Husbands and Household Management]', *Gekkan Shakai Kyōiku*, November 1958, pp. 7–8; Onodera Tetsu, 'Watashi no Oitachi [My Personal History]', *Gekkan Shakai Kyōiku*, August 1959, pp. 39–43; Mitsui, 'Fujin no Katsudō wa Kokomade Kiteiru', p. 13; and Kageyama Masako, 'Aru Nōson Fujin Gakkyū no Ayumi to Mondaiten [The Progress and Problems of a Housewives' Class in One Farming Village]', *Gekkan Shakai Kyōiku*, January 1961, pp. 55–8.
128 Saitō Takichi, 'Hyakushō wa Riekini Tsunagaraneba [Unless Farmers Recognize Self-interest]', *Gekkan Shakai Kyōiku*, September 1960, pp. 43–6; *Economist*, 5 July 1960, pp. 8, 15–16; and Amano Hiroko, *Sengo Nihon no Josei Nōgyosha no Chii: Danjo Byōdō no Seikatsu Bunka no Sōzō e* [The Status of Female Farmers in Post-war Japan: In Order to Create a Lifestyle Based on the

Equality of Men and Women], Tokyo: Domesu Shuppan, 2001, p. 44. While residents in rural areas are said to have been generally indifferent to the *Anpo Tōsō*, grassroots groups in the farming community of Oyamachō, Yamagata Prefecture, caught the attention of pundits with their vigorous movement to protest about a wide range of peace-related issues, including nuclear weapons, teacher work assessments, the Police Duties Law and the revision of the security treaty. But the movement does not appear to owe its growth entirely to farmers' initiatives, and their collaboration with local labour unions also seems to have played a significant role in stimulating grassroots activities. See Fujita Hideo, 'Machigurumi no Seiji Undō to Shuji no Yakuwari [A Community-Based Political Movement and the Role of Officers in Charge of Adult Education]', *Gekkan Shakai Kyōiku*, June 1960, pp. 52–7. For peace activities in rural areas, see also Nasuno Ryūichi, 'Seinen Katsudōka to Anpo Tōsō [Young Activists and the *Anpo Tōsō*]', *Gekkan Shakai Kyōiku*, September 1960, p. 50; *Fujin Minshu Shimbun*, 31 July 1960; and *Heiwa Fujin Shimbun*, 8 April 1960.

129 Maruoka Hideko, *Nihon Nōson Fujin Mondai* [Issues Concerning Japanese Women In Rural Areas], Tokyo: Domesu Shuppan, 1980, p. 194.

130 The 1960 census gives an indication of the size of the workload that women in farming communities had to handle. A total of 49 per cent of female farmers worked in their fields 8–10 hours a day and 19 per cent 10–11 hours. At the busiest time of the year, 58 per cent worked twelve hours or more. Women also took on the bulk of housework when not working in the fields. A total of 69 per cent said that when they were pregnant they worked till the day before giving birth, and more than 90 per cent of those with children complained about a lack of day care centres. Cited in Maruoka Hideko (ed.) *Nihon Fujin Mondai Shiryō Shūsei* [A Collection of Data on Women's Issues], 10 vols, Tokyo: Domesu Shuppan, 1981, ix, pp. 645 and 648.

131 A young girl in a farming village in Miyagi Prefecture complained that whenever she and her friends sang in a choral group, neighbours called them 'Reds' and that even young men were of the opinion that a good young girl was supposed to do nothing but stay home and work. She said that everyone in her family pressured her not to take part in peace activities because people would suspect she was involved with the JCP and that would hurt her and her sisters' prospects of finding a good husband. See *Heiwa Fujin Shimbun*, 14 August 1953; and *Fujin to Kyōiku*, July 1959, p. 10.

132 Saitō Takichi, 'Hyakushō wa Rieki ni Tsunagaraneba', p. 48; Nasuno Ryūichi, 'Seinen Katsudōka to Anpo Tōsō', pp. 53–4; and *Economist*, 5 July 1960, p. 8. Some activists who tried to organize protests against the security treaty in the countryside said that farmers were most concerned about whether rice prices would rise after the treaty was revised. See Shiratori Kunio, '*Anpo Tōsō* to Sākuru [The *Anpo Tōsō* and Societies]', *Kokumin Bunka*, 31 July 1960, pp. 2–4.

133 Tanabe Shinichi, 'Sensō Taiken to Shakai Kyōiku wa Naze Muenka [Why Adult Education Programmes Do Not Deal with People's Experience of the War]', *Gekkan Shakai Kyōiku*, December 1961, pp. 13, 16, 17, 19.

8 Reflections on war and self

1 Sōka Gakkai Fujin Heiwa Iinkai (ed.) *Kappōgi no Jūgo* [Aprons and the Home Front], Tokyo: Daisan Bunmeisha, 1987, p. 206. The poll was taken in the greater Osaka area in November 1986 of 1,200 women, of which 1,146 submitted valid responses.

2 Tsurumi Kazuko and Makise Kikue (eds) *Hikisakarete* [Torn between Duty and Emotion], Tokyo: Chikuma Shobō, 1959, pp. 262–3. See also Suzuki Yūko (ed.) *Ashibue no Uta* [The Song of a Reed Pipe], Tokyo: Domesu Shuppan,

1989, p. 239; and Setagaya Joseishi Hensan Iinkai. (ed.) *Setagaya Joseishi* [The History of Women in Setagaya], Tokyo: Domesu Shuppan, 1999, p. 350.
3 Interview with Numabe Tamiko on 6 October 2000.
4 Poll results published in the 21 November 1945 issue of *Mainichi Shimbun* show that of 299 women in rural areas around Japan, only 1.6 per cent said they were interested in women's voting rights and 39.1 per cent said they had some interest, while 57.1 per cent were not interested. Some respondents said it was too early to give the vote to women because very few of them had any idea what it meant for them to take part in politics or that if there were any women in rural areas who demanded the right to vote, they must be eccentrics. Cited in Kageyama Saburō, 'Seichō Shinpo wa Shitakeredo [Though Women Have Made Progress]', *Fujin Shidōsha*, September 1958, p. 44.
5 *Yamagata Shimbun*, 6 September 1946.; *Gekkan Shakai Kyōiku*, March 1956, p. 68; and Sudō Katsuzō (ed.) *Murano Hahaoya Gakkyū* [School for Mothers in Rural Areas], Tokyo: Shinhyōronsha, 1956, p. 105.
6 Iwasaki Kikue and Ōki Motoko (eds) *Kusanone no Hahatachi* [Mothers at the Grassroots], Tokyo: Domesu Shuppan, 1991, p. 17.
7 Interview with Kondō Yūko on 14 January 1999.
8 Interview with Maruoka Akiko on 23 September 2000. Maruoka was born in 1921 in Pusan, Korea, and finished today's equivalent of high school under the pre-war school system. After getting married, she went to live in Japan following the war's end and became a member of Kusanomikai in the mid-1950s after her letter, in which she wondered how the wife of an average office worker could make ends meet, appeared in *The Asahi Shimbun*. She subsequently became actively involved in the peace movement and community service. She waited until the 1970s before joining the JCP for fear that her affiliation with the communists might cause her husband difficulty while he worked for a bank.
9 Interview with Ozawa Kiyoko and Kojima Senoko on 22 September 2000; Kodomo o Mamoru Fujin no Atsumari (ed.) *Izumi wa Dokokara* [Where Do the Springs Originate?], Kōchi: Kōchishi Shiritsu Shimin Toshokan, 1959, p. 36; *Asahi Shimbun*, 18 July 1951, 14 April 1955, evening edn, and 9 January 1960, evening edn; and *Gekkan Shakai Kyōiku*, March 1958, p. 53.
10 Satō Yōko, *Jiyū to Jiritsu eno Ayumi* [Progress towards Liberty and Independence], Tokyo: Asahi Shimbunsha, 1984, p. 154; and Makise Kikue, 'Haha toshite Shufu toshite [As a Mother and a Housewife]', *Kokumin Bunka*, 31 July 1960, p. 10.
11 Maeno Tokiwa, 'Shukensha Ishikini Mezamete [Awaking to People's Sovereign Rights]', in Iwasaki and Ōki (eds) *Kusanone no Hahatachi*, p. 42.
12 Numabe interview. Numabe was born in 1921 and studied homemaking at a junior college. She later began working for the then Great Asia Ministry, which was incorporated into the Foreign Ministry after the war, before getting married.
13 Prior to a lower house election in 1952, Shimizu Keiko, for example, said it was more important for women to decide for whom to vote by thinking about how they could become happy, rather than by acquiring broad knowledge about politics or the economy. See *Asahi Shimbun*, 16 September 1952, evening edn.
14 Fujin Minshu Kurabu Nijūnenshi Hensan Iinkai (ed.) *Kōro Nijūnen: Fujin Minshu Kurabu no Kiroku* [A 20-year Voyage: The Records of the Women's Democratic Club], Tokyo: the Women's Democratic Club, 1967, pp. 47 and 56–7.
15 *Fujin Yūkensha*, 1 March 1952.
16 Yoneda Sayoko, *Rekishi ni Jinken o Kizanda Onnatachi* [Women who Helped Human Rights to Take Root In Japan], Kyoto: Kamogawa Shuppan, 1996, p. 86.
17 Kobayashi Tomie, *Hiratsuka Raichō*, Tokyo: Shimizu Shoin, 1983, p. 198.
18 Interview with Kojima Senoko on 22 September 2000. The view is echoed by Maruoka Akiko, another JCP member, who recalled that many joined the JCP in

order to address actual problems facing people rather than practise Marxist ideology. Maruoka interview. Kojima was born in 1916. She graduated from high school and worked for the government postal savings bureau before getting married to become a housewife prior to the end of World War II.
19 Interview with Ozawa Kiyoko on 22 September 2000. Ozawa Kiyoko was born in 1915 and graduated from today's equivalent of high school under the pre-war school system.
20 Kojima and Ozawa interviews. One opinion poll taken in July 1959, where women were asked the question 'What do you think of the new China?', suggests that in general more women voiced scepticism or held a negative view of China under the new communist government rather than expressed a liking for it (see Table 8.2 below).

Table 8.2 Women's responses to the new China (shin chūgoku) (expressed as a percentage)

	No response	Reports about the new China are propaganda	Don't like the new China	Like the new China	The new China is wonderful	Total (%)
Chūo Ward, Tokyo	13	23	37	3	24	100
Suginami Ward, Tokyo	12	26	13	7	42	100
Kawasaki, Kanagawa Prefecture	2	29	57	6	6	100
Utsunomiya, Tochigi Prefecture	12	32	19	1	36	100
Average	10	27	25	5	33	100

Source: Tatewaki Sadayo *et al.*, *Sengo Fujin Undōshi* [The Post-war Women's Movement], Tokyo: Ōtsuki Shoten, 1960, p. 193.

21 Tsurumi and Makise (eds) *Hikisakerete*, pp. 58–9 and 274–5; Yamagata Fumiko, 'Mizukara Egaita Miraizu O [Mapping Out a Course for the Future on Your Own]', *Gekkan Shakai Kyōiku*, December 1961, p. 24; Izuminokai Sensō Taikenki Hensan Iinkai (ed.) *Shufu no Sensō Taikenki* [Accounts of Housewives' Experiences of the War], Nagoya: Fūbaisha, 1965, pp. 31 and 168; and Kusanomikai Dainana Group (ed.) *Sensō to Watashi* [The War and I], Tokyo: Kusanomikai Dainana Group, 1963, pp. 77 and 96.
22 *Fujin Kōron*, September 1952, pp. 38–9.
23 Yamashiro Tomoe, *Watashi no Mananda Koto* [Things I Have Learned], Tokyo: Komichi Shobō, 1990, pp. 77–8.
24 Matsushita Ryūichi *et al.*, *Samazamana Sengo* [Various Post-war Experiences], Tokyo: Nihon Keizai Hyōronsha, 1995, p. 5.
25 *Fujin Minshu Shimbun*, 16 August 1959. Another woman, who was the mother of a five-year-old boy, said that she named her son after the Chinese novelist Lu Xun because she made up her mind never to lose her son to those who would plot another war, nor let her son or any other Japanese men repeat the barbarous

acts Japan had committed against China and Korea. See *Asahi Shimbun*, 7 October 1955, evening edn.
26 *Heiwa Shimbun*, 9 September 1956.
27 Kondō interview. The writer Nakamoto Takako also pointed out that the Japanese government had done nothing to atone for its conduct after taking an estimated 10 million Chinese lives. She added that many groups, however, followed their conscience by opposing the revision of the security treaty, which could cause comparable damage to China again. See Nakamoto Takako, *Watashi no Anpo Tōsō Nikki* [My Diary on the *Anpo Tōsō*], Tokyo: Shinnihon Shuppansha, 1963, p. 22.
28 *Fujin Minshu Shimbun*, 15 April 1950.
29 *Ibid.*
30 NHK Educational TV, 15 August 2000. For a similar view, see also Toyoda Masako, 'Ichinenki: Sensō de Shinda Futarino Otōto [The First Anniversary: My Two Brothers Who Died in the War]', *Fujin*, June 1948, pp. 21–2.
31 Tanigawa Gan, 'Hahaoya Undō eno Jikigen [Straight Talk on the Mothers' Movement]', *Fujin Kōron*, October 1959, pp. 124–8.
32 Awata Yasuko, 'Shufu no Mezame to Chiisana Kōfuku [Housewives' Awakening and Small Happiness]', *Shisō*, October 1959, pp. 130–5.
33 Makise Kikue, 'Iwayuru Bitoku o Kanaguri Suterutameni [Casting Off So-called Virtues]', *Gekkan Shakai Kyōiku*, November 1959, pp. 21, 36–9.
34 *Ibid.*, pp. 38–9; *Fujin Kōron*, June 1960, p. 26; and Kusanomikai Dainana Group (ed.) *Sensō to Watashi*, p. 152.
35 Tsurumi and Makise (eds) *Hikisakarete*, pp. 275–6; Makise, 'Iwayuru Bitoku', pp. 37–8; and Makise Kikue, 'Haha toshite Shufu toshite', *Kokumin Bunka*, 31 July 1960, p. 9.
36 *Fujin Minshu Shimbun*, 13 March 1955.
37 Makise, 'Iwayuru Bitoku', pp. 21 and 36–9.
38 Tsurumi Kazuko, *Social Change and the Individual*, Princeton: Princeton University Press, 1970, p. 99.
39 Tsurumi and Makise (eds) *Hikisakarete*, pp. 62–3.
40 Ōe Michi, 'Osoikedo … Kenpō o Yomu Hahanokai [Mothers' Society That Began Reading the Constitution Belatedly]', *Asahi Shimbun*, 22 June 1960, evening edn.
41 *Fujin Minshu Shimbun*, 11 August 1957.
42 Makise, 'Haha toshite Shufu toshite', p. 9.
43 *Ibid.*, pp. 9–10. See also Yoshimura Hiroko, 'Watashino Seikatsu no nakade [Within My Personal Life]', *Sekai*, July 1961, p. 70. A similar view was expressed also in *Asahi Shimbun*, 22 May 1957, evening edn.
44 Iris Morgan Young argued that humanist feminism defines women's oppression as the inhibition and distortion of women's potential by a society that allows the self-development of men. It considers femininity as the primary vehicle of women's oppression and calls upon male-dominated institutions to allow women the opportunity to participate fully in public world-making activities of industry, politics, art and science. In gynocentric feminism, the oppression of women consists not of being prevented from participating in full humanity, but of the denial and devaluation of specifically feminine virtues and activities by an overly instrumentalized and authoritarian masculine culture. Cited in E. Patricia Tsurumi, 'Visions of Women and the New Society in Conflict: Yamakawa Kikue versus Takamure Itsue', in Sharon A. Minichiello (ed.) *Japan's Competing Modernities: Issues in Culture and Democracy 1900–1930*, Honolulu: University of Hawaii Press, 1998, p. 350.
45 Makise, 'Iwayuru Bitoku', pp. 36 and 38.
46 *Asahi Shimbun*, 15 August 1959, morning edn.

47 According to the 3 October 1957 evening edition of *Asahi Shimbun*, 23 per cent of women who sent letters to the editor between 21 August and 20 September 1957 asked the paper not to print their names. The reason most women cited was that they feared criticism from their families or acquaintances. Tsurumi and Makise (eds) *Hikisakarete*, pp. 214–15 and 220–1; and *Fujin Asahi*, September 1955, p. 177.
48 *Ibid.*, p. 36.
49 Nihon Kyōshokuin Kumiai (ed.) *Daisanshū Nihon no Kyōiku: Daisankai Zenkoku Kyōiku Kenkyū Taikai Hōkoku* [Tertiary Education in Japan: Reports to the Tertiary National Pedagogical Research Conference], Tokyo: Kokudosha, 1954, p. 133; and *Hahaoya Shimbun*, 1 January 1961.
50 Kusanomikai (ed.) *Kusanomi Sanjūnen no Kiroku* [30-year Records of Kusanomi], Tokyo: Kusanomikai, 1984, p. 2.
51 Katsudō Shūdan Shisō Undō Fujin Undō Bukai (ed.) *Hansen Heiwa to Josei Kaihōshi* [Campaigns Against War, Peace and the History of Women's Liberation], Tokyo: Ogawamachi Kikaku, 1983, pp. 54–5.
52 Amano Masako, *Feminism no Ism o Koete* [Transcending the Ism of Feminism], Tokyo: Iwanami Shoten, 1997, p. 122.
53 Kawata Tōru, 'Onna toshiteno Tatakaikara [Women's Struggle]', *Gekkan Shakai Kyōiku*, August 1960, p. 35.
54 Yamashiro Tomoe, *Minwa o Umu Hitobito* [People Who Create Folklore], Tokyo: Iwanami Shoten, 1958, p. 29.
55 Kansai Shufu Rengōkai (ed.) *Shōhisha Undō Sanjūnen: Kansai Shufuren No Ayumi* [30 Years of the Consumers Movement: The History of Kansai Shufuren], Osaka: Kansai Shufuren, 1976, pp. 50–1.
56 *Fujin Kōron*, December 1956, pp. 78–85; and *Fujin Minshu Shimbun*, 21 June 1953.
57 Isono Fujiko, 'Fujin Kaihōron no Konmei [The Stalled Debate over the Emancipation of Women]', *Asahi Journal*, 10 April 1960, pp. 14–21.
58 Ishigaki Ayako 'Shufu to iu Daini Shokugyōron [Housewifery as a Second Occupation]', *Fujin Kōron*, February 1955, pp. 48–53.
59 Takagi Tadao, 'Fujin Undō niokeru Rōdō Fujin to Katei Fujin [Working Women and Housewives in the Women's Movement]', *Shisō*, December 1960, pp. 142 and 144.
60 *Fujin Kōron*, March 1955, p. 296.
61 Awata, 'Shufu no Mezame', *Shisō*, October 1959, pp. 130–5.
62 Kusanomikai also suffered a division between activist housewives and those who sought to live up to the traditional image of a model housewife. See Kusanomikai, *Kusanomi Sanjūnen no Kiroku*, p. 220; and *Hahaoya Shimbun*, 1 January 1960. Although the number of women surveyed is quite limited, the results of one opinion poll conducted of 497 housewives in July 1959 are indicative of the generally held idea of an ideal family among women around 1960. Women were presented with three types of family and asked which one they considered to be ideal (see Table 8.3 below).
63 *Fujin Asahi*, May 1958, pp. 282–4.
64 Kusanomikai (ed.) *Kusanomi Sanjūnen no Kiroku*, p. 28.
65 Nakajima Mineko, 'Shufu no Kimochi [A Housewife's Feelings]', *Kokumin Bunka*, no. 20, 1961, p. 27.
66 *Asahi Shimbun*, 11 April 1955, evening edn.
67 Morisaki Kazue, 'Onna wa Nando demo Tatakau [Women Will Never Give Up Their Fight]', *Gekkan Shakai Kyōiku*, November 1959, pp. 50–3 and December 1961, pp. 88–9.
68 Shimizu Keiko, 'Shufu no Jidai wa Hajimatta [The Age of Housewives Has Just Begun]', *Fujin Kōron*, April 1955, pp. 119–23.

Table 8.3 Women's views of an ideal family

Area	No response	Husband plays central role	Husband is breadwinner, wife works at home	Double-income family	Total (%)
Chuo Ward, Tokyo	2	23	45	30	100
Suginami Ward, Tokyo	2	5	62	31	100
Kawasaki, Kanagawa Prefecture	2	12	76	10	100
Utsunomiya, Tochigi Prefecture	0	11	45	44	100
Average	1	12	55	32	100

Source: Tatewaki *et al.*, Sengo Fujin *Undōshi*, p. 178.

69 *Ibid.*
70 Itō Yasuko, 'Sengo Kaikaku to Bosei [Post-war Reform and Maternity]', in Wakita Haruko (ed.) *Bosei o Tou* [Studies of Maternity], Kyoto: Jinbun Shoin, 1985, pp. 245–6.
71 Fukao Sumako, 'Risōkyō no tameniwa [To Create an Ideal World]', *Josei Kaizō*, March 1951, p. 32.
72 Kōra Tomi, 'Heiwa ni Shitsubō Shitewa Naranai [We Should Never Lose Faith in Peace]', *Josei Kaizō*, April 1954, p. 94.
73 Interviews with Kojima, Tanaka, Hashiguchi and Numabe; Dairokkai Nihon Hahaoya Taikai Jikkō Iinkai (ed.) *Watashitachi wa Ayumi Tsuzukeru* [We Continue Our Progress], 1960, p. 99; *Asahi Shimbun*, 28 September 1959, evening edn, and 23 April 1960, evening edn.
74 Maruoka interview. For various opinions expressed by ordinary women on the rearmament issue, see *Fujin Kōron*, October 1956, pp. 155–71 and *Fujin Asahi*, March 1951, pp. 50–1.
75 The results of one opinion poll taken in July 1959 are as shown in Table 8.4 below.
76 *Fujin Asahi*, November 1952, pp. 51–2.
77 Goseki Setsuko, 'Same no Ejiki ni sareta Korani Inoru [Praying for the Children Who Were Preyed on by Sharks]', in Sōka Gakkai Fujin Heiwa Iinkai (ed.) *Ano Hoshino Motoni: Heiwa eno Negai o Komete 1: Hikiagehen* [Under that Star: Praying for Peace 1: Repatriation After the War], Tokyo: Daisanbunmeisha, 1981, pp. 141–8.
78 Nakano Jirō, 'Akarui Seikatsu o Mezasu Hahaoya no Ayumi [The Progress of a Mother Who Seeks a Bright Future]', *Gekkan Shakai Kyōiku*, May 1959, pp. 20–2.
79 Makise, 'Iwayuru Bitoku', p. 21.
80 Kyoto no Fujin no Ayumi Kenkyūkai (ed.) *Kyoto no Fujin no Ayumi* [The Progress of Women in Kyoto], Kyoto: Kyoto no Fujin no Ayumi Kenkyūkai, 1976, p. 55.
81 Tsurumi Kazuko, *Seikatsu Kiroku Undō no Nakade* [Amidst the Movement to Record One's Life], Tokyo: Miraisha, 1963, p. 193.

Table 8.4 Women's views on rearming Japan

Area	No response	Japan needs a strong military	Japan should be rearmed to a degree in case of foreign aggression	Japan should stay neutral	Japan should possess no armed forces	Total (%)
Chuo Ward, Tokyo	9	2	50	23	16	100
Suginami Ward, Tokyo	4	1	29	35	31	100
Kawasaki, Kanagawa Prefecture	4	2	39	39	16	100
Utsunomiya, Tochigi Prefecture	6	3	34	30	27	100
Average	6	2	37	32	23	100

Source: Tatewaki *et al., Sengo Fujin Undōshi*, p. 191.

Conclusion

1 Yasui Kaoru, 'Humanism to Heiwa [Humanism and Peace]', *Heiwa*, November 1954, p. 18.
2 The writer Matsuoka Yōko also expressed respect for ordinary women who would demonstrate in the streets at the risk of being branded as 'Reds'. She argued that they defied public censure because the experience acquired from their personal lives told them something was wrong or unjust, and she saw an intrinsic value in ordinary people's sensibilities shaped primarily through their daily struggles to sustain their modest existence. See *Fujin Kōron*, March 1961, p. 154.
3 John W. Dower, *Embracing Defeat: Japan in the Wake of World War II*, New York: W. W. Norton and Company, 1999, p. 30.
4 Charles Douglas Lummis, 'Japan's Radical Constitution', in Tsuneoka Setsuko *et al.*, *Nihonkoku Kenpō o Yomu* [Reading the Japanese Constitution], Tokyo: Kashiwa Shobō, 1993, pp. 156–8.
5 Rekishi Kyōikusha Kyōgikai (ed.) *Nihonkoku Kenpō o Kokumin wa Dō Mukaetaka* [The Japanese People's Response to the New Constitution], Tokyo: Kōbunken, 1997, pp. 132–5.
6 Opinion survey results cited in Wada Susumu, 'Keizai Taikokuka to Kokumin Ishiki no Henbō [Change in Public Opinion Amid Japan's Growing Economic Prowess]', in Watanabe Osamu *et al.*, *'Kenpō Kaisei' Hihan* [The Critique of Proposed Constitutional Amendment], Tokyo: Rōdō Junpōsha, 1994, p. 143; and Tsurumi Shunsuke, 'Seishin Kakumei no Jitsuzō [The Realities of the Spiritual Revolution]', in Nakamura Masanori, Amakawa Akira, Yoon Keun Cha and Igarashi Takashi (eds) *Sengo Nihon Senryō to Sengo Kaikaku: Sengo Shisō to Shakai Ishiki* [The Occupation and Reform in Post-war Japan: Post-war Thought and Social Consciousness], 6 vols, Tokyo: Iwanami Shoten, 1995, iii, p. 14.
7 NHK Hōsō Seron Chōsabu (ed.) *Zusetsu Sengo Seronshi* [The Illustrated History of Post-war Public Opinion], Tokyo: Nihon Hōsō Shuppan Kyōkai, 1982, p. 169.
8 *Ibid.*, p. 171.

9 Kōsaka Masataka, *Saishō Yoshida Shigeru* [Prime Minister Yoshida Shigeru], Tokyo: Chūō Kōronsha, 1968, p. 104.
10 Charles Douglas Lummis, 'Japan's Radical Constitution', p. 184.
11 Yoon Keun Cha, *Kozetsu no Rekishi Ishiki* [An Isolated View of History], Tokyo: Iwanami Shoten, 1985, p. 63.
12 A member of one choral group formed by workers and students in Nara Prefecture, for example, said

> Each of us has been all by himself or herself for a long time and we had been looking for friends with whom we could bond to gain strength. There were too many troubles in our city and our schools. We found the gloomy atmosphere oppressive and thought it impossible to endure alone. One of the very few things we could do [to improve our condition] was to sing. After just several of us began choral singing three years ago, our group attracted 100 people in just three months. It was because everyone was looking for something that would dispel that gloomy atmosphere.

A group of female office workers at one Tokyo company began their studies of history, economics and literature in 1953 for a similar reason. They wanted to do something about the feudal employment practices at their workplace, their fears of losing their jobs, loneliness and other personal problems. See *Chisei*, November 1955, pp. 52 and 54.
13 The widow, Oguri Takeko, is quoted in Wada Susumu, *Sengo Nihon No Heiwa Ishiki* [Peace Consciousness in Post-war Japan], Tokyo: Aoki Shoten, 1997, p. 24.

Bibliography

Printed primary sources

Akahata.
Amakusa, T., *Chiiki niokeru Seinen Fujin tono Teikei nitsuite* [On Co-operation with Women and Youths in Local Communities], a report on activities in Miyazaki Prefecture to the 1954 women teachers' research conference.
Asahi Shimbun, Tokyo and Seibu editions.
Chisei.
Chūō Kōron.
The Economist.
Fujin.
Fujin Asahi.
Fujin Jihō.
Fujin Kōron.
Fujin Minshu Shimbun.
Fujin no Koe.
Fujin Sensen.
Fujin Shidōsha.
Fujin Shimbun.
Fujin to Kyōiku.
Fujin to Nenshōsha.
Fujin Yūkensha.
Gekkan Rōdō Mondai.
Gekkan Shakai Kyōiku.
Gekkan Sōhyō.
Gensuikin, The minutes of the international convention for anti-nuclear bomb campaigns, 13 August 1957.
Hahaoya Shimbun.
Hasegawa, T., Kimura, F. and Suga, T. (eds) *Kihonteki Jinken o Dō Mamorinukuka* [How to Defend People's Basic Human Rights], a report on the activities in Yamagata Prefecture to the 1954 women teachers' research conference.
Heiwa.
Heiwa Fujin Shimbun.
Heiwa Nihon.
Heiwa Shimbun.
Higuchi, T., *Onko Chishin* [Learning Anew from Things Old], unpublished paper, 1992.

——*Meshi to Tamashii to Sōgo Fujo* [Food, the Soul and Mutual Help], unpublished paper, 2001.
Irei Jikkō Iinkai News.
Ishikawaken Kyōshokuin Kumiai Fujinbu (ed.) A Report to the Tertiary Women Teachers' National Research Conference on the Activities of the Ishikawa Prefecture Teachers' Union, 1954.
Iwai, A, *Ippan Keika Hōkoku* [A Report on Past Events] at the Fifteenth Sōhyō regular convention, 31 July 1960.
Jichi Shimbun.
Jiyū no Koe.
Josei Kaizō.
Josei Shimbun.
Kinzoku Rōdōsha.
Kokumin.
Kokumin Bunka.
Kokutetsu Bunka.
Kokutetsu Rōdō Kumiai, *1951 Nendo Tōsō Hōshinsho* [The Policy for Fiscal 1951 Struggles], unpublished material compiled by Kokutetsu Rōdō Kumiai, c.1951.
Kokutetsu Shimbun.
Kōwan Rōdō.
Kōwa Shimbun..
Kyodo Printing Co. Union, *Kyōdō Insatsu Rōso no Taikai o Seikō Saseru Tameni* [To Ensure the Success of the Kyodo Printing Co. Union's Annual Convention], 1959.
Ministry of Labour, *Shōwa Nijūkunen Rōdō Keizai no Bunseki* [Analysis of the Labour Economy in 1954], Tokyo: Ministry of Labour, 1954.
Kyōiku Hyōron.
Kyōiku Shimbun.
Mainichi Shimbun.
Nagasakiken Kyōshokuin Kumiai Fujinbu (ed.) *Ronbunshū* [A Collection of Essays], unpublished material, a report to the 1954 women teachers' research conference organized by the Japanese Teachers' Union.
Negami, M., *Kokutetsu Rōdō Kumiai Undō no Ichiyoku o Ninatte* [Supporting the National Railway Workers' Union], unpublished writing.
Nihon Fujin Shimbun.
Nihon Kyōshokuin Kumiai (ed.) *Daisanshū Nihon no Kyōiku: Daisankai Zenkoku Kyōiku Kenkyū Taikai Hōkoku* [Tertiary Education in Japan: Reports to the Tertiary National Pedagogical Research Conference], Tokyo: Kokudosha, 1954.
Nihon Rōdō Kumiai Sōhyō Gikai, Material for the Sōhyō's second annual conference, 1951. Unpublished material prepared by Nihon Rōdō Sōhyō Gikai for internal use.
——*Sōhyō Wa Kaku Tatakau* [Thus Will Sōhyō Fight], 1952, 1956, 1957 and 1958.
——The minutes of Sōhyō's tenth regular convention on 21 July 1958.
——The draft policy on the protest movement against the Police Duties Law, 24 October 1958.
——The records of the twelfth regular convention, 26 August 1959.
——Materials for the thirteenth extraordinary meeting No. 1: Jōsei ni tsuiteno Nisan no Tokuchō [Several Characteristics of the Current Situation], 1959.
——The records of Sōhyō's thirteenth extraordinary meeting, 1959.
——Materials for the fifteenth Sōhyō extraordinary convention I, *Jōsei ni tsuiteno Nisan No Tokuchō* [A Few Characteristics of the Current Situation], 1959.

―― *Anpo Tōsō ni tsuiteno Ishiki Chōsa Chūkan Hōkoku* [Interim Report on the Opinion Poll Concerning the *Anpo Tōsō*], 23 November 1960.
Nihon to Chūgoku.
Ōhara Shakai Mondai Kenkyūjo Zasshi.
Ōkubo, T., *Nōson no Fujin ya Kodomo no Kaihō o Mezashite* [Aiming for the Emancipation of Women and Children in Rural Areas], an unpublished report on the activities in Fukui Prefecture to the 1954 Nikkyōso women teachers' research conference.
Ōnishi, T., *Heiwa to Fujin Kaihō o Mezashiteno Fujin Kyōshi no Shimei* [Women Teachers' Mission To Achieve Peace and Emancipate Women], an unpublished report on the activities in Okayama Prefecture to the 1954 women teachers' research conference.
Ono, K., *Chiiki no Fujin o Taishō toshita Ie ni taisuru Ishiki Chōsa* [An Opinion Survey on Family Issues Conducted Of Women in Local Communities], an unpublished report on the activities in Fukushima Prefecture to the 1954 women teachers' research conference.
Ōtsuka, M., *Watashi no Sengo* [My Post-war Life], unpublished writing.
Rōdō Sensen.
Sekai Heiwa.
Shakai Shugi.
Shakai Times.
Shin Josei.
Shin Sanbetsu.
Shufu no Tomo.
Shufuren Dayori.
Shufu Shimbun.
Shūkan Asahi.
Shūkan Rōdō Jōhō.
Sōhyō.
Suematsu, H., *Heiwa Kakuho no Tame no Kyōiku Jissen* [Educational Activities Aimed At Promoting Peace] an unpublished report on activities in Fukuoka Prefecture to the 1954 women teachers' research conference.
Suzuki, M., *Iwate, Shutoshite Nishi Iwai Chiku niokeru Seinen Fujin Teikei no Ayumi to Shomondai* [Co-operation with Youths and Women and Problems in Iwate Prefecture Including the Nishi Iwai District] an unpublished report to the 1954 women teachers' research conference.
Takeuchi, M., *Watashi no Sengoshi: Kakenuketa Seishun* [My Post-War History: Tumultuous Days of My Youth], unpublished writing.
Tanaka, F., *Heiwa Kyōiku wa Ikani Suishin Subekika* [How To Conduct Peace Education] an unpublished report on activities in Kōchi Prefecture to the 1954 women teachers' research conference.
Tokyo Chihyō.
Tokyo Chihō Rōdō Kumiai Hyōgikai, *Tokyo Chihyō no Genjō to Saikin no Omona Tatakai nitsuite* [The Current State of Tokyo Chihyō and Recent Major Labour Disputes], unpublished report, Tokyo, 1960.
Tokyo Shimbun.
Unesco Nippon.
Utagoe Shimbun.
Yamagata Shimbun.

Yamagishi, M., unpublished report to the third women teachers' research conference on the activities of teachers in Niigata Prefecture, 1954.
Yamaguchi, K, *Sengo Kakumei Mushuku* [A Wandering Post-war Revolutionary], unpublished writing, 2000.
Yomiuri Shimbun.
Zendentsū Bunka.
Zenei.
Zenkoku Kinzoku, *Sōgi no Tokuchō to Zenkokuno Kinzoku Rōdōsha Shokun e no Uttae* [The Characteristics of Labour Disputes and an Appeal to All Metal Workers of Japan], unpublished material, Tokyo, July 1959.
Zentei Bunka.
Zentei Jihō.
Zentei Shimbun.

Printed secondary works

Abe, Y., Ōuchi, H., Nishina, Y. *et al.* (eds) 'Sensō to Heiwa ni Kansuru Nihon no Kagakusha no Seimei [A Japanese Scientists' Statement on War and Peace]', *Sekai*, March 1949, pp. 6–9.
Akiyama, M., 'Heiwa Undō no Rosen [The Policy for the Peace Movement]', *Zentei Jihō*, July 1959, pp. 56–9.
Amano, H., *Sengo Nihon no Josei Nōgyosha no Chii: Danjo Byōdō no Seikatsu Bunka no Sōzōe* [The Status of Female Farmers in Post-war Japan: In Order to Create a Lifestyle Based on the Equality of Men and Women], Tokyo: Domesu Shuppan, 2001.
Amano, M., *Feminism no Ism o Koete* [Transcending the Ism of Feminism], Tokyo: Iwanami Shoten, 1997.
Aoki, Y, 'Watashi no Shittakoto [Things I Have Learned]', in Kusanomikai Dainana Group (ed.) *Sensō to Watashi* [The War and I], Tokyo: Kusanomikai Dainana Group, 1963.
Arase, Y., 'Nihonjin no Kokka Ishiki [The Japanese View of the State]', *Shisō*, August 1960, pp. 41–9.
Ariga, S., *Kokutetsu Minshuka e no Michi* [The Road to Democratization of the Japanese National Railway], Tokyo: Tetsurō Yūai Kaigi, 1989.
Ariyama, T., *Sengoshi no Nakano Kenpō to Journalism* [The Constitution and Journalism in Japan's Post-war History], Tokyo: Kashiwa Shobō, 1998.
Asahi Shimbun Tēma Danwashitsu (ed.) *Nihonjin no Sensō* [Wars as Experienced by the Japanese], Tokyo: Heibonsha, 1988.
Ashigara, S., *Tetsuro no Hibiki* [The Sound of the Rails], Tokyo: Rironsha, 1954.
Awata, Y., 'Shufu no Mezame to Chiisana Kōfuku [Housewives' Awakening and Small Happiness]', *Shisō*, October 1959, pp. 130–5.
Bix, H. P., *Hirohito and the Making of Modern Japan*, New York: HarperCollins, 2000.
Carter, A., *Peace Movements: International Protest and World Politics since 1945*, London: Longman, 1992.
Ceadel, M., *Pacifism in Britain*, Oxford: Clarendon Press, 1980.
—— *The Origins of War Prevention: The British Peace Movement and International Relations, 1730–1854*, Oxford: Clarendon Press, 1996.
Chatfield, C., *For Peace and Justice: Pacifism in America 1914–1941*, Knoxville: University of Tennessee Press, 1971.

280 Bibliography

Chino Y., 'Chiiki Fujinkai [Regional Women's Organizations]', in *Asahi Journal* (ed.) *Onnano Sengoshi* [Post-war History of Women], 3 vols, Tokyo: Asahi Shimbunsha, 1985, i, pp. 116–24.

——(ed.) *Shiryō Shūsei Gendai Nihon Josei no Shutai Keisei* [A Collection of Materials on Formation of Women's Identity in Modern Japan], Tokyo: Domesu Shuppan, 1996, iii.

Daigo Fukuryūmaru Heiwa Kyōkai (ed.) *Bikini Suibaku Hisai Shiryōshū* [Materials on the Bikini Hydrogen Bomb Test], Tokyo: Tokyo University Press, 1976.

Dairokkai Nihon Hahaoya Taikai Jikkō Iinkai (ed.) *Watashitachi wa Ayumi Tsuzukeru* [We Continue Our Progress], 1960.

Dower, J. W., *Embracing Defeat: Japan in the Wake of World War II*, New York: W. W. Norton and Co., 1999.

Eda, T., 'Wakazuma no Gakushū Katsudō wa Dou Hatten Shitaka [The Progress in Young Wives' Educational Activities]', *Gekkan Shakai Kyōiku*, November 1959, pp. 40–3.

Fujii, T., *Kokubō Fujinkai* [Women's Organization for National Defence], Tokyo: Iwanami Shoten, 1985.

——*Heitachi no Sensō* [Soldiers' Wars], Tokyo: Asahi Shimbunsha, 2000.

Fujime, Y., 'Reisen Taisei Keiseiki no Beigun to Seibōryoku [The Sexual Violence of US Servicemen During the Formation of the Cold War System]', in 'Josei, Sensō, Jinken' Gakkai Gakkaishi Henshū Iinkai (ed.) *Josei Sensō Jinken* [Women, War, Human Rights], Shiga: Kōrosha, 1999, no. 2, pp. 116–38.

Fujimoto, T. and Shimoyama, F., 'Nihon No Rōdōsha no Keizaiteki Jōtai [The Economic Condition of Japanese Workers]', *Keizai Hyōron*, April 1961, pp. 33–44.

Fujin Minshu Club (Saiken) (ed.) *Asu o Hiraku* [Paving the Way for Tomorrow], Tokyo: Fujin Minshu Club (Saiken) 2000.

Fujin Minshu Kurabu Nijūnenshi Hensan Iinkai (ed.) *Kōro Nijūnen: Fujin Minshu Kurabu no Kiroku* [A 20-Year Voyage: the Records of the Women's Democratic Club], Tokyo: the Women's Democratic Club, 1967.

Fujishima, U., 'Nihon no Tomoshibi [Lights of Japan]', *Fujin Kōron*, January 1957, pp. 233–7.

Fujita, H., 'Machigurumi no Seiji Undō to Shuji no Yakuwari [A Community-Based Political Movement and the Role of Officers in Charge of Adult Education]', *Gekkan Shakai Kyōiku*, June 1960, pp. 52–7.

Fujiwara, A. (ed.) *Nihon Minshū No Rekishi: Minshū no Jidai e* [The History of the Japanese People: To the Age of the People], 11 vols, Tokyo: Sanseidō, 1976, xi.

—— (ed.) *Shiryō Nihonshi: Guntainai no Hansen Undō* [Primary Materials on Japanese History: Anti-war Activities Within the Military], 13 vols, Tokyo: Ōtsuki Shoten,1980, i.

——'Jūgonen Sensō to Gendai [The 15-year War and the Modern Age]', in Fujiwara, A. and Imai S. (eds) *Jūgonen Sensōshi* [The History of the 15-year War], 4 vols, Tokyo: Aoki Shoten, 1989, iv, pp. 249–78.

Fujiwara, O., *Gensuibaku Kinshi Undō no Seiritsu: Sengo Nihon Heiwa Undōno Genzō* [The Formation of the Anti-nuclear Movement: the origins of the Japanese Post-war Peace Movement], Yokohama: Meiji Gakuin Kokusai Heiwa Kenkyūjo, 1991.

——'Sensō to Heiwa o Meguru Shisō no Shoruikei [Types of Thought Concerning War and Peace]', *Tokyo Keizai Daigaku Kaishi*, November 1992, pp. 29–64.

Fujiwara, T., 'Shicchi Kaifuku no Jidai [Time for Regaining Lost Ground]', *Fujin Kōron*, October 1959, pp. 85–8.

Fukao, S., 'Risōkyō no tameniwa [To Create an Ideal World]', *Josei Kaizō*, March 1951, p. 32.

Fukuda, R., 'Sākuru to Rōdō Kumiai [Workers' Societies and Labour Unions]', *Chisei*, November 1955, pp. 41–2.

Fukuokaken Keisatsushi Hensan Iinkai (ed.) *Fukuokaken Keisatsushi: Shōwa Zenpen* [The History of Fukuoka Prefecture Police: The First Volume for Shōwa Era], Fukuoka: Fukuokaken Keisatsu Honbu, 1980.

Funabashi, N., 'Rōdō Kumiai Soshiki no Tokushitsu [Characteristics of Labour Unions]', in Ōkōchi, K. (ed.) *Nihon no Rōdō Kumiai* [Japanese Labour Unions], Tokyo: Tōyō Keizai Shimpōsha, 1954, pp. 13–39.

Gekkan Shakaitō Henshūbu (ed.) *Nihon Shakaitō no Sanjūnen* [The 30-year History of the Social Democratic Party of Japan], Tokyo: Nihon Shakaitō Chūō Honbu Kikanshikyoku, 1976.

Gordon, A., 'Contests for the Workplace', in Andrew Gordon (ed.) *Postwar Japan as History*, California: University of California Press, 1993, pp. 373–94.

—— *The Wages of Affluence: Labor and Management in Postwar Japan*, Cambridge MA: Harvard University Press, 1998.

Goseki, S, 'Same no Ejiki ni sareta Korani Inoru [Praying for the Children Who were Preyed on by Sharks]', in Sōka Gakkai Fujin Heiwa Iinkai (ed.) *Ano Hoshino Motoni: Heiwa eno Negai o Komete 1) Hikiagehen* [Under that Star: Praying for Peace 1) Repatriation After the War], Tokyo: Daisanbunmeisha, 1981, pp. 141–8.

'Hamakaze yo Kibō o Nosete' Shuppan Iinkai (ed.) *Hamakaze yo Kibō o Nosete* [A Sea Breeze That Brings Us Hope], Yokohama: 'Hamakaze yo Kibō o Nosete' Shuppan Iinkai, 2000.

Hani, S. and Ogawa, T. (eds) *Fujin no Gakushū Kyōiku* [Learning and Education for Women], Tokyo: Aki Shobō, 1970.

Hara, T., 'Katasumi no Kiroku [A Record of Small Things]', *Shisō*, July 1961, pp. 136–40.

Hayashi, E., *Kaikyō no Onnatachi* [Women of the Straits], Fukuoka: Ashi Shobō, 1983.

Heiwa Mondai Danwakai (ed.) 'Kōwa Mondai ni tsuite no Heiwa Mondai Danwakai Seimei [A Heiwa Mondai Danwakai's Statement on the Issue of the Peace Treaty]', *Sekai*, March 1950, pp. 60–4.

Heiwa Mondai Danwakai (ed.) 'Mitabi Heiwa ni tsuite [For the Third Time on Peace]', *Sekai*, December 1950, pp. 21–52.

Hidaka, R., 'Taishūron no Shūhen [The Background of the Debate on Ordinary People]', *Minwa*, March 1959, pp. 2–10.

—— *Gendai Ideology* [Modern Ideology], Tokyo: Keisō Shobō, 1960.

Hidaka, R. and Shimizu, S., 'Kokumin Taiken wa Ikiteiru [The People's Experience Lives On]', *Sekai*, July 1961, pp. 42–58.

Higuchi, T., *Uyoku 'Rōsen Tōitsu' 'Hantai'* [Opposition to the Right-wing 'United Labour Front'], Tokyo: Tsuge Shobō, 1981.

—— *Nihon Rōdō Undō: Rekishi to Kyōkun* [Japan's Labour Movement: Its History and Lessons], Tokyo: Daisan Shokan, 1990.

—— 'Kakumei Senryaku to Kakumei Moral [The Strategy and the Morals of Revolutionaries]', in Watanabe, I., Shiokawa, Y. and Ōyabu, R. (eds) *Shinsayoku Undō*

Yonjūnen no Hikari To Kage [Light and Shadow of the 40-year New Leftist Movement], Tokyo: Shinsensha, 1999, pp. 179–245.

—— 'Akai Kakumei to Shiroi Kakumei [A Red Revolution and a White Revolution]', *Asu o Hiraku Tsūshin*, 1 April 2000, pp. 8–11.

Hino, S., *Rail yo Takarakani Utae* [Railway, Sing Out Loud], Tokyo: Kōyō Shuppansha, 1988.

—— 'Waga Seishun Jidai, Gyakkyō o Kirihiraku [The Days of My Youth: Overcoming Adversity]', in 'Hamakaze yo Kibō o Nosete' Shuppan Iinkai (ed.) *Hamakaze yo Kibō o Nosete* [A Sea Breeze That Brings Us Hope], Yokohama: 'Hamakaze yo Kibō o Nosete' Shuppan Iinkai, 2000.

Hirasawa, E., *Sōgiya* [Labour Dispute Handlers], Tokyo: Ronsōsha, 1982.

Hiratsuka, R. and Kushida, F. (eds) *Warera Haha Nareba* [Because We are Mothers], Tokyo: Seidōsha, 1951.

Hirayu, K., '1959 Nen Nihon PTA no Ugoki [The Activities of the National PTA Federation in 1959]', *Gekkan Shakai Kyōiku*, December 1959, pp. 34–7.

Hirokawa, T., 'Kokumin no Haisen Taiken [The People's Experience of the Defeat]', in Fujiwara, A. and Imai, S. (eds) *Jūgonen Sensōshi* [The History of the 15-year War], Tokyo: Aoki Shoten, 1989, pp. 49–85.

Hiroshima Joseishi Kenkyūkai (ed.) *Hiroshima no Onnatachi* [Hiroshima Women], Tokyo: Domesu Shuppan, 1987.

Hisae, M., *Kyūten Ichiichi to Nihon Gaikō* [The September 11 Terrorist Attacks and Japanese Diplomacy], Tokyo: Kōdansha, 2002.

Hokuriku Tetsudō Rōdō Kumiaishi Hensan Iinkai (ed.) *Hokuriku Tetsudō Rōdō Kumiai Gojūnenshi* [The 50-year History of the Hokuriku Railway Union], Tokyo: Rōdō Kyōiku Centre, 1996.

Hōsei University Ōhara Shakai Mondai Kenkyūsho (ed.) *Shōgen: Sanbetsu Kaigi no Tanjō* [Witness Accounts of the Beginning of Sanbetsu Kaigi], Tokyo: Sōgō Rōdō Kenkyūsho, 1996.

Hoshi, K. (ed.) *Shashinshū: Sunagawa Tōsō no Kiroku* [The Photo Collection of the Sunagawa Struggle], Tokyo: Keyaki Shuppan, 1996.

Howard, M., *War and the Liberal Conscience*, Oxford: Oxford University Press, 1978.

Hozumi, S., 'Ippan Fujinsō no Shakai Ishiki [The Social Consciousness of Ordinary Women]', in Fukutake, T. (ed.) *Nihonjin no Shakai Ishiki* [The Social Consciousness of the Japanese], Kyoto: Sanichi Shobō, 1960, pp. 255–69.

Ikeda, S., 'Chūritsu Shugi to Yoshida no Makki Gaikō [A Neutral Policy and Japan's Diplomacy in the Final Days of the Yoshida Government]', in Toyoshita, N. (ed.) *Anpo Jōyaku no Ronri: Sono Seisei To Tenkai* [The Logic of the Japan-US Security Treaty: Its Beginning and Development], Tokyo: Kashiwa Shobō, 1999, pp. 161–214.

Inomata Tsunao Chosaku Ikō Kankō Kai (ed.) *Ichi Kaikyū Senshi no Bohyō* [The Tombstone of a Class Warrior], Tokyo: Inomata Tsunao Chosaku Ikō Kankō Kai, 1975.

Inui, H., 'Shikarareta Hahaoya Taikai [The Mothers' Congress that Got a Scolding]', *Gekkan Shakai Kyōiku*, December 1959, pp. 46–9.

Inumaru, G., Tsujioka, S. and Hirano, Y., *Sengo Nihon Rōdō Undōshi* [The History of the Post-war Labour Movement in Japan], Tokyo: Gakushū no Tomo Sha, 1989.

Irokawa, D., *Kindai Nihon no Sensō* [Wars in Modern Japan], Tokyo: Iwanami Shoten, 1998.

Ishida, T., *Nihon no Seiji to Kotoba* [Language in Japanese Politics], 2 vols, Tokyo: Tokyo University Press, 1989, i.

Ishigaki, A., 'Shufu to iu Daini Shokugyōron [Housewifery as a Second Occupation]', *Fujin Kōron*, February 1955, pp. 48–53.

Ishihara, S., 'Rōdō Undō to Sengo Sedai [The Labour Movement and Post-war Generations]', *Shisō*, July 1959, pp. 29–38.

Ishii, A., 'Kusanomikai e: Kininaru Seikaku no Aimaisa [The Puzzling Ambiguity of Kusanomikai]', *Gekkan Shakai Kyōiku*, August 1960, pp. 94–6.

Ishii, H., *Watashi no Zentei Yonjūnenshi* [My 40 Years at Zentei], Tokyo: Zentei Fukushi Centre, 1993.

Ishikawa, A., *Shakai Hendō to Rōdōsha Ishiki* [Social Change and Workers' Attitudes], Tokyo: Nihon Rōdō Kyōkai, 1975.

Ishikawa, T., *Ningen no Kabe* [Human Walls], Tokyo: Shinchōsha, 1973.

Isono, F., 'Fujin Kaihōron no Konmei [The Stalled Debate over the Emancipation of Women]', *Asahi Journal*, 10 April 1960, pp. 14–21.

Itō, S., 'Rōdōsha ga Susumeru Nōson no Chiiki Katsudō [Community Activities Conducted by Workers In Rural Areas]', *Gekkan Shakai Kyōiku*, October 1959, pp. 32–8.

Itō Y., 'Sengo Kaikaku to Bosei [Post-war Reform and Maternity]', in Wakita, H. (ed.) *Bosei o Tou* [Studies of Maternity], Kyoto: Jinbun Shoin, 1985, pp. 219–49.

——*Sengo Nihon Joseishi* [Post-war History of Japanese Women], Tokyo: Ōtsuki Shoten, 1974.

Iwai, A., 'Sōhyō no Shin Undō Hōshinan ni tsuite [About the New Policy Proposals of Sōhyō]', in *Shakai Shugi*, July 1958, pp. 36–43.

Iwai, A., *Sōhyō to tomoni* [With Sōhyō], Tokyo: Yomiuri Shimbunsha, 1971.

Iwasaki, K. and Ōki, M. (eds) *Kusanone no Hahatachi* [Mothers at the Grassroots], Tokyo: Domesu Shuppan, 1991.

Izuminokai Sensō Taikenki Hensan Iinkai (ed.) *Shufu no Sensō Taikenki* [Accounts of Housewives' Experiences of the War], Nagoya: Fūbaisha, 1965.

Kageyama, M., 'Aru Nōson Fujin Gakkyū no Ayumi to Mondaiten [The Progress and Problems of a Housewives' Class in One Farming Village]', *Gekkan Shakai Kyōiku*, January 1961, pp. 55–8.

Kamisaka, F., 'Tokkō deatta Chichi to Watashi [My Father Who Was in the Thought Police and Me]', *Fujin Kōron*, August 1960, pp. 112–8.

Kanō, M., 'Nigai "Dokuritsu" [A Bitter Taste of 'Independence']', in Onnatachi no Genzai o Tou Kai (ed.) *Jūgoshi Nōto Sengohen: 'Dokuritsu Nihon' To Onnatachi* [Notes on the Post-war History of the Home Front: 'Independent Japan' and Women], Tokyo: Impact Shuppankai, 1987, pp. 6–26.

——*Onnatachi no Jūgo* [Women's Home Front], Tokyo: Impact Shuppan, 1995.

Kansai Shufu Rengōkai (ed.) *Shōhisha Undō Sanjūnen: Kansai Shufuren No Ayumi* [30 Years of the Consumer Movement: The History of Kansai Shufuren], Osaka: Kansai Shufuren, 1976.

Katsudō Shūdan Shisō Undō Fujin Undō Bukai (ed.) *Hansen Heiwa to Josei Kaihōshi* [Campaigns Against War, Peace and the History of Women's Liberation], Tokyo: Ogawamachi Kikaku, 1983.

Kawamura, Y., *Sokoku no Nakani Ikoku ga Aru*, in Kido, N. (ed.) *Shi to Jōkyō: Gekidō no Gojū Nendai* [Poems and the Situation: The Turbulent '50s], Tokyo: Bungaku Dōjin Menokai, 1992, pp. 90–1.

Kawata, T., 'Onnatoshiteno Tatakaikara [Women's Struggle]', *Gekkan Shakai Kyōiku*, August 1960, pp. 34–7.
Kido, N. (ed.) *Shi to Jōkyō: Gekidō no Gojū Nendai* [Poems and the Situation: The Turbulent '50s], Tokyo: Bungaku Dōjin Menokai, 1992.
Kimura, S., 'Kyōbōka suru Danatsu Seisaku to Tatakau Tameni [To Fight Worsening Repression]', *Zenei*, December 1959, pp. 62–7.
Kitagawa, R., Nakabayashi, K., Sasaki, H., Masujima, H., Satō, T. and Matsushita, K., 'Sōhyō to Zenrō' *Chūō Kōron*, April 1960, p. 103–25.
Koana, H., 'Heiwa no Mondai wa Dō Kangaetara Yoinoka [What We Should Make of Issues Over Peace]', *Zentei Bunka*, August 1959, pp. 25–6.
Kobayashi, S. 'Red Purge Hantai Tōsō ni tsuite [About the Protest against the Red Purge]', *Zenei*, December 1959, pp. 87–91.
Kobayashi, T., *Hiratsuka Raichō*, Tokyo: Shimizu Shoin, 1983.
Kobayashi, T. and Yoneda, S. (ed.) *Hiratsuka Raichō Hyōronshū* [Writings by Hiratsuka Raichō], Tokyo: Iwanami Shoten, 1987.
Kobayashi, T., 'Kakemeguru Jidōsha Bunko to Dokushokai [Travelling Car Libraries and Reading Societies]', *Gekkan Shakai Kyōiku*, October 1960, pp. 40–4.
Kōda, Y., 'Sōhyō Hanshuryūha no Undō Rosen [The Policies of Sōhyō's Non-mainstream Groups]', *Gekkan Rōdō Mondai*, October 1962, pp. 15–20.
Kodomo o Mamoru Fujin no Atsumari (ed.) *Izumi wa Dokokara* [Where Do the Springs Originate?], Kōchi: Kōchishi Shiritsu Shimin Toshokan, 1959.
Kohara, K., 'Nikkyōso Fujinbu to Heiwa Undō [The Women's Section of Nikkyōso and the Peace Movement]', in Onnatachi no Genzai o Tou Kai (ed.) *Jūgoshi Nōto Sengohen: Chōsen Sensō to Gyaku Kōsu no Onnatachi* [Notes on the Post-war History of the Home Front: The Korean War and Women amid the Reverse Course], Tokyo: Impact Shuppankai, 1986, pp. 46–61.
Kojima, T., *Chūgoku Seiji To Taishū Rosen* [Chinese Politics and the Mass Line], Tokyo: Keiō Tsūshin Kabushiki Kaisha, 1985.
Kōjiya, M., *Sensō o Ikita Onnatachi* [Women Who Experienced the War], Kyoto: Minerva Shobō, 1985.
Kokubun, I., *Atarashii Tsuzurikata Kyōshitsu* [New Essay-writing Class], Tokyo: Nihon Hyōronsha, 1951.
——'Heiwa Undō [The Peace Movement]', in Takeuchi Yoshimi (ed.) *Sengo no Minshū Undō* [Popular Movements in the Post-war Era], Tokyo: Aoki Shoten, 1956, pp. 121–39.
Kokutetsu Rōdō Kumiai (ed.) *Kokutetsu Rōdō Kumiai Nijūnenshi* [The 20-year History of the National Railway Union], Tokyo: Rōdō Junpōsha, 1960.
Kokutetsu Rōdō Kumiai Shizuoka Chihō Honbu (ed.) *Kokurō Shizuoka Sanjūnenshi* [The 30-year History of the National Railway Union's Shizuoka Chapter], Shizuoka: Kokutetsu Rōdō Kumiai Shizuoka Chihō Honbu, 1983.
Kokutetsu Rōdō Kumiai Tokyo Chihō Honbu (ed.) *Kokutetsu Rōso Tokyo Chihō Honbu Nijūnen* [The 20-year History of the Tokyo Headquarters of the National Railway Union], Tokyo: Rōdō Junpōsha, 1961.
Kominami, M., 'Hibachi no Hi wa Moetsuzukete [The Fire in a Brazier Burns on]', in Iwasaki Kikue and Ōki Motoko (eds) *Kusanone no Hahatachi* [Mothers at the Grassroots], Tokyo: Domesu Shuppan, 1991, pp. 97–111.
Kōra, T., 'Heiwa ni Shitsubō Shitewa Naranai [We Should Never Lose Faith in Peace]', *Josei Kaizō*, April 1954, pp. 94–5.

Kōriyama, Y., *Nikoyon Saijiki* [The Diary of Day Labourers], Tokyo: Tsuge Shobō, 1983.

Kōsaka, M., *Saishō Yoshida Shigeru* [Prime Minister Yoshida Shigeru], Tokyo: Chūō Kōronsha, 1968.

Koyama, H., *Sengo Nihon Kyōsantōshi* [The Post-war History of the Japanese Communist Party], Tokyo: Haga Shoten, 1972.

Kudō, M., 'Keijō to Watashi [Keijō and I]', *Asahi Shimbun*, 1 July 1950.

Kumagai, T. and Saga, I., *Nissan Sōgi 1953* [The 1953 Labour Dispute at Nissan Motor], Tokyo: Satsukisha, 1983.

Kumakura H., *Sengo Heiwa Undōshi* [The History of the Post-war Peace Movement], Tokyo: Ōtsuki Shoten, 1959.

Kusanomikai (ed.) *Kusanomi Sanjūnen no Kiroku* [30-year Records of Kusanomi], Tokyo: Kusanomikai, 1984.

Kyoto no Fujin no Ayumi Kenkyūkai (ed.) *Kyoto no Fujin no Ayumi* [The Progress of Women in Kyoto], Kyoto: Kyoto no Fujin no Ayumi Kenkyūkai, 1976.

Lummis, C. D., 'Japan's Radical Constitution', in Tsuneoka, S., Lummis, C. D. and Tsurumi, S. (eds) *Nihonkoku Kenpō o Yomu* [Reading the Japanese Constitution], Tokyo: Kashiwa Shobō, 1993, pp. 155–93.

Maeno, T., 'Shukensha Ishikini Mezamete [Awaking to People's Sovereign Rights]', in Iwasaki, K. and Ōki, M. (eds) *Kusanone no Hahatachi* [Mothers at the Grassroots], Tokyo: Domesu Shuppan, 1991, pp. 39–59.

Makise, K. 'Iwayuru Bitoku o Kanaguri Suterutameni [Casting Off So-called Virtues]', *Gekkan Shakai Kyōiku*, November 1959, pp. 21, 36–9.

——'Haha toshite Shufu toshite [As a Mother and a Housewife]', *Kokumin Bunka*, 31 July 1960, pp. 9–10.

Maruoka, H., 'Heiwa no Botai [The Mother of Peace]', *Fujin*, August 1948, pp.6–9.

——*Aru Sengo Seishin* [Spirit of the Post-war Era], Tokyo: Hitotsubashi Shobō, 1969.

——*Nihon Nōson Fujin Mondai* [Issues Concerning Japanese Women In Rural Areas], Tokyo: Domesu Shuppan, 1980.

——(ed.) *Nihon Fujin Mondai Shiryō Shūsei* [A Collection of Data on Women's Issues], 10 vols, Tokyo: Domesu Shuppan, 1981, ix.

Maruyama, M., *Gendai Seiji no Shisō to Kōdō* [Thoughts and Actions in Modern Politics], Tokyo: Miraisha, 1960.

Matsumiya, Y., 'Yusuburareta Kokurō Taikai [The Disturbance during the Kokurō Convention]', *Gekkan Rōdō Mondai*, October 1960, pp. 39–43.

Matsumoto, S., *Kuroji no E* [A Picture Against a Black Background], Tokyo: Kōbunsha, 1961.

Matsushita, R., Morisaki, K., Hirowatari, T., Kinoshita, M., Tomimori, K., Hayashi, K., Hiroshige, S. and Obara, R., *Samazamana Sengo* [Various Post-war Experiences], Tokyo: Nihon Keizai Hyōronsha, 1995.

Minaguchi. K., 'Anpo Tōsō eno Hitotsu no Hansei [Self-criticism about the *Anpo Tōsō*]', *Gekkan Shakaitō*, August 1960, pp. 6–14.

——*Anpo Tōsōshi* [The History of the *Anpo Tōsō*], Tokyo: Shakai Shinpō, 1968.

Ministry of Labour (ed.) *Shiryō Rōdō Undōshi* [Materials on the History of the Labour Movement], Tokyo: Ministry of Labour, 1951.

Mitsui, T., 'Fujin no Katsudō wa Kokomade Kiteiru [Advances in Women's Activities]', *Gekkan Shakai Kyōiku*, August 1960, pp. 12–9.

Miyamoto, Y., 'Watashitachi wa Heiwa o Tebanasanai [We Will Never Give Up Peace]', *Fujin Minshu Shimbun*, 12 August 1948.

286 Bibliography

Miyaoka, M., *Sunagawa Tōsō no Kiroku* [The Records of the Sunagawa Struggle], Tokyo: Sanichi Shobō, 1970.

Momii T., 'Kankōrō to Futō Rōdō Kōi Seido [Public-sector Unions and Their System of Unfair Employment Practices]', *Gekkan Rōdō Mondai*, October 1960.

Monogatari Sengo Rōdō Undōshi Kankō Iinkai (ed.) *Monogatari Sengo Rōdō Undōshi* [The History of the Post-war Labour Movement], 10 vols, Tokyo: Kyōiku Bunka Kyōkai, 1998, iii and iv.

Mori, N., *Kazoku Gurumi, Machi Gurumi* [Struggles Involving Workers' Families and Communities], Kyoto: Sanichi Shobō, 1958.

——'Soshikijin Keisei no Kadai [Problems Regarding the Education of Members of an Organization]', in Gendai no Hakken Henshū Iinkai (ed.) *Gendai no Hakken* [Discovery of Modernity], 12 vols, Tokyo: Shunjūsha, 1960, xii, pp. 33–80.

——*Kanazawa ni Ikite* [Life in Kanazawa], Kanazawa: Mori Naohiro, 1985.

Morisaki, K., 'Onna wa Nando demo Tatakau [Women Will Never Give Up Their Fight]', *Gekkan Shakai Kyōiku*, November 1959, pp. 50–3; December 1961, pp. 88–9.

Morita, F., 'Hitorini Natta Watashi [I Am By Myself Now]', *Sekai*, August 1959, pp. 123–5.

Muchaku, S. (ed.) *Yamabiko Gakkō* [School of Echoes in the Mountains], Tokyo: Seidōsha, 1951.

Mueller C. M., 'Building Social Movement Theory', in Aldon D. Morris and Carol McClurg Mueller (eds) *Frontiers in Social Movement Theory*, New Haven and London: Yale University Press, 1992.

Murakami, K., *Sōhyō Monogatari* [The Story of Sōhyō], Tokyo: Nihon Hyōronsha, 1960.

Nagahara, K., 'Josei Tōgō to Bosei [Organization of Women and Maternity]', in Wakita, H. (ed.) *Bosei o Tou* [Studies of Maternity], Kyoto: Jinbun Shoin, 1985, pp. 192–218.

Nagahara, K. and Yoneda, S., *Onna no Shōwashi* [Women's History of the Showa Era], Tokyo: Yūhikakusensho, 1986.

Nakagawa, N., 'Chūso no Ronsō [Debates between China and the Soviet Union]', *Gekkan Shakai Kyōiku*, October 1960, pp. 50–1.

Nakajima, M., 'Shufu no Kimochi [A Housewife's Feelings]', *Kokumin Bunka*, no. 20, 1961, p. 27.

Nakamoto, T., *Watashi no Anpo Tōsō Nikki* [My Diary on the *Anpo Tōsō*], Tokyo: Shinnihon Shuppansha, 1963.

Nakamura, K., *Shakai Shugi Kyōkai o Kiru* [In Criticism of the Japan Socialism Association], Tokyo: Nisshin Hōdō, 1977.

Nakano, J., 'Akarui Seikatsu o Mezasu Hahaoya no Ayumi [The Progress of a Mother Who Seeks a Bright Future]', *Gekkan Shakai Kyōiku*, May 1959, pp. 19–23.

Nakano, M., 'Fujin Daigishi [Female Legislators]', *Asahi Shimbun*, 2 September 1952, evening edn.

Naramoto, T., 'Nihon ni okeru Sākuru Katsudō no Hatten [The Development of Informal Group Activities in Japan]', *Chisei*, November 1955, pp. 37–9.

Nasuno, R., 'Seinen Katsudōka to Anpo Tōsō [Young Activists and the *Anpo Tōsō*]', *Gekkan Shakai Kyōiku*, September 1960, pp. 50–4.

NHK Hōsō Seron Chōsajo (ed.) *Zusetsu Sengo Seronshi* [The Illustrated History of Post-war Public Opinion], Tokyo: Nihon Hōsō Shuppan Kyōkai, 1975.

Nihon Hahaoya Taikai Jūnenshi Hensan Iinkai (ed.) *Hahaoya Undō Jūnen no Ayumi* [The 10-year History of the Mothers' Movement], Tokyo: Nihon Hahaoya Taikai Renrakukai, 1966.
Nihon Heiwa Iinkai (ed.) *Heiwa Undō Nijūnen Undōshi* [The 20-year History of the Peace Movement], Tokyo: Ōtsuki Shoten, 1969.
Nihon Rōdō Kumiai Sōhyō Gikai (ed.) *Sōhyō Jūnenshi* [The 10-year History of Sōhyō], Tokyo: Rōdō Junpōsha, 1964.
Nihon Sakubun no Kai (ed.) *Seikatsu Tsuzurikata Jiten* [A Reference Book on Essays on One's Own Life], Tokyo: Meiji Tosho Shuppan, 1958.
Nihon Tōkei Kyōkai (ed.) *Nihon Chōki Tōkei Sōran* [National Statistics of Japan], 5 vols, Tokyo: Nihon Tōkei Kyōkai, 1988, i.
Nikkyōso Fujinbu (ed.) *Nikkyōso Fujinbu Sanjūnenshi* [The 30-year History of Nikkyōso's Women's Section], Tokyo: Rōdō Kyōiku Centre, 1977.
Nissan Rōdō Undōshi Hensan Iinkai (ed.) *Zenji Nissan Bunkai: Jidōsha Sangyō Rōdō Undōshi* [The Nissan Chapter of the Autoworkers' Union Federation: The History of Autoworkers' Unions], 3 vols, Tokyo: Nissan Rōdō Undōshi Hensan Iinkai, 1992, ii.
Obara, T., *Ishikoroni Kataru Hahatachi* [Mothers Who Talk to Pebbles], Tokyo: Miraisha, 1981.
Ōe, M., 'Osoikedo...Kenpō o Yomu Hahanokai [Mothers' Society That Began Reading the Constitution Belatedly]', *Asahi Shimbun*, 22 June 1960, evening edn.
Ōe, S., *Sensō to Minshū no Shakaishi* [The Social History of Japan's Wars and People], Tokyo: Tokuma Shoten, 1979.
——*Nichiro Sensō to Nihon Guntai* [The Russo-Japanese War and the Japanese Military], Tokyo: Rippū Shobō, 1987.
Ogata, N., 'Fujin Shimbunron [On Women's Newspapers]', *Josei Kaizō*, March 1949, pp. 12–7.
Ōkōchi, K. (ed.) *Nihon no Rōdō Kumiai* [Japanese Labour Unions], Tokyo: Tōyō Keizai Shimpōsha, 1954.
——*Sengo Nihon no Rōdō Undō* [The Labour Movement in Post-war Japan], Tokyo: Iwanami Shoten, 1955.
——'Sōhyō Ron [Opinions about Sōhyō]', in *Sekai*, September 1955, pp. 63–73.
——'Taishū Undō no Gōrisei to Higōrisei [The Rationality and Irrationality of Mass Movements]', *Chūō Kōron*, May 1961, pp. 37–45.
Ōkōchi, K. and Matsuo, H., *Nihon Rōdō Kumiai Monogatari* [The Story of Japanese Labour Unions], Tokyo: Chikuma Shobō, 1969.
Ōkubo, K., *Kaze Wa Cuba Kara Fuitekuru* [Winds Blow From Cuba], Tokyo: Dōjidaisha, 1998.
Ōmura, A., 'Shinsō o Socchokuni [Frankly Tell Us the Truth]', *Asahi Shimbun*, 7 February 1952, morning edn.
Onda, S., 'Otto o Ugokashi Keiei o Ugokasu [Influencing Husbands and Household Management]', *Gekkan Shakai Kyōiku*, November 1958, pp. 6–11.
Onnatachi no Genzai o Tou Kai (ed.) *Jūgoshi Nōto Sengohen: Chōsen Sensō Gyaku Kōsu no nakano Onnatachi* [Notes on the Post-war History of the Home Front: Women during the Korean War and the Reverse Course], Tokyo: Impact Shuppankai, 1986.
——(ed.) *Jūgoshi Nōto Sengohen: Gojūgonen Taisei no Seiritsu to Onnatachi* [Notes on the Post-war History of the Home Front: The Emergence of the 1955 System and Women], Tokyo: Impact Shuppankai, 1987.

288 *Bibliography*

——(ed.) *Jūgoshi Nōto Sengohen: Mohaya Sengo dewa nai?* [Notes on the Post-war History of the Home Front: Is the Post-war Era Over?], Tokyo: Impact Shuppankai, 1988.

——(ed.) *Jūgoshi Nōto Sengohen: Onnatachi no Rokujūnen Anpo* [Notes on the Post-war History of the Home Front: Women's 1960 *Anpo Tōsō*], Tokyo, Impact Shuppankai 1990.

Onodera, T., 'Watashi no Oitachi [My Personal History]', *Gekkan Shakai Kyōiku*, August 1959, pp. 39–43.

Ōsawa, K., 'Nikkō Akabane no Tōsō Kiroku [Records of the Struggle at Nippon Steel's Akabane Plant]', *Shakai Shugi*, March 1953, pp. 60–3.

Ōta, K., 'Seitō to Rōdō Undō [Political Parties and the Labour Movement]', *Shakai Shugi*, October 1955, pp. 25–7.

——'Nihonteki Kumiai Shugi [Japanese Trade Unionism]', *Shakai Shugi*, March 1960, pp. 25–40.

——*Gendai no Rōdō Undō* [Today's Labour Movement], Tokyo: Rōdō Junpōsha, 1964.

——*Tatakai no Nakade* [Amidst the Struggle], Tokyo: Aoki Shoten, 1971.

——*Hibike Rappa* [Sound the Trumpet], Tokyo: Nihon Keizai Shimbun, 1974.

Ōta, K. and Iwai, A., 'Rōdō Undō no Atarashii Tenkai ni tsuite [About New Developments in the Labour Movement]', *Shakai Shugi*, January 1959, pp. 2–8.

Ōtake, H., *Sengo Nihon no Ideology Tairitsu* [Ideological Conflicts in Post-war Japan], Kyoto: Sanichi Shobō, 1996.

Ōtsubo, Y., 'Watashino Keiaishita Ōta Kaoru San no Seikyo o Itamu [Mourning the Passing of Mr Ōta Kaoru Whom I Respected and Loved]', *Shinpo to Kaikaku*, December 1998, pp. 4–9.

Packard, G. R., *Protest in Tokyo: The Security Treaty Crisis of 1960*, Princeton: Princeton University Press, 1966.

Rekishi Kyōikusha Kyōgikai (ed.) *Nihonkoku Kenpō o Kokumin wa Dō Mukaetaka* [The Japanese People's Response to the New Constitution], Tokyo: Kōbunken, 1997.

Rironsha (ed.) *Keihin no Niji: Rōdōsha no Kaihō Shishū* [The Rainbow of Keihin: Workers' Poems for the Liberation of the Nation], Tokyo: Rironsha, 1952.

Rochon, T. R., *Mobilizing For Peace: The Antinuclear Movements in Western Europe*, Princeton: Princeton University Press, 1988.

Saeki, Y., 'Tadashiku Miyō [Let's See Things as They Are]', *Fujin to Kyōiku*, July 1959, pp. 50–1.

Sagawa, M., 'Seikatsu Kiroku Undō no Keifu to Sono Konnichi no Mondai [The History of the Movement To Record Personal Histories and Its Current Problems]', *Gekkan Shakai Kyōiku*, September 1959, pp. 11–20.

Saitō, K., 'Kokutetsu Rōdōsha wa Heiwa to Tōitsu ni Susumu [National Railway Workers' Progress toward Peace and Unity]', *Zenei*, no. 53, 1950, pp. 69–73.

Saitō, S., 'Fujin Dantai no Gakushū Katsudō Hihan [A Critique of Educational Activities by Women's Organizations]', *Gekkan Shakai Kyōiku*, November 1959, pp. 12–21.

Saitō, T., 'Hyakushō wa Riekini Tsunagaraneba [Unless Farmers Recognize Self-interest]', *Gekkan Shakai Kyōiku*, September 1960, pp. 43–6.

Sakai, S., 'Hahaoya Taikai o Hirakumade [How We Organised a Mothers' Congress]', in *Gekkan Shakai Kyōiku*, July 1961, pp. 22–5.

Sakisaka, S., 'Hahatachi to Teo Tsunagu Jokyōshi [Women Teachers Allying with Mothers]', *Fujin Asahi*, April 1955, pp. 64–72.

Sakizaki, K., *Circle Katsudō Nyūmon* [An Introduction to Society Activities], Kyoto: Sanichi Shobō, 1957.

Saotome, K., *Sensō o Kataritsugu* [Telling Younger Generations About the War], Tokyo: Iwanami Shoten, 1998.

Sasaki, Y. [1] 'Nōkanki o Furikaette [Looking Back on the Time I Took off Farm Work]', *Asahi Shimbun*, 25 May 1953, evening edn.

Sasaki, Y. [2] *Umi o Wataru Jieitai: PKO Rippō to Seiji Kenryoku* [The Overseas Dispatch of the Self-defense Forces: The International Peacekeeping Legislation and the Political Establishment], Tokyo: Iwanami Shoten, 1991.

Sasaki-Uemura, W., *Organizing the Spontaneous*, Honolulu: University of Hawaii Press, 2001.

Satō, Y., *Jiyū to Jiritsu eno Ayumi* [Progress toward Liberty and Independence], Tokyo: Asahi Shimbunsha, 1984.

Seki, A., *Utagoe ni Miserarete* [Enchanted by Singing], Tokyo: Ongaku Centre, 1971.

Sekine, K., 'Hangaria Mondai ni tsuite [About the Issue of Hungary]', *Shakai Shugi*, March 1957, pp. 35–7.

Sekiya, R., 'Keishokuhō "Kaisei" o Meguru Fujinsō no Ugoki Nitsuite [Women's Activities against the Revision of the Police Duties Law]', *Shisō*, February 1959, pp. 36–43.

Sengo Rōdō Undōshi Kenkyūkai, 'Sengo Rōdō Undō no "Shinwa" o Minaosu [Reviewing the "Myth" about the Post-war Labour Movement]', *Sekai*, January 1999, pp. 280–96.

Setagaya Joseishi Hensan Iinkai (ed.) *Setagaya Joseishi* [The History of Women in Setagaya], Tokyo: Domesu Shuppan, 1999.

Shigematsu, K., 'Fujinkai Buchikowashi Ron [Women's Societies Should Be Broken Up]', *Fujin Kōron*, July 1959, p. 122–7.

——'Fujin Gakkyū Imamade to Korekara [The Past and the Future of Fujin Gakkyū]', *Gekkan Shakai Kyōiku*, August 1960, pp. 20–4.

Shijō, E., 'Sanshirō Ningyō no Kai [The Society for Making Sanshiro Dolls]', *Gekkan Shakai Kyōiku*, February 1958, pp. 54–5.

Shimada, T., 'Hahaoya Undō eno Kitai [Expectations for the Mothers' Movement]', *Gekkan Shakai Kyōiku*, September 1958, pp. 74–7.

Shimizu, K., 'Shufu no Jidai wa Hajimatta [The Age of Housewives Has Just Begun]', *Fujin Kōron*, April 1955, pp. 119–23.

Shimizu, S., 'Anpo Tōsō Sōkatsu no Ichidanmen [One Aspect of the Analysis of the Anpo Tōsō]', *Gekkan Shakaitō*, August 1960, pp. 22–9.

——*Nihon no Shakai Minshushugi* [Social Democracy in Japan], Tokyo: Iwanami Shoten, 1961.

——*Sengo Kakushin Seiryoku* [Post-war Reformist Forces], Tokyo: Aoki Shoten, 1966.

——'Sōhyō Sanjūnen no Balance Sheet [The Balance Sheet for the 30-year History of Sōhyō]', in Shimizu, S. (ed.) *Sengo Rōdō Kumiai Undōshi Ron* [Critiques of the Post-war History of the Labour Movement], Tokyo: Nihon Hyōronsha, 1982, pp. 315–72.

——*Sengo Kakushin no Hanhikage* [Semidarkness in the Post-war Reform Movement], Tokyo: Nihon Keizai Hyōronsha, 1995.

Shimizu, S., Nakajima, M. and Tatsui, Y., 'Takano-Hosoya Line no Koro [The Days of the Takano-Hosoya Axis]', pp. 88–119.

Shimizu Shinzō no Omoide Kankō Iinkai (ed.) *Kunshiran no Hanakage ni* [Under the Shadow of a Kaffir Lily], Tokyo: Heigensha, 1997.

Shinobu, S., *Anpo Tōsōshi* [The History of the *Anpo Tōsō*], Tokyo: Sekai Shoin, 1961.

Shinofuji, M., 'Shokuba Tōsō no Rekishiteki Keifu to Sōkatsu [The History of Workplace Struggles]', in *Gekkan Rōdō Kumiai*, February 1980, pp. 12–17.

Shin Sanbetsu Nijūnenshi Hensan Iinkai (ed.) *Shin Sanbetsu no Nijūnen* [The 20-year History of Shin Sanbetsu], 2 vols, Tokyo: Shin Sanbetsu, 1969, i.

Shin Sanbetsu (ed.) *Zoku Shin Sanbetsu no Nijūnen* [The 20-year History of Shin Sanbetsu: Sequel], Tokyo: Atlas Network, 1988.

Shiota, S., 'Rōdō Kumiai to Seiji [Labour Unions and Politics]', in Ōkōchi, K. (ed.) *Nihon no Rōdō Kumiai* [Japanese Labour Unions], Tokyo: Tōyō Keizai Shinpōsha, 1954, pp. 81–105.

Shiratori, K., '*Anpo Tōsō* to Sākuru [The *Anpo Tōsō* and Societies]', *Kokumin Bunka*, 31 July 1960, pp. 2–4.

Shishido, Y., 'The Peace Movement of Post-war Japanese Christians', in *Japan Christian Quarterly* (Tokyo) vol. 51, no. 4, fall 1985, pp. 215–24.

Shisō no Kagaku Kenkyūkai, *Kyōdō Kenkyū: Shūdan: Sākuru no Sengo Shisōshi* [Joint Research on Groups: The Post-war Intellectual History of Social Circles], Tokyo: Heibonsha, 1976.

Shitetsu Sōren Nijūnenshi Hensan Iinkai (ed.) *Shitetsu Sōren Nijūnenshi Shiryōhen* [Appendix to the 20-year History of the General Federation of Private Railway Workers' Unions of Japan], Tokyo: Rōdō Junpōsha, 1969.

Sodei, R., *Haikei Makkāsāsama* [Dear General MacArthur], Tokyo: Ōtsuki Shoten, 1985.

Sōka Gakkai Fujin Heiwa Iinkai (ed.) *Kappōgi no Jūgo* [Aprons and the Home Front], Tokyo: Daisan Bunmeisha, 1987.

Storm, H., 'Japanese Women and the Peace Movement in the 1950s: Opposition to Nuclear Testing', *Asian Profile* (Hong Kong) vol. 26, no. 1, February 1998, pp. 17–28.

Sudō, K. (ed.) *Murano Hahaoya Gakkyū* [School for Mothers in Rural Areas], Tokyo: Shinhyōronsha, 1956.

Sumiya, M., 'Rōdō Undō niokeru Hiyaku to Hatten [Development of the Labour Movement]', in Oka, Y. (ed.) *Gendai Nihon no Seiji Katei* [The Political Process in Modern Japan], Tokyo: Iwanami Shoten, 1958, pp. 412–20.

—— 'Rōdō Undō ni okeru Shinri to Ronri [The Psychology and Logic of the Labour Movement]', in Sei Itō, Ienaga Saburō, Odagiri Hideo, Katō Shūichi, Kamei Katsuichirō, Karaki Junzō, Kuno Osamu, Shimizu Ikutarō, Sumiya Mikio, Takeuchi Yoshimi and Maruyama Masao (eds) *Kindai Nihon Shisōshi Kōza* [Modern Japanese Intellectual History], 15 vols, Tokyo: Chikuma Shobō, 1960, v, p. 188.

—— 'Gijutsu Kakushin to Keiei Kazoku Shugi [Technological Innovation and a Paternalistic Management System]', *Chūō Kōron*, May 1961, pp. 90–9.

Suzuki, Y. (ed.) *Ashibue no Uta* [The Song of a Reed Pipe], Tokyo: Domesu Shuppan, 1989.

Taguchi, F., 'Sōhyō ni Okeru Leadership [Leadership in Sōhyō]', in Sei Itō, Ienaga Saburō, Odagiri Hideo, Katō Shūichi, Kamei Katsuichirō, Karaki Junzō, Kuno

Osamu, Shimizu Ikutarō, Sumiya Mikio, Takeuchi Yoshimi and Maruyama Masao (eds) *Kindai Nihon Shisōshi Kōza* [Modern Japanese Intellectual History], 15 vols, Tokyo: Chikuma Shobō, 1960, v, pp. 339–65.

Tahara, S., *Nihon no Sensō* [Japan's Wars], Tokyo: Shōgakukan, 2000.

Takabatake, M., 'Rokujūnen Anpo no Seishinshi [The History of Ideas Concerning the 1960 *Anpo*]', in Tetsuo Najita, Maeda Ai and Kamishima Jirō (eds) *Sengo Nihon no Seishinshi* [The Post-war History of Ideas in Japan], Tokyo: Iwanami Shoten, 1988.

Takada, Y., 'Sākuru Undō no Teitai o Yaburu [In Order To Revive Group Activities]', *Shisō no Kagaku*, July 1959, pp. 20–9.

——'Kōdō no Imi no Hakkutsu [Delving into the Meanings of Actions]', *Shisō no Kagaku*, August 1959, pp. 25–30.

——'Henkaku no Rinen ni Dō Chikazukuka [How to Deal With the Concept of Reform]', *Bungaku*, October 1959, pp. 100–13.

Takagi, I. (ed.) *Shimizu Shinzō Chosakushū* [A Collection of Writings by Shimizu Shinzō], Tokyo: Nihon Keizai Hyōronsha, 1999.

Takagi, T., 'Fujin Undō niokeru Rōdō Fujin to Katei Fujin [Working Women and Housewives in the Women's Movement]', *Shisō*, December 1960, pp. 135–45.

Takahashi, H., 'Kokumin Ishiki no Henka to Shakai Undō [Change In Public Opinion and Social Movements]', in Rekishigaku Kenkyūkai and Nihonshi Kenkyūkai (eds) *Kōza Nihon Rekishi II: Gendai 1* [Lecture Series in Japanese History: Recent History 1], Tokyo: Tokyo University Press, 1985, pp. 138–40.

Takahashi, M., *Rōdō Kumiai to Shakai Shugi* [Labour Unions and Socialism], Tokyo: Sangyō Keizai Kenkyū Kyōkai, 1990.

Takano, M., 'Kyūgoku Sensen eno Hossoku [The Beginning of the Popular Front to Rescue the Nation]', *Shakai Shugi*, November 1953, pp. 4–5.

——'Vittorio Apīru to Nihon no Rōdō Undō [The Vittorio Appeal and Japan's Labour Movement]', *Rōdō Jōhō Tsūshin*, 18 April 1956, Appendix p. 10.

——'Sōhyō Taikai o Mamore [Defend the Sōhyō Convention]', *Shūkan Rōdō Jōhō*, 19 August 1959, pp. 2–6.

Takano Minoru Chosakushū Henshū Iinkai (ed.) *Takano Minoru Chosakushū* [A Collection of Writings by Takano Minoru], 5 vols, Tokyo: Tsuge Shobō, 1976, i and ii.

Takaragi, F., 'Shin no Leader de atta Ōta Kaoru San [Mr Ota Kaoru, a True Leader]', *Shinpo to Kaikaku*, December 1998, pp. 10–30.

——'Ōta-san no Omoide ni Kanrenshite [Memories about Mr Ōta]', *Shinpo to Kaikaku*, February 1999, pp. 48–55.

Takashima, K., 'Takano san ni okeru Rōdō Undō to Tō [The Labour Movement and Political Parties for Mr Takano]', in Inomata Tsunao Chosaku Ikō Kankō Kai (ed.) *Ichi Kaikyū Senshi no Bohyō* [The Tombstone of a Class Warrior], Tokyo: Inomata Tsunao Chosaku Ikō Kankō Kai, 1975, pp. 4–13.

——*Sengo Rōdō Undōshi Ron* [A Critique of the History of the Post-war Labour Movement], Tokyo: Tsuge Shobō, 1977.

——'Kabu karano Tatakai o Jūshi Shita Haga San [Mr Haga Who Put Priority on Struggles from Below]', in Haga Tamishige San o Shinobu Kai (ed.) *Haga Tamishige San o Shinobu* [In Memory of Mr Haga Tamishige], Saitama: Haga Tamishige San o Shinobu Kai, 1996, pp. 74–5.

Tanabe, S., 'Sensō Taiken to Shakai Kyōiku wa Naze Muenka [Why Adult Education Programmes Do Not Deal with People's Experience of the War]', *Gekkan Shakai Kyōiku*, December 1961, pp. 13–21.

Tanaka, S., 'Hibakugo Hanseiki no Joseitachi [Women Half a Century after the Atomic Bombings]', *Gunshuku Mondai Shiryō*, August 1994, pp. 32–5.

Tanaka, S. (ed.) *Josei Kaihō no Shisō to Kōdō – Sengohen* [Ideas Informing Women's Emancipation and Action Aimed at Their Realization – Post-war Years], Tokyo: Jiji Tsūshinsha, 1975.

Tanigawa, G., 'Hahaoya Undō eno Jikigen [Straight Talk on the Mothers' Movement]', *Fujin Kōron*, October 1959, pp. 124–8.

Tatewaki, S., Hasegawa, A. and Ide, F., *Sengo Fujin Undōshi* [The Post-war Women's Movement], Tokyo: Ōtsuki Shoten, 1960.

Tatewaki, Sadayo and Shimazu, Chitose, 'Senzen Sengo no Fujin Undō o Megutte [On Women's Movements before and after the War]', *Rekishi Hyōron*, November 1966, pp. 16–7.

Tokyo Chihō Rōdō Kumiai Hyōgikai (ed.) *Sengo Tokyo Rōdō Undōshi* [The History of the Labour Movement in Post-war Tokyo], Tokyo: Rōdō Junpōsha, 1980.

Tokyōso Fujinbu Nijūgonenshi Hensan Iinkai (ed.) *Honoo no Yōni: Tokyōso Fujinbu Nijūgonen no Ayumi* [Just Like a Flame: The 25-year History of the Women's Section of the Tokyo Teachers' Union], Tokyo: Tokyoto Shokuin Kumiai Fujinbu, 1972.

Tokyoto Kyōshokuin Kumiai (ed.) *Fudangi no mamano Shōgen* [Accounts of Things as They Were], Tokyo: Rōdō Junpōsha, 1963.

Torigoe, S., 'Sengo Jidō Bungakushi no Kūhakuki: GHQ no Genron Tōsei o Kangaeru [A Lacuna of the Post-war History of Children's Stories: Reflection on the Controls on Free Speech by the GHQ]', in Prange Bunkoten Kirokushū Henshū Iinkai (ed.) *Senryōki no Genron, Shuppan to Bunka: Prange Bunkoten Symposium no Kiroku* [Free Speech, Publishing and Culture During the Allied Occupation of Japan: The Records of the Prange Collection Symposium], Tokyo: Waseda and Ritsumeikan Universities: 2000.

Toshiba Rōren Jūnenshi Hensan Iinkai (ed.) *Kumiai Undōshi* [The History of the Union], Kanagawa: Toshiba Rōdō Kumiai Rengōkai, 1964.

Toyoda, M., 'Ichinenki: Sensō de Shinda Futari no Otōto [The First Anniversary: My Two Brothers Who Died in the War]', *Fujin*, June 1948, pp. 21–2.

Tsuboi, S. and Onchi, T. (eds) *Nihon Kaihō Shishū* [Poems for the Liberation of Japan], Tokyo: Iizuka Shoten, 1950.

Tsujimura, T., *Sengo Shinshū Joseishi* [The Post-war History of Shinshū Women], Nagano: Naganoken Renraku Fujinkai, 1966.

Tsumura, T,, 'Takano Minoru to Inomata Kenkyū Kankō Undō [Takano Minoru and the Movement to Publish Inomata's Writings]', in Inomata Tsunao Chosaku Ikō Kankō Kai (ed.) *Ichi Kaikyū Senshi no Bohyō* [The Tombstone of a Class Warrior], Tokyo: Inomata Tsunao Chosaku Ikō Kankō Kai, 1975, pp. 14–23.

Tsurumi, E. P., 'Visions of Women and the New Society in Conflict: Yamakawa Kikue versus Takamure Itsue', in S. A. Minichiello (ed.) *Japan's Competing Modernities: Issues in Culture and Democracy 1900–1930*, Honolulu: University of Hawaii Press, 1998, pp. 335–54.

Tsurumi, K., 'Ōrakana Doryoku o [Laid-back Efforts]', *Sōhyō*, 1 January 1956.

——*Seikatsu Kiroku Undō no Nakade* [Amid the Movement to Record Events in One's Life], Tokyo: Miraisha, 1963.

——*Social Change and the Individual*, Princeton: Princeton University Press, 1970).

Tsurumi, K. and Makise, K. (eds) *Hikisakarete* [Torn between Duty and Emotion], Tokyo: Chikuma Shobō, 1959.

Tsurumi, S., 'Seishin Kakumei no Jitsuzō [The Realities of the Spiritual Revolution]', in Nakamura, M., Amakawa, A., Yoon, K. C. and Igarashi, T. (eds) *Sengo Nihon Senryō to Sengo Kaikaku: Sengo Shisō to Shakai Ishiki* [The Occupation and Reform in Post-war Japan: Post-war Thought and Social Consciousness], 6 vols, Tokyo: Iwanami Shoten, 1995, iii, pp. 1–24.

Tsutaka, M., 'Fujin no Sākuru Katsudō [Women's Group Activities]', in Ogawa, T. (ed.) *Shūdan Kyōiku Jissen Ron* [On Ways to Conduct Group Education], Tokyo: Meiji Tosho Shuppan, 1958, pp. 205–19.

Uchiyama, M., *Kanbu Tōsō kara Taishū Tōsō e* [From Leaders' Struggle to Rank-and-File Workers' Struggle], Osaka: Rōdō Hōritsu Junpōsha, 1954.

——*Shokuba Tōsō Shokuba Orugu* [Workplace Struggles and Organization of Workplace Activities], Tokyo: Rōdō Hōritsu Junpōsha, 1959.

——*Shokuba no Rōdō Undō* [Workplace-based Labour Movements], Tokyo: Rōdō Junpōsha, 1970.

Uehara, S., *Rekishi Ishiki ni Tatsu Kyōiku* [Education Based on Historical Awareness], Tokyo: Kokudosha, 1958.

Wada, H., *Chōsen Sensō* [The Korean War], Tokyo: Iwanami Shoten, 1995.

——'Sengo Nihon Heiwa Shugi no Genten [The Origins of Japan's Post-war Pacifism]', *Shisō*, December 2002, pp. 5–26.

Wada, S., 'Keizai Taikokuka to Kokumin Ishiki no Henbō [Change in Public Opinion amid Japan's Growing Economic Prowess]', in Watanabe, O., Miwa, T., Wada, S., Urata, I., Mori, H. and Urabe, N., *'Kenpō Kaisei' Hihan* [A Critique of the Proposed Constitutional Amendment], Tokyo: Rōdō Junpōsha, 1994, pp. 131–84.

——*Sengo Nihon No Heiwa Ishiki* [Peace Consciousness In Post-war Japan], Tokyo: Aoki Shoten, 1997.

Wakakuwa, M., *Sensō ga Tsukuru Joseizō* [Wartime Images of Women], Tokyo: Chikuma Shobō, 1995.

Watanabe, M., *Atarashii Asa no Hibiki* [The Sound of a Fresh Morning], Tokyo: Domesu Shuppan, 1992.

Watanabe, O., *Nihonkoku Kenpō Kaiseishi* [The History of Japanese Constitutional Amendment], Tokyo: Nihon Hyōronsha, 1987.

Watanabe, T., 'Rōdō Undō [The Labour Movement]', in Takeuchi, Y. (ed.) *Sengo no Minshū Undō* [Popular Movements in the Post-war Era], Tokyo: Aoki Shoten, 1956, pp. 95–120.

Women and Minors Bureau of the Ministry of Labour, *Fujin Kankei Shiryō Series Chōsa Shiryō: Fujin wa Nani o Kangaete Iruka* [Research Materials on Women: What Are Women Thinking About?], no. 10, July 1952.

——*Fujin no Genjō* [The Current Condition of Women], 11 August 1959.

Yamabe, Y., 'Shakaishugi Kyōkai Bunretsu no Koro [When the Japan Socialism Association Split Up]', in Shimizu Shinzō shi no Omoide Kankō Iinkai (ed.) *Kunshiran no Hanakage ni* [Under the Shadow of a Kaffir Lily], Tokyo: Heigensha, 1997, pp. 121–7.

Yamada, S., 'Chūshō Kigyō Rōdōsha no Soshiki to Tatakai [The Unionization and Struggle of Workers in Smaller Firms]', *Zenei*, December 1957, pp. 108–12.

Yamada, Y., '1970 Nen to Nihon Kyōsantō [The Year 1970 and the Japanese Communist Party]', *Keizai Hyōron*, extra edn, December 1964, pp. 75–84.

Yamagata, F., 'Mizukara Egaita Miraizu O [Mapping out a Course for the Future on Your Own]', *Gekkan Shakai Kyōiku*, December 1961, pp. 22–5.

Yamagataken Josei no Ayumi Hensan Iinkai (ed.) *Toki o Tsumugu Yamagata no Joseitachi* [Yamagata Women Record Their Times], Yamagata: Michinoku Shobō, 1995.

Yamagataken Taishoku Fujin Shokuin Renraku Kyōgikai (ed.) *Harukanaru Michi Naredo* [Though We Have a Long Way Ahead], Yamagata: Dewajikai Jimukyoku, 1984.

Yamamura, M., *Sensō Kyohi* [Non-cooperation with War], Tokyo: Shōbunsha, 1987.

Yamashiro, T., *Minwa o Umu Hitobito* [People Who Create Folklore], Tokyo: Iwanami Shoten, 1958.

——*Watashi no Mananda Koto* [Things I Have Learned], Tokyo: Komichi Shobō, 1990.

Yamaya S., 'Women and the Peace Movement', in *Peace Research in Japan*, Tokyo, 1976, pp. 72–7.

Yamazaki, S., *Shijitsu de Kataru Chōsen Sensō Kyōryoku no Zenyō* [Historical Facts about Japan's Co-operation with the Korean War], Tokyo: Hon no Izumisha, 1998.

Yasui, K., 'Humanism to Heiwa [Humanism and Peace]', *Heiwa*, November 1954, pp. 10–21.

Yokoi, K., 'Entenka 56 Nichi o Kōshin shite [A 56-day March under the Blazing Sun]', *Heiwa Nihon*, September 1959, pp. 28–31.

Yoneda, S., *Rekishi ni Jinken o Kizanda Onnatachi* [Women who Helped Human Rights to Take Root in Japan], Kyoto: Kamogawa Shuppan, 1996.

Yoon, K. C., *Kozetsu no Rekishi Ishiki* [An Isolated View of History], Tokyo: Iwanami Shoten, 1985.

Yoshida, R., 'Chōhei Kihi: Korosaretemo Iikara Korosumaito Omotta [Draft Dodging: I Was Determined not to Kill even if I Got Killed]', *Shūkan Kinyōbi*, 9 August 2002, p. 15.

Yoshimi, Y., *Kusanone no Fashizumu* [Grassroots Fascism], Tokyo: Tokyo University Press, 1987.

Yoshimura, H., 'Watashi no Seikatsu no nakade [Within My Personal Life]', *Sekai*, July 1961, pp. 69–70.

Yoshioka, T., *Minato no Undō Yonjūnen* [The 40-year History of the Port Workers' Labour Movement], Tokyo: Kasahara Shoten, 1991.

Yui, M., '1940nendai no Nihon [Japan in the 1940s]', in Asao, N., Amino, Y., Ishii, S., Kano, M., Hayakawa, S. and Yasumaru, Y. (eds) *Nihon Tsūshi: Kindai 4* [The Complete History of Japan: the Modern Era], 21 vols, Tokyo: Iwanami Shoten, 1995, xix, pp. 1–92.

Zenkoku Chiiki Fujin Dantai Renraku Kyōgikai (ed.) *Zenchifuren Jūnen no Ayumi* [The 10-year History of the National Federation of Regional Women's Organizations], Tokyo: Shōwa Shuppan Bunka, 1965.

Zenkoku Chiiki Fujin Dantai Renraku Kyōgikai (ed.) *Zenchifuren Sanjūnen no Ayumi* [The 30-year History of the National Federation of Regional Women's Organizations], Tokyo: Zenkoku Chiiki Fujin Dantai Renraku Kyōgikai, 1986.

Zenkoku Kinzoku Rōdō Kumiai (ed.) *Zenkoku Kinzoku 30 Nenshi* [The 30-year History of the National Trade Union of Metal and Engineering Workers], Tokyo: Rōdō Junpōsha, 1977.

Zennihon Kōwan Rōdō Kumiai (ed.) *Zenkōwan Undōshi* [The History of the All-Japan Harbour Workers' Union], 2 vols, Tokyo: Rōdō Junpōsha, 1972, i.

TV programmes

Iida, Hichizō, in a 28 May 1997 broadcast of NHK Educational Television.
Okabe, Itsuko, in a 15 August 2000 broadcast of NHK Educational Television.

Interviewees

Andō, Jinbei.
Fukuda, Reizō.
Hashiguchi, Kazuko.
Higuchi, Tokuzō.
Hino, Saburō.
Kobayashi, Tomie.
Kojima, Senoko.
Kondō, Yūko.
Maruoka, Akiko.
Negami, Masayuki.
Numabe, Tamiko.
Ōtsuka, Masatatsu.
Ozawa, Kiyoko.
Saitō, Tsuruko.
Seto, Sadao.
Takeuchi, Motohiro.
Tanaka, Satoko.
Uchiyama, Mitsuo.
Yokoi, Kameo.
Yoshioka, Tokuji.

Index

absolute pacifism 9, 11, 149, 200, 211
activism: emergence of activist workers 29–35; location of women's activism 172–5; revival of union activism 54–9; women activists 145–8
adult education 176–7, 180–1
Afghanistan: war on terrorism 2
African-American soldiers 115, 251–2
age: women's activism and 174–5
Akabane plant dispute 54–5, 58, 114, 116
All Japan Federation of Electric Machine Workers' Unions (Denki Rōren) 107
All Japan Harbour Workers' Union (Zenkōwan) 115–16
All Japan Seamen's Union (Kaiin) 59, 238
Amagasaki steel mill strike 82
Amano Masako 195
Anabaptists 9
Andō Jinbei 53, 236–7
Anpo Tōsō (anti-security treaty protest) 13, 215, 229–30, 250; disciplinary actions taken against participants 250; intellectuals 16–17; run-up to 89–93; unionists' peace movement and 79, 89–98, 102, 107, 112, 113, 205, 250; women and 170, 175, 178, 189, 192–3, 210, 265
anti-military base campaigns 78, 110–11, 196, 243; *see also* Sunagawa anti-military base campaign
anti-nuclear international conference, Hiroshima 1955 169, 196
anti-nuclear weapons movement 8, 11, 15, 228; unionists' peace movement 104–5, 106; women 166, 167, 169, 171, 172, 177

anti-security treaty protest *see Anpo Tōsō*
Anti-Subversive Activities Law 57, 238
anti-Vietnam War movement 210–11, 215, 219
Ariyama Teruo 119, 120
Asahi Graph 13–14
Asahi Shimbun 26, 86, 117, 160, 161, 235; editorials for women readers 132; remorse about World War Two 119–20; women's letters to 142–3, 160, 263, 272
Asian nations 121
austerity budget 37
auto workers' industrial federation 110, 117
Awata Yasuko 166, 197

ban-the-bomb movement *see* anti-nuclear weapons movement
Bikini hydrogen bomb test 8, 24, 169, 218, 228; emergence of women's peace network 167–8; stirrings prior to 152–62
black soldiers 115, 251–2
Blau, Peter M. 23
Britain 8–9, 12; CND 23
Buddhism 10, 211
bureaucratic inertia 19

Campaign for Nuclear Disarmament (CND) 23
capitalism 49, 88
catharsis 168
Ceadel, Martin 8–9, 12
censorship 142, 256
Central Chorus (Chūō Gasshōdan) 70, 73, 74, 75
Chatfield, Charles 8–9

Chiba Chiyose 153
China 7, 87; unionists and 64–6, 86, 87, 122, 123, 253; women and 187, 270
choral singing 72, 73–4, 75, 268, 275
Christianity 8–9, 10, 211; Christians and war crimes 141, 150, 257–8
Churchill, Winston 64
citizenry (civil society) 102
citizens' groups 211
class 23–4
coal miners' wives 198–9
Cold War 7, 216; and escalating labour strife 35–42; women's peace movement 133–41
collective action 211–12
collective bargaining 109
Cominform 47
communists 32; *see also* Japanese Communist Party (JCP)
community-based action 105, 248
community services, in poverty-stricken areas 154–6
Congress of Industrial Unions of Japan *see* Sanbetsu
conscientious objectors 5, 227
consciousness-raising 178–9
conscription 3; avoidance of 5
conservative backlash 7
conservatives 22, 146–7, 148; clashes with political left 137–41, 170–2; peace statements 150–1
Constitution 6, 15, 16, 184, 213, 222–3; absolute pacifism 11, 149; Article 9 214, 223; and Gulf War 1991 1, 2; preamble 213–14, 222; support for 211, 215; women and defence of 178; women and pacifism of 133–4, 149, 255; women's equality 131, 132–3, 183; workers and 100, 101, 206
corporate culture 103
cultural activities *see* group activities, informal
'cultured nation' (*bunka kokka*) 6–7

deaths, war 129–30, 189–90
democracy 6–7, 13, 212, 214; teaching 153; women and Constitution 132–3, 183
Democratic Liberal Party (Minjitō) 138, 141
Democratic Party 146–7
Democratic Socialist Party 95
desire to live up to one's values 13, 15

disarmament, movement for 3–4
Discussion Circle on Problems of Peace (Heiwa Mondai Danwakai) 8, 17, 48, 49, 61
dissidents 81–5
Dodge, Joseph 137
Dower, John W. 212
Dulles, John Foster 64, 146, 228; women's requests to 148–9, 156–7

economic growth 30–1
economic issues: unionists and 79, 110–12, 206; women and 142, 144, 156–7; *see also* wages
economic privation 10, 37–40; women and poverty-stricken areas 154–6
education: school education 169–70, 184, 264–5; of women 131–3
Egashira Chiyoko 153–4
Eisenhower, Dwight 88; administration of 228
emancipation of women 131, 194–5
empowerment 193–9
Enlightenment rationalism 8
essay-writing groups 162–7, 177–8, 190–3
evil vs good discourse 135–7
externalization of the labour movement 19

Far East Military Tribunal 6, 150, 218
farm cooperatives 176, 267
farming communities 175–81
fatal railway incidents 39, 40, 54, 120, 233
Federation of All Japan Metal Mine Labour Unions (Zenkō) 117
feminism 22, 193–9, 208, 271
feudalistic relations 12–13; family relations 155, 195; industrial relations 30, 114
Five Principles of Peace 65, 240
foreign policy 216
Fudankyō (Association of Women's Organizations) 139, 140, 141
Fujii Tadatoshi 128–9, 130
Fujime Yuki 258
Fujin 135
Fujin Asahi 143
Fujin Kōron 132
Fujin Minshu Shimbun 131, 133, 135, 156, 159–60
Fujin Yūkensha 145

Fujita Taki 225
Fujiwara Osamu 10
Fujiwara Tei 174
Fukao Sumako 200
Fukuda Reizo 75, 242
Fukui 178

Gauntlett Tsuneko 148–9, 151, 225
Gekkan Shakai Kyōiku 179–80
general strike of February 1947, aborted 37, 43, 118, 233
Gensuikyō 172
good vs evil discourse 135–7
Gordon, Andrew 25
Gotō Junichirō 118–19, 132
group activities, informal 7; women's groups 162–7, 177–8, 179–80, 190–3, 208; workplace societies 70, 72–5, 101–2, 241
Gulf War of 1991 1–2
gynocentric feminism 194–9, 271

Haga Tamishige 91
Hagerty, James C. 94
Hani Setsuko 131
Hashiguchi Kazuko 153, 158, 258
Hayashi Eidai 115
Heiwa Fujin Shimbun 158, 186–7
Heiwa Mondai Danwakai (Discussion Circle on Problems of Peace) 8, 17, 48, 49, 61
heiwa shugi (peace-loving attitude) 10
Heiwa Yōgo Nihon Iinkai (Japanese Committee for Protection of Peace) 42
Hidaka Rokurō 7, 16, 102
Higa Masako 259
Higuchi Ryū 130
Higuchi Tokuzō 32, 35, 76, 82, 130, 232
Hinata Group 166
Hino Saburō 43, 44, 53, 123, 234, 235, 237; choral singing 70, 74
Hirabayashi Taiko 225
Hirano Yoshitarō 156
Hirasawa Eiichi 36–7, 116
Hiratsuka Raichō 136, 148–9, 151, 185–6, 200, 225
Hirosawa Kenichi 67
Hiroshima 11, 218
Hitachi 37
Hokuriku Railway Union 76, 110–11
horrors of war 201
Hoshika Kaname 56–7

Hoshino Yasusaburō 192
Hosoya Matsuta 48, 118
household spending 46
housewife debate 197
housewives' classes 176, 176–7, 267
housewives' peace movement *see* women's peace movement
human frailty 219–20
human life, sacred nature of 179, 210
humanist feminism 194, 271
humanitarianism 210–11
Hungary 86, 244

Ichikawa Fusae 128, 140, 185, 225
ideal family, women's views of 272, 273
idealism 133–5
ideology 209
ie system 127–8, 131, 176, 196, 254
Iida Hichizō 40, 233
Ikeda Shintarō 228
Ikegai Motor union 117
Imperial Rule Assistance Association (Taisei Yokusankai) 128
imperialism 49
independence 70–1
inflation: beating by buying too much 143
informal group activities *see* group activities, informal
Inomata Tsunao 62, 91
inspiration, sources of 182–7
institutional reform 13–15
intellectuals 7–8, 16–17; and unionists' peace movement 31–5, 61, 78, 242; and women's peace movement 185–6; young 31–5
internalization of the labour movement 19
International Confederation of Free Trade Unions (ICFTU) 51
international influences 85–9, 206
Iraq: Gulf War of 1991 1–2; post-war in 2003 2
Irokawa Daikichi 227
Ishida Takeshi 4
Ishigaki Ayako 175–6, 197
Ishikawa Masaharu 251
Ishikawa Tatsuzō 260
Ishimota Tadashi 7
isolation policy 3, 226
Isono Fujiko 196–7
Itō Yasuko 199, 266

Iwai Akira 77, 77–8, 79–80, 85, 95, 96, 98
Iwanami Shoten 184
Iwate 179

Japan-China Friendship Association (Nicchū Yūkō Kyōkai) 122
Japan Housewives' Association 142, 187
Japan-US Mutual Security Act (MSA) 62–3
Japan-US security treaty 70, 180, 217, 229–30, 268; see also Anpo Tōsō
Japanese Coal Miners' Union 58, 122
Japanese Communist Party (JCP) 234; Anpo Tōsō 93–4, 95, 246–7; members in labour movement 84–5; new platform 1951 240; 'peaceful revolution' policy 39; Sanbetsu and 35, 36; Shin Sanbetsu and 48, 49; Sōhyō and 52, 53; and Soviet invasion of Hungary 86–7; Takano and 61, 239; united action 66–7; women's peace movement 138, 140
Japanese Convention in Defence of Peace (Heiwa Yōgo Nihon Taikai) 40
Japanese Democratic Women's Association (Minpukyō) 138
Japanese Federation of Iron and Steel Workers 99
Japanese Federation of Textile Workers' Unions (Zensen) 59, 107
Japanese Federation of Trade Unions see Sōdōmei
Japanese People's Congress for Promotion of Peace (Nihon Heiwa Suishin Kokumin Kaigi) 120
Japanese Socialist Party (JSP) 19, 95, 145, 206, 226; peace campaign 158, 159; peace forces debate 68–9; platform 69; Shin Sanbetsu and 47–8, 49
Japanese Teachers Union see Nikkyōso
Japanese UN Association 147
Jōdai Tano 148–9, 225
Josei Kaizō 132, 140
Josei Shimbun 137, 150

Kaishintō party 228
Kakushin Dōshikai (Association of Reformers or Kakudō) 92
Kamen, Henry 9
Kamichika Ichiko 225
Kamisaka Fuyuko 100–1

Kanba Michiko 193, 265
kangaroo courts 118
Kanō Mikiyo 129, 149
Kansai Housewives' Association (Kansai Shufu Rengōkai or Kansai Shufuren) 196, 259
Katō Shizue 131
katsudōka (independent activists) 20, 85
Kawamura Yasuo 71
Kawasaki Natsu 195
Khrushchev, Nikita 86
Kido Noboru 72
Kihara Minoru 49
Kike Wadatsumi no Koe ('Hear the Voices from the Sea') 189
Kishi Nobusuke 80–1, 94, 97, 230
Kitamikado Jirō 227
Kobayashi Tomie 237
Koizumi Junichiro 2
Kojima Senoko 186, 187, 270
kokoro no heiwa ('peace in people's hearts') 138
Kokubō Fujinkai (Women's Society for National Defence) 128–9, 130, 254
Kokubun Ichitarō 40, 162, 163, 177
Kokurō (National Railway Workers' Union) 54, 56, 204, 236; informal activities 70, 75; and Korean War 44–5, 235; leadership power struggle 56–8; strike during Anpo Tōsō 109, 249
Kokutetsu Shimbun 56
Kondō Yūko 146, 183, 189, 257
Kōra Tomi 188, 200
Korean War 14; impact on labour movement 43–6; involvement in work related to 114–18; opinion polls and 161; Takano and 60–1; unionists' peace movement and 50–1, 59, 87, 114–18; women's peace movement and 21, 142–8, 157–8
Kōsaka Masataka 217
Kuno Osamu 16
Kusanomikai (Seeds of Grass) 170, 174, 184–5, 197, 198, 263, 272; organization by female principles 195
Kyōdō Printing 93, 107–8

labour movement: decline of 98–103; impact of Korean War 43–6; leadership power struggles 56–8; Takano's approach to 60–4; women

and 170, 195–6; see also unionists' peace movement
large company unions 112–14
leadership power struggles 56–8
League for Democratization of Sanbetsu see Sanbetsu Mindō
League of Women Voters of Japan (Shin Nihon Fujin Dōmei) 131, 137, 138, 140, 174
learning, desire for 165
left-wing women activists 148, 156–8, 186–7; clashes with conservatives 137–41, 170–2
letters to newspapers 142–3, 160–1, 165, 194, 263, 272
Liberal Democratic Party (LDP) 170, 265
Liberal Party 139, 146–7
liberalism 8–9
liberation of self 71–5
Liberty and Civil Rights Movement 4, 16
Liu Shaoqi 65, 75
living standards: living standards improvement movement 176, 180; rise in 13–15
Lummis, C. Douglas 213, 217

MacArthur, General 70, 212
Mainichi Shimbun 6, 263
Makise Kikue 163–4, 190–3, 194, 202
managers 118–19
Martin, David A. 9
Maruoka Akiko 183–4, 269, 269–70
Maruoka Hideko 136, 166, 180, 184, 185
Maruyama Masao 16, 227–8
mass line approach 7; Takano 65–6, 67; unionists' peace movement 75, 105, 108, 205, 248
mass media 132; see also newspapers
Masuda Tetsuo 110
Masuyama Tasuke 119
materialism 101
Matsu 87
Matsukawa fatal railway incident 84, 233, 243–4
Matsumoto Seichō 251–2
Matsuoka Komakichi 36
Matsuoka Yōko 138, 274
May Day 1950 (Anti-War May Day) 38
Meiji era 3
military 3, 11; views on 3, 229
Minaguchi Kōzō 246, 247
Mindō leaders 77–81, 83–4, 95–6, 204, 205

Ministry of Education 176
Ministry of Labour Women and Minors Bureau 166, 172–3
Mitaka fatal railway incident 233
Mito Nobuto 48, 50–1, 236
Mitsui Miike coal miners' dispute 1960 80, 98, 99
Miyamoto Kenji 94, 96
Miyamoto Yuriko 131, 135, 136, 185
Mizuno Aki 52
'modern', meaning of 12–13
modernization 99, 206–7
Moji 115, 251
moral duty 136
morality 207, 220
Morisaki Kazue 188, 198–9
motherhood 136, 185–6, 194; propaganda 127
Mothers' Congress 154, 170, 177, 186–7, 195, 265; demographic shift 175; remorse about Second World War 188–9, 190; rise of 167–9, 171
mothers' and teachers' groups 154
Muchaku Seikyō 162, 163
Muroran steel mill strike 82
mutual security act, Japan-US (MSA) 62–3

Nagahara Kazuko 163
Nagano Prefecture 178, 267
Nagasaki 11, 218
Nagasaki housewives' group 166
Nakajima Michiko 195
Nakamoto Takako 271
Naramoto Tatsuya 7, 74
National Congress to Block the Revision of the Japan-US Security Treaty 93–4, 96, 246
National Congress of Culture in Japan (Kokumin Bunka Kaigi) 75
National Congress for Promotion of Peace (Heiwa Suishin Kokumin Kaigi) 52
National Council of Anti-Nuclear Signature-collecting Movements 167
National Federation of Industrial Organizations (Shin Sanbetsu) 20, 46–50, 50–1, 246, 252
National Railway Workers' Union see Kokurō
National Trade Union of Metal and Engineering Workers (Zenkoku Kinzoku) 112
nationalism 33–4, 53
Negami Masayuki 39, 56, 73, 233, 235

negative pacifism 209
Nehru, Jawaharlal 65
networking: by teachers 152–6; by unionists 89–98
neutrality 49
new social movements 15
newspapers 132; censorship 142, 256; labour disputes related to war crimes 119–20; letters to 142–3, 160–1, 165, 194, 263, 272; *see also under individual names*
Nihon Fujin Shimbun 139, 140, 147–8, 160, 257
Nihon Kōzan Rōdō Kumiai (miners' union or Nikkō) 50, 51
Nihon Shakaitō *see* Japanese Socialist Party
Nikkyōso (Japanese Teachers Union) 7, 20, 35, 196; and women's grassroots activities 152–6, 168, 177, 260
1932 thesis 39
Nippon Steel Akabane plant 54–5, 58, 114, 116
Nissan Motor union 99, 110, 117, 249
Nogami Yaeko 148–9, 225
non-activists 142–4
North Korea 217
Numabe Tamiko 175, 182, 184–5, 269

Ōe Shinobu 3
Oguri Takeko 220, 275
Ōji Paper 99
Oka Saburō 158
Okabe Itsuko 189–90
Ōkōchi Kazuo 19, 30–1, 82, 114
Ōmi Kenshi 107
ordinary workers 29–31
Ōta Kaoru 51, 64, 77–8, 85, 95, 114; Haneda airport demonstrations 94; Police Duties Law protest 78–9; protest based on consensus 98; socialism 79–80; strike by Kokurō 249
Ōtake Hideo 25, 53–4, 111
Ōtsuka Masatatsu 31, 32, 35
Oyamachō grassroots groups 268
Ozawa Kiyoko 186, 187, 270

Pacific War 4
pacificism 9, 10, 11, 229
pacifism 214–15; absolute 9, 11, 149, 200, 211; defining 8–11; Japanese compared with Western 211; women's peace movement and 133–5, 149, 199–203
Packard, George R. 25

parent-teacher associations (PTAs) 156, 159, 166, 170, 177, 184, 265
Parkin, Frank 23
paternalistic employment practices 30
peace education 153, 154
peace forces debate 64–9, 85–6
peace groups' newspapers 42, 234
peace treaty 121, 156–7, 253
peace treaty debate: unionists' peace movement and 46–54; women and 148–51
'peaceful nation' (*heiwa kokka*) 6–7
Pearl Harbour 5
people-first pacifism (*seikatsu heiwa shugi*) 207
personal issues 212–13
Police Duties Law 78–9, 92, 170
Police Reserve 11
political affiliation, housewives without 158–62
political culture 12–17
political issues, women's degree of concern with 261–2
popular attitudes to peace 2–8
Popular Front Incident 1937 61
popular pacifism 11
post-war transition 219
Potsdam Declaration 6
private-sector unions 99, 103, 106–9
productivity improvement movement 80, 99
propaganda 33, 128, 134, 144
prostitutes 153, 258
Protestantism 8
public-sector layoff 1949 39–40
public-sector unions 103, 106–9

Quemoy 87

radicalization of workers 37–40
railways 30, 39–40, 44–5; fatal incidents 39, 40, 54, 84, 120, 233, 243–4; Hokuriku Railway Union 76, 110–11
rape 123, 153
rearmament 149, 161, 200–1, 262, 274
Red Purge 40, 43, 52, 55, 107, 145, 152, 234
reformism 83
regional women's organizations 171–2, 174
religion 8–9, 10, 211; *see also* Christianity
remorse about Second World War: unionists' peace movement 118–23; women's peace movement 187–93

reparations, war 121–2, 149–50, 253
repression 4, 128
resource mobilization thesis 13–15
revolution 83, 97
Rice Riot 1918 30, 209
riots 3, 4, 30, 209
Rōdō Sensen 40–1
Rōdōsha Dōshikai (Workers' Association) 58, 61
romanticism 33–4
Rōnō Party 92, 233
Rōnō school of Marxism 61
rural areas 154, 183, 269; peace movements in 175–81
Russo-Japanese War 1904–5 3, 4

Saga Ichirō 117
Saitō Kiku 139
Saitō Tsuruko 264
Sakamoto Yoshikazu 13
Sakisaka Itsurō 87
samurai spirit 203
San Francisco Treaty system 162, 163
Sanbetsu (Congress of Industrial Unions of Japan) 20, 34, 40–1, 42, 44, 115, 205; split 35–7
Sanbetsu Mindō (League for Democratization of Sanbetsu) 36, 37; peace treaty debate 47, 48; *see also* Mindō leaders
Sangyō Hōkokukai (Movement of Industrial Service to the Nation) 29
Sasaki-Uemura, Wesley 24
Sata Ineko 131
SCAP (Supreme Commander, Allied Forces) 6, 59, 213, 228; austerity budget 37; censorship 142, 256; clampdown on labour unions 37; creation of Police Reserve 11, 45; emancipation of women 131; encouragement of grassroots women's groups 131, 133; imposed reform 16; labour unions' youth and women's sections 152, 258; Sōhyō and 52, 53, 54; support for labour unions 29, 31; suppression of peace movement 14
school education 169–70, 184, 264–5
Second International 18
security 216–18
Seki Akiko 73, 74
Sekine Katsuhiko 244
self, liberation of 71–5
Self-Defence Forces (SDF) 1, 2, 11, 215–16, 217

Seto Sadao 45, 73, 235, 239
Shimizu Keiko 166, 185, 199, 269
Shimizu Shinzō 19, 54, 58, 83, 102, 103, 112–13; JSP platform 69; Takano 61, 68
Shimoyama incident 233
Shin Sanbetsu (National Federation of Industrial Organizations) 20, 46–50, 50–1, 246, 252
Shōriki Matsutarō 119
short-term contract workers 46
Shufuren Dayori 142
Shūkan Rōdō Jōhō (Labour Information Weekly) 81
singing movement 72, 73–4, 75, 268, 275
Sino-Japanese War 1894–5 3, 4
Sino-Japanese War of 1930s 4
Sino-Soviet conflict 87–8, 244
small companies 90
small company unions 112–14
Smedley, Agnes 65
Snow, Edgar 65
social mobilization paradigm 13–15
social movements 24; new 15
social studies 190–1
socialism 16, 18, 49, 210; international influences on unionist peace movement 85–9
Socialism Association (Shakaishugi Kyōkai) 61, 69, 239
socialization for death 33, 192
societies *see* group activities, informal
Society for the Protection of Children 167, 174, 264
Sodei Rinjirō 7
Sōdōmei (Japanese Federation of Trade Unions) 34, 58–9; split within 35–7
Sōhyō (General Council of Trade Unions of Japan) 19, 20, 42, 104, 206; *Anpo Tōsō* 94–8; creation 43–4; informal group activities 75; international influences 85–9; Korean War 44, 46, 114, 118; leadership 56, 58, 60, 205; leadership rivalry 77–85; mass line approach 105; MSA 62–3; peace forces debate 64–9; peace principles 47, 50–2, 54; policy shift 50–4; reparations 122; secession of major unions 58–9; Takano *see* Takano Minoru; workplace struggles 75–6
Sōka Gakkai 182, 183
Sone Eki 68, 240
South Vietnam 122
Soviet Union 49, 64–5, 66, 187; invasion

of Hungary 86–7; U-2 aircraft incident 88–9
spectre of war 37–40
speculative buying 143
standard of living *see* living standards
stevedores 115–16, 251
strategies for peace 199–203
students 192–3
Suginami housewives' group 166
Sunagawa anti-military base campaign 196; unionists' peace movement 78, 86–7, 89–90, 105, 108, 112, 243, 250
survival 5
Suzuki Mosaburō 68

Taguchi Fukuji 63
Tahara Sōichirō 4
Taishō era 3–4, 16
Takabatake Michitoshi 16–17
Takada Yoshitoshi 33–4, 71–2, 101
Takahashi Hikohiro 41
Takano Minoru 36, 60, 91–2, 103, 117; and his allies 81–4, 92; approach to the labour movement 60–4; Mindo leaders and 77–8; National Congress of Culture 75; peace forces debate 64–9; and reparations 121
Takaragi Fumihiko 86
Takashima Kikuo 58, 60–1, 62, 77, 83, 85–6, 239
Takeuchi Motohiro 32–3, 83, 84, 92, 123, 232, 253; *Anpo Tōsō* 97–8
Tanaka Satoko 172, 265, 266
Tanigawa Gan 190
Tanpukyō 198
Tatewaki Sadayo 129, 170
teachers 20, 260; networking by 152–6; *see also* Nikkyōso
third force 49, 52, 85–6, 149
Third Peace Declaration by Women of an Unarmed Japan 149, 224–5
Thorez, Maurice 47
Tibet 87
Toa Wool Spinning and Weaving Company 72
Togliatti, Palmiro 47
Tōjō Hideki 4
Tokyo Congress for Joint Struggles to Preserve Peace and Democracy 90–1, 92, 93, 94, 96, 245
Tokyo Local Council of Trade Unions (Tokyo Chihyō) 83, 91, 92–3, 245
Toshiba Corporation 107; Horikawachō plant, Kawasaki 35
toys, war 153, 259

Tsumura Takashi 62, 91
Tsurumi Kazuko 33, 100, 185, 192, 262; essay-writing groups 163, 191; samurai spirit 203
typhoon 83

U-2 spy aircraft 88–9
Uchimura Kanzō 9
Uchinada anti-military base campaign 111, 196
Uchiyama Mitsuo 33, 75, 254
Uemura Tamaki 138, 148–9, 151
Umegaoka housewives' group 166
UNESCO (United Nations Educational, Scientific and Cultural Organization) 138, 159, 160, 261
Union for Democratic Scientists (Minka) 56
union heroism 100–1
unionists' peace movement 17–20, 23–4, 27–123, 204–7; Cold War and 35–42; compared with women's peace movement 23, 202–3, 209, 210–11; decline in activism 98–103; dissidents 81–5; early years 29–42; elements of peace activities 104–23; emergence of activist workers 29–35; impact of Korean War on labour movement 43–6; international influences 85–9, 206; involvement in Korean War 114–18; left-wing Mindō leaders 77–81, 83–4, 95–6, 204, 205; link with economic struggles 110–12; major actors 77–85; under Mindō 77–103; networking at the grassroots 89–98; peace forces debate 64–9, 85–6; peace treaty debate 46–54; public- vs private-sector unions 106–9; remorse about Second World War 118–23; revival of union activism 54–9; rise of grassroots activism 70–6; small vs large company unions 112–14; Takano's approach to labour movement 60–4
united action 66–7
United Nations (UN): unionists and 44, 45, 51, 59, 206, 235; women and 142, 147, 149
United States (US) 3, 8–9, 49, 54, 228; anti-military base campaigns *see* anti-military base campaigns, Sunagawa anti-military base campaign; Bikini H-bomb test *see* Bikini hydrogen bomb test; black soldiers 115, 251–2; end of occupation 70–1; military

bases 70–1, 153, 155, 157, 161–2, 177; MSA 62–3; prostitution and US soldiers 153, 258; SCAP *see* SCAP; U-2 spy aircraft 88–9; unionists and anti-Americanism 45, 53
urban migration 30
US-Japan security treaty 70, 180, 217, 229–30, 268; *see also Anpo Tōsō*

Vietnam War 14; anti-Vietnam War movement 210–11, 215, 219
Vittorio, Giuseppe Di 91–2

Wada Haruki 14
wages 99, 106, 113
war crimes 6, 118–19, 218; military trials of war criminals 6, 150, 218
war reparations 121–2, 149–50, 253
war responsibility 24, 218; unionists' peace movement and 118–23; women's peace movement and 149–50, 187–93
war toys 153, 259
war-weariness 5, 11, 227
Watanabe Michiko 141
Watanabe Osamu 228–9
weapons production 116, 117–18
Wild Rose Society 263
Woddis, Jack 66–7
Women's Day demonstration 1950 139–40
Women's Democratic Club 131, 133, 138, 146, 151, 156, 186–7
women's organizations 145–8; participation in 172–4
women's peace movement 17–18, 21–2, 24, 125–203, 207–10; after Bikini H-bomb test 167–72; clashes between conservatives and political left 137–41, 170–2; Cold War 133–41; compared with unionists' peace movement 23, 202–3, 209, 210–11; emergence of nationwide peace network 167–8; essay-writing and other grassroots groups 162–7, 177–8, 179–80, 190–3, 208; feminism and empowerment 193–9; housewives with no political affiliation 158–62; Korean War 21, 142–8, 157–8; left-wing activists 148, 156–8, 186–7; location of activism 172–5; peace movements in rural areas 175–81; peace treaty debate 148–51; political outlook 168–70; pre-war and war years 127–30; revival of grassroots activities and post-war education of women 131–3; sense of remorse 187–93; sources of inspiration 182–7; stirrings prior to Bikini H-bomb test 152–62; strategies for peace 199–203; teachers' networking 152–6; third peace declaration 149, 224–5; three statements 148–51
workload, women's 268
workplace societies 70, 72–5, 101–2, 241
workplace struggles (*shokuba tōsō*) 75–6
World Federation of Trade Unions (WFTU) 39, 66, 86, 92
World Peace Council 41
World War Two 5–6, 13–14, 213, 219–20; experiences of and worker activism 31–5; remorse about 118–23, 187–93; women's experiences 127–30; women's responses to end of 182–3
writings 202; essay-writing groups 162–7, 177–8, 190–3; letters to newspapers 142–3, 160–1, 165, 194, 263, 272

Yamaguchi Kenji 123
Yamakawa Kikue 129
Yamamoto Kenkichi 197–8
Yamashiro Tomoe 188
Yamashita Asayo 169
Yamataka Shigeri 139–40, 171, 196, 265
Yasui Kaoru 166, 209
Yokoi Kameo 76, 123, 242
Yokoyama Toshiaki 57
Yomiuri Shimbun 119, 120
Yoon Keun Cha 218–19
Yosano Akiko 3
Yoshida Shigeru 233
Yoshida Sukeharu 29, 31
Yoshioka Tokuji 64, 74, 239
Young, Iris Morgan 271
young intellectuals 31–5
young workers 99–101, 103
YWCA 137, 140–1, 146–7, 170

Zenei 44–5, 85, 235
Zenrōren 38–9, 145
Zentei (Japanese Postal Workers' Union) 51, 109, 204
Zentei Shimbun 38
Zhou Enlai 65